To Chris — I want to shar
of my recollections of our work
you for your friendship — Jus

Have I Told You About...?

Knitting Together the Yarns of My Life

Justin Lawrence Wyner

As told to Steve Maas

*Published in cooperation with Wyner Family Jewish Heritage Center,
home of the American Jewish Historical Society's New England archives.*

The Wyner Family
**Jewish Heritage
Center**™
at NEW ENGLAND HISTORIC
GENEALOGICAL SOCIETY

Have I Told You About ...?
Knitting Together the Yarns of My Life

Justin Lawrence Wyner

As told to *Steve Maas*

ISBN : 978-1-54396-844-6

Copyright © 2018 Justin Lawrence Wyner

Registration No. TXu 2-095-594

All rights reserved. No part of this publication may be reproduced, distributed, or transmitted in any form or by any means, including photocopying, recording, or other electronic or mechanical methods, without the prior written permission of the publisher, except in the case of brief quotations embodied in critical reviews and certain other noncommercial uses permitted by copyright law.

To the love of my life, Genevieve, who has made our 63-year journey together magical.

TABLE OF CONTENTS

Foreword 1

Introduction 3

PART I: THE PEOPLE WHO MADE ME 5

PART II: GROWING UP 59

PART III: THE HOME FRONT 109

PART IV: BUSINESS WORLD 158

PART V: ON THE SEA 219

PART VI: PASTIMES 253

PART VII: MR. FIX-IT 275

PART VIII: BROOKLINE CITIZEN 314

PART IX: SWEPT UP IN HISTORY 330

PART X: RINGSIDE AT TEMPLE ISRAEL 349

PART XI: BODY AND SOUL 362

APPENDIX 386

The author, Justin Wyner, sits on bench dedicated in his honor by the condo association at Rowes Wharf in Boston.

Foreword

I have found that when I tell a story to someone in person, it comes out more interesting than if I were writing it for an unseen audience. That's because if I feel I'm losing my listener's attention, I can skip about until I regain it.

In thinking about how I would write this book, I had the excellent example of how my wife, Genevieve, went about fashioning her memoir. As a matter of fact, I finally started in on my own memoir because of the wonderful way hers turned out and her urging me to write my own. Genevieve told her stories to an experienced memoir facilitator, who recorded them. The young woman would transcribe the sessions, and Genevieve then would polish up the text.

Before I set about looking for such an assistant, Steve Maas, a retired *Boston Globe* editor, profiled my family for *The Jewish Journal*. I liked the way that he interviewed me and recounted my anecdotes so much that I decided to talk with him about my interest in writing a book. At first, I thought that it would be reasonably compact. As I shared family stories for the benefit of future generations of Wyners, Steve turned out to be such an avid and inquisitive listener that I felt encouraged to tell him more and more.

While drafting chapters based on our interviews, he'd ask me more questions to fill in gaps. That prompted me to recall people and situations I hadn't thought about for years. And, as an outsider, he found fascinating things that I had taken for granted and pressed for more details. Sometimes, we exchanged drafts four or five times. Although the process was painstaking, this working relationship made writing the book more enjoyable and produced a result far better than I could have achieved otherwise. And as a byproduct of our working together, Steve and I developed a wonderful friendship.

In the end, I was surprised by how much territory we had covered. But it is important that everyone understand that this is not intended to be a complete history. I have many friends with whom I have had delightful experiences who were not included. Often, it was simply the result of the haphazard way memory works. That doesn't mean I cherish their friendships any less.

The stories I have chosen to tell don't necessarily reflect our daily lives. It's more of a newscast of my life: events that proved to be turning points; anecdotes about incidents comical, poignant, instructive or, in some cases, hair-raising; and people who were inspirational, colorful or otherwise unforgettable. For instance, the stories of our sailing adventures hardly touch on the decades of glorious sailing trips in the Northeast and the Caribbean, where we would drop anchor in local gunkholes, swim a little, and then barbecue dinner as we watched the sun set over remote crescent beaches.

While I devote much space to the people who shaped my childhood and my adult life, I devote much less to the treasured experiences Genevieve and I have had with our sons as adults, their spouses and our grandchildren. Those stories are for them to tell, and I encourage them to do so.

And now, as I settle into total retirement in our new home at NewBridge on the Charles, I look back with great pleasure at the chapters in my life: a close family childhood; 40 years in business with my father; and 20 years in business with Genevieve and one or more of our sons.

Before I close, I want to express my appreciation to Dr. Michael Feldberg, a longtime colleague and dear friend, for his comments and suggestions on draft chapters of the book. I want to offer the same gratitude to Judi Garner and Stephanie Call, my longtime colleagues at the New England Archives of the American Jewish Historical Society. Judi and Stephanie, who are now the mainstays of the new Wyner Family Jewish Heritage Center, provided not only insightful feedback on the book, but also invaluable help digging through my family's records to clarify my sometimes-muddled memories. I also tapped my cousin Dick Ember's deep reservoir of family lore.

I must note that for Steve, this was a family project: His wife, Judith, copyedited the book, smoothing the flow and sharpening the content; his sister, Ann Maas, restored photos from the ravages of old age. Further backstopping the project was David Richwine, a longtime *Globe* copy editor and unusually careful reader. As to any remaining mistakes, however, I must take full credit.

Michael, Judi and Stephanie, along with Genevieve, always offered encouragement at just the right time when I – it was never Steve, who was always full of energy and enthusiasm – seemed to run out of steam.

Introduction

Many years ago, I was driving to work along Route 1 in Dedham when I noticed scores of people standing by their cars as they watched flames leap 50 feet into the air from a building set back from the highway.

As I looked on for a moment, I realized that no firefighters were around. It seemed ridiculous to contemplate, but everyone evidently assumed that someone else had already called in the alarm. I went to a pay phone – this was decades before cell phones – and dialed the Dedham Fire Department. Sure enough, officials there knew nothing about the fire. Fortunately, no one was hurt, but the building was gutted by the time the trucks arrived. Since then, whenever I run across a problem, I never sit back and assume that someone else has taken steps to address it.

But the fact of the matter is that I couldn't have acted in any other way than I did that morning. When I see something wrong, I try to fix it.

I am a product of my upbringing. My father drilled into me such lessons as your word is your bond, and doing the right thing is its own reward regardless of whether anyone notices.

I know it sounds corny, but when I first heard the story from my mother of how George Washington owned up to chopping down that cherry tree, I believed it. Not only that, I found myself looking around for ways in which I could demonstrate the same quality of honesty.

And to this day, I'm inspired by another George, my father's father, who arrived in the small South African town of Malmesbury an exotic stranger – a Jew from Lithuania – and left as a beloved pillar of the community. I treasure my copy of the letter the leading citizens of Malmesbury wrote in tribute to my grandfather when his family left South Africa in 1899:

"We can assure you, you have always shewn in every possible way, not only by your sterling business qualities, but in all matters relating to the welfare and progress of the Town and District, your hearty, cordial and loyal cooperation for the benefit of the whole community."

I feel that my life is a link in two chains. The first is that of the Jewish people. When I was a boy, my father would often say to me that people had fought and died for 3,000 years so that I could be born a Jew. Who was I to decide to break that chain?

The second chain consists of the creed of my family. The best way I could honor my parents and grandparents was to live a life of integrity and service.

When I was a child, I would listen with admiration as my parents and grandparents recalled times in their lives when they had to make tough, sometimes painful decisions. I grew up on the stories about how my father's father built a Boston landmark while helping the city's Jews build a community, and about how my father's mother, Gussie, helped establish Boston's first Jewish hospital while raising money and traveling to Palestine to help Henrietta Szold build a Jewish hospital there.

I don't want to paint my family as a collection of high-minded, self-sacrificing saints. They had their foibles and idiosyncrasies. They made their share of mistakes and harbored not a few secrets. But they knew how to balance work and play, community and home.

I watched my widowed father travel with his grandchildren, always taking two – one of my sister's boys and one of ours. First, they would go fishing in Northern Canada or the Caribbean, learning to appreciate nature. Then they advanced to Europe, visiting museums and historical sites. Finally, they toured Israel, where they saw the grave of my great-grandfather Rabbi Abraham Yitzhak Edelman on the Mount of Olives, and the fruits of the work for Hadassah of his daughter and my grandmother Gussie.

I was doubly blessed in that my mother's family left a deep impression on me as well. Her father, Samuel Goldberg, escaped the prospect of 25 years in the clutches of the czar's army by fleeing the country under a new name. In Boston, he went from itinerant watchmaker to owner of a prominent downtown jewelry store. He used his earnings to bring over his widowed father and many other relatives, helping them establish new lives in America. My cousins have told me that my grandfather Goldberg was revered as a hero in their families.

My Goldberg relatives inculcated in me the importance of family. As a child, I would spend Sundays with my mother's family. Every day, I would hear my mother's long phone conversations with her mother and sisters.

Since I've shared more than two-thirds of my life with my wife, Genevieve, many of the stories I tell in this book are our stories. And the lessons that we hope to pass along reflect a blending of those of our two families, the Wyners and the Gellers, as well as those that Genevieve and I have come to embrace over our years together.

As I look back at my experiences, I see them in a new light. Genevieve has broadened my horizons in so many ways, not the least of which is teaching me to be more empathetic. By her example, I have learned the importance of taking time to listen to people with whom I disagree, so as to see things through their eyes.

I had hoped it would be simple to gather my grandchildren around me to pass along family stories just as I had learned them. When they were young, I could do so on occasion. But now, children face many more demands and distractions than I or even my own sons did. If that's not enough, there are so many more stories to tell if I add my own to those of previous generations.

I don't expect anyone to read this book all in one sitting, but I hope my grandchildren and nieces and nephews will pick it up now and then, and perhaps pass it along to their children.

Some of the stories are amusing, some embarrassing, some serious. I hope that all are instructive, if only to explain the heritage and experiences that shaped their less than perfect author.

The most important bequest I can leave my children and grandchildren is not material. Rather, it's the values that will help them forge their own links in the chains of our family and our people.

PART I: THE PEOPLE WHO MADE ME

- **George Wyner:** From the shtetl to the Ritz

- **Gussie Wyner:** Turning dreams into reality

- **The Goldbergs:** My mother's daring, debonair family

- **Rudolph Wyner:** Not your run-of-the-mill factory owner

- **Sara Wyner:** A mix of pride, probity and playfulness

- **Edward Wyner:** Harvard rogue to Ritz legend

- **Two of a kind:** Cousin quizzes Picasso; aunt outwits Nazis

GEORGE WYNER

*How my grandfather journeys from the land
of the shtetl to the top of the Ritz*

AMONG MY EARLIEST MEMORIES of my father's father are vacations on Nantasket Beach, where the extended Wyner clan would gather for the summer. We'd go for early-morning swims, my grandfather – wearing a full wool jersey bathing suit complete with modesty skirt – plowing right into the chilly waters while I skittishly followed. Even in his 70s, he was in robust health. When he tossed me a medicine ball, it packed a punch that shook my reed-thin body.

To think, he was born the week before Abraham Lincoln signed the Emancipation Proclamation. I doubt, though, that there was much talk of the far-off American Civil War in Lithuania, a land still under the rule of the Russian czar. George (Gershon Eleazar) was born on Dec. 26, 1862, the last of four children of lumber dealer Yehuda Leib Wyner and his wife, Rachel. At the time, the family was living in Antakalnis, a northeast suburb of Vilna next to Butrimonys.

My great-grandfather Yehuda Leib Wyner.

Jews had been living in the Vilna area since the fourteenth century, coming under various rule as Poland, Lithuania and Russia contested the region. In the nineteenth century, Lithuania was part of the Pale of Settlement, the swath of territory that today spans Ukraine, Poland and the Baltic States. Unless they received special permission, Jews could live nowhere else in the Russian Empire. Many eked out a living in shtetls like that buffed up a bit in *Fiddler on the Roof*. They were subject to the fickle whims of nature and the brutal anti-Semitism – often state-sanctioned – of their Christian neighbors.

Despite their perilous environment, many Jews flourished. Vilna came to be known as the Jerusalem of Lithuania. Before World War II, Jews made up nearly half its population. Among them were merchants, writers and musicians, teachers and scientists. At its peak, the Jewish population numbered 240,000. But after Hitler was finished, only a tenth of that number remained.

ESCAPING THE TSAR

But that would be some 80 years, one world war and one revolution into the future. For now, my grandfather's greatest fear was being dragooned into the Russian army. His oldest brother, Baruch, had been spared that fate and saw to it that his younger brothers would be as well. Born a decade before George, Baruch is believed to have gone into the lumber business with his father and to have achieved such success that he was allowed to travel outside the Pale – and that freedom put him in a position to help his brothers emigrate.

At age 5, George already had a job, according to his daughter, Frances. He was entrusted with keeping wild animals away from the apple orchards leased by his father. George also gave Frances a glimpse of the poverty of the times. He loved the cooked prunes that relatives served at dinner, but his parents would admonish him not to eat the last one on his plate; they didn't want him to humiliate the hosts should they have no more to serve.

Only 13, George's brother Henry left Lithuania in 1870 with Baruch's help. He wangled his way aboard a ship as a cabin boy and traveled as far as Australia. Along the way, he hooked up with an enterprising fellow Jew, who went by the exotic name of "Singapore Joe" Fisher. They launched various businesses together in Australia, including a circus. Hearing about opportunities in South Africa, Henry settled in Stellenbosch, outside of Cape Town, in the late 1870s. He kept in touch with his family back in Lithuania, returning home briefly around 1880 to marry the bride they had picked for him, Annie Potruch.

Annie was the granddaughter of Zalmen Solomon Mickleshanski, a close friend of Yehuda's who was also in the lumber business nearby. Among Mickleshanski's other grandchildren was the famed art historian Bernard Berenson, who was born two years after my grandfather.

Around the time his brother Henry married, George began his own journey to South Africa. He went by way of London, where he visited Henry's sister-in-law Julia and her husband, Leon Eyges.

MONKEY BUSINESS

Family lore has it that when George joined Henry in South Africa they teamed up as itinerant peddlers. They would buy various supplies in Cape Town, load them up on mules and horses, and travel the countryside selling to Boer farmers. In his history of the family, Frances's grandson (and my cousin) Dick Ember writes that the brothers were so poor at first that they had to rely on a one-eyed horse. One of my grandfather's yarns sounds like a case of Tarzan meets John Wayne. By this time, the brothers had acquired a couple of horses. As they rode them one day, they ran into heavy traffic – of the wildlife variety. Here is Dick's version of the story:

> They encountered a large troop of baboons, crowding around them on the sides of a trail. Henry was scared and wanted to turn back. With time and supplies limited, the 19-year-old George insisted on forging straight ahead. The baboons appeared ever more menacing, at least to Henry, who finally spurred his horse to a gallop to get past the threat. At this point, George would, in his storytelling, recall that Henry was no great horseman, and Henry's horse instantly became an out-of-control runaway. George, in the best Tom Mix cowboy fashion, chased after Henry, and while holding the reins of his own horse, pulled the frightened Henry onto his saddle as Henry's horse ran off into the distance.

Dick told me another story he heard from his grandmother that suggests that George was as willing to stand up to bigots as to baboons:

> George arrived at the home of a Boer farmer the same day as three other Jewish peddlers. In the evening, the Boer farmer gathered them together and asked, 'Are any of you Jewish?' The three were silent, but George spoke up and said proudly, 'Yes, I'm Jewish.' The Boer farmer then replied: 'You, Wyner, you're an honest fellow; you can stay overnight in the house. The rest of you, you can sleep in the barn with the horses.'

The brothers set aside enough money to open a grain warehouse in Malmesbury, where George become the town's first Jewish resident. Henry and his family lived nearby in Stellenbosch, before moving to Boston in 1894 to be near his wife's sisters. For many years, a picture of George standing below his business sign, "G. Wyner," has graced the front cover of our family Haggadah.

My grandmother Gussie Wyner flanked by her father, Rabbi Avraham Edelman, and by
her husband, George, probably after her 1891 marriage in New York.

GUSSIE'S SPELL

By now in his late 20s, George was ready to marry. His father had arranged a match for him, too: Masha Potruch, Annie Wyner's sister. Masha was then living in Boston with Julia and Leon Eyges, who had emigrated from London. George booked passage to the United States. Landing in New York on the way to Boston, he stayed with his sister, Sarah, who was married to Isaac Snitkin. The doting sister told George that she wanted to introduce him to a lovely girl. George was reluctant, though, because his father had specifically directed him to go to Boston and marry Masha. But Sarah persisted, and George finally agreed to wait in Central Park for a chance to see this special girl walk by. He promised that if he liked what he saw, he would call on her. Once he set eyes on Gertrude (Gussie) Edelman, Masha in Boston didn't have a chance. George was enchanted by the 20-year-old native of Minsk.

Not wishing to cross his father, George wrote him that Sarah had introduced him to a wonderful girl, the daughter of Rabbi Avraham Edelman. The dutiful son asked his father for his blessing to marry Gussie rather than Masha. Instead of writing back, Yehuda – who must have been doing well in the lumber business – hopped a trans-Atlantic steamer to check out the prospective bride. He was impressed with her, but not with the hustle and bustle of New York City. Within a couple of days, he was back aboard the same ship on its return trip to Europe.

After their marriage in 1891, Gussie agreed to return with her new husband to South Africa, but made him promise that they would move back to America in a decade if she was not happy. They prospered in Malmesbury, as George expanded his business into raising cattle and ostriches. (I once saw an ostrich egg he kept as a souvenir; it must have been 10 inches wide.) The newlyweds quickly set about raising a family. Frances Rose arrived on Dec. 8, 1892; Isadore Alfred (better known as IA), on Nov. 14, 1893; my father, Rudolph Harold, on April 28, 1895; and Edward Newton, on August 20, 1897. One of the few surviving pictures from Malmesbury shows the family together with their staff. In a letter written some 75 years later to one of his nephews, my father describes the photograph as showing him "in the arms of a nursemaid on the 'stoop' of my home in Malmesbury." Rudolph is dressed in a gown that he may have worn for his bris. It has stayed in the family for years, and our grandson Samuel wore it for his circumcision ceremony.

And, in 1895, my father made three: George and Gussie Wyner with baby Rudolph and his older siblings, Frances and Isadore Alfred (soon to be known as IA).

George Wyner's Malmesbury store sold grain and, as the little sign says, Cadbury chocolate, among other sundries.

A SAD SENDOFF

With signs of another Boer War – pitting the British against the Dutch Afrikaners as in 1880-81 – Gussie called in her 10-year chit for the family to return to America. Some 40 Malmesbury residents signed a farewell letter. Dated June 16, 1899, and addressed to "Mr. George Wyner, Merchant," it reads:

> We the undersigned, residents of the town of Malmesbury, having learnt of your early departure from amongst us, do hereby wish to express to you our regret on your leaving us.
>
> During the time you have been amongst us, we can assure you, you have always shown in every possible way, not only by your sterling business qualities, but in all other matters relating to the welfare and progress of the Town and District, your hearty, cordial, and loyal cooperation for the benefit of the whole community.
>
> And now that you are retiring, we have much pleasure in expressing the hope, that you will enjoy the leisure, one so richly deserves after years of toil and business worries, which are invariably the necessary evils in connection with all undertakings of so extensive in nature, as those, in which you were engaged.
>
> We, all, wish you, and family, a safe and pleasant voyage; a happy reunion with all, who are near and dear to you, and Mrs. Wyner; and should you decide once more, to return to South Africa, we need hardly inform you we will all hail, with delight, your presence amongst us.

The signatures include names that would become prominent in South African history: Smuts, Botha and de Klerk. Later, in New York, several South Africans presented George with a silver tray engraved with a similar message and set of signatures. (See Appendix for copy of document.)

On the way to America, the family spent several months in London. My father, who was about 4, recalled that at one point during the stay he feared he might never see his parents and siblings again. During a visit to the Greater Britain Exhibition in 1899, he wandered off and got lost. A policeman, who happened to be a Sikh, noticed the crying child. He hoisted Rudolph up on his shoulders and walked around in the crowd. What a sight it must have been, this little white boy being carried around by a bearded, turbaned bobby. Incidentally, my father said the family rented rooms in London at 221 Baker Street, which would have put them right next door to Sherlock Holmes (221B Baker Street). I'm not sure if they were aware of the fictional detective.

The family arrived in New York in August 1899. Murray, the last of the children, was born there on June 15, 1900. After having been the proverbial big fish in a small pond back in South Africa, my grandfather must have found the New York commercial world overwhelming and impersonal. He opened an ostrich feather store, catering to the hat business and representing many of the South African ostrich farmers in sales across the United States. Accustomed to sealing deals with a handshake, he was an easy target for unscrupulous businessmen. He was said to have lost a fortune by putting his faith in people who failed to keep their word. Some four decades later, at the ceremony held for the unveiling of my grandfather's memorial, Selig Edelman, Gussie's brother and a prominent attorney, referred to this period in his eulogy:

> I saw him many years ago under the stress of adversity, when he was badly hurt by the treachery of those whom he had trusted implicitly because of his general faith in human nature. There was no bitterness or rancor on his part, no vengeful spirit, no vindictiveness; he remained true to himself whether fortune smiled or frowned upon him.

BUILDING A LIFE IN BOSTON

In 1903, the family moved to Boston. Their first house was at 9 Gaston Street in Roxbury, which was then predominantly Gentile. Indeed, at the turn of the century, according to *The Jewish Advocate*, "There were so few families of the Hebrew faith that it was seldom that a 'minyan' could be assembled from the neighborhoods of Dorchester and Roxbury together." But within a few years, several hundred Jewish families had settled in Upper Roxbury and Dorchester. Although not religiously devout, George donated the land for the majestic Adath Jeshurun, better known as the Blue Hill Avenue Shul, which opened in 1906. Around 1910, the family moved about a mile south to 61 Charlotte Street.

The street was home to several other Jewish families: A few doors up were the Goldbergs, my mother's family. Other neighbors included the Rabbs (then Rabinovitz), later of Stop and Shop fame, and Judge Jacob Kaplan and his family. During the first few years of their marriage, my Aunt Frances and her husband (and cousin), Francis Solomon Wyner, lived in my grandparents' spacious corner house. To avoid confusion, Francis was called Sol. Soon, another Wyner took up residence there: the first grandchild,

Anne. With three doting uncles, she must have been one spoiled little girl. When their nest finally emptied, my grandparents settled in a townhouse at 9 Marlborough Street in Back Bay.

Brothers Henry and George Wyner flank Henry's daughters Gertrude and Margaret. That's George's first granddaughter, Anne, in front, and his Charlotte Street house in background.

While my grandparents would ultimately live in four different locations in Boston, George's office remained throughout at 18 Tremont Street. He had a corner suite on an upper floor with a view of Boston Common. I still have his chairs in my office at the family business. Brother Henry already had an office in the same building. Later, Henry's sons would have their law offices there.

George's original stationery lists his business as "ostrich feathers." Among his business connections was brother-in-law Sam Edelman, who had followed sister Gussie to South Africa. As the feathers became less fashionable, George added "real estate" to his letterhead. By 1915, "ostrich feathers" were off the letterhead, but my father's name was on it.

George Wyner in his office at 18 Tremont Street, where he managed his real estate dealings for more than a quarter of a century.

AN EYE FOR PROPERTY

With an eye for value, George purchased properties all over Greater Boston. In Harvard Square, he invested in the Read Block building, which for decades was home to the Wursthaus and the Tasty restaurants. When his partner backed out after a year, George returned his share of the investment. Some four years later, the man once again had regrets. "I made a terrible mistake," he told George. "I should have never gotten out of the deal." George let him buy in again for the same amount (his descendants are still our partners). You can see why the South Africans were so won over by the immigrant who first came to them without a penny.

While he may have been overly trusting in New York and uncommonly generous to his business partners, George was a canny investor. One story the family fondly remembers concerns the purchase of a Back Bay property. After touring the building and listening to the real estate agent go on and on about how it was such a terrific place, George said, "I'll take it." But the agent kept enumerating its virtues, concluding: "And, Mr. Wyner, the cellar is dry as a bone."

"Cellar? I never looked in the cellar," my grandfather said. "Let's go look." They walked down to the basement, and it was wet. So much for that deal.

Decades later, whenever I became overeager about something, my father would tell me: "Remember the wet cellar."

George's biggest project was the Ritz-Carlton, overlooking the Public Garden. Originally, he intended to build an apartment house at the Newbury Street site, but Mayor James Michael Curley prevailed on him to build a luxury hotel instead. Working with Curley had its advantages, such as an exemption from the height limit. At 16 floors, it was the tallest building on Newbury Street. But what really gave the hotel stature was the Ritz name. It became only the second in America, after New York, with official ties to the original Ritz in Paris. The son of the Paris hotel's founder would later attend my grandfather's funeral.

RED-FACED IN THE RITZ

When the Ritz opened in 1927, my grandfather put my Uncle Eddie in charge. Later, my grandparents would move to a small apartment on the 16th floor. Though he wasn't running the hotel, my grandfather did have a pass key to all of its rooms – he used it instead of the key to his own apartment. One night, he took the elevator to the 15th floor instead of the 16th. Not realizing his mistake, he walked to what he thought was Unit 1604. He opened the door, ambled into the bedroom, took off his shoes and stretched out on the bed. Then he heard unfamiliar voices inside the apartment. When he stepped into the living room, he was met with the stares of strangers. Then it dawned on him that he was on the wrong floor. Leaving his shoes and coat behind, he rushed out in embarrassment. He asked a porter to retrieve his things, and he turned the passkey over to Eddie.

If Grandfather were to come back today, he'd be lost. The Ritz is now the Taj Boston, and the new Ritz is on the other side of the Common.

Once his business was firmly established, my grandfather would frequently start his day with a trip to Long Pond in Plymouth. Sacco, his chauffeur and all-around fix-it man, would drive Grandfather at 4 a.m. to go fishing. After a few hours, he'd head in for work.

When my grandmother traveled on Hadassah business to Palestine, my father wrote her detailed letters that included Grandfather's fishing exploits. In a letter dated July 5, 1927, Father makes a special point of clarifying the number of fish grandfather had caught on an excursion from Nantasket:

> The great event of the week-end of course was Father's fishing trip, and about this we have already sent you a radio [telegram]. The count was fourteen pickerel and one bass. In sending the [cable], however, we put it down as fifteen pickerel, because at the rate of twenty-one cents a [word] we did not think it worth while to distinguish the exact classification of the catch. We trust that you will pardon this inaccuracy and assure you that in a case of any such diversions from the truth in order to eliminate the excess cost of radio messages, we will always clear it up in a confirming letter.

In the same letter, my father assured his mother that her new maid, who replaced "the little Helen," was working out, although my grandfather admired her for more than her housekeeping skills: "Father finds her more agreeable to the eye than Helen was, but I am watching most carefully and assure you that I will protect your interest."

As I noted earlier, Sacco's duties extended beyond driving the car. In the absence of my grandmother, he basically took over. Again, from that July letter:

> Sacco is the man who is in charge of the department which I would call 'Special cuisine for Mr. Wyner.' He seems very proud of the fact that he has the most intimate knowledge of what Father might like and is giving various directions at all times with regard to the quantity of scallion that should be placed in the beet soup, the particular kind of scallion Mr. Wyner likes, etc.

Morris Sacco was with my grandfather to the end. Early on the morning of January 2, 1943, my grandfather was lacing up his boots to go fishing out at Long Pond when he suddenly died of what was believed to have been a stroke.

My grandfather, right, with one of his regular fishing companions at Long Pond in Plymouth in 1920.

A LIFE LED TO THE FULLEST

A "large and significant gathering of men and women from all walks of life [including] representatives of the outstanding religious and philanthropic institutions of our community" gathered for the unveiling of my grandfather's memorial at Adath Jeshurun Cemetery in Roxbury, as the *Advocate* reported.

Rabbi Joshua Loth Liebman, the nationally renowned rabbi of Temple Israel in Boston, officiated along with Rabbi Chaim Goldin of the synagogue my grandfather helped establish, Adath Jeshurun Congregation. The *Advocate* account of the event primarily quotes from the eloquent eulogy I cited earlier by Gussie's brother Selig. In it, he enumerated George's many qualities:

Courage. "As a youth, in the spirit of a pioneer, he left his childhood home and his parents, and went into the wilderness of the dark continent of Africa, to establish his fortune in the opening of a new and dangerous frontier. ... And in the later decades of his life, he exhibited courage that exceeded even the courage of his early years, the courage to live each minute of his life to its [fullest], without fear of the future or the end of life."

Humbleness. "He would not disdain anyone, nor display rude impatience or haughtiness towards others. His geniality was for all. ... His lips, as his heart, were clean of contumely or hate."

Generosity. "He gave as if it were a debt he owed for his material success – a success not attained by trampling upon the rights of others, but bestowed upon him by God as the fruit of honest effort and diligent application of such capacities as he was endowed with."

Good nature. "George Wyner had his delectable lighter side, his jokes, his jovial companionship, his early morning fishing parties with his cronies, that ever-present humorous vein which ran through all the realities of life and robbed them of their grimness."

My grandfather died when Franklin Roosevelt was in the White House. As I mentioned at the start of this chapter, he was born when Lincoln was president. Fittingly, Selig cited the 16th president at the close of the eulogy:

So, we here today have come, as Abraham Lincoln said at Gettysburg: not so much to dedicate a monument to George Wyner, as to dedicate ourselves, the living, that we may emulate his way of life and draw upon the rich store of spiritual treasures which he cultivated during his life and which he would wish to transmit to us as a heritage and a guide in our earthly journey.

GUSSIE WYNER

From Boston to Jerusalem, my grandmother turns dreams into reality

AS A LITTLE BOY, I was a bit overwhelmed by my grandmother Gussie Wyner. She would greet me with a big, juicy kiss right on the lips. But then everything about Gussie was big: her personality, her presence, her devotion to causes. I picture her standing in the kitchen with her maid, Hazel, fussing over a giant coal stove and shooing me out of the room. The community pictured her rallying troops on behalf of Beth Israel Hospital, Hadassah and other Jewish causes.

One of six children of Rabbi Avraham Edelman and his wife, Esther, Gussie came to America from Minsk as a teen. Before marrying George, she helped support the family by running a garment business out of their home.

To my grandmother, Israel was not some biblical ideal or far-off dream. Both her father and his father moved to Palestine in their later years to study. Both are buried there. In Boston, she was among the founders of the local chapter of Hadassah, which early on raised $50,000 for the organization's hospital in Jerusalem. Gussie launched America's first Junior Hadassah chapter and installed my mother as its president.

In 1912, Gussie was 42 years old and the mother of five children.

17

BEFRIENDING HENRIETTA SZOLD

In the 1920s, Gussie traveled to Palestine on several occasions, both to see her father and to research medical needs, taking a particular interest in eye care for Jewish and Arab children. On one trip, she accompanied Hadassah's legendary founder, Henrietta Szold, who became a friend. We have a letter to my grandmother from Henrietta, written in March 1926 on the stationery of Cunard liner RMS Berengaria. She thanks Gussie for sending her a portfolio-like briefcase, noting that she was touched that the card accompanying it closed with the words "your sincere co-worker." She continues:

> The signature made me glad, for there is still so much work ahead to be done by us, and the ranks of our co-workers must be enlarged indefinitely if we are to achieve it in the proper spirit and according to approved standards.

Gussie had entrusted her friend with a mission, as Henrietta writes:

> Please be assured that everything will be done to get the check and your messages to your father. I may not be able to deliver them myself before Pesach. If that should be the case, some reliable person will deliver them to him before Pesach, and I shall see him during the holiday week. But I shall make every effort to deliver them myself.

Eventually, Henrietta did find the time to visit my great-grandfather, but he wasn't home. Instead, she talked with his landlady, who asked her to relay a message to Gussie. Apparently, her father was giving all the money she sent him to his yeshiva and neglecting his own needs. The rabbi was walking around in socks with holes and shoes that were falling apart. I have no further information on how my grandmother responded to this news, but knowing her, I am sure she took action to fix matters.

Gussie and her father head off to Israel.

CHAMPIONING BETH ISRAEL

Back in Boston, Gussie was equally devoted to Beth Israel Hospital, Boston's first Jewish hospital. She saw it from its first home in a Roxbury mansion to its sprawling campus off Longwood Avenue, serving three decades as treasurer of the women's auxiliary. My father would joke that she'd never tell how much money she had in the kitty; but whenever someone asked for something the hospital needed, she was ready with a check.

If you go into the main entrance of the East Campus of Beth Israel and take the corridor that heads to the Rabb building, you'll see large plaques on both sides of the hallway, each designating a different year's roster of people who became Life Members of the hospital. At the bottom of many of the plaques, you'll see inscribed "Mrs. George Wyner, Treasurer." Gussie invented the concept of Life Membership to encourage large gifts for the hospital's endowment and capital drives. She later adapted the idea for Hadassah, as Perpetual Membership. The fundraising tool has since been copied by all sorts of charities across the nation.

Just as with Hadassah, Gussie didn't just raise money for Beth Israel; she kept a close eye on how it was spent. She pushed for the hospital's first maternity floor (which would bear her name), as well as for a surgical research lab and a children's pavilion. At the time of her death in 1948, she was still treasurer of the auxiliary as well as a member of the hospital's board of trustees.

My grandmother went on to become involved in other Jewish organizations, including the Women's Committee for Brandeis University and Boston University's Hillel House, where she was the first female charter member.

Gussie around 1940, surrounded by her children (from left): Rudolph, IA, Frances, Murray and Edward.

19

DONATE, DAHLING

Gussie always seemed to be raising money for some cause or another. And she wouldn't take no for an answer. "Dahling, you know I need an ad," she'd say to each of my father's suppliers as she solicited for charity publications. In her later years, she was known as this tough little Jewish lady with round thick glasses. She put many, many miles on her chauffeur-driven car. So many women over the years have told me my grandmother was their mentor. When she was on a trip to Palestine in 1927, my father wrote her about how much she was missed by the local Hadassah chapter:

> Mrs. Kalman writes that they will never do as well as they do when you are around. She says that she can see your face in her dreams, and that you speak to her every night urging her on. Mrs. Lurie also says they cannot tell how much they miss you. Last year at this time, they tell us they had over $1,200, of which almost $600 had been collected personally by you. This year they have about the $600 that you did not collect and are short about the $600 which you did collect. In other words, they have a total so far of $600.

The welfare of the Jews was always on her mind. One family story – which may be apocryphal – tells of Gussie standing outside the Ritz, worrying about the cracks in the sidewalk. In her heavily accented English, she was said to have asked: "Is that good for the Jews or not good for the Jews?" (I wondered if that accent was part of her shtick. Her brother Selig spoke mellifluous English.)

A GOVERNOR PAYS HIS RESPECTS

An overflow crowd – including Mayor Curley and Governor Paul Dever – attended my grandmother's funeral at Temple Israel after her death on April 17, 1949. In his eulogy, Rabbi Irving A. Mandel called her

> one of that early band of pioneers, a true woman of valor, who felt the needs of her community and then did something about it. She was both an architect and engineer, both strategist and tactician, one who was inspired in her tasks and who generated enthusiasm in others: that is the definition of a leader. … The thought of the world has been molded by its scholars. The technology of the world has been fashioned by the scientists, but the soul of the world is cultivated by noble individuals such as Gussie Wyner who made philanthropy and community endeavor her spiritual vocation.

Noting how Gussie had influenced Hadassah worldwide by introducing life memberships, Judith Epstein, honorary national vice president of Hadassah, told the mourners: "Her belief that good would conquer evil was a bulwark in our times, and her faith in the coming generation made her an influence for training them in leadership."

The president of Boston's Hadassah chapter, Romayne Goldberg, added:

> Long before most of the world acknowledged the necessity for the recreation of a Jewish homeland, she had the prophetic vision to sit with the engineers who were drawing the blueprints for the return of the exiles. She planned and directed when she and Hadassah were young; she planned and directed when she became older in years but never in spirit or mind. She died in the driver's seat, mapping out a clear and direct road on which others were to carry the torch.

On behalf of my grandmother's other great cause, Beth Israel Hospital, the women's auxiliary president, Mrs. Joseph Levy, said:

> From our midst has gone a light – a light which has led the way steadily, persistently and unswervingly. ... Hers was a loyalty which could never be questioned and hers was a vision which inspired all who were fortunate enough to work with her. We mourn her passing but we are thankful for the privilege we enjoyed in having had her with us these many years.

In her will, grandmother didn't forget the long-time helper at home who helped free her to devote so much time to the community. She left enough money for Hazel to enroll at Boston University. She graduated at the age of 80.

THE GOLDBERGS

How my grandfather evaded the tsar, weathered a police strike and became the family hero

LET'S START WITH THE name: the Goldbergs. It's fake.

The real name was Zakon.

My mother's father, Sam, slipped out of Russia by changing his name to Goldberg. Had he used his real name, he might have been arrested at the border if officials had him on a draft list. Many young Jews left under similar circumstances. While non-Jews faced only two years of service, Jews were drafted for up to 25 years.

Samuel Udey Zakon was born in St. Petersburg in 1870, the first of seven children of Yehuda Halevi and Elizabeta Leah Zakon. Elizabeta was called die Sheine Leah for her beauty; Yehuda was known as der Reite Rebbe (the Red Rabbi) because of his red beard. Village children were said to shout, "Here comes the Red Rabbi!" when he made his rounds outside of St. Petersburg to teach and serve as a shochet for the kosher slaughter of animals. While he was not an ordained rabbi, Yehuda was a tzaddik – a pious person who has devoted his life to studying Torah.

My great-grandfather Yehuda Halevi Zakon was known as der Reite Rebbe (the Red Rabbi) because of his red beard.

My great-grandmother Elizabeta Leah was such a beauty in her youth that she was called die Sheine Leah.

Because he taught Jews in service to the czar, Yehuda received special permission to live in St. Petersburg. But in the late 1890s, he ran afoul of the authorities – supposedly for marrying a couple without official permission – and he and his family were exiled for two years to Polotsk in Belarus, within the Pale of Settlement. There, his daughter Sadie befriended Anna Heifetz, the future mother of the violinist Jascha Heifetz, who will figure later in the Goldberg family story; I'll talk about that in a chapter on my first trip to Europe.

By the time of his father's exile, Sam was starting a family in East Boston and making his way in the jewelry business. They lived at 376 Sumner Street. He had arrived around 1890 and four years later married Gertrude Katherine Finklestein, better known as Katy. He was 24; she was 16. Katy had come to America with her mother, who had owned and operated an inn in Pisalotas (Pushelot) near Panevezys in central Lithuania. It had been the family business for two generations.

My grandmother Gertrude Katherine (Finklestein) Goldberg.

My grandfather Samuel Goldberg, who changed his name from Zakon to escape the onerous Russian draft.

IN THE THICK OF THE POLICE STRIKE

Sam and Katy would have five children, beginning with Louis in 1895; followed by my mother in 1899 (named Sadie, but called Sara to avoid confusion with other Sadies in the family); Harry in 1902; Florence in 1903; and Dorothy in 1906.

After starting out as a watchmaker, Sam established his own store, Studio Jewelry. The shop faced the Boston Common, sitting at the corner of Tremont Street and Temple Place (today, it's the site of a deli and convenience store). The location had its downside. The store was ransacked the first night of the riots that followed the 1919 Boston police strike. In an article illustrated with a photograph of the store's smashed windows, *The Jewelers' Circular* (Sept. 17, 1919) described the attack:

> The Studio Jewelry Co. … one of the best lighted stores in town, was one of the first to suffer among the many establishments looted by the crowds, who seemed to have been obsessed with the spirit of Bolshevism, and who pillaged and destroyed with utter disregard of the consequences.

> Led by a bluejacket [sailor], Carl J. Boles, who, with eight other rioters, smashed the eight plate-glass windows of the Studio jewelry store, the mob simply helped themselves to everything in sight. All kinds of jewelry, toilet articles, china and cut-glass were seized. Not a single article was left. … In addition, the vandals broke up all the fixtures and fittings, including more than 100 trays, the fragments of which were scattered about the store and the street. The diamond goods, however, had been removed to the safes, so that these escaped.

> The following day the sailor was arraigned in the municipal court, his head swathed in bandages. He was charged with breaking and entering in the nighttime the Studio Jewelry Co.'s store. His head, the volunteer police said, had been cut by glass.

In his 1975 book *A City in Terror*, Francis Russell wrote: "Police opened fire directly on the plunderers in the Studio Jewelry Company at Temple Place."

According to one story that I haven't been able to verify, my mother's brother Louis tried defending the store with a gun.

IN-LAWS IN THE TURRETS

In the early 1900s, the Goldbergs moved to Dorchester, first to 9 Page Street and then to a large Victorian house at 44 Charlotte Street, not far from my father's family. By then, two grandparents had joined them. Sam had brought over his father in 1908 after his mother's death. Katy's mother, Rachel Finklestein Abrams Quint, moved in after being thrice-widowed. From all accounts, there was little chance of the Red Rabbi becoming husband No. 4; the two in-laws did not get along. Sam's father lived in one of the house's two commanding turrets, and Katy's mother in the other.

Sam and his father were among the founders of Congregation Beth El, better known as the Fowler Street Shul, which was dedicated in 1912 and modeled after the 1763 Touro Synagogue in Newport, Rhode Island. Its congregation moved to Newton in 1967, and the building was razed in 1998 to make way for housing. While my grandmother Goldberg wasn't a force of nature like grandmother Wyner (I don't think one family could accommodate two such people), she did volunteer for Hadassah and synagogue women's groups.

The Goldbergs were very family-centered. Besides his father, Sam brought over all his siblings: brothers Yale and Louis, and sisters Bronya, Haya, Sadie and Bessie. As sponsor, he had them use the name of Goldberg (his father's gravestone has both names). Communitywide, Sam was esteemed for his generosity and integrity. Among his admirers was Joe Gann, who started out as a traveling watchmaker. My grandfather was his first customer, Joe told me. And like Sam, Joe went on to found his own successful jewelry business. If the name sounds familiar, that's because his family donated the money that made possible Gann Academy in Waltham.

After retiring from the jewelry trade at age 55, Sam invested in retail store properties for the rental income. As a child, I recall accompanying him and my mother as they visited his merchant tenants in North Cambridge, Codman Square, Roxbury and Whitinsville (a village in Northbridge).

Sam and Katy would later move to the Jamaicaway, just a few blocks from where my family rented a house when I was a toddler. They followed us when we moved to Brookline, eventually living around the corner.

I still have my grandfather's old-fashioned jewelry scale, the kind in which one pan is balanced against another. It reminds me of the scales of justice. When I think back to how my grandfather led his life, that's a fitting image.

RUDOLPH WYNER

A Shakespeare scholar becomes a mill owner

THERE IS NO COMPLIMENT I value more highly than hearing people speak of me as they did of my father. To this day, I run into people who say, "I knew your father. He was a wonderful man." It was not so much because he did tremendous things, but because of the indelible impression he left. People thought he was brilliant. They thought he was funny. Whether friends and relatives or hard-boiled competitors, everyone enjoyed his company.

My father, in uniform, but much too young for battle.

When I look back at his childhood writings, I see glimmers of the man he would become, but mostly I'm struck by how quickly this South African native took to life as an American boy.

Writing his mother from a YMHA camp in Bournedale on Cape Cod, he boasts of the fishing and boating awards he and his brother Isi [IA] won. He blames his "shaky handwriting" on having just caught more than 20 fish. The only trouble is a bee's nest between two tents that has the campers in a tizzy. He closes by giving his love to his brothers and sisters, and asking his mother, "Are you having a good time?" Perhaps he figured that having him and IA out of the house was like a vacation for her.

Reading my father's diary from the year 1909, when he was 14, I find him by turns playful, thoughtful, curious, generous and mischievous.

At the time the family was living on Gaston Street in Boston. Rudolph describes a typical winter day during school vacation: davening in the morning, followed by twirling around the Gaston Street Skating Rink (as he has dubbed the ice patch in his yard), a trip to the movies and perhaps falling asleep with a Peck's "Bad Boy" book by his side.

A big fan of the movies, Rudolph writes of taking the trolley to movie palaces with names long since forgotten, like the Scenic Temple in the South End. Here he writes about how embarrassed he was when he didn't have the money for the fare (notice that his friends were Irish lads):

> When we rode home I thought Shaw was going to pay my fare as I had paid for him going there, but he thought I was going to pay for him both ways. Fortunately we met Al Maguire on the car and he lent us the money to pay our fares. I never felt so embarrassed in all my life, because we made the conductor wait a full minute for his fare and he kept saying, "Hurry up," so everybody could hear him.

Perhaps recalling his own shame, Rudolph told of another trip, when the conductor gave him two transfers by mistake. "I gave one to a poor working man next to me who had not paid his fare," he wrote.

> If you find the T to be a challenge today, it was even more of an adventure a century ago. Rudolph describes a hair-raising commute, to and fro, to music lessons. First, a man attempted to jump aboard as the trolley was moving, "but only got half of his body on and his legs were dragged along the street. He got into a fight with the conductor and he said he would complain. I signed my name as a witness for the conductor's side." On his return home, "the car in front of ours went off the track and ours had to go through Copley Square in a very roundabout way to Dudley Street."

'MAMMA, GOD BLESS HER'

With evident pride, Rudolph writes of his mother's charitable activities: "Mamma, God bless her, is treasurer for the [illegible] Ball. She was also treasurer for the Chanukah Play at the shul." Later, he notes, "Mamma's picture was in the *Post* and in the *Globe* to-day because she is treasurer for the Hadassah Ladies Auxiliary."

He keeps us abreast of his schoolwork. On one report card, he got all A's and B's, except for a "C" in neatness. One day he tells us he wrote 11 pages in Latin, and many of his diary entries are in French. *Pride and Prejudice* and *The House of the Seven Gables* were on his assigned reading list. His critique: "The first is a very good book, but is altogether different from the second, as one is a novel and the other a book full of ghosts. The conversations [in] some parts of 'Pride + Prejudice' [are] very brilliant. I like P+P better because it isn't so gloomy."

He was not always an angel at school. On March 4, he writes: "Taft was inaugurated to-day as the 27th President of USA, Sherman Vice-Pres. ... I had to stay 1 hour after school with Quincy for misbehavior."

Nor was he always an angel at home. On April 4: "First day of Passover. I went to Temple in the morning. Played ball in the afternoon. I got a scolding from Pa in the evening for not going to Temple for evening services."

Many of the entries concern sports. Referring to his brother, he writes, "I went to the B.A.A. marathon finish with Ed [and] Hibbard from [Roxbury Latin School], and I lifted [brother] Ed on our shoulders and he saw fairly well."

ONE DEGREE OF SEPARATION FROM LINCOLN

Scattered among notes about everyday life are news flashes from the outside world. The juxtapositions can be jarring, as in this entry from January 7: "Almost froze on the way to school. Earthquake in Messina, Italy. … Over 75,000 killed." Over subsequent days, he keeps tabs as the death toll rises to 200,000.

Reading the diary reminds us of how close – generation-wise – we are to what seems to be distant history. February 12 that year came on the centennial of Lincoln's birth. At a school assembly, the students were addressed by the president of the board of trustees, "who saw Lincoln." Rudolph vows: "I am going to take Lincoln for my ideal. I think he is a noble character, and although I cannot be as good as he, I will strive as well as I can to do as he did in regard to honesty, and justice, and all moral things."

Rudolph was on his way to achieving that goal, at least in the view of his mother's brother Selig. In response to a letter from Rudolph, Uncle Selig writes:

> Your charming little letter of the 14th pleased me very much. I liked the sentiments expressed by you, and above all, your sincerity. Of course, sincerity is a part of you, and it is apparent as well in your letter as it is in your conduct and speech. … Sincerity simply means the honesty of one's emotions and feelings. It means that the person who possesses it is true to himself and to all other human beings. … The heart is as visible and can be read as easily as the face. Therefore, the sincere boy or man will attract to himself and be loved by others who are sincere and true, and will get the most goodness, truth and beauty out of life.
>
> Matthew Arnold once said that as we grow older 'we unlearn the poetry of life and learn its prose.' He means that we stifle all that is noblest and purest in our hearts, and saturate ourselves with the purely material, and even the mean, vicious and ignoble things in life. He didn't mean that it was so in every case, but as a general rule. We can fight against it. Therefore, I say to you, keep on in a manner and bearing which accurately mirrors and reflects your inner self.

I would say that Dad met the challenge.

At Roxbury Latin, Rudolph demonstrated both his athletic and academic skills. He competed on the crew team, serving as its captain at one point. Among his teammates were two future college presidents, James Bryant Conant of Harvard and Bancroft Beatley of Simmons.

In a handwritten essay he composed when he was 16 or 17, Rudolph presents a sophisticated argument against the United States fortifying the Panama Canal as opposed to placing it under international control. Presciently, less than a decade after the Wright brothers flew their first plane, he cites the growing threat of aerial bombardment: "There is hardly a scientist who does not concede that aviation will be a great factor in our wars."

Rudolph left Roxbury Latin after his junior year, having passed an exam that qualified him to start his studies at Harvard. The trickiest part was showing proficiency in a foreign language. Using the Yiddish he had picked up from his parents, he passed the German test.

Rudolph, in his late teens, with the family Pierce-Arrow.

SHOWING UP A SHAKESPEARE SCHOLAR

His Harvard class of '15 included an assortment of people who would go on to establish themselves in very different ways. Among them: Edward Estlin Cummings, the poet better known by his lower-case pen name, e. e. cummings; the composer Roger Sessions; Christian Archibald Herter, who would serve Massachusetts as governor (1953-57) and the United States as secretary of state (1958-61); John Phillips (J.P.) Marquand, who would go on to chronicle Boston Brahmins in his Pulitzer Prize-winning novel *The Late George Apley* but gain his greatest fame by creating the fictional detective Mr. Moto (played by Peter Lorre in the movies); and Charles Lee Smith, who founded the American Association for the Advancement of Atheism and was the last known person convicted of blasphemy in the United States.

Rudolph wasn't a big joiner in college (unlike me, as you will come to see). He participated in crew, but only for his freshman year. He also belonged to the Menorah Society, a predecessor to Hillel, and the Argo Club, a Jewish fraternity. Jews made up 13 percent of his entering class.

Rudolph distinguished himself as a voracious scholar, one not cowed by the university's eminent roster of professors. He enjoyed recounting the time he challenged George Lyman Kittredge, a professor of English literature and a Shakespeare expert, about his use of a particular word (I don't remember anymore what it was). The professor, of course, disagreed with this young upstart. So at the next class Rudolph cited the *Oxford English Dictionary* as backing him up. "Does it?" Kittredge responded. "I'll have it changed." Lo and behold, Kittredge was an editor of the dictionary.

My father would point to that story as an example of why I should never hesitate to question authority or, for that matter, take anything on face value. His innate skepticism probably explains in part why later as a factory owner he would pull apart every piece of new machinery.

Knowledge stuck in my father's memory as if attached by one of the most resilient adhesives used by Shawmut Corporation, the company he would found. When he saw me breaking my teeth on the Latin of Caesar and Cicero at Roxbury Latin, he would amaze me by quoting at length from them both.

Rudolph could also quote almost every Shakespeare play, from beginning to end. I once ran into a fellow who said he took a course on the Bard from my father at Brandeis. "What are you talking about?" I asked him. "My father never taught at Brandeis." Well, it turned out that when my father, then in his 80s, attended a Shakespeare class there, he ended up appearing to lead it because he knew so much more than the teacher. I still have all of my father's copies of Shakespeare's plays, marked with his notes from studying under Kittredge.

By the way, the professor figured in another funny story my father told of his college days. It seems that Kittredge was never quite able to master the clock with the same precision as he did the Bard. Harvard had a rule that if a professor was late to class (I believe it was by five or 10 minutes), students didn't have to wait. Dad recalled that he and his classmates would stand at the classroom window watching Kittredge, supporting himself with a cane, make his way slowly across Mass. Ave. Noticing his students, the professor would stop in mid-street and check his watch. If he concluded he would be late, he'd abruptly turn around and totter away.

THE WOULD-BE DEVELOPER

After receiving his B.A. with honors, Rudolph joined his father in the real estate business. His first major ambition was to acquire and develop a property of his own. For nearly a year, he scoured the Boston area for a suitable spot. He decided to invest in an estate on Townsend Street in Roxbury. When he proudly announced the deal, his father said, "Congratulations on signing the purchase and sale agreement. I know you have spent a long time on this, but you know your mother has been raising money to build a hospital where Jewish doctors, rejected by other hospitals, will be able to practice. We have decided that your Townsend Street property is where it should be – so here is your money back."

Rudolph, who was still living at home at the time, didn't feel he was in the position to question his father – or, no doubt, take on his indomitable mother. So what he hoped would be his launching pad as a real estate tycoon became the first home of Beth Israel Hospital.

I didn't get the impression my father was all that angry about turning over the product of his months-long labor. Perhaps his heart wasn't in real estate. More likely, by the time my father told me the story, Shawmut was already such a successful company that he had buried any regrets.

The original Shawmut building (right) dated to 1795 and housed the oldest knitting mill in America.

Inspectors examining fabric just off the knitting machines and mending where necessary in photo taken between the wars.

THE RUN OF THE MILL

How did a Jewish boy born in a small South African town end up buying the oldest knitting mill in America? I wish I could answer that question, beyond saying that Rudolph's foiled foray into real estate left him looking for some other field in which to make his mark.

In 1916, he invested in the French and Ward Knitting Mill in Stoughton, which dated to 1795, and renamed it Shawmut Woolen Mills. Perhaps it was his cousin Leon Rubenstein who got Rudolph interested in textiles. Leon was a partner in the purchase along with Abraham Persky. My father would eventually buy each of them out after they went on to establish their own mills: Leon, Security Mills in Newton, and Abraham, Worcester Knitting Mills.

And so that is how our company, Shawmut, and Beth Israel Hospital both came to be founded in 1916.

Another early shareholder was Gilbert Harris, who had joined French and Ward in the early 1890s and advanced to the position of superintendent. I'm not sure how he liked reporting to my father, who was little more than half his age. I've heard Harris had a short fuse. He eventually left the company after some sort of disagreement. Apparently, he was the type who carried a grudge – as I was to discover decades later when I was blackballed in my initial attempts to join the Masons in Stoughton. The embarrassed lodge members eventually traced the blackballing back to Harris, and I was subsequently admitted.

My son the sailor: my father and grandmother.

My father's ham radio skills helped get him promoted to ensign.

The veterans: brothers IA, left, and Rudolph.

Just a year after launching the company, Rudolph joined the Navy and asked his father to help run the business in his absence. George said he would, provided Rudolph agreed to take his brothers into the business when they returned from the war, which he did. After graduating from the submarine school in New London, he was commissioned as an ensign on a sub that patrolled the East Coast. Because he had been a radio ham operator, he was made communications officer. He would joke that his most important responsibility was to be prepared to dump the lead-encased codebooks overboard should the sub come under attack. But by the time he was on active duty, the war was nearly over.

While he didn't have any war stories, Rudolph did come back with a harrowing tale of his training. To qualify for sub duty, he had to enter an enormous water tank through a lock at the bottom and then shoot up to the surface far above. He was equipped with a breathing apparatus like those used by trapped coal miners.

After the war, Dad returned to the factory. Even as he got the business off the ground, he did find time for a social life. Rudolph must have cut a dashing figure, as he picked up dates in his chauffeur-driven car. The only problem was that the driver, a fellow named James, wouldn't always be around to take him home. Rudolph and his date would be left hunting for a cab after the theater let out. One morning after

James had pulled his disappearing act, the chauffeur turned up walking with crutches. He had a big bandage wrapped around his ankle and a cock-and-bull explanation for what had happened to him. Rudolph would sometimes get so fed up with James that he would fire him – and then inevitably hire him back.

But all the while that my father was gallivanting about town, it turned out that the woman who would capture his heart was living just down the street.

SARA (GOLDBERG) WYNER

A surprising mix of pride, probity and playfulness

Dec. 4, 1923

"A memorable day. Blanco became 1 year and 4 mos old and incidentally we were married."

And so my mother began her honeymoon diary with this entry dated Dec. 4, 1923.

The passage captures so much about my mother. First, of course, her wry sense of humor. Then there's her fondness for dogs. And finally, while not intentionally, it reflects my mother's modesty. She did not like to draw too much attention to herself.

The passage continues: "The deed was done at the Hotel Somerset, about 7:15. Both of us paced our rooms nervously until the fatal moment and then came down and went through the ceremony gloriously."

The bride: "Incidentally we were married."

The Somerset is that giant U-shaped Mediterranean-style building that stands at the border of Back Bay and the Fenway. Today, it consists of condominiums. When my parents married, it had just celebrated a quarter century as one of Boston's finest luxury hotels.

In her wedding portrait, Sara looks like fairy tale bride. Her slender frame is enveloped in a gossamer gown that flows to the floor. Wearing a snug flower-bud headdress over her short wavy hair, she holds a heart-shaped bouquet.

Sara's maid of honor was her younger sister Florence; my father's best man was his younger brother Eddie. Rabbi Harry Levi, who by then had been leading Temple Israel for more than a decade, presided over the Tuesday evening ceremony.

"Rabbi Levi quite justly said we were the best couple he saw in the last twenty years," my mother wrote. In between the lines, she squeezed: "He liked our manner – was very much impressed and felt very optimistic about our future."

I'm sure my mother took great pride in that compliment. "Manner" meant a lot to her.

The couple spent their honeymoon night at a more recent addition to Boston's luxury scene. "I had already inscribed 'R H Wyner and wife' on the annals of the Copley Plaza [the previous] day," Sara wrote of her advance visit. She had inspected their quarters (Room 229) "and had the key in my pocket." So like my mother to be so meticulously prepared.

As to the couple's first night together, she keeps it succinct: "About twelve thirty we got to bed. (Curtains)."

Fashionably dressed for an outing in 1924.

Unusual for a woman of her day, my mother was a college graduate when she married (Boston University, '23) and did graduate work at Radcliffe. At BU, which was in Copley Square back then, Sara (known there as Sadie) studied philosophy – one of only three in her class with that major. The year she graduated, BU had 9,646 students, 4,011 of them women.

Sara was auditor of the Gamma Delta social organization, "her probity and sound observation, gained in the study of Philosophy, eminently qualifying her for this position of trust," according to the 1923 yearbook entry. She also served on the Standing Committee of the Sociological Society and on the Constitutional Committee of the Philosophical Society. "Her friends are many and deserved," the year-book entry concludes.

Lest Sara come off as sounding too serious, her photo in the 1922 yearbook is accompanied by the following poem, the first letter of each line spelling out her name:

She drives her car the most convenient way,
And takes her chance with bad breaks [sic] and the law,
Drawing the angry injured to her side,
Inimitable smile, the scowls soon thaw,
Each victim wishes her a pleasant ride.

MAD DASH TO THE SHIP

It's that fun, breezy side of Sara that lights up the pages of her honeymoon diary.

After their night at the Copley, they headed for New York, their first stop before a Caribbean cruise. "Our chief topic of conversation on the train was furniture and home decoration. Also Einstein's theory, etc. Yea, sure."

That night they took in a Broadway musical, *Spring Cleaning,* returning to their hotel "in a hansom cab, where the doors … opened and closed by an invisible agency. … I laughed until my appendix appealed for mercy."

Harrowing rather than hilarious would describe their cab ride to the docks. They caught a taxi at 9 a.m., the time they were supposed to be at the ship. When they hopped in, Sara told the driver "to beat it for the pier," but "[t]he dumbbell went the wrong way first."

As the minutes ticked by, the bride was a nervous wreck. But they arrived in plenty of time. At 9:20, Sara sighed in relief as she spotted their destination, Pier 9.

"It was lucky we rushed to get there," she wrote, tongue in cheek, "because the ship shoved off promptly at 1:45 p.m."

Sancho, their porter, treated the breathless newlyweds "like a couple of babes in the wood," Sara says, adding, "The funny thing is we like it. "

Just as they were unpacking, they experienced their first shipboard emergency: Their camera was broken. "After the entire ship's engineering force gave it up, the mechanical genius fixed it (that is, Rudolph thinks he fixed it)." Sara was already wise to the ways of the male ego.

That night, they donned their finest. "We dressed for dinner. We and no others. We became characters."

After playing mahjong, they turned in. "The lower berth was very comfortable. Also slept in the upper."

Over the next days, Sara reports skipping rope, playing checkers and keeping her eyes peeled for flying fish. "Damn things don't exist," she announces after one week.

The next day, though, she saw plenty of flying fish, but heavy seas confined her to her cabin. "They say that whenever there are any religious people aboard, the sea is very rough. We have five 'sisters of mercy' and, oh my! I wish they would have mercy."

While she ate in the cabin, "Rudy" (in later years, she would call him Ru or Ruey, and he called her Dolf) lunched in the dining room. There he found the portholes blocked and only one other companion. "His service in the submarine corps during the war proved of great value for that one meal – but I don't think from his description that its influence will carry through many more under these conditions."

A MACHETE MEMENTO

On their two-week anniversary, they arrived in Panama, where an elderly worker regaled them with "fairy tales about the canal." Shepherded around by a "chauffeuress," they saw "sugar cane, coconuts, coffee, bananas, pineapples, old ruins … and native children sans clothes."

In Panama City, Sara bought two ivory cigar holders and a machete. She doesn't report using it, though it sounds as if it might have come in handy. One evening she witnessed a man "drunk and trying to force the door of his stateroom which his wife had locked from inside."

No such marital spats for the Wyners, though. On their last night at sea, "We drank cocktails, smoked cigarettes, and took our last fling at everything on the ship that would be prohibited in the States in the morning." Prohibition was heading into its fourth year.

As 1923 came to a close, they arrived back in Boston. After stopping off at Charlotte Street to visit their families, the couple settled down to married life:

We rode 'home' – HOME – to our love nest at 33 Halifax St. Jam Pl.

Rudy, great lover that he is, true to ancient tradition, carried me over the threshold of our new home. May the peace and happiness and bliss that we found therein permeate it throughout the years we spend together here and may we be able to carry it with us to any other place, better or worse, that we leave this one for.

So ends the first chapter of the 'sweetest little story ever told.'

About a year and a half later, I would join the story. For what happened in between – and for that matter before – I can only rely on photos and a few stories from my mother and father that went with them. For example, there is a picture of my mother with a shotgun on the dunes in Barnstable at a gunning camp my parents shared with their best friends, Llora and Mark Bortman. I still have a decoy from their duck hunting days, as well as their guns. My mother was also an avid golfer (I still have some of her clubs) and an accomplished pianist.

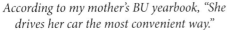

According to my mother's BU yearbook, "She drives her car the most convenient way."

Shooting ducks on the Cape.

I have home movies from a Hadassah party in the mid-'20s at my grandmother Gussie's Nantasket home. The women arrived in chauffeur-driven limousines. Zaftig ladies, thin ladies – they all wore cloche hats and long, loose skirts. But my mother stood out among them. She was so graceful and so beautiful, with her bobbed hair and stylish attire.

Throughout her life, my mother was independent-minded, but I do think she was a little afraid of her mother-in-law. Who wasn't? Gussie was, after all, a bossy lady. She organized people and told them what to do – period. Perhaps that's how my mother wound up as the first president of the Junior Hadassah chapter in Boston.

But nothing came between my mother and her family. Among her brothers and sisters, she was the pillar, the one who stood strong when the others let emotions get the best of them. Her grace under pressure served as an example to me later in life. She was dedicated to her parents, and they to her. She was at their home or on the phone with them every day. Not long after my grandfather died, my mother insisted on her mother moving in with us. Her sisters were a bit miffed, having been given little say in the matter. When her brother Harry became ill, my mother swooped in and smothered him with the attention that she felt his wife, Florence, had failed to provide.

Not that she would have rebuked Florence to her face. My mother spoke her mind only to those closest to her. She wasn't one to embarrass others in public. That just wasn't done. And on the flipside, she wouldn't let what others said bother her.

I opened this chapter by painting a portrait of a playful Sara. I don't wish to close it with her perched on a pedestal. She was human, after all. On one subject, in particular, she could be quite sensitive: her age. When she was in her 50s, she stopped talking to her sisters for several weeks because they said she was born in 1899. She insisted the year was 1901. I suspect that my aunts were right, but if you look at our family tree on Geni, you won't see her birth year.

THE MANY SIDES OF UNCLE EDDIE

From Harvard rogue to Ritz legend and friend of the stars

Uncle Eddie in 1918, the year he should have graduated from Harvard.

MY UNCLE EDDIE — who had prospective guests vetted before granting them reservations at the Ritz-Carlton Boston – would probably have never allowed his younger self anywhere near his exclusive hotel.

His 1961 *Globe* obituary says Eddie graduated from Harvard in 1918. True, he was a member of the class of '18, but he never graduated. His Ivy League education came to an abrupt end late one December night in the chilly waters of the Charles by the Esplanade.

"Lets Girl Drop Into River; Says it was 'Joke,'" read the headline on the *Boston Record* of December 11, 1916. The story reports that Eddie and Gertrude Weston, 19, of Brooklyn, New York, were:

> … sauntering along the Esplanade after riding down to the river edge in an automobile about midnight. Wyner seized the young woman playfully about the waist and lifted her to the top of the railing.

She lost her balance, and before Wyner could grasp her, she fell into the water. Wyner then plunged in after her and rescued her before other assistance arrived.

Aside from suffering chills and embarrassment, the pair were unhurt. But after Harvard administrators saw the news in the paper, they firmly asked Eddie to leave the university. In a January 29, 1917, letter appealing the decision, Eddie wrote: "The whole affair was a mere accident and it is only the foolish but harmful publicity given it by the paper which makes it appear questionable." He said he and a friend had taken two girls to the movies and for hot chocolate at a drug store. After they dropped one of the girls off, their car had a flat tire in Back Bay. While the friend, who owned the car, took it to a garage for repair, Eddie and Gertrude decided to take a stroll (according to weather records, the temperature would have been in the 30s). Eddie continues:

> The Esplanade being right there we naturally walked down by the River and at her request, she being very light, I playfully lifted her up on the rail. She was no sooner seated there than she lost her balance and fell backwards before I could help her. The water was not deep and she was more frightened and cold than hurt.

Eddie went on to state that he and his friends had not "entered any place where liquor was sold" and that the girls were "both of excellent character and from respectable families." He asked to be readmitted in the fall. "I feel that this six months away from college will let me see its true value and comprehend a feeling of responsibility."

The college turned down his appeal. It didn't help Eddie's case that he was already on academic probation for multiple missed classes and poor grades.

Until we recently found the records with the details of the incident, there existed only my father's telling of the tale. According to his version, Eddie's splash-mate was a showgirl. In a low voice, Dad would add, with a smile, "There are some who say he may have pushed her in first to create this rescue scene."

That was just an example of the lore that surrounded Uncle Eddie, who to me as a teenager was this wondrous, mysterious character with the most fascinating attributes: All his clothes were painstakingly custom-tailored by Boston's august F.L. Dunne & Co. (New York's Metropolitan Museum of Art exhibits one of its suits online); his shoes were handmade to include a Jones Bar, a therapeutic insert between the inner and outer soles. Eddie knew many of the celebrities of his day; he was a "scratch" golfer; and he was choosy about the company he kept. As he didn't have children until late in life, I was among the few he welcomed into his world.

For a man at the pinnacle of the hospitality industry, he could be oddly abrupt. On the phone, he never said "hello" or "good-bye." He just launched into conversation and when he thought enough had been said just hung up – you'd hear a click, and he was gone. (Admittedly, at times I'm guilty, too, of dispensing with the niceties and immediately getting down to business.)

And he valued his privacy. Once when visiting the hotel, I made the mistake of dropping in on him unannounced. When I rang his doorbell, no one answered, but I could hear a shuffling sound. I rang again. This time, I heard Eddie ask, "Who's there?" When I said it was me, he answered the door. "Hi kid," he told me. "It's not like I don't love to see you, but don't ever come up and just ring the doorbell again.

Have them call ahead to say who's coming up – I don't like to have people ring my doorbell and not know who they may be."

But that was the adult Eddie. From what I know of the younger, seemingly carefree version, Eddie would have graduated Harvard summa cum laude – that is, if it offered a major in sowing wild oats.

'SUCH AN OUTLAW'

I can only imagine the fits that their second youngest son gave Gussie and George. After Harvard dropped him, Eddie literally spent time in the wilderness. He journeyed to the Gulf Coast, where he tried to make his fortune in the oil fields. My father told me that his parents became so worried that they hired a private investigator to track him down.

In November 1919, Eddie wrote his mother:

> I dreamt of oil fields and of me walking along the road only to accidentally kick some oil in my eye + thus reveal the world's greatest oil well. I now realize that those dime novels exaggerate the world's opportunities.

By the early '20s, the prodigal son had returned and joined his father in the real estate business. The reformed rascal was a natural.

In October 1926, Eddie partnered with George and his good friend and attorney, John S. Slater, to form the Arlington Trust to construct an apartment house to be called the Mayflower on a third-of-an-acre parcel at Arlington and Newbury streets. It was after construction had reached the second floor that Mayor Curley stepped in and prevailed upon the partners to build a luxury hotel instead. The Ritz-Carlton opened on May 18, 1927; rates for its 300 rooms ran from $5 to $15 a night; suites cost $40 a night.

THE LAIR OF A RECLUSE

The youthful playboy shunned the social whirl as an adult. Eddie ran the hotel as if all its guests were as anxious to avoid other people as he was. That turned out to be an early key to its success.

The lobby of the hotel was located one level above the first-floor entrance. I don't recall any chairs on that first floor, save for one that could be brought out when the occasional dowager was awaiting her limo. You went directly to the elevators, where the operators were instructed never to allow unrelated parties to ride together – no danger, then, of rubbing shoulders with a stranger in such intimate quarters. Eddie had small kitchens installed on every floor. If you wanted a steak at 2 a.m., a porter was on duty and fully trained in how to prepare it. It did not take long for word to spread among Boston's elite about the Ritz's exquisite service and respect for privacy. A number were so impressed that they made the hotel their home. Eventually, permanent residents occupied a third of the rooms.

No one could just come in off the street and get a room at the Ritz. Guests had to make reservations through other reputable hotels or allow management to check their credentials. Sometimes, Eddie called my father to look up a name in Dun & Bradstreet, to which Shawmut subscribed. Eddie's executive secretary and assistant manager, Eleanor O'Neil, told the *Globe* for a 1976 article, "When I first came here 28 years ago, we couldn't take a reservation unless we knew who the person was. We would check the name with the social registers, Poor's Directory of Executives and our previous guest files."

Uncle Eddie makes sure his parents get the Ritz treatment.

Eddie was so confident in his vetting process – and protective of his guests – that in 1934 he barred police from searching the hotel to check out a tip that three brothers wanted for murder were holed up there. "Absolutely not," Eddie was quoted in the *Globe* as telling the officers. "I can give you the pedigree of every person in the hotel." And, according to the story, Eddie did just that. The police backed down. They eventually found the brothers elsewhere in town.

During that time – the midst of the Depression – there wouldn't have been many guests. But Eddie kept the lights blazing in all the rooms to retain the illusion that the hotel was flourishing. Tactics like that helped the hotel achieve one of the highest occupancy rates in Boston, as people tried to reserve the Ritz first.

SNOB APPEAL

Many people assumed that the Ritz-Carlton's exclusivity extended to barring "people of the Hebrew persuasion," but Jews numbered among its permanent residents, including my grandparents and Eddie.

My father tried to set the record straight about the Ritz-Carlton in a 1977 letter to the editor of *Boston* magazine, following a feature about the hotel. Noting that he had been one of the hotel's three directors, Dad wrote that on occasion people called him to complain that Eddie was anti-Semitic. If Eddie were guilty of anything, it was bruising egos. "His policy of selling the Hotel to the snob and elegant section of the public gave offense to anyone who aspired to acceptance by the Ritz and did not receive it," Dad wrote.

While not an observant Jew, Eddie stocked the Ritz-Carlton kitchen with kosher meats from my grandmother's butcher in Brookline (only non-kosher cuts were purchased elsewhere). For him, it wasn't a religious thing; he just loved his mother's cooking and thought that it owed much of its flavor to kosher meat. I wonder how all those Yankees who dined at the Ritz would have reacted if they'd known that their steaks came from Alter Brothers Kosher Meat Market on Harvard Street.

Speaking of religion, the Ritz-Carlton had the distinction of being one of the few hotels without a Gideon Bible at bedside. "When the Ritz opened in 1927, Edward N. Wyner, the owner, said that he didn't want to foist religion on anyone. Therefore he refused to put Gideon Bibles in the rooms," Evans F. Houghton, the hotel's public relations counselor, told the *Globe* in 1973. However, guests could ring a bellhop for a Bible or peruse the holy books in the hotel's library, which owned several versions of the Bible, along with the Torah and Koran.

For his time, Eddie was enlightened about race, too. In her interview with the *Globe*, Eleanor, who started at the Ritz in 1948 as a reservations clerk, recalled booking the hotel's first black guest: Eddie Anderson, best known as Jack Benny's fictional sidekick, Rochester. Eleanor said when she checked with her boss, "Mr. Wyner told me it was up to me. He said he didn't object to black guests." Rather, it was a matter that none had sought to stay before.

THE FASHION COP

While Eddie didn't give a toss about people's race or creed, he could be a stickler on their behavior and dress. My uncle had a rule that no unescorted women could eat in the Ritz café between 11 and 3. He feared they would commandeer the tables and gossip for hours. Since the café charged lower prices, it depended on high turnover to make a profit. How Eddie managed to enforce his policy, I don't know. Eddie decided that male diners would be on their lunch break and thus wouldn't loll away the afternoon.

Women were not allowed to wear slacks if they wanted to eat in the dining room. Even Katharine Hepburn, Ritz lore has it, was told by a maitre d', "Sorry, you have to wear a skirt." Supposedly, she then dropped her trousers and had her shirttails serve as a substitute.

It would be interesting to know when this supposed wardrobe adjustment occurred. During the late '30s, Hepburn had an affair with Howard Hughes. When he visited Boston, the multimillionaire recluse would rent out an entire floor of the Ritz-Carlton. I'm sure Uncle Eddie had no trouble sympathizing with Hughes's passion for privacy.

By the way, when it came to attire, Eddie didn't just pick on women. In a two-page, single-spaced 1947 memo to employees regarding admittance to the Street Bar, he singles out the sport coat as indicative of unwelcome clientele. Ostensibly, his concern is just keeping out underage drinkers, but he's not taking any chances:

Not properly dressed means the college boy uniform of odd coat and pants. Odd coat means a coat not part of a regular suit. It is sometimes called a sports jacket. It usually comes in bright patterns and is very appropriate dress for college wear; that is, on the college campus going back and forth from the classroom, in and around Harvard Square in the stores. It is not, however, proper dress to patronize the Ritz bar. If you are still in doubt as to what a sport coat or odd coat is, the Manager's office will have several samples to show you and it may be that one will fit you and you can buy it so that you will always know what an odd coat and sport coat is. … Actually, there is nothing wrong with a sport coat, the Duke of Windsor wears them and many other men who are considered to be well dressed. I do not consider myself in this group.

That last declaration is interesting in light of a photo taken a decade before of Eddie, Benny Goodman and me. Benny is dressed in a suit; both my uncle and I are wearing sports jackets and white slacks – Eddie isn't even wearing a tie!

Eddie did give his staff room to use their own judgment, even when it came to the sport coat:

[O]ne of the waiters recently said he was confused with the odd coat regulation because Mr. Thomas Yawkey, age 45, the gentleman who owns the Red Sox Baseball Club, made it a practice to come into the bar with a sport coat. The waiter said Mr. Yawkey looked young and he was not sure whether or not he was a student. He said that after a consultation with other employees in the bar it was decided to serve Mr. Yawkey without asking him for his automobile license. I think that this discussion and the right conclusion is ample testimony that we have the basis of building a fine crew in the bar who can logically think a problem out.

I strongly suspect that Eddie's tongue was firmly planted in his cheek when he wrote that memo (see Appendix for copy). He was so proud of it that he sent copies to his close friends and relatives. But he did have serious reason to be concerned about under-age imbibers – and not just because they put his liquor license at risk.

One particular diner really got to Eddie. Presumably using his family's credit account, a grown-up-looking Phillips Exeter Academy student passed himself off as an adult. After getting sloshed in the bar, he went up to the 14th floor and squirted the fire hose all over the place. Afterward, his father not only refused to pay for the extensive damage, but sued the hotel for serving his son liquor. He claimed that the incident got his son kicked out of Exeter, which was all the more painful because the father had donated a fortune to get the less-than-brilliant lad accepted.

The episode made Eddie even more wary about extending credit to customers. Instead of issuing credit cards, he instituted a policy that gave diners one shot at proving their trustworthiness. When they had their first meal in the dining room, guests could sign with their name and address. If they paid up after being mailed a bill, they could pay on credit in the future. If they turned out to be deadbeats, they were never allowed in the Ritz-Carlton again.

'MONEY DIDN'T IMPRESS HIM'

Eddie may have used snob appeal to his commercial advantage, but he wasn't all that star-struck by the rich and famous, according to his son George. "My father always judged people on the basis of ethics and character. Titles didn't impress him. Money didn't impress him," George told the *Globe*, which interviewed him in 1987, when he took his own star turn as Irwin Bernstein on "Hill Street Blues."

Based on my father's correspondence, Eddie did take delight in the Ritz-Carlton's fame. In a July 27, 1927, letter to my grandmother when she was on a trip to Palestine, Dad wrote:

> Eddie said he had a dream when the Ritz-Carlton was being built that some day they would have to call the police to keep the crowd away from the hotel. I wrote you at your last port that Lindbergh was going to stop at the hotel, and when he did stop Eddie's dream was certainly realized. It took about 200 policemen to keep the crowd back from the hotel, and the affair was a huge success. Now they have added to the trip which they take sight-seers thru the hotel the "Lindbergh Suite."

The next month the Ritz was again the center of much excitement because Governor Alvan T. Fuller holed up there to write up his decision refusing to intervene in the Sacco-Vanzetti case. "The hotel has been surrounded the last few days by police squadrons and armed private detectives who were protecting the Governor," my father wrote to his mother on August 5.

While as a rule, Eddie didn't socialize with the guests, he did give a personal welcome to the most prominent among them, including English and Hollywood royalty (Shirley Temple, who looked just like my sister, had a birthday party at the hotel). Eddie wasn't enamored with celebrities, but felt that as the hotel owner he had a duty to provide them personal attention. For example, in 1949, at Winston Churchill's request, Eddie had an entire suite redone in the statesman's favorite colors of Chinese red, black, and gold.

BACKSTAGE WITH EDDIE CANTOR

As much as he valued privacy – for his guests and himself – Eddie was not antisocial. In the comfort of his close circle of friends and family, he had a ready smile and hearty laugh. They included celebrities, but he liked them for themselves, not their fame. As you might expect, many of them were Jews, including Eddie Cantor, Benny Goodman, Al Jolson, and George Jessel.

Jolson was a guest at one of my grandfather's birthday parties. My uncle took me to meet Cantor between shows at the Keith Boston Theater, an old vaudeville house that's now a Chinese restaurant. We met him in his dressing room. To avoid the fans at the stage door, Cantor took us out through the main part of the theater. With his hat shoved down over his trademark bug eyes, no one recognized him. As we pressed our way through, people complained that we were blocking their way to see Eddie Cantor. He didn't say a word as he led us out the front door.

Another friend and frequent guest, Moss Hart, set his play *Light Up the Sky* in a suite at the Ritz-Carlton. It's about a leading lady of a Broadway-bound play in Boston for a trial run. I like to imagine Hart returning from a long night of rehearsals and ordering the hall porter to rustle up steak and eggs. Not long before her death in 2007, I had a chance to reminisce with Hart's widow, Kitty Carlisle, about the Ritz-Carlton; we were at a party at the 92nd Street Y in New York celebrating the birthday of a mutual friend, the philanthropist Dan Kaplan.

Broadway tryouts brought other show-biz luminaries to the hotel, including Irving Berlin, Jule Styne, Noel Coward and Cole Porter. According to a *Globe* account of Ritz-Carlton historical highlights, it was where Richard Rodgers and Lorenz Hart wrote "Ten Cents a Dance" in 1930, and Tennessee Williams, scenes for *A Streetcar Named Desire* in 1947.

Yes, that's Benny Goodman, and he really did let me hold his clarinet. We were on the Ritz roof at an afternoon rehearsal for his night-time big band show.

On the walls of the café at the Taj Hotel, which took over the Ritz-Carlton building, you can see photos of Eddie and his illustrious guests. In one of them, you'll see Benny Goodman and Uncle Eddie (I was cropped out). Benny is pictured with his clarinet, but he did pay me the ultimate compliment of letting me hold it. "Be careful with that reed, kid," he told me. Benny and his big band would broadcast their national show from the French Room on the hotel's second floor. I attended a few times. It was like a private concert because there wasn't much room for an audience, unlike the Roof Garden, where he also frequently performed. Despite his fame, Benny was an unassuming, friendly fellow. It was amazing to watch how he played that clarinet with such ease and simplicity.

MY NEAR FATAL SWING

If Eddie wasn't at the hotel, he was likely at one of the half dozen country clubs where he was a member. But, contrary to convention, he'd always change into his golf shoes in his car rather than use the men's locker room in the clubhouse. That wasn't surprising, considering how he didn't like to socialize with people he didn't know.

He frequently played mornings at Woodland Golf Club in Newton with Boston radio host Carl ("Beantown Varieties") Moore and Eddie Ryan, whose family-owned Ryan Iron Works helped pioneer welding technology.

Eddie partnered with pro Ted Bishop in many pro-am tournaments before television turned them into sports spectaculars. My uncle was so good that even Ted Williams asked him for pointers on his swing – his golf swing, that is. In the Taj photo gallery, you can see a picture of the pair practicing on the roof of the Ritz-Carlton. I was among Eddie's protegees, too; he bought me my first pair of clubs when I was 8.

Before he had a family, my uncle had a corner of the roof fenced off to serve as a driving range. My memories of it are tinged with alarm, thanks to a time I visited him on the roof when he was practicing with, I believe, Bishop or Williams. Seeing me, Eddie said, "Hi kid; hit a few balls." By then I was in my 20s, but I was so nervous and anxious to impress his famous guest that I shanked the ball. It hit off a pipe in the far corner, bounced back over my head and then slipped through a narrow opening behind us. There was dead silence. We looked at one another in horror, imagining the ball dropping 16 floors onto someone's head. After what seemed to be an eternity, but was probably only two minutes, the roof phone rang. It was the doorman. "Mr. Wyner," he said to my uncle. "I have your golf ball. Do you want it brought up?" Eddie asked, "What happened?" The doorman told him, "Well, just as it was bouncing, a car was turning the corner and the ball hit under it. The driver thought something had exploded in his car. And while he got out to look, the ball dribbled into the gutter, and I picked it up."

Around the same time, I again made a golfing spectacle of myself – this time without being a public nuisance. I happened to arrive at Belmont Country Club one day to learn that Eddie was starting out on the course with another of his golfing friends, the great Sam Snead. I met them on the first tee. "Come on kid, do you want to play with us?" Eddie asked. He then warned Sam, "This kid has a terrible swing." I didn't take offense. That was my uncle's way of showing affection, that he enjoyed my company on the golf course even if my abilities paled next to those of his regular partners.

The first hole was a par 4; I managed to get the ball onto the green in three, and holed out with a par. The next hole was also a par 4. To my astonishment, for my second shot I hit a fairly long iron, and it went into the cup for a 2 – a feat that I've never repeated.

That eagle got Sam's attention. Now I was really getting nervous. I knew this kind of luck couldn't hold. On the next hole, a par 3, I took an iron for my drive and shanked the ball. It went way off to the side. I decided there was no way I could continue to play with Sam. As I finished my swing, I grabbed my back and yelled out in pain. I then excused myself and limped off to the clubhouse. And that's the story of my two holes with Sam Snead.

I think that Eddie probably played golf every day during the golf season. My father said that his brother was always able to find the time because of his clean-desk philosophy. When it was time for a game, Eddie would sweep any papers left on his desk into the wastebasket. He believed that if any of them were important, the people would write him again. I envied his confidence in that theory as much as I doubted that he really operated that way. The Ritz-Carlton always had a reputation as a well-run hotel.

Still, I was often tempted to resort to the Eddie method when confronted with a desk piled high with paper at the end of a long day of work.

A SECRET WEDDING

Eddie must have been among Boston's most eligible bachelors, but he didn't marry until he was in his 40s. Even then, he initially lived separately from his wife in a small apartment at the hotel and kept the wedding secret from nearly everyone. That was because his bride, the former Helen Crowley, was a Roman Catholic.

In that 1977 letter to *Boston* magazine, my father disputed the article's portrayal of Eddie as being indifferent toward his mother's distress that he intended to marry a Catholic. "She knew nothing of his intention and I was present when Edward first spoke to my mother about his marriage, which was then about a year old," Dad wrote, elaborating:

> Probably the only individuals associated with the Ritz who knew of Edward's marriage to Helen Crowley were [assistant manager] Eleanor O'Neil, Charles Banino and myself. Edward knew that my mother would be distressed and he found it difficult and therefore put off telling her. Helen lived in an apartment outside the hotel. We had many discussions about when and how to tell mother, because Edward was seriously concerned. Helen indicated her willingness to be converted to Judaism and we decided under those circumstances my mother would accept the situation. I was asked by Helen and Edward to make the arrangements for someone to properly perform the conversion ceremony. I contacted the Rabbi and the ceremony was performed on Woodrow Avenue in Dorchester. The officiating Rabbi brought two other Rabbis with him and they assisted in the ceremony which included the immersion in a ritual bath, a wedding ceremony according to Jewish tradition and the signing of a "Ketubah" or marriage contract. I signed as a witness.

> Armed with the "Ketubah," Edward and I visited my mother. She was decidedly unhappy at the news, but threatened no suicide. She took the announcement far more calmly than either of us expected and the feelings that she might otherwise have had were mollified by the consideration that Helen had shown of mother's religious background.

My father went on to add that "Helen was very kind and considerate in her relations with my mother." She became as devoted to Judaism as she had been to Catholicism. Helen joined Hadassah and other Jewish women's groups. The family belonged to Temple Israel, where Helen "faithfully went to Holiday services, usually without Edward," according to my father's letter. She also saw to it that all their children attended religious school, hoping that one of them would become a rabbi. They had six sons in six years – Eddie kept hoping for a daughter.

My aunt was a lovely person, extremely cultured and refined. She endeared herself to everyone. Helen was included in Gussie's will along with her other daughters-in-law, receiving a platinum chain with 45 diamonds.

SOX PLAY NANTASKET

After Helen moved into the Ritz-Carlton, the couple removed the walls of adjoining apartments to accommodate their growing brood. In summer, Eddie's family took over the house at 95 Manomet Avenue in Nantasket Beach that George and Gussie had used as a retreat for so many years. He fenced in the lawn and created a camp for his boys. Eddie arranged for Red Sox players to come by on their days off and act as counselors. You'd think the attention from baseball stars would be enough to keep the kids on the reservation, but Eddie had the gates locked just to make sure no one wandered away. Whenever the Red Sox players were around, the neighborhood kids would clamor to be locked in, too.

With the Nantasket house came a shared tennis court. It sat on property straddling Eddie's and that of neighbors Arthur and Annette Lurie. My grandparents and their neighbors had had it built back in 1905; it was probably the first private tennis court on Nantasket. Apparently, Eddie liked golf far more than tennis. In the middle of the night, he had a landscaper install a fence down the middle of the tennis court and sod his half. My father told me that Eddie decided that no one was using the court anymore, so it didn't matter. I don't know how the owners of the other half of the court reacted, but I heard that the neighbors living behind Eddie became nervous. Some of them had built houses on an abandoned railroad right-of-way. By rights, Eddie owned half that property, too. They worried that they would wake up one morning and find a fence at their doors. Eddie never went that far to assert his property rights.

THE GOOD BROTHER

With family and friends, Eddie was generous. On occasion, he would give my father custom-made slacks from F.L. Dunne. In a 1943 letter on the occasion of my father's birthday, Eddie acknowledges how obsessive he can be about fashion. He also reveals something of his feelings toward his brother and his father:

> I have exaggerated your capacity and understanding to so many people for so many years, that I hardly need try to deceive you. I guess my best audience and the most gullible was the mighty George himself. I will reiterate, however, that you have always been a good brother who did good things.

> Ever since I reached adolescence, I have wanted to own a white cashmere sweater. I have had many garments of cashmere; socks, suits, coats, and sweaters of various hues, but never a white sweater. Some years ago in New York, I spent a whole day visiting every store that dealt in the luxurious fabric, but no one knew where you could get a sweater of pure white. Only a few days ago I received a letter from my New York agent with the good news that he was in possession of the long-sought-after garment, and in my size. Needless to say, the orders and directions for packing and sending were minutely discussed and proper precautions arranged. The priceless article arrived.

> Mother reminded me last night that today was the anniversary of your birth. I brought the cashmere sweater upstairs with me to let her see it with her own eyes. My inner conscience, the "categorical imperative" that Kant talks about, kept saying "It's just the thing for Rudolph." With its clean, friendly warmth, it seemed to symbolize all my appraisals of you and so I am much happier in giving it to you than in keeping it.

By the way, when I graduated from Harvard Business School, Eddie presented me with a custom-tailored tuxedo from F.L. Dunne. I still wear that tux to formal events.

EDDIE, THE LEGEND

After Eddie died in 1961, the hotel went through several owners before relocating across the Common. Covering the hotel's 50th anniversary gala in 1977, the *Globe* wrote that the hotel "remains as a monument to its builder and president who carefully managed its high standards for more than 30 years – the late Edward N. Wyner, who probably was the person best and most fondly remembered last night."

At the gala when the Taj replaced the Ritz in 2006: Longtime hotel doorman Norman Pashoian is flanked on left by Uncle Eddie's son (and Ritz baby) Franklin Wyner and his wife, Carel; and on right by Genevieve and me.

When the Taj took over the building in 2006, it revived the Wyner family story as a way of giving the hotel a sense of tradition. At the request of Eddie's sons, I accepted an invitation to represent the Wyner family at a private celebration for the staff. For about an hour, I told anecdotes and answered questions about Eddie. I was especially struck by the lineup of what seemed like 50 chefs, all in their tall white hats. I think the entire event would have come as a surprise to Eddie. Remember that memo he sent to his staff about keeping out the college boys? In it, he expressed little concern about them holding a grudge:

> When these college boys grow up to become important men of the country this hotel will probably be a garage but they will nevertheless have more respect for it when they look back and no doubt, if they live in the vicinity, will store their cars here as a token of their appreciation.

TWO OF A KIND

Cousin Anne questions Picasso; Aunt Frances outwits the Nazis

Aunt Frances in 1912: Cars would play a major role in her life.

MY COUSIN ANNE EMBER and her mother, Aunt Frances, could have been characters in Herman Wouk's novel *The Winds of War*. Toward the end of their lives, they could have appeared in the TV comedy *The Golden Girls*.

As the first Wyner granddaughter born in America, doted over by a bevy of uncles, Anne did not lack for confidence. The daughter of a brilliant if eccentric judge, my Uncle Sol, she did not lack for brains, either. Where others saw barriers, she saw opportunities. Nothing got in her way, be it a chauvinistic Henri Matisse or Nazi thugs.

Three generations of Wyner women: Frances, Anne and Gussie.

Anne, who was born in 1915, was already a veteran international traveler at age 12. She accompanied her mother and Gussie to Palestine to make funeral arrangements for Gussie's father. As a fourth or fifth grader, I remember Anne visiting us when she lived on Dean Road. Tall and lanky, she dressed more like a tomboy than a sophisticated girl.

After graduating from Brookline High School in 1933, she attended Wellesley College. Anne majored in art history, and her mother in pampering. It seemed that Frances was out there every morning, placing fresh flowers in Anne's dorm room. After graduating in 1937, amid the mounting tensions in Europe, Anne and Frances set off for Paris. They studied painting at the École des Beaux Arts for two years – despite being told by Matisse that women painters would be better off as "couturieres" (dress designers).

Anne found Pablo Picasso to be much more liberated in his attitude toward women. "Just because you're dressed in a skirt and I in pants doesn't make any radical differences between us," he told her, according to a draft of a story that she had planned to submit to a Wellesley College publication. She describes Picasso, then in his 50s, as well-mannered and unpretentious, but at times prickly.

As she climbed the stairs to his atelier, she anticipated that he would be gruff and aloof. She noted that the studio was located on the top floor of a business building, far from the artists' quarter of the city. But he disarmed her from the start: "He immediately gave the impression of a comfortable person, stocky in build, friendly and careless as was the atmosphere of his studio."

Anne was amused by the "artistic litter which reigned in the large rooms." Scattered on a farm table was an old bread roll, leather-bound Spanish books, manuscripts and sketches, and a large chalk-white bust of the artist himself. "A very long faced, solemn-eyed dog" lounged on a sofa.

When she took out her notebook, she was met with a sharp rebuke. "If you're going to do that, I won't say anything. I thought we were going to talk like friends."

Picasso told her that if she asked point-blank questions, she'd only get glib responses. "How can I explain my art to you in words?" he asked. "I can't master two trades: painting is one and words another."

Anne refused to let him off that easy. "It's really your duty to clarify [your paintings for] the public a bit," she recalls telling him. "So many specious explanations have been [foisted] on them. For instance, many prominent critics claim that your latest paintings are an exposé of the subconscious mind."

To that, Picasso smiled and dismissed such commentary as a *blague*, a joke.

Standing in front of one of the artist's earlier, more realistic works, Anne confessed that she was baffled by his "surrealist" turn. "He comforted me," she writes, telling her: "It's natural to appreciate better the form we are accustomed to." Pointing to a "two-eyed profile of a blue and yellow lady," Picasso said, "I hope that the public will become accustomed to this."

He said he would prefer to be remembered for his more abstract work than for his harlequins and blue boy prints. "[W]hat I'm doing now is something I have been striving for," he told Anne. "I'm continually trying to learn about the technique of painting, about the way to achieve more strength, and more solidity of construction."

He elaborated: "I always start from reality. … When I paint a wooden table, I'm constantly aware of its woodiness, of its shape and form and of its solidity. I may paint it green instead of brown, but I do that simply because it has no importance."

When she asked if he still felt any sort of spiritual connection to his earlier works, "Picasso retaliated. 'Do you still believe in dolls?'"

Chastened, Anne realized that she would learn more if she just let the conversation take its own course. "[I]n our casual talk he patiently helped me to clarify my ideas."

When the discussion turned to Anne's artistic aspirations, she ventured that "perhaps women are more timid."

In response, Picasso blamed men. Because women have lived so long under their domination, "it's only natural that they should be still a bit weak. Their trouble is that they try to think like men. … It's easy to understand why a man paints a nude woman; that's natural. But why should women paint nudes in the same way? Why don't they paint nude men?"

Picasso became most passionate when talking about the Spanish Civil War. "I was surprised that after having lived almost forty years in France, he felt so personally attached to Spain," Anne writes. "When he talked of the fleeing refugees pursued by machine gun fire, his black eyes showed more than mere humanitarian indignation. He acted out the machine guns."

The draft of the interview is not dated, but Picasso's fury suggests that it took place after the Germans bombed the Basque town of Guernica in spring 1937 – the subject of one of the artist's most famous paintings.

While she braved no bombs, Anne would soon have her own harrowing encounter with the Nazis.

SEIZED IN SALZBURG

In early 1938, just weeks after Hitler marched into Austria, Anne and Frances traveled to Vienna to see what life was like under the Nazis. Back in Brookline, Frances's husband was frantic, visiting my father every night wondering what to do about the adventurous pair. Later, Frances would admit that before making the journey she and her daughter had underestimated the Nazi threat.

Spending about 10 days in the Austrian capital, Frances and Anne met Jews seeking to flee Europe. With my father helping from America, they cleared the way for journalist Otto Zausmer and his wife, Elizabeth (Liesl), to emigrate. Their help was too late for Liesl's father, who during their stay was arrested. Shortly later, her father, despite having served as an Austrian army captain during World War I, was shot and killed by the Nazis.

Frances and Anne's assistance went beyond rushing through paperwork. Liesl asked the pair to pack a number of antique silver plates in their luggage, since emigrating Jews were allowed to take only the most basic possessions. While Liesl and Otto traveled by train to Paris without incident, Frances and Anne were arrested after their luggage was searched in Salzburg. Discovering the silver, the Nazis pulled them off their train and detained them. Thanks to the intervention of the US consul, mother and daughter were released after a day and allowed to resume their journey – without the silver.

Later, they traveled to Europe's next trouble spot, Czechoslovakia. While Hitler was fulminating about the plight of Czech Germans in the Sudetenland, the pair toured Prague. They saw the Czech people in their last few months of freedom. That September would see the infamous Munich conference, after which British Prime Minister Neville Chamberlain would declare "peace in our time" and the Nazis would seize all of Czechoslovakia.

Once settled in America, Otto Zausmer was hired by *The Boston Globe*, even though he spoke little English. Assigned to monitor Hitler's weekly radio broadcasts, Otto listened at home with his shortwave radio. With Liesl's help, he translated the speeches into English and clued readers in to when Hitler was being sarcastic or threatening. I was at Otto's Brookline home when we heard over his Hallicrafter receiver that the Japanese had attacked Pearl Harbor.

LIKE MOTHER, LIKE DAUGHTER

Anne moved to Baltimore in 1943, where she married Theodore Ember and raised two sons, Aaron and Richard (Dick). She painted and sculpted, and later developed an interest in the innovative Montessori teaching techniques. During our sailing years, Genevieve and I had a memorable visit with the Embers in Baltimore. After we had sailed into the harbor in our beloved Seabiscuit and settled into a slip, we called Anne and Teddy about getting together. We had been instructed to wait for them at a waterfront-area hotel that had a large, one-way circular driveway. We waited and waited, and finally a car pulled up from the wrong direction. Anne was at the wheel with Teddy in the passenger seat. They told us how happy they were to see us and that they were going to take us to a very special restaurant outside of town. Sitting in the back and engrossed in conversation, I didn't notice at first that Anne kept drifting onto the wrong side of the road. When I did finally notice, I grew increasingly nervous until I thought up an excuse for us to pull over. I persuaded Anne to let me take the wheel the rest of the way. The special restaurant turned out to be an all-you-can-eat buffet.

Eccentricity must have run in Anne's genes. According to family lore, her father, Sol the judge, lost most of his personality when he was a student from spending too much time on the trolley with his nose in his books. Frances apparently survived the marriage by living apart in Florida. In the 1950s, I made a surprise visit to her after my Georgia-bound flight was diverted to Sarasota by bad weather. Being Aunt Frances's favorite nephew, I knew she wouldn't mind. I took a cab over to her place. "Oh, I'm so glad to see you," she gushed, before abruptly announcing that she had an art class and would be back in two hours.

Sol and Frances would visit one another. He would take the train, but travel only by day. At dusk, he'd get off wherever the train happened to be and find a hotel. In the morning, he'd catch another train. The trip could take him three days. Once he arrived in Sarasota, he'd stay overnight, and inevitably the two would get into a fight. Then Sol would hop onto the next train north – once again traveling only in the daytime.

Frances traveled by car. She fancied convertibles, replacing them every couple of years. I always picture her pulling into Brookline with the back of the car jammed with papers and assorted junk. When she arrived at her house, she'd wash the pile of dishes Sol had abandoned in the sink and clean up whatever mess he had made. Just as in Florida, the two of them would soon find something to fight about (yes, I know it sounds like they didn't get along, but I truly believe they loved one another in their own peculiar fashion). The next day or so, Frances would be off again. She loved to drive – and it didn't seem to matter in which direction. Once on her way back to Sarasota, she took a detour through Maine – or was it Montreal? And this was when she was in her 80s.

Eventually, age took its toll on her driving skills. One day as Frances was driving to art class, her rear fender struck a man as he stepped off a curb. She stopped the car, got out and saw him lying on the ground. Learning that someone had already called an ambulance and seeing that he didn't appear to be seriously injured, she announced she was late for class and continued on her way. The police took her license away for leaving the scene of an accident, even if it wasn't her fault. By then, she was living in a retirement community that provided all her meals. But she could still drive on the property, and evidently did so with gusto. Somehow, the complex managers got my name and called me to complain about her terrorizing the other residents.

Frances drove the management to distraction in other ways, too. For one thing, she was living too long – these places counted on turnover so they could resell the homes at higher prices. I think the managers would have liked nothing better than to have seen her declared no longer of sound mind and packed off to a nursing home. One afternoon, a manager called me, all in a dither. "You've got to do something. Your aunt has called the sheriff." I asked, "Why has she called the sheriff?" He said she claimed her lunch hadn't been delivered on time. So, I told the manager, "I don't know whether the sheriff will decide to take this on as his own responsibility, but there is a very simple solution. She's entitled to have her meal, and there are certain hours, and you're either delivering it on time or not."

Speaking of food, Frances never threw anything out. It was frightening what she would exhume from her refrigerator and offer to Genevieve and me when we would visit. "Have this wonderful, beautiful thing," she would say.

Even in her 90s, Aunt Frances was telling off doctors.

STARTLING A SURGEON

As frustrating as Aunt Frances might have been at times, Genevieve and I could not help but admire how she maintained her independence and self-assurance well into her 90s. She never asked us for help, managing instead to surmount difficulties in her own inimitable way. On occasion, however, she would allow me – and apparently only me, among her relatives – to intervene.

Just a few years before she passed away, Frances seriously bruised her leg. Ignoring the injury, she allowed it to fester to the point of gangrene. When I learned of her condition, I suggested that she come up to Boston, where I would arrange to have her treated by the leading vascular surgeon at Beth Israel Hospital. She agreed after I pointed out that it would only be fitting for her to go to the BI since her mother had been instrumental in its success.

I picked her up at the airport and whisked her off to the hospital, where the surgeon was expecting us. As soon as we arrived, she was placed on a gurney and wheeled into an examining room. The doctor came out a few minutes later and told me that the wound was much worse than had been described to him. He said that the only way to prevent further damage was to amputate the leg, a procedure that none of us had anticipated. The doctors said, "Do you want me to tell her my recommendation or would you rather do it?" I suggested that we do so together.

I watched in amazement as my aunt listened attentively and calmly to the startling news. At the end, the surgeon asked her how she wanted to proceed. Perfectly composed, she responded, "Doctor, I didn't travel all the way up here to tell you what to do. Just answer one question: Is this what you would recommend for your own mother?" Visibly surprised by her directness, the doctors answered yes. "Then let's do it right away," she said. "I have a lot to do at my home in Florida and want to get back there as soon as possible. Just one thing, can you make the cut here?" She pointed to a spot below the knee, but above the injury. The disconcerted doctor found himself negotiating inches with a patient whom he had expected to have been traumatized by the prospect of amputation.

The operation was a success. Frances, with great determination and no self-pity, transferred to the Spaulding Rehabilitation Center. After three weeks of physical therapy and learning how to walk with a temporary prosthesis, she announced that she was ready to fly back to Sarasota. She brushed aside our suggestion that we fly up her aide from Florida to accompany her home. A few days later, I saw her to the plane, which she boarded with the assistance of a crutch.

Aunt Frances died just two months shy of turning 100. For Genevieve and me, she was a role model of how to grow old.

INDOMITABLE ANNE

In later years, Anne had a difficult relationship with her mother. Frances could be very hard on her, putting her down with biting remarks. Genevieve and I were with Frances when she received a birthday gift from her daughter. Before even opening it, Frances was disparaging Anne's taste. It turned out to be a beautiful pocketbook. When Anne called to ask her mother if she liked it, Frances called the pocketbook a waste of money since she didn't need one. Her tone wasn't angry, but I'm sure her lack of appreciation left Anne in tears at the other end of the line. Afterward, Frances defended her remarks, criticizing Anne for sending her useless gifts rather than visiting.

As Anne grew older, she became somewhat of a recluse. After her husband died, she refused to leave Baltimore or even her house. Finally, at 88, she decided to rent a place in Houston, where her son Dick lived. After a few weeks, she announced that she liked the city, but wanted her other son, Aaron, to move there, too, which he did.

Some years later, Anne and Aaron took a trip to Sarasota, Florida. It was supposed to be for just two weeks, but they announced they planned to stay for good. It took a lot of coaxing from Dick, with some help from me, to persuade the pair to return to Houston.

Shortly before she died at 98, Dick told me about his mother's unconventional way of seeking medical advice. "My mother called 911 and was taken by ambulance to the hospital last night," Dick said. "You won't believe it, but she had been concerned about a new medication Aaron's doctor had prescribed for him and decided this was the best way to gain access to another doctor for a second opinion." Like her mother, Anne was resourceful to the end.

PART II: GROWING UP

- **Brookline boy:** Horse-drawn wagons and bomb parachutes

- **Big man on campus:** The birth of a joiner

- **B-School days:** How being brash got me into Harvard

- **A Yank in Europe:** A grand tour and a mysterious uncle

- **The single life:** Tasting the high life from Havana to Miami

- **My one and only:** Wooing and wooing back Genevieve

BROOKLINE BOY

From horse-drawn milk wagons to parachutes for bombs

Mother holds me at age 1 month.

A FAMILY FILM FROM when I was a year old shows a couple of kids wearing caps pushing me around in a baby carriage. My parents told me that the boys' father was Mayor James Michael Curley.

The Curleys lived around the corner from my family in the house with the famous shamrock shutters overlooking Jamaica Pond. We lived in a modest, brand-new two-family duplex at 33 Halifax St.

The scene of my birth, August 6, 1925, was right out of a Gothic novel. That's how my father described it to me in a letter marking my 20th birthday: "[T]he rain and lightning deluged and crashed about the hospital on the hill [as] your mother went so bravely, and so hopefully, into the unknown trial of her first motherhood."

I was anything but a stormy baby, judging by letters Father wrote to his mother when she was traveling to Palestine. In fact, I must have been downright placid. One night in July 1927, when I was just a month shy of 2, our street was roused in the wee hours by the blaring of a neighbor's car horn. The next morning, my father asked me if I had heard anything. According to the letter to my grandmother, I responded: "No, Father, I did not hear the horn blow at all. I enjoyed my sleep very much and my repose was unbroken." I suspect that Dad took a few liberties with my vocabulary.

CLOMP, CLOMP, CLOMP

When I was 3, we moved to a two-story colonial-style clapboard house at 144 Clark Road, Brookline. The street parallels the tracks that today serve the D branch of the Green Line; the Boston & Albany Railroad rumbled down them at that time. When we moved in, houses had yet to go up on the railroad side of the street. The hill behind our house rose up into a big wooded estate. In the winter, I'd sled down the slope.

The neighborhood was new, but it retained sights and sounds of a soon-to-vanish world. A lamp-lighter tended to gaslights on Clark Road. Several mornings each week, I'd hear the clomp, clomp, clomp of the milkman and his horse-drawn buggy. He would load up his carriers and walk from one backyard to another, depositing bottles into insulated boxes and collecting the empties. He would stop at several houses before returning to the cart for more milk. Amazingly, the horse always knew just where to meet him.

We stored the milk in an icebox. Whenever we needed more ice, we'd indicate the number of pounds by turning a square card in the window of the house. Each of the card's four sides had a different number. The ice man would go by the number that was right side up. Using tongs, he would carry blocks as heavy as 50 pounds around to our back door and deposit them in the icebox.

Our knives were sharpened by a man who cycled down our street in a three-wheeled vehicle. Gypsies came by occasionally, asking to pluck the dandelions from our lawn to use in their salads and soups. I remember seeing a woman in her long, loose Old World clothes with her two children snapping up these weeds, which we considered a terrible blight. An organ grinder, a monkey on his shoulder, entertained the neighborhood kids.

When I was growing up, the big Tudor-style building that dominates the corner of Beacon and Harvard streets in Coolidge Corner housed the grocer S.S. Pierce & Co. Clerks from the store would come to our door to take our order, which would be delivered later.

When I was in fourth grade and now had a 4-year-old sister, Elizabeth Jane (Betty), our family moved a mile west to a large brick house at 237 Dean Road. Built in the 1880s, it had three floors and two fireplaces. The top floor had two maids' rooms and an unfinished attic, which I took over for my hobbies. But when we first moved in, it wasn't that the house was so much bigger that struck me but that the yard was smaller. I missed roaming the hillside behind Clark Road.

The extended Wyner family gathers in early 1930s. Back row: Murray, Francis (Frances' husband), Edward, Rudolph and IA. Middle row: Dolly (Murray's wife); Frances; patriarch George and wife Gussie; Amelia (IA's wife) and Sara (Rudolph's wife). Front row: cousins Anne (Frances' daughter); me; Estelle (IA's daughter); Norman, Hilda and Donald (all Murray's children); my sister, Betty; Arlene (Murray's daughter); and Lester (IA's son).

TRANSFORMING A NEIGHBORHOOD

We were among the first Jewish families in the neighborhood; most of the other residents were Yankees. But that balance switched during the half century we owned the house, with my extended family contributing to the demographic switch. Considering the list of relatives who lived nearby, I wonder why we didn't buy the entire neighborhood:

- My mother's parents, Samuel U. and Gertrude K. Goldberg, first lived at a house they rented at 284 Dean Road. They then moved to a house they built around the corner at 175 Eliot Street.

- The next occupants of that 284 Dean Road house came from the Wyner side of my family. It was purchased by my father's sister, Frances, and her husband and first cousin, Francis (Solomon) Wyner. They moved in with their daughter, my cousin Anne.

- Reuben Wyner, Sol's brother, lived on the other end of Dean Road, at number 78, with his wife, Helen, and their two children, my cousins Bob and Betsy. Reuben and Sol shared a legal practice at 18 Tremont Street in Boston, where my grandfather George Wyner had an office for many years.

- My mother's sister Florence and her husband, MIT professor Alvin Sloane, built a house on Eliot Street, across from my Goldberg grandparents. When we were children, we saw our cousins, Arthur and Bobby Sloane, every Sunday.

- My mother's brother Harry Gilbert (changed from Goldberg) bought the house next door to his parents on Eliot Street. His wife, Florence, was the daughter of one of the more famous heads of Beth Israel Hospital, Dr. Charles Wilinsky.

- My mother's other sister, Dorothy, bought a house on nearby Clinton Road, with her husband, Dr. Gustave B. Fred, an ear, nose and throat specialist who was born in Waco, Texas.

We had some eminent neighbors on Dean Road when I was growing up, including conductors Arthur Fiedler of the Boston Pops and Erich Leinsdorf of the Boston Symphony, but I can't claim them as relatives. Besides music, one of Fiedler's favorite sounds was a siren. He was well known to firefighters around that time, following their trucks to watch them battling blazes.

SPOILED GRANDSON

Surrounded by grandparents, aunts, uncles and cousins, I experienced the warmth of family life that few in today's generation can enjoy. Not only were families less spread out, but kids' schedules weren't packed with soccer practice, music lessons and play dates.

After returning to Shawmut Woolen Mills from the Navy, my father kept his promise to his father and took on two of his brothers as partners. Every night after work, he'd call his dad to talk about what came up that day. My dad and his siblings all called their father George, but their mother was always Mother.

On Saturday afternoons, my mother would often drive her parents and me to the movies. She'd drop us off at either the Paramount Fenway Theater, which is now part of the Berklee School of Music, or the Loews Orpheum, farther down Massachusetts Avenue. I remember the shorts they'd show before the main feature. One of my favorites featured a plucky kid named Skippy. He'd toss rocks at trains to provoke the engineer into retaliating by throwing back lumps of coal. Skippy took the precious coal home for the family stove. His plight brought tears to my young eyes.

Grandfather Goldberg was a dapper dresser who never went about without a homburg hat, coat, tie and a walking stick that had an embossed silver knob (I still have it). My earliest memories of him are from Sunday visits to his house, where I'd find him smoking a cigar in his easy chair. My Uncle Louis, who had changed his last name to Gilmore, would also be there. He'd take the train up from Providence to Back Bay station and then hop a cab (which I thought terribly extravagant) to play pinochle with his dad. Meanwhile, my grandmother would be in the kitchen, cooking with a young Irish girl who lived in as a maid.

Another memory of my Goldberg grandparents is spending the second day of Rosh Hashanah in their front-row pew at Congregation Kehillath Israel, which they joined after moving to Brookline. My family's Reform synagogue, Temple Israel, celebrated only the first day of the New Year.

By the time I got to know him, my grandfather had retired from Studio Jewelry, his store on Tremont Street across from the Common, and was dabbling in real estate. I recall accompanying him and my mother as they made the rounds of store buildings he owned. I believe one of them was the original Jordan's Furniture in Waltham.

With my grandfather George at Nantasket Beach, the Wyner summer getaway.

I was the first grandchild on the Goldberg side, so my mother's parents – whom I called Nana and Papa – paid a lot of attention to me, always asking what I was up to and how school was going. Since cousin Anne had arrived before me, I wasn't such a novelty for my father's parents, whom I called Grandma and Grandpa. They had a corner apartment on the 16th floor of the Ritz, overlooking the Public Garden. It wasn't lavish: a bedroom, living room and small kosher kitchen. Most of their furniture was at their summer house at Nantasket Beach. Most of my early memories of my Wyner grandparents are from Nantasket Beach. In a letter to his traveling mother dated July 7, 1927, my father wrote how taken I was with my grandfather:

> He is getting more friendly with Father all the time and … when he wants company and comfort, the first thing he hollers more than anything else is 'Nampa.' He is firmly convinced that the absolute ownership of every stone, train and stick on the beach is positively 'Nampa's' and if you hand him anything at all, except things that he considers his own property like his playthings, he will tell you that they belong to "Nampa."

My father spared no detail in his account (August 8) to his mother of my second birthday party at the beach house:

> We had a big gang over to the house. … Most of the presents were in the way of something on wheels. There were automobiles, kiddy cars, bicycles, push carts, and various other vehicles and then a collection of Lindy dolls, two aeroplanes, balloons, two sets of furniture consisting in one case of two chairs and a table and in another case of one chair and a table, clothing and other items of interest. It was simply just one damn thing after another as far as the baby was concerned, and he dropped the thing he had and picked up the thing that came next. There was considerable screeching, and quite a lot of interpretation on the part of the child's mother, and toward the close of the afternoon a little spanking

on the part of the child's father. However, as such things go, it was undoubtedly a big success, and baby was initiated into his second anniversary with the proper gusto.

Among our many family movies is one of a party for my third birthday held at my grandparents' beach house. It shows a clown and lots of kids. When each guest arrived, I immediately reached for the present. Afterward, I behaved a bit more graciously; I even kissed one of the little girls (Sylvia Grossman). All of the kids were Jewish, and we'd become reacquainted years later as members of the Belmont Country Club.

'WE DON'T DO THOSE THINGS'

With so many doting relatives, I was always hearing "Justin is a good little boy." I did get into trouble on occasion, such as the time when I tripped up Roger Sonnabend with a hoop on the kindergarten playground at the Lawrence School. I don't think I did any permanent damage; Roger went on to follow his father into the hotel business (the Sonesta, among others). My mother, though, was furious. "We don't do those things," she told me. I knew I was in trouble when my mother called me Justin, or if she was really steamed, Justinian (maybe she thought I considered myself to be some sort of Roman emperor). She never hit me, but on occasion would warn me that I'd get a spanking when my father got home.

The few times that my father did discipline me, it was for disobeying my mother. He would never punish me for something I didn't mean to do. When I was 10, my father gave me a really nice gold ring that he had worn as a boy. It was at the start of a vacation in Butlers Cove along Buzzards Bay. The first day I wore it I went swimming, and I lost it. I was a skinny kid, and the ring must have slipped off my finger. My dad didn't get mad, but I felt so guilty. He had worn that ring throughout his childhood, and I couldn't keep it for more than a day. I spent the rest of the summer combing the rocks in search of that ring. Maybe some other kid found it and is wearing it today – or passed it along to his son.

As long as I'm confessing transgressions, when I was 10, I somehow hit poor little Betty Lipshitz (later Betty Singer) on the head with a ping-pong paddle while we were playing a game in the basement of her home at Nantasket Beach. She was in tears, and my parents made me apologize profusely. But it didn't end our friendship. Indeed, eight decades later we were still joking about it.

I recall being a happy kid, but I'm not one to remember unpleasant things. My mother instilled in me great pride in my family. But with that pride came a sense of responsibility. She emphasized that how I behaved reflected on my family. She also said if people saw that I was well brought up, they would respect me. "You don't want to be like the children on Erie Street," she would tell me, contrasting them with the well-bred kids like her who had grown up on Charlotte Street. When I was little, I thought those streets must be miles apart; actually, they're within a few blocks of each other in the old Jewish neighborhood of Roxbury and Dorchester.

We may have been better off than most people, especially during the Depression, but that wasn't something I noticed. I was told it was bad breeding to talk about money and the things you own. It wasn't that there was anything wrong with having it, only that making money shouldn't be an end in itself. My mother would often deride what she called the "nouveau riche," the people for whom everything had to be glitzy to show they were a success.

My parents would spend extra money for quality – furniture and clothes that would last a long time – but they didn't lead a lavish lifestyle. We rarely went out to restaurants. We proudly wore the McKem children's outfits made at Shawmut Woolen Mills, such as our winter snowsuits and my sister's Shirley Temple outfits. Not wanting to show up his employees, my dad didn't drive a flashy car.

We did have household help, which wasn't unusual even for middle-class families in those days. After Betty was born in 1930, we had a nurse, Miss Flagg, for a while; a maid, Ada; and a laundress, who came in several times a week. That was before washing machines, when clothes had to be hand-scrubbed on a washboard. We also had a chauffeur, Dickson, who doubled as a handyman, since my father was often out of town on business.

THE BOTTLE BOY

As a little kid, I earned spending money by pulling weeds – a penny for five plants – and redeeming bottles for two cents at a store in Cleveland Circle. I'd load up my little red wagon with our family's bottles and those of our next-door neighbors. The store owner got angry with me because I was bringing in so many bottles, but my mother came to my defense and lectured him right back. I was really proud of her when she threatened to take her business elsewhere.

My mother didn't depend on someone else's approval or feel compelled to climb some social ladder. If I expressed concern about what other kids thought, say about clothes she bought for me, Mom would say, "You should hold your head high, and maybe they'll wonder if they should have worn what you wore."

She told me to brush aside teasing or insults. "Sticks and stones will break my bones, but names will never hurt me" she would quote whenever I felt hurt by some kid's taunt. If I let my anger show, she said, my tormenters would be the winners. Over and over, she reminded me: "If you are confident in yourself, if you try to do the right thing, then you don't have to worry."

My mother had very firm ideas about what was the right thing – perhaps too firm, as she had me so inculcated in her ways that it was hard for me to accept that the ways of other families – like those of my future wife – could be right, too. Mother insisted that properly raised people don't show their emotions in public. Her attitude was that if you felt unhappy, you shouldn't let it show; if you wanted to mope, you should go someplace private.

When she was dying of cancer, Mother concealed her pain even from her own sisters. Through much of my life, I tried to emulate my mother's stoicism. When I got involved in Marriage Encounter much later in life, I learned how to share my feelings with Genevieve. I came to realize that feelings were neither right nor wrong – they just were.

In matters of food, my mother was also strict. The kitchen was virtually off limits to all but her and her housekeeper. No snacking between meals, though I was allowed to patronize the Good Humor Man (I liked the coconut-covered chocolate ice cream on a stick). Dinner was 6 sharp; to be late was unthinkable.

The food was brought in plated, and asking for seconds a no-no. If I didn't like what was served, I still had to clean my plate. Remember the starving Armenians, I was admonished.

My mom, though, did worry about my weight. As I said, I was skinny. When I was in my early teens, she would have me drink a glass of Guinness Stout with dinner to fatten me up. Among the more bitter brews, it turned me off to beer until I was well into college. Other than Shabbos wine and my grandfather's schnapps, I don't recall much alcohol growing up.

Unlike many other Jewish households, ours did not revolve around food. Dinner was a place for good conversation. And sometimes that conversation could get pretty intense. My mother was a big fan of Franklin Roosevelt. My father was not. Like many other businessmen, he resented FDR's meddling in the economy.

Betty and I in the great outdoors with Mom and Dad around 1940.

Betty in her late teens.

SAYING NO TO THE WHITE HOUSE

Good breeding, of course, demanded good manners. No elbows on the table. No leaving the table without asking to be excused. No reading at the table. Such a contrast with so many family tables today, where kids – and some adults – can't resist checking their iPhones.

But it wasn't so much a matter of rules for the sake of rules. My parents drilled home the importance of courtesy. Treat everyone with respect, no matter how humble. When I was a little boy, I was punished for speaking rudely to our housekeeper. That drove home a principle that I would try to follow throughout my life. I made it a point to treat everyone with the same interest and care, from the fellow who swept the factory floor to corporate CEOs and community leaders. And if I ever needed reminding, I had the example my father set over the 40 years we worked together: His office door was always open to everyone.

There were occasions, though, when I thought Mom took etiquette to an extreme, such as when my parents' close friends Mark and Llora Bortman were honored at the White House. An immigrant from Romania, Mark made his fortune in manufacturing. He was so proud of his new citizenship that his true love became collecting Americana, especially manuscripts and antiques. As soon as he had a little savings, he started buying Paul Revere silver (much of his collection is now at the Museum of Fine Arts). In 1964, the Bortmans donated a silver coffee urn once owned by President John Adams and his wife, Abigail, to the White House. It was a particularly appropriate gift, as the Adamses had been the first occupants of the presidential mansion. My parents were invited to lunch and the presentation ceremony, which was hosted by then-president Lyndon Johnson and his wife, Lady Bird. My mother declined. "You don't send an invitation to somebody from out of town to come to lunch," I recall her saying. It's just not proper. We're not going to go." And they didn't.

CAMP TIMES

Now I don't want to make mother out as being stuffy. As her honeymoon diary revealed, she had a sense of fun and adventure. We have photos of her driving a white convertible right out of the Roaring Twenties.

When we spent summers at Butlers Cove, Mother would take my sister and me out sailing on weekdays while my father was at work. The 26-foot catboat, which had a small inboard motor, was half as wide as it was long. When the entire family was aboard, Mother would cook down below in the cramped, primitive galley. Every once in a while, she would pop up – green in the face – for fresh air, but she remained good-natured about it.

At least twice a month, my father would take the night boat to New York on business, and Mother would drive us to a spot on the shore of the Cape Cod Canal where she knew the boat would pass at 8:05 p.m. Sure enough, the boat was there when she said it would be. We'd yell across the water, "Hi Daddy," and he'd wave back at us.

In my early years, my mother was an ever-present part of my life. Even in the summer of 1934 when I went to Camp Wigwam in Maine, she rented a house for herself and my sister right outside the gates. It seemed that whenever I was out marching with the other campers, the pair would be waving and yelling, "Hi Jerry!" Looking back, I'm amazed at my mother's devotion in following me to camp, but at the time I just felt embarrassed by the attention (not that I would have told her).

Genevieve's brother, Jack Geller, was at the camp at the same time, though I didn't know him then. I do remember the camp directors Arnold "Pop" Lehman and Abraham "Mandy" Mandelstam.

Mandy wasn't particularly good with names. Whenever he greeted one of his charges, he would pat the camper on the back and sneak a look at the name tag that had to be sewn into our collars. Our camp outfits were supplied by a clothing company with a name that began with Alexander. Mistaking the company's label for our name tags, he would call half the kids "Alex." Another memory from that camp isn't as funny. I came down with a severe case of poison ivy – so bad that about the only activity I could do was target shooting. I spent all day at the rifle range. I returned from camp with a bunch of medals from the National Rifle Association. Unfortunately, I lost my marksmanship skills as an adult.

Showing off my prize catch on my first salmon fishing trip with my father to New Brunswick, Canada.

TAKING THE BAIT

I wasn't big on sports as a kid. Occasionally, my dad and I would toss around a baseball, but I have more memories of us fishing. I liked fishing from my first outing when I was 6 or 7, but it was at the dinner table that my dad taught me one of the most important lessons about the sport. When he saw that I wasn't eating our catch, he admonished me that it wasn't right to catch and kill fish just for entertainment. If I couldn't eat the fish, I couldn't go fishing. Eventually, I developed a taste for fish.

Later, my dad would take me fishing with his friends. We'd use clams for bait, the same kind of cherrystone quahogs that I enjoyed eating raw in the half shell. I didn't make myself particularly popular with the crew when I devoured half the bait.

Like just about every kid in New England, I loved to go sledding. When I was about 10, my parents gave me the ultimate Chanukah gift: a Flexible Flyer. It was made from beautiful dark wood and stood out from all the other kids' sleds, which were light in color. For its first run, I took it to the hill at the Heath School. As I hurtled down the slope, I spied two of the tough Irish kids from the neighborhood converging on me. Just as I reached bottom, they crashed into me. The sled was slightly damaged, my feelings more so. I never went back to that hill.

In warmer weather, I tooled around in a bicycle that had a sidecar. Little Betty was a frequent passenger. Being five years older, I was her big brother and could do no wrong. Our relationship remained close, even when she was in her teens and entering college. When we were older and the age gap was less yawning, I dated some of her friends. I know she put in a good word for me. She was very proud of her brother.

Getting back to the bike, it was at the center of a valuable but painful lesson I learned about life. When I was 11, I became enamored with a pocket knife owned by a kid who was a grade ahead of me.

He came from an old Yankee family, and I think he was a bit wiser to the world than I was. He offered to swap his knife for my bike, and I took him up on the deal. When my parents learned about how I had been snookered, they talked about stepping in. But they decided not to. They had always stressed that your word is your bond: If you agree to something, you have to follow through.

After I split the end of a finger nearly to the bone playing with the knife, my parents took it away from me. But while I lost both the bike and the knife, I did end up with a permanent reminder of my folly. Look at the index finger of my left hand today, and you'll see it has a square top.

ARMCHAIR ADVENTURES

Indoors, I escaped into books and hobbies. I read the Tom Swift science fiction books, Hardy Boy mysteries and the Peck's Bad Boy series. When my father went on his business trips to New York, he would always pick up the latest Big Little Book for me. They were hardcover comics about 3½ inches by 4½ inches in size. The big part was that they were an inch and a half thick – more than 400 pages. The title characters included Dick Tracy, Little Orphan Annie and Tarzan. I also used to read Western-themed pulp magazines, but I got over that habit after I was bedridden with stomach flu. Uncle Louis brought me a bunch of the Westerns to help me through my convalescence. I must have read them all, because ever since I haven't been able to look at those magazines without my stomach turning over.

My appetite for travel was whetted by Richard Halliburton's accounts of trips to just about every exotic corner of the globe. He followed the route of Cortez through Mexico and of Ulysses on his way home from Troy. I was so enthralled by Halliburton's adventure in Jerusalem's biblical tunnel of King Hezekiah that I retraced the route as an adult.

Inspired by the railroad across from our first house on Clark Road, I was laying my own tracks before I was 5. I got one of the first models of the Streamliner locomotive, a celebrated super-fast diesel electric engine. My hobby got a big boost when my older cousin Lester, who lived in New York, gave me his model trains. I then had a big setup, with multiple trains, in the attic of our Dean Road house. I called it the JL Wyner Railroad.

I loved mechanical and electrical things, but there was only so much tinkering I could do with model railroading. Later, I moved from train sets to crystal sets – and from there to the wonders of talking to people on the other side of the world.

DON'T BE LIKE UNCLE SOL

Unlike the trains that ran at all hours through my neighborhood, the JL Wyner Railroad ran on a schedule constrained by its namesake's homework. At my mother insistence, I had to complete all my assignments before doing anything else. She instilled in me the habit of never putting anything off. Even today, if I have e-mails waiting for answers, I find it hard to tear myself away from the computer for a game of golf.

I was a good student, but more because I wanted to be than because of pressure from my parents. My father joked that he would take the strap to me if I got straight A's. He didn't want me to turn out like Uncle Sol, the husband of his sister, Frances.

Sol earned straight A's right through Harvard and Harvard Law. He'd ride the trolley for hours because that's where he did his best studying. As I mentioned in an earlier chapter, many in the family believe Sol's pursuit of scholastic perfection turned him into somewhat of a pedant. Great things had been expected of Sol. His Harvard Law roommate was Robert Taft, a future U.S. senator and the son of a former president. With his connections and brilliant mind, many thought Sol would eventually be named to the Supreme Court. I thought he was the most boring man in the world. I spent endless hours at his house as he droned on about some subject or another. But to give Sol his due, close family friends who were his clients worshipped the ground he walked on.

Sol served most of his career as a municipal court judge in Brookline. He was about as straitlaced as one could be. When my mother appeared before him to appeal a parking ticket, he recused himself. But people used to tell me that his wife – my Aunt Frances – would go behind his back and persuade his clerk to fix tickets for almost anyone who asked her.

My formal education began with the Brookline Playschool, overseen by a man named Huberman. I remember that a station wagon would pick us up at our doors. On the way home we'd often stop at Irving's Toy and Card Shop on Harvard Street. I'd buy these special pictures that would appear when the paper was exposed to the sun. The founder's daughter was still running the store until her death in December 2015. She was 101.

When I was in fifth grade, my mother moved me from the Runkle School to Rivers Country Day, a private boys school. Mom felt it offered a better athletic program than the public schools. Rivers was then located just behind the houses on the other side of our street. Its main entrance was on Eliot Street, opposite the public Heath School, which drew students from a rough section of town. Heath boys were notorious for pouncing on Rivers students as they left school. I managed to avoid being ambushed by taking a back path that let out on Dean Road not far from my house. I don't have many memories of Rivers itself, beyond being the youngest boy on the basketball team and somehow always managing to be first or second in my class in grades (my main rival was the son of the headmaster).

In seventh grade, I transferred to the all-boys Roxbury Latin School, where my father and two of his brothers had gone. In my father's day, it was actually in Roxbury. When I attended, it was at its current location in West Roxbury. The toughest part of school was all the homework, which made that at Rivers seem like nothing. Since we had to stay after school for athletics, I didn't get home until 4:30. By the time I was finished with homework and dinner, it was 8.

The grading was tough, too. Even the top-ranked students didn't get all A's. I didn't set out to be a standout student, but when the rankings came out, I usually was at or near the top. People used to fight to sit next to me at exam time. While I wouldn't move my arm so they could see my answers, I admit I would be less than totally protective. I didn't want to alienate the in crowd, but I still felt a bit guilty.

AT 44, I GET MY HIGH SCHOOL DIPLOMA

Here's a head scratcher: How is that my father and I both received our high school diplomas in the same year?

Although my dad finished Roxbury Latin in 1911 and I in 1942, we both weren't recognized for our success until the 1969 commencement. That's because we each started college ahead of our high school classmates.

When my father was at Roxbury Latin, juniors could take the entrance exams for Harvard; seniors could take those they had skipped or repeat ones they had failed. My father, as far as we know, was the first student to pass all the exams in his junior year. That allowed him to skip his senior year and go directly to Harvard. I entered college after the Christmas holiday of my senior year at Roxbury Latin.

When I returned to Roxbury Latin for the 25th reunion of my class, I told the headmaster that it did not seem right that my father and I were listed as only attending the school and not graduating. I told him that this suggested we had either dropped out or transferred to another high school. Shouldn't the fact, I argued, that we had both directly entered college be proof enough that we qualified to be considered Roxbury Latin graduates?

The headmaster passed my request to the board of trustees, which agreed with me. Dad and I received our diplomas at the graduation ceremony the following year. As I told a *Globe* reporter at the time, we wanted our sheepskins to show "that Roxbury Latin satisfactorily prepared us for college."

My biggest moral dilemma was the time when several students found the mimeographed stencil of an upcoming physics exam in a wastebasket. They ran off copies, and someone sent me one. I didn't want to be a cheat, so I tossed it in the trash without looking at it. Physics was one of my easiest subjects; it just came naturally to me. Afterward the culprits were caught. When the headmaster asked me if I had looked at the copy, I pointed to my test score. It was the lowest mark I had ever received on a final. While almost everyone else scored 90 to 100, I received a 75.

Looking back, I'm surprised anyone felt the need to cheat. The school bent over backward to help students succeed. The administration felt that if a student failed, doubts would be raised about the school's admission standards. Still, I was amazed to see some of my less-than-diligent classmates go on to Harvard and actually graduate.

I wanted to go out for crew – which my father had captained when he was at the school – but the medical exam revealed I had a heart murmur. No doctor ever found a murmur again, but that one time was enough to keep me off the rowing team. I was crestfallen. But I found another outlet in the drama club, not as an actor but as a salesman. I became the darling of the club's faculty adviser, Professor Joseph Sasserno. As business manager, I filled the playbills with advertising from my dad's suppliers, who had offices on Summer Street in what was then known as Boston's Wool District. When I called on them, all were all happy to contribute because of how much they liked and respected my father.

That's me with the mustache in a Roxbury Latin play. At least I didn't have to dress as a girl like my fellow actor at the all-boys school.

THE OPPOSITE SEX

Roxbury Latin gave me an excellent grounding in the classics, but left me clueless about the opposite sex. My first real exposure to girls was Saturday afternoons at the Charlotte Orlov School of Dance, which was located above a garage in Cleveland Circle. Many of Boston's leading Jewish families sent their teens there to learn ballroom dancing. I was reunited with kids from playschool, and many of the same students had attended Sunday school with me at Temple Israel.

There were about 30 of us in the class, evenly split between boys and girls. The boys wore coats and ties, and the girls wore dresses. The instructor, Charlotte Orlov, made sure we danced every number. She mixed up our partners, occasionally making an exception for her niece, Betty Ann Orlov, who was going steady with my cousin Bob Wyner (the match didn't last). I became pretty good at dancing and have enjoyed it ever since.

I occasionally went to parties hosted by someone from the dancing school. Since I couldn't drive and was still pretty shy around girls, I didn't date much. I do remember, though, going out with Sissy Cohen. She picked me up in her father's chauffeur-driven car, and we went to an afternoon movie.

This is one of the bomb parachutes I worked on as a teen at Shawmut.

I have my mother to thank for helping me overcome bashfulness with girls. In my teens, I worked summers at the Shawmut factory. Being the boss's son didn't come with any perks. I had the privilege of sweeping the shipping-room floor under the supervision of Leonard Gimpel, who I thought at the time must have been the grumpiest manager in the factory. I remember Mr. Gimpel saying to me, "Your father told me you weren't to receive any special treatment, so you be sure to get down on your hands and knees and sweep under every one of those bins." The summer when I was 16, I was pressed into service tying and inserting cords for parachute shrouds. The chutes were for bombs, not people. One type was for 22.5-pound fragmentation bombs dropped by dive bombers. The chute slowed the bomb after it was released, giving the pilot time to climb out of the dive and escape the blast. Later, we worked on bomb parachutes that contained camouflaged antenna wires. It was all top secret. The man who delivered the plans carried them in a briefcase handcuffed to his wrist.

Besides being mysterious, the work was tedious. It would take something like 100 half hitches to fasten the cords of a single chute. My mother was so appalled by how sore my hands were at the end of the day that she hatched a plan to spring me from the factory. When we went up to visit my sister at Camp Dunmore in Salisbury, Vermont, I discovered that I wasn't going home. Unbeknownst to me, Mom had had my clothes sent up. The camp's owners, Joe and Kitty Jacobson, were related to a business partner of my father, Ray Franks. My mother had arranged for me to have a specially created job: the counselor responsible for taking the girls out fishing once a week. The rest of the time I was to spend looking for good places to fish. I couldn't complain. It sure beat sweeping floors and tightening parachute cords – and I was the only guy among a bevy of female counselors.

The following fall, two of the counselors visited me. I took them out to the Totem Pole Ballroom at Norumbega Park in Newton. Back in the '40s, all the big bands would play at the Totem Pole. Afterward, as I was driving the counselors home, I heard on the radio that the main roads into the city were closed because of a big fire. I had to detour around Boston to take the girls to the Revere house where they were staying with friends. When I finally got back to Brookline, it was 1:30 in the morning. My parents were frantic. That was the night of the Cocoanut Grove Fire, which killed nearly 500 people. My parents didn't think I was at the Boston nightclub, but they couldn't be sure until they saw me step out of the car.

MY EXODUS CONNECTION

Regular Sunday guests at the home of my Goldberg grandparents were Dewey and Anne Stone. Anne was my mother's first cousin and her closest childhood friend.

The Brockton couple didn't have children, but they treated their many nieces and nephews as if they were their own. Dewey ran a number of businesses, including the Converse Rubber Company (best known for making "Chuck Taylor" sneakers). But his big passion was Israel, which he promoted first as a leader of the Jewish Agency and then of the United Jewish Appeal. Little did I realize it at the time, but this short, gregarious relative was smuggling weapons to Jews in pre-state Palestine. He helped arrange the purchase of the refugee ship "Exodus," which became the subject of a Leon Uris novel and Paul Newman movie.

Dewey used his business to help support the Zionist cause, storing contraband in his warehouses and – if the stories are to be believed – soliciting contributions from customers in exchange for selling them goods. My father bought cotton woven goods from Dewey's Harodite Finishing Company in Taunton. During the war, when factories had to abide by fixed prices and quotas, Dad said Dewey requested a "voluntary" donation to the Stone Charitable Foundation for each yard of fabric purchased. It was all part of Dewey's mystique, but I do recall reading that when he became chairman of the UJA in the mid-1940s, he donated a half-million dollars to a single year's annual campaign. That was the largest gift by far in the history of the appeal, making headlines in the Jewish press across the country.

After Genevieve and I married, the Stones often hosted us at their summer home in Brewster. You never knew who else would be there. Abba Eban, the legendary Israeli diplomat, was among Dewey's famous guests. Dewey was also close to Chaim Weizmann, Israel's first president. In fact, Dewey helped orchestrate the White House meeting where Weizmann persuaded President Harry S. Truman to support a Jewish state. Dewey was the founding chairman of the board of governors of Israel's Weizmann Institute of Science.

In the 1960s, when Genevieve and I first visited Israel, we happened to tour the institute the week that it dedicated the Stone Administration Building.

BIG MAN ON CAMPUS

In which I challenge a captain, unplug the women's dorm
– and join just about every club that would take me

I WAS SUPPOSED TO go to Harvard, following in the family tradition. I had even been accepted under the college's policy of waiving entrance exams for any Roxbury Latin boy ranking in the top 10 percent of his class.

Harvard, though, wouldn't let me start classes until the summer session began in June 1943. With the United States already at war, I was anxious to get my degree so that I could enter the service as an officer rather than as an enlisted man. Students majoring in math or science, as I intended, could be deferred from the draft so long as they graduated by June 1945. I didn't have a moment to waste: I needed to finish college in less than two and a half years. I could just make it by taking seven courses a semester and extra classes during summer and winter breaks.

With the help of my Uncle Alvin Sloane, a Tufts College graduate and then a professor of mechanical engineering at MIT, I was admitted to the Medford school in January 1943. My plan was to transfer to Harvard, which had agreed to accept my Tufts credits, after my first semester. But I instantly took a liking to Tufts, and the college to me.

Tufts had yet to establish the national reputation it enjoys today; half the students then commuted from home. But Tufts did have one big advantage back then over Harvard: The classes were co-ed. The last time I had attended classes with girls was in fourth grade. I missed out on the boy-girl friendships that flourished in public schools.

THAT HEADY FEELING

Entering Tufts in midyear, I was not only one of the youngest students, but the other freshmen had a semester's head start on making friends. To meet people, I became even more of a joiner than I had been in high school, where I was a member of *Tripod* magazine and the debating and drama societies. My services were very much in demand by campus clubs and my company by the gals at Jackson, Tufts's sister school. I'd like to say that the reason was my charisma, but the fact of the matter was that many of my male colleagues had little time for extracurricular activities because they were in uniform, primarily in the Navy's new V-12 officer-training program. Still, being so popular was a heady feeling.

But there was a flip side to my charmed life. I felt increasingly uncomfortable about being out of uniform when so many people my age had signed up. So, I decided one day to put school on hold and enlist in the infantry. I gave my parents only a day's notice of my intentions. My mother was startled and a bit alarmed, but didn't try to stop me; she knew it was an important war. As it turned out, I was rejected – not because of the heart murmur that had kept me out of crew at Roxbury Latin (the problem didn't even come up), but for having flat feet that required prescribed orthotics. The military didn't want to deploy servicemen who might need replacement equipment that was not readily available in the field. I could only hope that it would not be an issue when I graduated and planned to enlist in the services with a commission. I would never find out: By the time I received my degree, the war was winding down. The closest I got to battle, as I'll write later, was as a civilian simulating air-to-air combat.

By senior year, I would become involved in more activities than anyone else, according to a student survey. Among them: editor of the newspaper *Tufts· Weekly*, associate editor of the literary magazine *Tuftonian*, member of the debating society, vice chair of Pen Paint & Pretzels (the dramatic society also known as 3 P's) and head of the Traditions Society (a playful club that enforced made-up rules, such as by paddling freshmen for walking on the grass). And to think that my original plan was to leave Tufts for Harvard after my first semester.

Editing The Tufts Weekly with Betty Lundgren.

THE PARTY ANIMALS

Since I was among a handful of students entering college at midyear, I was placed in an upperclassman dorm, West Hall, the gingerbread-looking building on the main academic quad. Built in 1871, it was already old when I lived there. My two roommates had horrible study habits. One would regularly go out drinking and come back sick. As it happened, he and I shared bunk beds. Initially, I was in the lower bunk. After lying awake a few unpleasant nights, wondering what might stream down from above, I persuaded him to switch bunks.

Early on, I hung out with a group of students who would drink and study at the Jumbo Café in Teele Square in Somerville, just a five-minute walk from the campus. I didn't like alcohol; at first, I couldn't even stand the smell of beer. But I wanted to be sociable, so I would nurse a brew while everyone else downed several. Eventually, I was able to tolerate beer. Some nights, I would even drink several bottles, quenching my thirst from the salty peanuts. I must have had a hollow leg. Those who reordered when I did often would leave plastered, while I was still, strangely, unaffected and steady on my feet.

Thanks to the rigors of Roxbury Latin (Tufts was easier by comparison) and my mother's insistence on homework before pleasure, I had little trouble adapting to academic life at Tufts. I'd work on assignments every spare moment so that my evenings would be free. I'd read textbooks while waiting in line and write papers while eating lunch. I sharpened my skills by tutoring others. If you explain things out loud, it helps you remember them. It certainly helped me master that most dreaded of science courses, physical chemistry.

I majored in chemistry, because I already had my eye on entering the family business and thought that would be the most helpful specialty. As a result, I had to attend labs as well as classes. Because I was accelerating college, one semester I had seven three-hour labs a week. I was forced to become a master organizer. I'd work simultaneously on lab assignments from different classes. But that was the easy part. Cleaning up was the real challenge, until I developed the special Wyner wash-up routine. While other students accumulated a huge pile of dirty glassware after finishing their experiments, I found it much more efficient to clean, dry and store test tubes and beakers as soon as I was done with them. To this day, I'm the same way in the kitchen as I was in the lab, washing pots and pans and other utensils as I go along.

I also got in some studying – and not a small amount of socializing – when I subbed for a friend who worked the college switchboard after hours. I worked for nothing. My pal needed the money more than I did; besides, the job was a lot of fun. I was familiar with switchboards from watching the Shawmut operators, but now I had an opportunity to run one. It was the old-fashioned kind that that you see in old movies, with plugs attached to long retractable cords. The college didn't receive many outside calls at night, so I sometimes would call friends in different places and hook them all up for a conference call.

Seeking cushier quarters, I occasionally transferred the operations to the dean's office by routing the calls through his phone. Late one night, as I was on the phone chatting up a girl, my feet resting on his desk, the dean walked in to catch up on work. Seeing my shock at his appearance, he broke out in laughter. We became good friends. The dean, Nils Yngve Wessell, went on to serve as Tufts president from 1953 to 1966.

POWER OF THE PRESS

Outside of schoolwork, the Tufts weekly newspaper took up much of my time. In addition to serving as editor, I wrote a gossip column about men on campus (there was a separate column for women). It was a big deal, as I was in a position where I could promote or criticize anyone. My pen wasn't particularly venomous, though. Lots of people became my new best friends, anxious to be quoted in the column.

In addition to writing and editing, I furtively tinkered with printing the newspaper. It was set on a linotype machine run by two old guys in a print shop located next to the campus police and the gym. Much to my frustration, they jealously guarded access to the linotype machine. But I got to do the makeup, which involved moving around lines of metal type, and setting the headlines, letter by letter. At night, after the printers had gone home, I'd do a last check before locking up the pages for the press. I got pretty good at slicing off lines of type that contained errors. One time, though, surgery wasn't enough. I had to heat up the lead and set a few lines of type myself. The printers must not have read the paper the next day; otherwise, they would have noticed lines they hadn't set.

I became a hero of the V-12 Navy men when I wrote an editorial chastising a Navy captain for restricting a sailor to quarters for several months because he had returned late to his dorm. The sailor had been at a Pen Paint & Pretzels party with other cast members the final night of a play. Captain Preston B. Haines, who commanded the Tufts Naval Training Unit, wasn't accustomed to having his orders challenged. Furious, he called the president of the college, who in turn called me into his office to tell me that Haines had demanded that I apologize. I did go to see the captain, but I didn't apologize. As a civilian, I felt every right to express my opinions. I told him that grounding the sailor was extreme punishment for celebrating after a school play that he had been authorized to participate in. Haines was a tough guy; he didn't change his mind. But I think I won his respect. We got along OK afterward.

We donated a splinter from the tusk of college mascot Jumbo the elephant to the SS Tufts, a Navy transport ship.

I did please the Navy brass with another story. It involved the launch of the SS Tufts, one of a series of Victory transport ships that bore the names of colleges and universities. The faculty adviser to the paper, Celia Van Auken, also happened to be public relations director of the university. We came up with the idea of donating a plaque to the ship bearing a splinter from the tusk of the college mascot, Jumbo the elephant. As editor of the college paper, I presented the plaque – and got my picture in newspapers across the country. Jumbo, by the way, had been a star attraction of the Barnum & Bailey Circus until he was struck dead by a train in 1885. P.T. Barnum, a benefactor and trustee of Tufts, donated the mounted body to the college. The 12-foot-tall elephant stood in Barnum Hall, a museum on campus, until he went up in flames with the rest of the building in 1975.

The V-12 program swelled in size during my second semester. The servicemen wore white sailor suits in the summer and navy blue in the winter. No matter the season, they wore round white sailor caps. Every evening, they marched in formation down Professors Row to their mess hall. At the foot of the street, where it intersects with College Avenue, the sailors passed two women's dormitories. One of the residents had a boyfriend in the Crane Theological School who was lucky enough to have his own car. They would often be necking inside it when the sailors passed. The guy – unforgettably named Frazier Kearsted – would taunt the servicemen, knowing full well that they couldn't break ranks. One evening, though, the sailors got even. Though they weren't on duty, they marched down the street in uniform and in formation. When the wisecracking Romeo started in with his jibes, they suddenly spread out around his car, heaved it up – with the young lovers inside – and deposited it on a ledge just above the sidewalk.

The Navy men did not hold my civilian status against me. In fact, some of them became close friends. After they went overseas, I corresponded with them, printing some of their letters in the paper. They also must have trusted me. Some of those who had left behind brides or girlfriends at Jackson asked me to escort them to dances and the movies.

PREACHER AND PRANKSTER

The Navy presence was so large on campus that the rest of us had to scramble for housing. In my two and one-quarter years on campus, I lived in five places. For a while, I roomed with divinity students at Crane Theological School, a now-closed seminary that taught a combination of Universalist and Unitarian creeds. One would think the students would have had their eyes on heaven, but they were real hell-raisers. They also seemed to have ever-changing religious outlooks. I never knew from day to day which faith they were practicing. Sometimes their services were much like those I attended at Temple Israel. Since I knew the Union Prayer Book, widely used by Reform synagogues, I was in big demand to help write sermons for their student pulpits.

At another point, I lived in a rooming house with four other students on Bromfield Road, opposite the engineering school. We bonded over pinochle, staying up half the night playing for small amounts of money – though sleep-deprived tempers sometimes flared in the wee hours. The landlady was a formidable unmarried woman in her 60s. She was stingy, to the point that she demanded that we call her before bathing so she could measure the height of the water in the tub. She limited us to so little hot water that we couldn't even cover ourselves. I ignored that rule and somehow escaped her wrath. But one of my roommates, a dignified young pre-dental student from Jamaica named Basil Henriques, wasn't as fortunate. One night when he was bathing, she banged on the door, insisting that she be let in. She then made him get out of the tub so she could make sure he wasn't cheating her. (The experience evidently didn't sour Basil on the college; he later became an accomplished professor at Tufts Dental School.)

Later, I was proctor at Phi Epsilon Pi. Previously a Jewish fraternity house, it, like other fraternities, had been taken over for general use during the war. Although I was the head of the house, I admit that at times I suppressed my "good Justin." We decided one of the members needed more of a social life. So, we sent out about 50 postcards signing him up for various things, from a course on growing mushrooms in the cellar to a trial period with a piano (which he managed to cancel before delivery). The guy didn't know what hit him. Suddenly, he was the center of attention, but I think he probably enjoyed finally being noticed. We weren't looking to scar anyone for life; we just wanted to have a little fun.

Tufts was pretty tolerant of pranks. When someone told me that you could fill up a room by balling up every single page of the *Sunday New York Times*, I decided to conduct my own experiment. While the student who lived across the hall from me was out, some of us balled up two entire papers. When he returned and opened the door, he found his room stuffed topped to bottom. I was peering in from the fire escape to see his reaction. As he started to push his way through all the crumpled paper, I decided I'd better skedaddle. In my haste, I fell through the rusty stairs and punctured my leg on a rusty rod. To be safe, I went to the Somerville hospital. I told the doctor that I had fallen from a fire escape, but didn't elaborate. I still have the scar – and a subscription to the *Times*.

LIGHTS OUT, LADIES

During exam week one year, I snuck into the girls' dormitory. This was no spur-of-the-moment escapade. Beforehand, I had persuaded a campus cop to lend me his master key, saying that I had lost the key to a building where I had an activity. Before returning it, I made a copy. Even though I had a girlfriend in the dorm, I resisted the temptation to go upstairs. I stuck to my mission: pulling out all the electrical fuses in the basement. Suddenly, a dorm full of girls frantic with last-minute studying found themselves in the dark. My reputation must have preceded me, because they instantly knew whom to blame. I can still see it today: about 50 girls in nightgowns and bathrobes dashing across the campus to the Phi Epsilon Pi house to shake their fists at Jerry Wyner.

It was all in good fun and, besides, civilian men were in short supply on campus. We were outnumbered by the women. That gave us a distinct advantage at night, when the sailors were restricted to quarters. Our male status also stood us well when the dining hall at Jackson became the only civilian cafeteria.

Much to my mother's consternation, most of the women I dated at college weren't Jewish. I knew of only one Jewish gal living on campus, and she was the daughter of a Tufts graduate. Many of us wondered if the dean of Jackson had been disinclined to admit Jews, although I don't recall her making any anti-Semitic remarks.

In the paper's April Fool's edition, we ran a photo of my co-editor Ray Thompson and me (right) under the headline "Police Raid Dean's House."

Besides possibly being bigoted, the dean struck us as inordinately stuffy. On several occasions, we took the opportunity to knock her down a few pegs. At midnight one evening, we called a dozen taxi companies and sent them to her house on Professors Row. We told them that they should toot their horns because the doorbell didn't work. We then scrambled to the top of a hill overlooking the street and watched as the cabs converged on the dean's house. It looked like the theater district when the plays let out. Every time a cab honked, the bewildered dean would pop out and wave the equally clueless driver away.

On another occasion, we used the newspaper to needle the dean. At a time of day when we knew she wouldn't be at home, Ray Thompson, my co-managing editor at the paper, and I had our picture taken on the front steps of her house, handcuffed to two campus policemen. We were wearing only our long johns. In the April Fool's edition – called the *Wufts Teekly* – we ran a photo with the title "Police Raid Dean's House."

MAESTRO OF PROPS

I was involved in a little onstage drama as well, but for the most part I worked behind the scenes as co-director of Pen Paint & Pretzels. Our adviser, Professor John Woodruff, liked to experiment, and set up a permanent theater-in-the-round in the former Jackson gym. It was one of the first in the country. We mounted a revival of William H. Smith's temperance play *The Drunkard; or, The Fallen Saved*. The run marked the 100th anniversary of the play's premiere in Boston, which was produced, incidentally, by our old pal, P. T. Barnum. For a more sensory experience, we set up a mock tavern at the edge of the stage and served beer to the audience. My job was to come up with the beer steins, which – like other consumer goods – were in short supply because of the war effort. I managed to borrow some from the downtown German restaurant Jacob Wirth. By the way, on the same night our production debuted, a professional version was banned just hours before it was to open in a Boston nightclub. The city's licensing board ruled that the play was inappropriate for "a place licensed to sell alcoholic beverages." I wrote about the brew-ha-ha (sorry) in my weekly newspaper column, under the heading "An immoral moral play":

> 3 P's got a gift when Boston banned "The Drunkard," the temperance play, as being immoral & too suggestive of over-indulgence of alcoholic beverages. The last two performances in the gym saw people flocking to the play from all over the state, & last Sat. saw more outsiders at the gym than at any other single night in our memory. People were being turned away at the gates by the dozens.

For other specialty props, I turned to the Howard Athenaeum, a burlesque theater better known as the Old Howard. It was in then-notorious Scollay Square, which was later bricked over to become Boston's Government Center. Built in the 1840s, the Howard retained the gothic look of the church that originally stood on the site. The religious appearance gave the theater a respectable air at a time when actors were viewed with suspicion. For many years, the Howard presented plays of the day, and so its prop room was like a theatrical museum. Rummaging around, I found gems such as 18th-century dueling pistols.

Ray, my newspaper colleague, and I organized Tufts Night to ogle the risqué shows at the Old Howard. It started out as a joke, but before we knew it, we had two busloads of guys and gals signed up.

C FOR SUCCESS

To achieve my goal of graduating in June 1945, I had to cram in extra courses on other campuses. One summer, at the Boston University intersession, I took a six-week course in German: 90-minute classes five days a week. Afterward, I passed an exam in scientific German that normally required two years of study. In my last semester, I still needed another class in organic chemistry to qualify for my major. With nothing scheduled that spring at Tufts that I hadn't already taken, I enrolled in a graduate-level course at MIT in the emerging field of heterocyclic compounds (synthetic rubber, for example).

By all rights, I should not have been in the course, as I hadn't taken the necessary preparatory classes. So, I was completely lost when the professor would say something like, "I'll skip the next 15 steps because you had that in course 4432." The only place I could find background on the material was in a German-language periodical. But I had trouble deciphering it with my limited German from the crash course at BU. I wound up with a C in the course. That was good enough for Tufts, from which I graduated cum laude. Meanwhile, I got a letter from MIT saying that because I had not maintained a B average, I had flunked out of graduate school.

Besides helping me graduate from Tufts, the MIT course led to another milestone in my life: my first car. I had to have one to get from Cambridge to Medford in time for all my classes. My father bought me a used Packard from a Newton fellow, a prominent liquor dealer who reputedly had made his money as a bootlegger during Prohibition. He had a turntable in his garage to accommodate all the cars he owned. The Packard cost $495. I didn't check the trunk.

That's me in my first car, a used Packard, in front of our Dean Road house.

With Mom at my Tufts graduation.

A $1,000 INSULT

When it comes to keeping track of people, the FBI has nothing on college alumni offices. Yes, universities take pride in the success of their progeny, but they're particularly vigilant of dollar signs; after all, they've got buildings to build and salaries to pay.

About five years after I graduated, I was solicited for a Tufts capital campaign by a young alumnus, Alan Wolozin. I knew him from when he had worked at Uncle Eddie's makeshift kids' camp on Nantasket Beach. We met for lunch at a restaurant in Brockton. I gave Alan a check for $1,000, which was big, big money for me in those days. Alan, though, had apparently believed that I had access to much more than that because I worked in the family business. He took one look at my check and tore it up. One long rip. Perhaps he had read in some book that such theatrics were an effective way to shame people into larger donations. "You're my key to raising a lot of money," he told me. I responded that his behavior was so insulting and irritating that I wouldn't give him a cent. As time went on, however, I did give a modest annual gift, but prompted only by the annual mail solicitation from my class agent.

About 15 years later, Genevieve and I were approached by Sol Gittleman, a long-time provost at Tufts whom we had gotten to know and like after he spoke at the annual Wyner lecture at Temple Israel. Sol sought to persuade us to support the school in a more substantial way. When I told him how I had been turned off by my experience with Alan, Sol asked that we keep an open mind as he considered ways to win us back.

A short time later, he told us about a special project that he thought we might find particularly worthy of support, a movie about the university's international educational initiatives that was to be shown to children in the Soviet Union. The project did indeed appeal to us, so we donated $10,000 toward it – the largest gift we had given to anyone up to that point.

When we received a copy of the program that was distributed at the movie's premiere, we noticed that we were listed as "Justin and Genevieve Wiener." While we hadn't craved the recognition, we felt that if we did receive credit, our last name should be spelled correctly. Sol assured me that the spelling would be correct in the movie credits. Curious to see how our contribution had been acknowledged, we asked for a copy of the film. After what seemed like forever, it arrived. The film concluded with a bunch of credits followed by our names, but they had an unprofessional appearance and were in a different color and typeface. This time, we were listed as Jerry and Genevieve, which was not how we had submitted our first names.

That error, along with the long delay in sending the film, reinforced our suspicion that our names had been tacked onto our copy only and were never planned to be included in the credits until the program misspelling issue arose. I told Sol that I felt a bit insulted that someone had thought we'd be taken in and flattered by such a crude ploy.

"I guess we really goofed," Sol sheepishly responded. I suggested that Tufts, besides soliciting us for the annual class gift, leave us alone for a while.

We have remained good friends with Sol and, some years later, opened our checkbook again to Tufts. We focused our support on its wonderful Hillel chapter and its charismatic director, Rabbi Jeffrey Summit, who had impressed us as a Wyner Lecturer at Temple Israel. One big check went toward an elevator for Hillel's new building. As I note in the chapter on Beth Israel Hospital, the Wyner family is especially generous when it comes to elevators.

B-SCHOOL DAYS

How being brash helped me get into Harvard

I WASN'T ON MY best behavior at my interview for Harvard Business School.

After a year working at Shawmut, I didn't see the need for a master's in business. After all, my father didn't have one. But my mother thought I started my career too young at age 19, and kept after me until I applied to Harvard in 1947.

When I went to the interview, I took the attitude that I would be happy with the outcome either way. I guess I might have come off a bit cocky, which was out of character for me. I boasted about my recent business experience. Thinking I was talking myself out of acceptance, I did just the opposite.

Although I had already had a year's work experience, I was still among the younger students in my class. Many of the other students had just been discharged from the service and were resuming their educations. Among my better-known classmates were Jack Valenti, who headed the Motion Picture Association of America for 38 years; Al Casey, CEO of American Airlines and later the government's point man for cleaning up the savings and loan scandals of the 1980s; and Walter Curley, ambassador to France.

By taking courses in the summer, I completed business school in 16 demanding months. Besides taking classes, I had to write a 15- to 20-page paper every week and meet regularly with a study group. As it does now, the school used the case method. We'd diagnose real-life business problems and propose solutions. Just as in the real world, there was never one right answer.

MR. EFFICIENT

I churned out my papers in a way that would have impressed Frederick Winslow Taylor, the time-and-motion guru. I would read the case, making notes of points to raise with my study group. After the discussion, I'd dictate my paper on a recording disc that I sent to my secretary at Shawmut to type up. My theory was that I was putting in the same effort as if I were writing a four-hour final exam. Even if I got a grade as low as a C-plus, I could reassure myself that the teachers would assume I had spent at least 20 hours on the paper, as did everyone else. I figured that if I turned in similar-quality work for the finals, I could count on a much higher grade. In the meantime, until everyone else in my group had finished their papers, I had to avoid them at dinner or risk hearing ideas that would tempt me to rewrite my report. My system worked. I never got less than high pass on my papers (the HBS equivalent of a B) and did even better in the finals.

HBS allowed me to take two courses at the law school, including one taught by Professor Warren Abner Seavey, a renowned expert in the field of agency. In legal jargon, an agent is appointed by someone else, the principal, to act on his or her behalf, such as by entering into contracts with a third party. While the legalese may sound mind-numbing, I found the topic fascinating and later very useful in my business life. At the end of the course, I went to him with a problem: His final exam was scheduled a few days after I was to graduate, and I needed the credit. I asked to take the exam early. He said not to worry; he would just give the average grade that I was getting in my courses in the business school.

My other law school professor, Robert Braucher, was not as generous. But Braucher, who was Seavey's son-in-law, did let me take the final exam early for his course in bills and notes, and I did reasonably well.

CHARTING MY OWN COURSE

I was a different sort of student than many of my classmates. They were focused on how they could jump-start stellar careers. For them, being a business success was everything. Influenced by my father, I viewed work as a means, not an end. I wanted to be able to provide for my family and to contribute to my community. Yes, I sought the excitement of running a business, the pride of making products that were the envy of the competition and the satisfaction of providing employees secure jobs at a company they held in high regard. But I knew that would never be enough for me – just as that had not been enough for my father.

One classmate called me a year after graduation to find out whether I was president of Shawmut. Relieved to hear that I was not, he said, "I wanted to be the first graduate who became a president." So far as I was concerned, he was welcome to enjoy that distinction.

At my 30th Harvard Business School reunion: from left, me, George, Genevieve, James and Daniel.

Mom was right, though, to push me to enroll at HBS. Learning accounting, for example, taught me how to analyze a balance sheet and recognize when a company was in trouble. Studying how other companies went wrong trained me to anticipate problems. Courses in marketing and advertising also helped me when I returned to Shawmut. Most of all, HBS's signature case study method taught me not just how to solve problems, but how to identify them before they became obvious – training that has stood me in good stead throughout my career.

I was very proud when our son James decided to leave the business to attend HBS. I was even prouder when he bettered his old man by graduating as a Baker Scholar, the school's top honor.

A YANK IN EUROPE

In which I nearly lose my shirt, skirt a riot and meet a mysterious cousin

Those were the parting words of French native Gerard Regard to me and our fellow Harvard Business School grads in spring 1948. "Why not?" I thought to myself, as did a number of my classmates.

Some weeks later I was on the SS Ernie Pyle, a WWII-built C4 troop carrier that had been transformed into cheap trans-Atlantic transportation for students and young travelers like me. I was lucky to have only five bunkmates; others had as many as 50. Accompanying me was my long-time friend from Brookline, Paul Lubell.

Soon after the ship got underway we found ourselves in extremely rough seas. We were among the few passengers who already had our sea legs. Often, we would be the only people in the dining room. Everyone else – who wasn't down in the hold shooting dice – seemed to be racing around for a place by the outside rail to throw up. Paul and I stuck to the windward side of the deck to avoid being in the line of fire. One day, though, I watched in horror as a woman with a green face rushed up to the railing. Before I could warn Paul, she had tossed the contents over the side and into the wind. It blew back on Paul in a fine spray from head to toe. It was not to be our last clothing calamity.

For me, the most dangerous part of the ship was deep in its bowels, where men who didn't know if they would be alive the following year were engaged in a high-stakes crap game. They were a contingent of what would eventually number a thousand young North Americans who defended Israel during its War of Independence. They became known as the Machal (an acronym of the Hebrew for "volunteers from abroad"). One of my roommates, a friendly Canadian named Sidney Leizer, confided to me that he was among the future fighters. Sidney persuaded me to venture down to the hold. Little did I know that I would be walking into an atmosphere of "tomorrow we die; today we gamble."

"Hey, I'm hot," my new friend told me. "Give me some of your money, and I'll bet it for you, too." I handed over some cash, then some more, and suddenly, I was down $150; he urged me to let him win it back. I had only brought $850 for the entire summer. Each time he lost, he insisted his luck would change with the next roll. That's when I realized how awful gambling can be. The more you lose, the more logical it seems to your temporarily twisted mind that it can't be snake eyes forever. Let me tell you, it changed my life for the future. I couldn't believe it. In a few minutes, I was down to my last hundred dollars. I said, "Dear God, if I get this back, I'll never gamble again."

Well, God was apparently listening. When I came out about even, I quit. I can't say I kept my promise never to gamble again – in fact, I would break it later on that trip – but I've never again put more money on the line than I thought was worth admission to the activity. I took enough chances in my life just running a business.

After 10 days at sea, we landed in Le Havre – hard to believe we were in Normandy just four years after the D-Day invasion. But not all the passengers disembarked with us. The Machalniks continued on to the next destination in southern France. I learned later that after the ship left Le Havre, British soldiers boarded the ship and removed a number of Canadian air aces who were part of the Israel-bound contingent; eventually, though, they did make it into the fight.

A couple of years ago, the American Jewish Historical Society held a major event honoring the Machal. Looking over the casualty list, I discovered that among the very first to be killed in battle was my shipboard friend, Sidney. He was just 19.

LOST IN TRANSLATION

Our first stop was Paris, where Gerard, our Harvard classmate, had booked rooms for fellow business school grads. It was at the Hotel Royal, at 33 Avenue de Friedland in the heart of the city. The rate was $1.75 a night. But we almost didn't get past the lobby. The hotel clerk told us that he had no record of our reservation. Struggling with my schoolbook French, I tried to explain that we were among the group from Harvard. Just in time, a classmate who had arrived a few days earlier came downstairs and to our rescue. In English, he told the clerk, "For Christ's sake, why don't you give them a room!" And I said, "He speaks English?" We got the room. A few years ago, when I was last in Paris, I checked on the price of the same room; it was more than $300 a night.

This was my first time in Europe. Paris was packed with students, and it seemed that every one of them ended up at the American Express office at Place de l'Opera at least once a week to pick up mail or cash traveler's checks. I ran into many of my contemporaries from Brookline and Newton there. One of them was Jane Bortman, daughter of my parents' best friends. Jane, who was paying just 75 cents a night for lodgings on the Left Bank, became a frequent member of the gatherings at our hotel.

After spending a few days in Paris, Paul and I hopped on a train for Marseilles. We sat in a third-class compartment. Next to me was a mother trying to soothe her baby with a swig of wine. The baby apparently didn't like the vintage; he (or she) smacked the bottle, and the wine spilled all over my pants. Paul, having had his own experience with unwelcome fluids, got a big kick out of the scene. But I had the last laugh. We were both wearing seersucker suits. That night, I realized I had on my jacket but his trousers.

Along the Riviera, we splurged by staying at the famed Hotel d'Paris in Monte Carlo. We had the suite that appeared in the movie *The Red Shoes*. We paid $3.50 a night. Now a one-bedroom suite at that hotel is listed at more than $4,000 a night!

I felt I couldn't visit Monte Carlo without seeing its famed casino. In the exclusive Salon Privé, I broke my promise to swear off betting. I bought some 100-franc chips, the equivalent of a quarter in those days, and watched a game called Trente Quarante (30/40). After I thought I had the hang of it, I placed my chips. With each spin of the wheel, it seemed I was winning more and more. But the next time I reached for my winning chips, the croupier suddenly swept them away. I turned to him and said, "You've made a mistake." As I was to learn, no one tells the croupier in the Salon Privé that he has made a mistake. Everything came to a halt. The table was closed. The manager came out and escorted me to his office.

After a humbling lesson in Trente Quarante, I came to appreciate that the game was much more complicated than I had thought. Despite setting back U.S.-Monaco relations, I managed to win about 1,700 francs in Monte Carlo. That was a little over four dollars. I still have one of the 100-franc chips.

MOBS AND MUMPS

We went from Monte Carlo to Italy, visiting Florence, Venice (where we stayed in a *pensione* near the Bridge of Sighs) and Rome. We arrived in the Eternal City amid political upheaval in mid-July. The head of the Italian Communist party, Palmiro Togliatti, had just been shot and nearly killed, setting off a general strike and widespread rioting. Somehow, though, we avoided it all. Safely ensconced in the Grand Hotel, we didn't even take the matter seriously until I received cables and a phone call from my frantic mother, who wanted us to come home at once. From thousands of miles away, she probably knew much more about what was going from the news than we did sitting in the middle of it. Our only experience with the rioting was secondhand. The hotel asked the guests to stay inside for a day or so, shutting its gates when protesters started tossing cobblestones. Soon, we were back to sightseeing.

If a spate of rioting wasn't going to curtail our journey, neither was a case of the mumps. It struck me in Switzerland. Paul, I'm afraid, was not particularly helpful. First, relying on his very garbled knowledge of German, he told a doctor I was crazy when he meant to say I had a bad headache. Then he left me to recuperate on my own, saying he didn't want my illness to ruin his trip.

Fortunately, I had my trusty list of ham operators whom I had contacted throughout the world. One of them was in Zurich. He recommended a doctor and visited me as I recovered, bringing me back issues of ham radio magazines.

THIS WAS LONDON

Britain was the last stop on our Grand Tour. London was still in the early stages of recovering from World War II. Large swaths of bombed-out buildings remained near Buckingham Palace and the Houses of Parliament. Rationing was still in effect. Restaurants were prohibited from charging more than five shillings – a dollar – for a meal. Those with tablecloths could charge a shilling more. You had your choice of ordering chicken or, well, chicken. For heartier fare, you could join a club for three dollars to five dollars. There, you could get steak for eight shillings. I later was told it was horsemeat, but I thought it tasted pretty good.

The British seemed to love Americans. When some of our fellow passengers on our train ride to Scotland learned we were Yanks, they could not stop extolling the virtues of the soldiers who passed through Britain during the war. They insisted on buying us lunch to express their gratitude. Such a gesture was particularly generous considering how precious food was at the time.

Before going overseas, I had contacted our former housekeeper, Isabelle, who had retired to Scotland. She sent me a list of tinned goods to bring from America. Dutifully, I had been lugging a 70-pound parcel for her around Europe. When she met us at the station, I had to overcome this elderly woman's insistence that she should carry the burden the rest of the way home.

Isabelle had relatives who took good care of us and recommended golf courses, including the famed Old Course in St. Andrews. There I had a formidable caddy who had guided my Uncle Eddie's golfing partner the summer before. It's a challenging course; you need a ladder to reach some of the sand traps. The caddy told me exactly how to putt. And at one point on the fairway, I was about to nudge a ball out of a bare spot. He laid down the law: "If you move that ball, I won't sign your scorecard."

THE MYSTERIOUS MISCHA

While in Britain, besides visiting our former housekeeper, I met up with one of the more mysterious members of my extended family. Mischa Sinelnikoff was a first cousin of my mother. Born in the early 1890s in St. Petersburg, he and his brother immigrated to England. He had three sisters as well, several of whom I used to see at my grandparents' house in Brookline. The story I had been told (but haven't been able to confirm) was that Mischa had married a Russian-born countess whom he had met in England. They had one child, Michael, who was born in 1928. Mischa moved among many worlds. He invented a mortar-firing rifle, according to Michael's website; traveled for a time with the violinist Jascha Heifetz as his agent; and made his own name as a book dealer.

He was a large and somewhat jolly man, clean-shaven and extremely solicitous of us. Mischa took Paul and me to lunch at Parliament, where he seemed to be a familiar figure, and on an excursion to Oxford. In return, I served as his courier to America. He gave me $300 to pass along to relatives, and a wrapped package that he told me contained an important book. I managed to get it through customs without being asked to open it. I don't recall whom I delivered it to, and I never saw what was inside. Some people have speculated that it contained a very rare volume. Later, I learned that Mischa had provided Yale University with its copy of the Gutenberg Bible. Perhaps that was what was in the mystery package – at least, I'd like to think that it was.

I never did meet the countess. At some point, the two divorced, and she moved to Canada. So did their son, who became an actor. The son has written a novel based on his family that portrays Mischa as having drowned in 1959 in Switzerland, a presumed suicide.

Paul and I returned to America on the S.S. Veendam of the Holland America Line. The ship had suffered heavy bomb damage during the war, when it had been commandeered by the Germans to billet U-boat crews between missions. After undergoing extensive repairs, the Veendam was put back into trans-Atlantic service a year before we sailed on it. Compared with the voyage over, the one home was in relative luxury. One night, we even got to sit at the captain's table.

THE SINGLE LIFE

*In which I cross paths with Winchell, Batista
and Roy Cohn's right-hand man*

While my social side emerged at Tufts, it was at Harvard Business School that I really came into my own as an adult. In large part I owe that to a lovable rascal from Pittsburgh.

The first time I saw Allen Brunwasser was when he pulled up to the business school dorm, Morris Hall, on his bicycle. Although it was summer, he was wearing a raccoon coat over a seersucker suit. Intrigued, I introduced myself and suggested that we get together sometime. "Let me write your name down on this $5 bill," he said, "because I'll never spend it. I'll always have it with me." And so I was introduced to Allen's special brand of humor and outlook on life.

We were both living in Morris C Entry while taking summer classes. Actually, I went to classes; Allen, who was in the law school, rarely did. He would read the assigned cases in the morning and nap in the afternoon, when I would study. Then the two of us would go over to Adams House for dinner and later perhaps downtown to a jazz club (he didn't always come back with me, but in those days people didn't brag about their conquests).

I tipped Allen off to a labor relations class offered at the business school, for which he could earn credit toward his law degree. Considered one of the easiest courses on the schedule, it was mostly lectures and drew several hundred students. True to form, Allen never went to a class. The professor, Benjamin M. Selekman, rarely called on anyone, but one day he happened to pluck Allen from his roster. Perhaps Allen had stood out as being from the law school. Getting no answer, Selekman made it a habit to call on Allen every class. I told Allen that he had better attend class or risk flunking out. Allen wouldn't budge, even refusing to attend meetings on the only paper that the professor had assigned. Feeling responsible for having suggested that Allen take the class in the first place, I helped him along with the paper, and he managed to eke out a credit.

Not that Allen was one to ruminate over his academic standing. He brimmed with confidence. He was a short, pudgy guy with a less-than-chiseled face, but it was his charisma that captured everyone's attention. You could take him to even the most prim and proper of places, and within 30 minutes he would be the center of attention. He would tell story after story, hilarious tales, often at the expense of the friends surrounding him. But that was his way of pulling others into the conversation. However, if someone tried to upstage him, he could be merciless.

THE WISDOM OF ALLEN

For a long time, we were inseparable. If Allen saw me heading off somewhere, he'd ask, "Where are you going?" If I replied, "I'm going to a party," he'd say, "And you didn't invite your best friend?" So, he'd tag along. Once he talked me into taking him along to the Martha's Vineyard fishing derby. He knew nothing about fishing, but there he was in the middle of the night chatting away with my dad, Uncle Murray and Murray's partner, Horace McCormick. He didn't land any fish, but he did catch a good time.

At first, Allen's brashness made me uneasy at times. But I soon came to admire the forcefulness of his personality. Even my dad and mother fell for him. Allen loved Sunday dinner at my parents' house, raving about how he had never eaten better. Telling me how lucky I was to come from such a wonderful family, he said he was surprised I wasn't more outgoing in social settings. It wasn't that I lacked confidence, but Allen was right: I did tend to be reserved. I worried that if I spoke up more, people would think I was hogging the conversation or someone would try to put me in my place. With Allen's encouragement, I overcame my reticence. In the years since, I've never been hesitant to join a conversation if I felt I had something to add. Now, when I'm invited to community meetings, I make it clear that I'm no shrinking violet. If I have an opinion, I'll speak up, even if my views are contrary.

After graduation, Allen moved back to Pittsburgh to practice law. With his rapid-fire mind, he must have been a whiz in the courtroom. But rather than boast of his legal triumphs, he would joke about how he represented all the prostitutes. When he visited the detention cells, he told me, all the women would cheer him on, saying, "There's my buddy."

Allen married a woman seven years his senior. They had one child, Ina. Not surprisingly, given Allen's mercurial ways, the marriage didn't last. After the couple divorced, they lived on different floors of the same apartment building so they could raise Ina together.

Allen attended my wedding, but after that we saw less and less of each other. Judging by what I've read about him on the Internet, the legal profession hasn't succeeded in taming his eccentricities; if anything, he's turned the court into his stage. Take for example a suit he filed against TWA to force it to un-cancel a flight.

Allen Brunwasser with his daughter, Ina, and me in the 1970s.

In February 1981, Allen bought tickets for himself and Ina on a direct flight from Pittsburgh to London scheduled for September 1. Several months after he booked the trip, TWA announced it was scaling back direct service from daily to three days a week. As a result, the September 1 flight was canceled. Allen refused the options the airline offered: taking a connecting flight, a direct flight on another day or a full refund. He insisted on "specific performance," namely, that he get exactly what he had paid for. To give the case extra oomph, he made it a class-action suit by enlisting Ina as a fellow plaintiff. Somehow, he was able to get a hearing in federal district court that August. In his ruling, Judge Gerald J. Weber captured the essence of Allen:

> We must note Attorney Brunwasser conducts lawsuits like a commanding general of a theatre of operations. There are preliminary skirmishes, diversionary attacks, a main thrust, a fall-back position, and leapfrogging maneuvers, all conducted on a coordinated basis. Another difficulty of Attorney Brunwasser's pleadings is his literary style. When I was in college, which would be near the time of Allen N. Brunwasser, students tried to play the sedulous ape to certain prevailing literary styles. Most in favor was the strong, simple, direct prose of Ernest Hemingway, which is also the model of the Federal Rules of Civil Procedure. Others tried a bit of John Dos Passos, with its insertion of newsreel items of current events and portraits of prominent characters of the time, irrelevant to the story, but contemporaneous to its events. Allen N. Brunwasser's pleadings contain a good bit of this, and we are never certain whether we are reading an attempted assertion of a legal claim, or some side remark that popped into Brunwasser's mind at the time. But more than that, Brunwasser's pleadings and briefs reflect principally the style of the stream of consciousness school, so popular in that generation. We were able to understand dimly the action in 'Ulysses,' [while] today it is explained by shelves of guides, commentaries, companions and concordances. As Joyce grew older he became more difficult and nobody understood 'Finnegan's Wake' until the guides and commentaries began to appear. No one supplies us with guides to Brunwasser's pleadings.

Some 2,000 words later, Judge Weber denied Allen's claim. I'm not sure whether he ever got to London. But if he did, it was not on a direct TWA flight on September 1, 1981.

The last time I saw Allen, he joked, "Let's promise to go to each other's funerals."

STEPPING OUT WITH SCHINE

At one of our dinners at Adams House, Allen introduced me to an undergrad living there who five years later would become a household name: G. David Schine. Several years after graduating from Harvard, David assisted Roy Cohn, the chief counsel to Senator Joe McCarthy, at the height of his red-baiting campaign. When the army drafted David in 1953, Cohn tried to pressure the brass into granting his protégé special privileges and a commission. The hot-headed lawyer badgered his way up the chain of command to the secretary of the army. This time, the McCarthy team misjudged its power to intimidate. The subsequent congressional investigation – known as the Army-McCarthy hearings – turned the tide against the demagogue from Wisconsin.

I would never have guessed that future for David. It was his pomposity, not his politics, that I remember. He was dining alone when Allen pointed him out to me. "There's my friend Schine, sitting all by himself," Allen said. "Nobody will sit with him."

Allen had given David a big buildup about me, that my family was even richer than his. It perked up his interest a bit. But I never boasted to David about myself. Not that I think he would have paid much attention; he was too self-absorbed. David was a tall, very good-looking guy, but he felt compelled to show off. He loved to impress the girls with his convertible. He'd sit outside Adams House, with the top down, chatting away on his car phone – then a status symbol.

Allen loved telling stories about how "ridiculous" David was, particularly when it came to money. Although he came from a wealthy family, David never seemed to have any cash. So Allen, the poor kid from Pittsburgh, was always giving him loans. Frustrated about never being paid back, Allen got David to write him out a check on a napkin. Back then, banks would accept makeshift checks, so long as they included the right account number and signature. The bank would have taken this one, had it fit through the canceling machine.

I suppose that in the end I tolerated David because I liked his sister, Renee, who was much more down-to-earth than her brother. She invited me several times to the family's home on West Caroga Lake in Upstate New York State. Her dad, J. Myer Schine, had made his fortune after switching from selling candy and dresses to buying up theaters and other real estate. As I heard the story, he would walk into a small-town theater, make an offer to buy it and, when rebuffed, threaten to build a cinema across the street. Ultimately, the wheeler-dealer amassed scores of theaters, posh hotels in Florida and California, and a string of broadcast outlets. When he tried to unload his $150 million empire in the mid-'60s, he wound up in a messy court fight with, among others, Harry B. Helmsley (later better known as Mr. Leona Helmsley).

But though mine was just a bit part in the Schine family saga, it did offer some memorable glimpses of glamour. Once again, Allen played a pivotal role. Always looking for what he called a "free flop," he arranged for us to stay at Miami's Roney Plaza, which the Schines then owned.

Built a quarter-century before, the Roney was Miami Beach's first oceanside grand hotel. Rising more than 10 stories and capped by a gothic-style tower, it hosted royalty, socialites and movie stars. The notorious gossip columnist Walter Winchell was a winter regular, always wearing his trademark hat.

Several times I saw him dancing with David's mother, Hildegarde. Allen cracked that in return Winchell scored a free flop.

It was at the Roney that I first met Renee – not that David had bothered to introduce us. Perhaps he didn't want his sister dating his friends or, more likely, it just hadn't occurred to him.

Once while Allen and I were at the hotel, David called us from another of his family's resorts, the lavish Boca Raton Club. "Come on up," David said. Allen and I hopped in a car and made the 50-mile drive to Boca Raton. That night at the club, a half-plastered patron stood up and began singing with the band. He seemed to be making up the lyrics as he went along, stringing together medical terms. Allen turned to David and said, "How can you allow this?" David made sure the guest would be gone in the morning. The next day I learned that the inebriated singer was Dr. Michael Greenfield, my future brother-in-law, and that among his party was a Wellesley College student whom I had just met a few weeks before. Her name was Genevieve. But I'm getting ahead of myself.

Through me, David was able to play golf at Belmont Country Club. He and I would occasionally hit balls late in the afternoon. Several times, I invited him to my parents' house. On his way over, he'd call us on his car phone. "This is G. David Schine, and I'm in my car," he'd intone. "I'm on Commonwealth Avenue. Please tell me how do I come to your house?" When he arrived at our street, he'd call again to announce, "I'm now here."

At Allen's suggestion, we took David with us on an outing on Uncle Murray's boat. David came with a girl. She seemed nice enough, but David wasn't particularly sociable. I remember him making a public show of smooching with her, leaning up against a cabin window of the boat.

I would later hear another tale about David's love life from, of all people, my father. He got a call one night from the Ritz, where David was trying to book a room for the night. The staff was wary because they spotted a girl standing behind a pillar. "We don't want to let him in, and he's using you as a reference," they told my dad. He responded, "Just tell them you don't have any rooms." After that, David would go to the Statler or Copley Plaza for his trysts.

I pretty much lost touch with David after Harvard. In 1957, he married a former Miss Universe, Hillevi Rombin of Sweden. I wasn't invited to the wedding, though I doubt I would have gone. The marriage lasted nearly 40 years. In 1996, they both died in a private plane crash, along with the pilot, who was one of their six children.

The last contact David had with my family was around 1970. He was producing a movie and asked my father to invest in it. But Dad wasn't willing to risk money on Hollywood or on David. The picture, by the way, was *The French Connection*.

Dancing the Charleston at the Mount Washington Hotel in New Hampshire in the days before I met Genevieve.

HAVANA'S HIGH LIFE

Another friend, Phil Richards, opened the door for me to another slice of the high life, this one some 230 miles south of Miami, in Cuba. I met Phil thanks to the hop, skip and jump of radio waves, as I recount in the chapter on ham radio. Phil was five years older than me and a Navy veteran of World War II. I'm not sure if he ever had a real job, although his 1997 death notice in *The New York Times* said his family owned an electronics business. He implied at one point that he had something to do with the CIA, but who knows?

Although not Jewish himself, Phil lived on a trust fund established by his uncle, the Jewish philanthropist Lucius Nathan Littauer. After attending Harvard in the late 1800s, where he was the first head football coach, Littauer became a successful glove manufacturer. He also was active in politics, advising his old Harvard roommate, Theodore Roosevelt, and serving in Congress for 10 years. The one blot on his life was a conviction in 1914 for smuggling a diamond and pearl tiara in from Europe. He said it was a gift for his wife, but he neglected to inform customs about it. By the time of his death in 1944, he was best known for his generosity, which included providing Harvard the seed money for the Littauer School of Public Administration, now known as the Kennedy School of Government. As I would learn later, he was also a supporter of the American Jewish Historical Society and Harvard's Judaica collection.

I often stayed with Phil and his lovely Cuban-born wife, Lily, on trips to our factories in Georgia and later Puerto Rico – an extra $75 would allow me to add Havana to my itinerary. They fixed me up with the girl next door, Maria Louisa Fonz, whose father had the contract to print Cuba's banknotes. When Maria was not horseback riding, she was relaxing at the country club or dining out on the town. But she abided by the strict social codes of Cuba's elite society. When I took her out, we had to be chaperoned. Usually her mother and an aunt would accompany us, sitting at a separate table. I suspected that they loved the chance to get out of the house. Given all the attention showered on her, Maria was surprisingly unspoiled and quite down-to-earth.

Out on the town in Havana with Maria Louisa Fonz. Her mother would sit nearby to keep us in line.

Phil and Lily served as our chaperones one night when they invited us to an expensive French restaurant. Since the place was packed, we had to wait to be seated. Phil and Lily took the opportunity to head off to the bar. By the time our table was ready, our hosts had seemingly vanished. Finally, we spotted a very sloshed Phil being stuffed into a cab. Meanwhile, Maria and I had ordered steaks, but she was nervous about us being seen together without a chaperone. "People will know me," she said. "My reputation will be ruined." I was more worried about how I was going to pay for the steaks. And once they arrived, I certainly wasn't going to let them go to waste. After a hurried dinner, I took Maria home.

I can't say I was too surprised by Phil's premature departure. He was a bit too partial to liquor, and the customary way Cuban bars served drinks didn't help matters. The bartender would give you a glass and the bottle. However much you poured in the glass counted as one drink. But once you set the bottle down and picked it up to pour again, you were charged for another drink. It's hard for someone new to this system to resist filling the glass to the rim. I got very drunk on whiskey – an experience I never wanted to repeat. I learned that just because something seems to be a steal, it's not necessarily wise to take it to excess.

Another memorable date with Maria was a New Year's Eve party at the exclusive Marianao Country Club. That was in the early '50s, when Cuba was under the iron – and corrupt – rule of Fulgencio Batista. The strongman himself crashed the party. As he sat at a table with four bodyguards, everyone went up to him to say "*Feliz año nuevo! El Presidento.*" But as soon as he left, they all spat at the door. Tracing their ancestry back to Spain, Havana's elite despised Batista for all kinds of reasons, including that some of his ancestors were black.

My relationship with Maria never advanced beyond the stage of giving her a kiss goodnight. The last I heard she had left Cuba and married a wealthy Mexican. When Castro took power, Phil and Lily moved to Fort Lauderdale, and we kept in touch.

*   *   *

One footnote: My Harvard and Brookline lives would overlap in 1970 during my first campaign for town moderator. Among the people who endorsed me was a Brookline acquaintance, Joseph Welch. As you may recall, the Boston attorney was McCarthy's main nemesis. At the Army-McCarthy hearings – the televised confrontation sparked by David Schine's draft notice – Welch famously scolded the senator: "Have you no sense of decency, sir? At long last, have you left no sense of decency?"

My sister, Betty, at far right on the Adhara, the yacht that later nearly cost her and my dad their lives.

WHEN DAD WAS BLOWN SKY-HIGH

While I was on the course at Belmont watching the nation's elite golfers, my father and sister were jumping for their lives into the choppy waters off Onset.

Over the last weekend of August 1949, Belmont Country Club hosted a match between the U.S. Ryder Cup Team and Byron Nelson's team of pros. I served as a marshal at the event, helping to keep the spectators in line.

My father and my sister, Betty, were spending a dad-daughter weekend on a luxury cabin cruiser. With them were my dad's longtime friend Mark Bortman and his 22-year-old daughter, Jane, and Dean Road neighbor Louis Hayes and his 19-year-old daughter, Frances (known by her nickname, Fuzzy). My father had been offered use of the boat and its full crew by Maurice Guerin, owner of the River Mills Corp. of Fall River, which supplied Shawmut with wool yarns. As was often the case with my father, his relationship with Maury had started out as purely business but developed into a long-time friendship.

The 42-foot cruiser *Adhara* was anchored in the outer harbor when an auxiliary engine automatically switched on to recharge the batteries. Evidently, it set off sparks that ignited gas fumes, sending flames flashing over the boat. Amazingly, no one suffered more than minor burns, scrapes and bruises. My father, who was just stepping out of the cabin, was blown straight up in the air. He landed in the water, but not before suffering minor burns as he glanced off the hot engine. Their clothes aflame, Betty, Jane and Fuzzy jumped into the harbor. Betty credited *The New York Times* with saving her from serious injury. She had the paper spread out before her, leaving only her legs exposed. With the tide heading out, the four were plucked from the waters by the Coast Guard and speedboaters.

Those who appeared more seriously injured, including Betty, were taken to the hospital. My father was put ashore at Onset. On his way to see Betty, he decided to buy a pair of trousers. Soaked and in his undershorts (he had doffed his pants to better maneuver in the water), he walked up the street. Before he could get to a store, he was stopped by a Shawmut employee, who apparently saw nothing unusual about my father's attire. "Oh, Mr. Wyner, I'm so happy to see you," the woman said. "You're the first familiar face I've seen down here."

When Dad finally got to a store and asked about buying underwear and pants, the clerk nonchalantly said, "I suppose you want the same kind as you're wearing now." The salesman didn't display the slightest curiosity about why Dad was walking around in wet underwear. But he did express interest in the Coast Guard vehicle racing up the street, its siren blaring – not that he put two and two together. From then on, whenever my mother would stop my father from leaving the house because he had on mismatched socks or the like, he'd scoff and say, "People aren't interested in anything but themselves. Nobody's going to notice."

I learned about the accident when my mother called me at the club with the news. She had first found out about it from a reporter, who told her he was calling for information about her husband and daughter who had been blown up in a boat. He had no information about how they were or even if they survived. Fortunately, my father called just a few minutes later and assured her everyone was OK.

The story made page 1 of *The Boston Globe* on August 29, headlined: "4 Leap Overboard, Clothing Afire, as Cabin Cruiser Explodes at Onset." The subhead: "Greater Boston Quartet Saved 40 Minutes Later." Naturally, the *Globe* chose to put headshot photos of the daughters on the front page. The less photogenic dads appeared inside with the jump.

MY ONE AND ONLY

How I nearly lost the great love of my life

"I WOULDN'T GO UP there if I were you."

I was climbing the final flight of stairs to a mixer at a Wellesley College dorm with Malcolm Gordon, whom I'd known since childhood, and a couple of other friends. Intent on reaching our third-floor destination, I hardly glanced at the group of girls heading down the stairs. But then I heard a voice from below call out, "Don't go up there. It's no good!" I turned around and asked, "Why is it no good?"

I had no idea what the person with the voice looked like, but I was intrigued by the answer that followed.

"Because nobody will dance with me."

"Come back up, and I'll dance with you," I responded.

Before she came back into view, I began to wonder what I had gotten myself into – and then, to my great delight, there appeared a tall, slender, very attractive brunette with a smile on her face that struck my heart.

And so it was on a Wellesley College staircase in fall 1950 that Genevieve's life and mine were changed forever.

While it was her good looks that I first noticed, it was Genevieve's vivaciousness that captivated me.

After the mixer, we all headed over to Howard Johnson's. Genevieve, Malcolm and I shared a booth. As she spotted friends across the low dividers, Genevieve kept up a running exchange of wisecracks with them while not missing a beat as she chatted with us. I marveled at how at ease she was – and how funny. My infatuation with her was obvious. "Make sure to invite me to the wedding," Malcolm said. And, as it would turn out, we would.

My future wife well before I knew her.

When I next saw Genevieve, she was playing the lead in the Junior Show at Wellesley. Wearing a pith helmet and waving a cigar, she swaggered across the stage as Sex'L B. Demolished. She had the audiences convulsing in laughter; Cecil B. DeMille himself couldn't have topped her act. That night, I met her parents, Max and Ida Geller, who had come up from their home in New Rochelle, N.Y., for the show.

As Genevieve and I got to know each other, we realized we had a lot in common. Besides both being Jewish, we could swap stories about editing our schools' papers and working on plays. Her exuberance was infectious. I liked the way she spoke her mind, so unlike other girls who, although very bright, would take their cues from the guys.

Genevieve and I are all decked out for the Wellesley College Junior Prom.

Over her last year and a half at Wellesley, I dated Genevieve more and other girls less. I scored a lot of points by arriving at the doorstep of her dormitory one stormy winter day. I had promised to pick her up at 8:30 in the morning to take her to the train station for a trip to New Rochelle. Seeing the heavy snow, Genevieve figured that she wouldn't even need to call me to say that she had decided not to go. She certainly didn't expect me to brave the weather. So, she was astonished when I arrived right on time. "What did you expect?" I remarked nonchalantly. "I said I'd be here at 8:30, and it's 8:30."

A BATTLE OF WILLS

It was storms of the emotional variety that challenged our relationship. For one thing, both of us were strong-willed. That meant that one of the qualities I most liked about Genevieve – her outspokenness – would irritate me when we disagreed. I was trying to have it both ways. Another problem was that because I cared so much about Genevieve I scrutinized everything she did and said to a degree that I hadn't with other girls. In some ways, our growing together also pushed us apart. It was as if we were fighting for our lives, our individual lives.

I was brought up a certain way and clung to the belief that it was *the* right way. I felt as if I should fix everything about Genevieve that wasn't like *my* mother. I must have made Genevieve feel extremely self-conscious, as if with my every glance I was rendering judgment. And so our relationship ran hot and cold.

After graduating from Wellesley, Genevieve worked for a newspaper in Mamaroneck, N.Y., and then for a small public relations firm in New York City. In Manhattan, she lived in the legendary Barbizon Hotel for women. Dormitory in style, but exclusive in reputation, the Barbizon required potential residents to present letters of recommendation and to possess poise and immaculate manners. Over the years, it was home to budding luminaries including Joan Crawford, Grace Kelly, Liza Minnelli, Cybill Shepherd, Candice Bergen and Joan Didion – not to mention Genevieve Geller!

As it happened, I had to go to New York at least several times a month on business. I found myself looking forward to those trips more and more, but I continued to date other girls in Boston. (At an event not long ago, Genevieve and I were chatting with three women, when one of them said, "Isn't it interesting; we've all dated Jerry.")

On more than several occasions, I nearly drifted away from our relationship. But Genevieve would lure me back with a well-timed letter. In 1953, on a trip to New York, I proposed, and she accepted. But six weeks before the wedding date, just before the invitations were to go out, we went out to her country club for dinner and by evening's end it appeared we'd be splitting for good.

It wasn't that we had discovered something irreparable about our relationship, some profound disagreement that defied reconciliation. The fact is, we got into a fight over her glass of water. Genevieve complained that there was something in it. I said it was probably remnants of food she had eaten before taking a sip. As ridiculous as it might sound, we just kept arguing. Finally, we realized that if we were going to quarrel over such trivial matters, we'd never be able to live together.

We didn't formally break up that night. But I went back to Boston discouraged. And Genevieve went home to New Rochelle and cried for three straight days. After our fathers talked by phone about the frayed relationship, the wedding was called off. Genevieve's mother remained optimistic; she carefully packed the wedding invitations away in the attic.

A picture of true love, snapped in a photo booth.

THE MAGIC EARRINGS

Neither of us felt good about what had happened. Over the next couple of years, though I dated other women, I could not get Genevieve out of my mind. Had I spoiled my future out of sheer stubbornness?

I finally decided to follow my feelings. On a trip to New York, I bought a pair of earrings and went to the lobby of Genevieve's office building. Without giving my name, I had someone bring the gift up to her. Earrings had been the source of an inside joke between the two of us, probably because she didn't have pierced ears. When she saw the anonymous gift, she knew immediately who must have sent it. She rushed downstairs and found me on the street.

Shortly after that, Genevieve's mother pulled those unsent wedding invitations out of the attic, crossed out the old date and wrote in the new. This time the invitations made it to the post office.

Genevieve with her parakeet on our wedding day.

It was so hot at the reception that my father and I broke with Wyner decorum and doffed our jackets to sing the family favorite "Shine on, Harvest Moon."

We were married on July 3, 1955, at Temple Israel in New Rochelle. The reception was held there that night. It was so hot that my father, who would never remove his jacket and tie at dinner, turned to me and said, "Jerry, this is a matter of life and death; we have to take our jackets off." The historic moment was preserved for posterity in a photo of us singing the Wyner family song, "Shine On, Harvest Moon," with the wedding band.

We stayed the night at the St. Regis Hotel in Manhattan and then set off for Bermuda. It was to have been the first stop on our honeymoon. We had planned to go from there to South America. But as we continued to adjust to living our lives together, we decided to keep it simple and spend our entire honeymoon on the island of Bermuda.

After a week's stay at the Princess Hotel (I have movies of the two of us playing tennis), we moved to the Four Ways Inn. We stayed in one of its 10 rooms and dined and played darts in its traditional British tavern. Then, at a cottage overlooking Marley Beach, we took our first plunge into housekeeping.

Genevieve still kids me about how embarrassed I was when a guest walked by the kitchen window and saw me doing the dishes. It just goes to show how attitudes about gender roles have changed. Today I can only laugh at myself for fretting to Genevieve, "People have seen me washing the dishes – what are they going to think?"

The honeymooners.

HELL'S ANGELS WE'RE NOT

In other chapters, I'll write more about the honeymoon, such as how our picture ended up in a ham radio magazine and how I chucked chivalry overboard on a sailing trip. But I do have one final honeymoon anecdote to tell here.

At that time, tourists to Bermuda couldn't rent any vehicles other than a motor-assisted bicycle. But if you remained for at least a month, as we did, you could get a motorcycle license. Even then, the government didn't make it easy on visitors. There weren't any motorcycle rental places, so we had to "borrow" one (for a fee, of course). We met up with a guy in a Hamilton parking lot who agreed to "lend" us his machine.

As we were sitting on it, listening to him explain the instruments, the cycle somehow slipped into gear. Before I knew it, I was driving in the middle of rush hour traffic on Front Street, and Genevieve was waving goodbye to the cycle's shocked owner. As we were heading out of town, Front Street took a sharp turn to the right. I leaned into the curve. That's what you're supposed to do on a cycle.

Unfortunately, Genevieve didn't know that. Thinking we were tipping over, she leaned the other way to straighten us out. As a result, we drove right off the road, fortunately not striking anything before I was able to bring the cycle to a stop.

The bike wasn't damaged, and neither were we – save for suffering severe embarrassment. It was our first lesson in the importance of communications and teamwork. Such lessons would help carry us through turbulent waters, both figuratively and literally.

PART III: THE HOME FRONT

- A home of our own: Husband, dad and mountain climber

- My other father: Swept up in whirlwind world of Max Geller

- A transformative weekend: Magic of Marriage Encounter

- This new house: Our televised encounter with the future

- Rowes Wharf: Forging community, fighting City Hall

- Home away from home: Falling in love with the Vineyard

A HOME OF OUR OWN

In which I learn to be a husband, dad and mountain climber

OUR FIRST HOME WAS in a residential building on Beacon Street across from what is today the Holiday Inn in Brookline. Our building was then called the Hampton Court Hotel. We lived there just a month, but it's memorable for two dinners.

Our first guest for a home-cooked meal was my old pal Paul Lubell. Just before he arrived, Genevieve was in tears. She insisted that she had ruined the main course, a chicken. Maybe it was just first night jitters. Paul went on and on about how the chicken was the best he'd ever eaten. I don't recall how the chicken tasted, but Paul had earned himself a lifetime of dinner invitations.

The other dinner was on the occasion of a visit from Horace McCormack, Uncle Murray's partner and the "McK" part of the McKem division of Shawmut. Horace had a reputation as a playboy, sweetheart and drunkard, all rolled into one. When the department store buyers came to New York for show weeks, he'd take them on the town. They were women and tough cookies. But Horace's charm stripped away all their defenses – and who knows what else.

On one of his trips to our Stoughton plant, I invited him over for dinner. We served cocktails, and I made the mistake – several times, I'm afraid – of offering to freshen his glass. Soon he was plastered. He stood up on his wobbly legs, went over to Genevieve and – not really knowing what he was doing or saying – whispered in her ear what he wanted for dessert. Except, he didn't use that word, and he wasn't referring to food.

The proposition took Genevieve very much by surprise. I quickly came to her rescue, firmly suggesting to Horace that it was time for him to get back to his room. Even though he was staying in our building, this turned out to be easier said than done. It was like a scene out of a Hollywood farce. Horace was a big guy and top-heavy. As soon as I'd get him on his feet, he'd start to tip forward, and I'd run as fast as I could to keep him from falling flat on his face. When we reached a corner, I'd turn him in the right direction and then rush ahead to catch him. In such a manner, we lurched our way to the elevator, and somehow I got him bedded down.

Genevieve got over the shock. She realized that Horace was just a harmless old guy who couldn't hold his liquor. Poor Horace would have been mortified if he ever remembered what he had said.

THE BIRDHOUSE

I couldn't wait until we had our first house, if only so that I could move my ham radio equipment from my parents' place. For $90 a month, we rented a 1,000-square-foot three-bedroom house in the new development of Stonybrook Village in Hyde Park. I erected my radio tower in its tiny backyard. Genevieve's mom came up several times to shop with her for furniture and housewares. Among her mother's gifts was a Steinway grand piano. It was so grand that it wouldn't fit into the living room. I figured out that if we removed the back leg, the piano could sit partially over the stairway that ran up from the front door, and the keyboard would project into the living room at the perfect level. Vladimir Horowitz might not have approved, but it was OK with Genevieve.

In March 1956, New England was walloped with two blizzards over four days. The *Globe* reported 68 people killed, thousands stranded and drifts of up to 10 feet high. "Not in the era of the motor car has any one single cause so crippled such a wide area," the paper stated. I managed to drive through the storm from work, making it all the way to the foot of our street. We lived at the top of a hill, and the plow had yet to come through. Blasted by the winds, I staggered though waist-high drifts to our front door. I was wiped out, but Genevieve wouldn't let me in. "You'll get snow in here," she said. "Go around back." She had plugged up the gap under the front door to keep the snow from blowing in. I dutifully waded through more snow and entered through the back. The things a newlywed will do. Genevieve had no idea of the struggle I'd had getting up the hill until I was safely inside recounting my ordeal.

Mother Nature created a stir at the house on another occasion, this time in the form of a giant bird. Genevieve had been sitting in the living room when it smashed through the picture window. With the bird lying stiff on the floor, she rushed next door for help from an older woman who had taken a liking to us. When they returned to the house, the bird was gone. Genevieve said the neighbor looked at her as if she were crazy. There was a hole in the window, but not even a single feather remained as evidence of our visitor.

The home on Marthas Lane where we raised our three sons.

A MAN OF HIS WORD

In 1956, we found a bilevel ranch house, typical of the period, in a small development on Marthas Lane in the southern part of Brookline. The builder, Ben Gold, had finished just about everything except for the kitchen and a back room when he defaulted on his mortgage. The note was held by an investor who lived nearby, Billy Cohen. The house was to have gone on the market for $45,000. When I told Mr. Cohen I was interested in buying it, he asked what I was willing to spend. I told him $33,000. The house was due to go on the auction block the following day, but Mr. Cohen advised me to stay away. He assured me that I'd end up getting my price. I don't know why he wanted to work it this way, but I trusted him.

Feeling confident that the house would be ours, I showed it to my parents. Ben the builder interrupted our tour, insisting that he had offered Mr. Cohen a very good price and was going to get it. I went back to Mr. Cohen. "I don't care how much more anyone else might offer me – I gave you my word, that's it," he assured me. "You'll have the house." And the next day, indeed it was available, and for the $33,000 price we had offered. I would remember Billy Cohen's honesty years later when we sold the house – and it was my turn to be a man of my word.

A WOMAN'S PLACE ...

I took great pride in being able to afford a house. I know I've talked about how my family wasn't into status symbols, but this was something different. Back in those days, it was important for a young fellow starting out in the world to prove he could stand on his own two feet and support his wife and family without outside help. But I felt as if one of those feet had been tripped up when I got home from work one day and Genevieve greeted me with the announcement that she had been offered a job reporting for a local newspaper. I was flabbergasted. Women in the Wyner family did not work, they volunteered – as my grandmother Goldberg would later decree to Genevieve. None of the wives in our family's social circle worked.

While Genevieve was excited about exercising her journalistic skills, all I could think about was appearances. I told her that people would look at us and say she had to work because I couldn't earn enough to support us. I don't recall how long we argued over the matter or whether there was yelling, but there may have been tears. In the end, out of consideration for my fragile male ego, Genevieve turned down the job. Looking back, I can't believe what a male chauvinist I once was. But you have to understand that that term wasn't even part of our vocabulary in the mid '50s.

I did play a role in what Genevieve now calls "the best job I ever had": raising our three sons. Like seemingly everything else in our lives, it was an adventure right from the start.

With our firstborn, George, who arrived in a snowstorm.

THE SNOW BABY

Just as Genevieve was due to deliver our first son, George, in February 1958, Boston was expecting a severe snowstorm. When my father heard that we were still at home, he was aghast. "You're going to sit there and wait until she has to go to the hospital and you can't get out of Marthas Lane? You've got to check into a motel," he told us.

So, we went to the Brookline Motor Court (now the Holiday Inn). But before we could settle in, Genevieve began feeling labor pains. I rushed her to Beth Israel Hospital, where she was whisked to the upstairs maternity wing. I wanted to accompany her, but that simply wasn't done in those days (not even for me, the grandson of the wing's namesake, Gussie Wyner). In fact, there wasn't even a waiting room for expectant dads. Despite all my family's connections to the hospital, I had to sweat it out all night in the lobby on the first floor. As the hours passed, without any word from above, my imagination concocted all sorts of horrible scenarios.

Meanwhile, Genevieve's mom – whom I had alerted when we went to the hospital – had hopped the overnight train from New York and was calling me from stations along the way. By the time she got to the hospital, I was a wreck. Then we finally got the news: All was well. I rushed upstairs and got my first sight of George, nestled in his mother's arms. That's when it hit me: I was a dad.

I launch George on his academic career.

George was an easy baby, always smiling. And, taking after his dad, he was a good boy. Maybe, in a way, too good. Whenever something went wrong, he decided he must have been at fault. He's carried that sense of responsibility with him all his life.

At two-year intervals, Daniel and then James arrived – the youngest on the very same date as the oldest four years before. I didn't suffer nearly as much nail-biting with the delivery of the younger two. I had managed to wangle a cot in a staff sleeping room on the maternity floor and received frequent updates on Genevieve's progress from our obstetrician, Dr. David Kopans. It was to be the mid-1970s before the medical profession in Boston got the point and allowed fathers into the delivery room.

FAMILY TIMES

Marthas Lane back in the late '50s and the '60s was a great place to raise kids. The neighbors were young families like ours. Just as had been the case when I was growing up, our home was a popular gathering place. Genevieve, though, was more laid back as a mother than mine had been. I was the one who would remind the boys to mind their manners at the dinner table, to the point that Genevieve suggested I was too controlling. She had been raised in a more relaxed household, and as the one who was mostly at home, she set the tone for ours. One of James's friends said he loved coming over to our house because there were no rules.

Even though George was the oldest, he was often the butt of jokes. His brothers took advantage of his sweet nature. Daniel would be the plotter, and James would happily follow along. Always a bit of a rascal, Daniel pulled a fast one on me when I took the boys to an amusement park on the North Shore. We had a great time – perhaps too great a time. Daniel didn't seem to want to leave. As we were about to go home, he snatched the car keys and threw them in the bushes. We hunted and hunted, but couldn't find them. Genevieve had to make a half-hour drive to bring the spare keys. I couldn't really get mad at Daniel. After all, he was only 5.

At home, we had our own little amusement park in the backyard. The main attraction was a space trolley, the predecessor to the zip lines of today. The rider sat on a bar suspended from a line that ran between two widely spaced trees. The slope of the line was just right so you could go flying down from one side with enough speed to make it up to the other. Kids came from all over the neighborhood to ride it.

Our basement became a workshop for building things as we raised a new generation of Wyner tinkerers. On a large table, I reassembled the J. L. Wyner Railroad from my childhood. We also had a variety of miniature racing cars, both electric- and gravity-powered. One of my favorite projects was building a soapbox derby car with Daniel. We sandpapered the wood to a super-smooth finish and painted the wheels with bright colors. I don't think it won any races, but it drew many admiring glances.

I tried to interest the boys in ham radio by buying them a Heathkit radio, but I think I probably did most of the assembling. They were more attracted to computers. This was well before the advent of the personal computer. For a time, the computer center at the Museum of Science became like a second home for them. Along with a friend, Stanley Kugell, they'd hog the workstation by signing up for consecutive half-hour sessions. After a couple of months, they got so proficient at programming that they managed to change the operating system. They had the computer doing things it was never meant to do. I became so alarmed that they had crashed it with their attempts to write games that I went to see the museum's head, Brad Washburn. I had to walk a delicate line. I didn't want to get the kids into trouble, but I did want to make sure they hadn't done any permanent damage.

The computer weathered the Wyner onslaught, and it helped prepare James and Daniel for brief careers in computer gaming. While in college, the pair broke the Atari code and created the game *Meteorites*. Without Atari's blessing, it became a cult hit in the early 1980s. The copy on the box reads: "Blast off into space to fight for survival through a never-ending field of meteorites and alien attack ships." You can still find it on eBay. Note the copyright: 1983 Wyner Bros.

The extended Geller family gathers in late 1950s. Back row (from left), Jack and Suzanne Geller; Michael and Harriet (Geller) Greenfield; Max and Ida Geller; Marjorie (Geller) Brody and husband Gene; Genevieve holding George; and me. Front row: John, Jamie, Kenny and Andy Greenfield; Joanne, Susan, David and Bruce Brody.

With the birth of James in 1962, our family is complete (from left): Daniel, Mom, James, Dad and George.

CLASS ACTS

Teachers were to play pivotal roles in our sons' lives, beginning with Ann Jackson of the Jewish Community Center nursery school near Cleveland Circle. All our sons grew attached to Ann (who would later work on my campaign for Town Meeting moderator). Without forcing it, she instilled in them a sense of Jewish tradition. I remember, for example, George coming home one day and telling us that we ought to have two challahs on Shabbos. That was to commemorate the Jews receiving two portions of manna every Friday when they were wandering in the desert.

For their elementary years, the boys attended the Baker School in South Brookline. Its principal, Robert Newbury, was strict and vigilant. Many parents and teachers thought he was old-fashioned. But Genevieve and I thought he was what made the school great. He monitored teachers' performance and arranged to transfer those whom he thought were shortchanging their students. His dress code required girls to wear dresses and boys to dress neatly. Kids could run all they wanted on the playground, but never in the hallways – Dr. Newbury saw to that. He knew all 600 students. He could even recognize them by the back of their heads.

George set a high bar for his brothers as he progressed through school. Both he and Daniel were class presidents at the Baker. James wasn't interested in school politics, and by the time he reached Brookline High, he wasn't much interested in school, either. He couldn't be bothered with studying subjects he felt were not important or taught by teachers he deemed incompetent.

Emotionally, it was a difficult time for James. He felt self-conscious about his 6-foot-3 height. He'd go so far as to shave down his heels to appear shorter. To make him feel better about his stature, I introduced him to a 6-foot-4 business acquaintance who was an executive at J.P. Stevens, the textile company. I wanted James to see that far from being a liability, height can be a big asset, particularly for a leader.

Meanwhile, it got to the point that James practically was refusing to go to school. He'd just stay home. Frustrated, Genevieve called the truant officer. The high school's headmaster, Dr. Carmen Rinaldi, saw potential in James that others had either missed or lacked the patience to nurture. Dr. Rinaldi assigned James to his office for homeroom and kept tabs on whether he was attending class.

WHEN I WAS A CROW

With the demands of work, Town Meeting and other activities, I didn't have as much time as I would have liked to spend with the kids. I made the most out of the weekends, though. Just as I would later enjoy plotting sailing trips, I got a kick out of planning outings for the family.

Early on, we'd explore the acres of woods that stretched behind the nearby Brookline transfer station. George recalled I would tantalize his brothers and him with tales of a lost pond. What I remember is having everyone lay on their backs in complete silence. Then I'd cry out, "Caw, caw, caw," in my best crow imitation. Soon dozens of the birds would flock around us – no doubt disappointed to find a quartet of two-legged creatures rather than one of their feathered friends.

When George was in his early teens, he and I tackled Cannon Mountain in New Hampshire. Since we weren't used to mountain hikes, I suggested that we take the chairlift up and then walk down. Dumb move. It may sound counterintuitive, but your legs take more of a pounding hiking downhill than up. When we were two-thirds of the way to the bottom, my knees hurt so much that I had to walk backward.

But we didn't let that experience sour us on hiking. We joined the Appalachian Mountain Club and tackled the trails of the White Mountains. We slept at night in the club's huts, which were like bunkhouses. Volunteers cooked the meals. After a dinner at Lonesome Lake, a naturalist took us on a tour of the night skies. The planets and constellations stood out sharply, unobstructed by the lights of civilization. Head out to the middle of nowhere in the middle of the night and look up: There really is a Milky Way.

Another favorite hike was along Zealand Falls. On hot summer days, we'd climb past a long series of waterfalls and cool off in the pools below them. It was at a hut there that Genevieve learned just how strict the AMC was about its carry-in, carry-out policy, which was intended to keep sites as pristine as possible. After dinner, she ate a tangerine. The next morning, the peels were left on a table for her to take out of the park.

When the kids were young, I served as Sherpa. I carried a 50-pound pack loaded with clothing and food. A veteran mountaineer suggested that when I felt fatigued, I should take baby steps. He said if I resisted the temptation to stop when I felt exhausted and instead forced myself to push on just a bit longer, I would get a second wind, just like a long-distance runner. The advice worked. In fact, I applied to the office what I learned on the mountains. When faced with seemingly overwhelming tasks, I'd force myself to push on – even if I was only taking baby steps. Inevitably, I'd get over the hump. Now, I'm so concerned about losing my forward momentum that I'm reluctant to take a nap in the afternoon.

In winter, when the kids were young, we all took up skiing – unwittingly putting George's budding dramatic career at risk. To climb the slope, he took a button lift, otherwise known as a Poma lift, clinging to a round disk attached to a pole fastened to a rope tow. Once, as he was going up, one of his skis turned out of the track and jammed in the snow. The lift kept moving, and the stuck ski twisted his ankle to the breaking point. From afar – too far – Genevieve and I powerlessly watched. The scene seemed to unfold in slow motion. Poor George was helpless against the unrelenting lift. At the time of this real-life drama, George had been preparing for the lead role in a play at the Baker School. When he hobbled into school, his teacher wasn't pleased. But George was a trouper. He worked a cast and crutches into his costume, and the show went on.

A birthday party at the Ritz (from left) in early '60s: My sister, Elizabeth Mark; her sons Peter and Johnny; grandparents Sara and Rudolph; David Mark; and my son George.

UP, UP AND AWAY

I wasn't above using my business connections to arrange some of our more spectacular family outings. Visiting Genevieve's parents in Florida, we hitched a ride on a Goodyear blimp. I had to employ my glibbest sales pitch to talk our way onto the airship, which was reserved for Goodyear's best customers. There were only about 10 of us, including the pilot, in the airship's comfortable gondola. No experience can compare with hovering thousands of feet above the ground, the only sound the low grumble of the engine. Before we landed, the crew yelled, "Go get it" and dropped ropes to a team that pulled the giant helium-filled craft to the ground. On another occasion, one of our suppliers arranged a helicopter ride for the kids. The copter landed at the landfill near our house, and we were treated to a bird's-eye view of Brookline, Boston and Newton.

As much as I tried, I couldn't top my father in the trip department. After my mother died, Dad would travel during every school vacation, always taking two grandchildren: one of our sons and one of my sister's sons. Both sets of three grandsons are about the same ages. This way the cousins really got to know each other – and their grandfather. After starting them off with fly fishing in northern Canada, he took the grandkids to the Caribbean, then Europe and finally Israel. In Europe, they stayed at luxury hotels. I'm sure the boys must have been popular with management and the other guests, especially when they sent paper airplanes sailing down the hallways of London's posh Claridge's Hotel.

My father was having the time of his life. But one of the trips nearly gave Genevieve and me heart failure. Dad took Daniel and his cousin Peter by plane to a remote fishing camp in Canada. With no word from them after a couple of days, I called the outfitter. He told me that he hadn't heard from the pilot, who should have returned by then. As I was trying to persuade him to send out a search and rescue team, he reported that the pilot had finally checked in. It turned out that heavy fog had delayed his return flight, and he had been out of radio range. As to my father and the boys, they were having a great time. Besides fishing, my sons found a new sport: playing pranks on a business colleague whom Dad had brought along.

I envy my father's relationship with his grandchildren. Nowadays, my sons' children are so booked up with extracurricular and summer activities that they simply don't have time to globetrot with their grandparents.

THE LOOK ON HER FACE

As I hinted earlier, we sold our house on Marthas Lane in much the same manner as we had bought it: on the strength of a promise.

When we put the house on the market, agents descended on us to get the listing. We signed up with one and watched as weeks went by without prospective buyers. I rejected advice to lower the price. That would have amounted to bidding against ourselves, we thought, since so far nobody had expressed interest in buying. After our contract with the realtor expired, we took the house off the market.

Then we settled on a new strategy: We listed the house ourselves. I called interested brokers to a meeting and announced that whoever sold the house would receive full commission. The incentive worked. It wasn't long before we received an offer from an airline pilot and his wife who were moving here from California. Since it was well below the asking price and only the first to come in, I turned it down. Then another couple offered to pay just $10,000 below the asking price. I said OK.

Just as the wife was returning with a deposit and a purchase and sales agreement, the phone rang. It was a call from California. The pilot and his wife had reconsidered. They really wanted the house. I explained that it was too late and that I was right in the middle of making a deal. The California couple offered $25,000 over the asking price. As we were talking, I could see the other buyer with tears in her eyes as she picked up the gist of the phone conversation. When I got off the phone, I told her that we had bought the house on the basis of a guy keeping his word and that was how we would sell it. I said that the fact that we hadn't signed the P & S yet didn't make any difference.

It would be impossible to put a price on how wonderful I felt to see the look of gratitude on that woman's face.

SOME OF LIFE'S QUIRKS

The Wyner diet: When it came to food, Genevieve and I were raised in different worlds. The consequences would play out in my waistline and how we raised the kids.

Except for an occasional treat from the Good Humor man or a stop at a Howard Johnson's ice cream stand, eating between meals was a no-no in my house when I was a child.

I couldn't go raid the ice box or cupboards for snacks. My mother didn't leave dishes of candy or nuts sitting around the living room.

Our meals were served plated, not family-style. And there was no asking for seconds. And if we didn't like what was served, too bad. If I didn't finish dinner, I might well find my leftovers sitting at the table for me the next day. Wyners did not waste food.

Genevieve's mom had an entirely different philosophy about food – and it put us on a collision course for a while. While she fretted that her guests wouldn't have enough to eat, I worried that good food would go to waste. So, as I kept finishing my plate, she kept bringing out more food for me, all the while panicking that she'd run out. I must have gained 20 pounds visiting Genevieve's family while I was courting her.

When we had our own family, Genevieve took after her mother. What stands out in my memory is my behavior, especially when the family went out to eat. Usually, I wouldn't order anything. Instead, I'd just eat what my sons left on their plate. Their eyes were always bigger than their stomachs. Over my objections but with their mother's approval, they ordered everything they desired. And so, I would always leave full.

To this day, you'll find me assembling lunches and even dinners out of leftovers and whatever else I can scavenge from the refrigerator. My refrigerator regimen is to eat the oldest (but still edible) food first, resisting the dictates of my taste buds; this way, nothing languishes so long that it must be tossed out. Oddly enough, I've received compliments for creating delicious, if unusual meals, by combining ingredients based on my first-in, first-out fridge formula. I guess, as in so many other instances in life, it is all about the presentation!

* * *

My churchgoing days: I grew up in a family where household help was common. Genevieve didn't. And this could be a source of contention.

In the immediate weeks after the kids were born, Genevieve's mom arranged to have the same nurse, Charlotte, stay with her as had helped her other daughters. But beyond that, Genevieve preferred to run the house herself.

But with three sons born within six years, Genevieve had a lot to handle. On one of my regular visits to our Puerto Rican plant, I interviewed a lovely woman named Ramona Matos, who agreed to travel to Brookline to be our housekeeper.

Ramona arrived in Boston in the middle of a winter storm. In those days, passengers didn't deplane directly into the terminal, but rather descended a mobile staircase to the tarmac outside. Also at that time, security wasn't a major concern. Passengers could be met at the bottom of the stairs.

Ramona looked scared to death. She had never experienced snow before and had no idea what to make of the flakes falling all around her.

I went about trying to make Ramona feel as at home as possible in Brookline. She didn't speak much English, so she had difficulty making her desires known. I assumed that as she was Catholic, she would want to go to church. I first took her to St. Lawrence in Chestnut Hill, where it turned out that the monsignor was a man I knew. While I was Town Meeting moderator, I had invited him to give the invocation at an opening session. When Ramona and I walked into his church, the monsignor greeted us enthusiastically and, somewhat to my embarrassment, escorted us to the front row. We went to St. Lawrence on several occasions, Ramona mystified by the language and I by the liturgy.

I then suggested that we try the cathedral on Shawmut Avenue in Boston, which I had just learned held a Mass in Spanish every Sunday. After accompanying Ramona to services there, I suggested that in the future I could drop her off and pick her up afterward. "Mr. Wyner," she told me, "if you don't want to go to church, I don't want to go church."

It finally dawned on me that Ramona really didn't want to go to church. While my intentions were good, she was going just to please me.

* * *

Out of the mouths of babes: Just as my dad had with me, I used to take my children to work on occasion. There, James as a little boy demonstrated traits that decades later would help make him an excellent company president. He had an advantage over me on these visits. Everything he saw was new to him.

"Daddy, why are they doing that?" James would ask about one process or another. That forced me to stop and look closely at something I might have walked by a hundred times. Thanks to him, I found problems that otherwise I never would have noticed. It wasn't that he was an engineering prodigy; he just had an eye for the irrational.

I drew a couple of lessons from James's talent for catching flaws others missed. First, I realized that as a youngster, he had yet to be socialized into worrying that people would think he was asking a stupid question. To him, there were no stupid questions. It would probably save us adults a lot of trouble if we were to shed our inhibitions and follow his example. Think of "The Emperor's New Clothes."

Second, James made me realize just how often we look at things without really seeing them. In part, this is our mind's way of warding off sensory overload. But there are pitfalls to becoming so focused that we blind ourselves to the big picture.

I used to attend meetings with executives from other companies to discuss common business problems. At each meeting, one of us would present a program in which we showed how we addressed a production or logistical challenge. One participant, who headed a produce department at a local supermarket, told how he had streamlined the process of breaking down bulk loads of oranges for display out front. He filmed the process so that he could study it frame by frame to make sure not a single motion was wasted. He showed us a movie to demonstrate how he had reduced orange processing down to a science.

As we watched the movie, laughter started rippling through the audience, growing louder and louder. This wasn't at all what our presenter had expected. He couldn't see what was so funny. He had watched the film so many times that he hadn't noticed the little drama going on in the background. A worker unloading a stack of orange cartons was climbing on the boxes rather than using a ladder. The boxes began tipping over, spilling oranges onto the floor. His scrambling to pick up the fruit looked like a scene out of an episode of Laurel and Hardy.

Too bad the supermarket guy hadn't asked James to preview his movie.

MY OTHER FATHER

Yoo-hoo, Yogi and other business escapades with Max Geller

THANKS TO MY FATHER-IN-LAW, I did business with Yogi Berra and a business mogul with an apparent fondness for cocaine. Such were the wide variety of characters I encountered through Max A. Geller's entrepreneurial adventures.

Max was a people person. Outgoing and brilliant, he had a genius for marketing – starting with himself.

Speaking English without a trace of an accent, he fooled everyone – including his own children – into believing that he was born in Lexington, Kentucky. It was only when Genevieve was in her 30s and happened to visit her uncle's office that she learned the truth. One of her uncle's colleagues told her that he had attended "gimnazjum," middle school, with her father in Poland. When Genevieve confronted her dad, the truth came out. He had immigrated to the United States several years before the outbreak of World War I.

Max told his daughter that upon seeing the Statue of Liberty he tossed his coat overboard and symbolically everything else that had to do with the old country. He became a fiercely proud American. Entering grammar school in the fourth grade, he was teased by other children because of his accent. Max asked a teacher to help him with his pronunciation. In time, he trained himself to speak like an aristocrat. The only trace I ever detected of his roots was at synagogue, when he was invited to the bimah to chant the blessings over the reading of the Torah. Hearing him say "baruch a-too-eee," I asked myself, "Where did that come from?" Much later, I learned of his Polish childhood.

My in-laws, Ida and Max Geller.

Max earned a bachelor's degree from City College in 1919 and a law degree from New York University the next year. After practicing law for several years, he became so interested in the business of one of his clients – an advertising agency – that he decided to go into advertising himself. Over the next 15 years he worked as sales manager for *Liberty* and *Cosmopolitan* magazines. In 1941, he teamed up with Ed Weiss of Chicago to form the advertising firm Weiss & Geller. It was most famous for its slogan for a home permanent treatment: "Which twin had the Toni?" The company was also known for its use of psychologists to help shape ad campaigns. Its philosophy was that to sell the product, you have to know the customer. Consulting in the 1950s with Ed about his latest scientific methods, we learned how the eye roamed a newspaper ad. As a result, we modified ads for our Vanta line of baby clothing, such as by softening sharp-edged typefaces.

One of the traits that made Max successful was that he invested himself in his clients by learning everything he could about them. After World War II, he became so caught up in the fate of New Haven Clock that he helped save it from bankruptcy. As the company had taken on several federal government contracts, Max went to Washington to plead its case. The government agreed to give New Haven Clock a loan, but only if Max took over as its CEO. He did so well in that role that the company's union presented him with a Cadillac for saving their jobs. Max later stepped in to save Waltham Watch Company.

In 1951, with the encouragement of his children, Max completed the doctoral studies in American history at NYU that he had abandoned during the Depression. His dissertation, *Advertising at a Crossroads: Federal Regulation vs. Voluntary Controls,* became a very successful book.

A DAY AT THE RACES

Besides engaging in such varied enterprises as advertising, soda pop and clocks, my father-in-law dabbled in race horses. That's how Genevieve and I ended up joining Max and Ida in Saratoga, New York, in the early '60s – an experience that recalls lessons I learned about high society and horse manure.

I'll start with the less aromatic subject. In Saratoga, we stayed at the Gideon Putnam, a plush resort near the racetrack that was owned by my old Harvard acquaintance David Schine. We saw him there, along with his wife, the former Miss Universe. Luxury accommodations were a treat for us at the time (and, no, David didn't give us a discount). So, when it came time to drive over to the racetrack, I suggested to Genevieve that we hitch a ride with another guest. After all, just about everyone was heading to the races. That way I wouldn't have to call for our car and tip the attendant. Genevieve was shocked at the idea of asking someone for a lift. "Nobody does that at the Gideon Putnam," she said.

Admonished, I ordered up the car. While I waited for Genevieve to come down from the room, a man and a woman came along. "Are you going to the track?," the man asked me. "Would you mind giving us a ride?" I told him, sure. The couple got in the back, and Genevieve sat in the front. I turned around and said, "My name is Jerry Wyner, and this is my wife, Gen." And the man responded, "I'm Alf Vanderbilt, and this is my wife, Jean." Yes, a grandson of Cornelius Vanderbilt II was not above hitching a ride. Later, we saw Alf – a renowned horseman – bid $100,000 for a yearling with no record yet, always considered a major gamble.

While at the races, we did a little gambling ourselves. I used a system that my father and I, with tongues firmly planted in our cheeks, had devised when we went to Suffolk Downs a few times in its early days. My father had theorized that the more comfortable a horse felt, the faster it would run. We would gauge comfort by whether the horse had just had a productive bowel movement. Before each race, we'd visit the paddock to look for a signal. Sometimes, several horses left deposits on their way to the track; other times, none did. We would only place our two-dollar bets when just one horse had answered nature's call. We had to keep a sharp eye out. A stable boy usually followed the horses to scoop up their deposits. Ostensibly, that was to keep the paddock clean, but Dad and I joked that the real reason was to thwart spies like us.

Getting back to Saratoga, I noticed everyone scrutinizing the statistics in the racing newspaper before placing their bets. I didn't put much stock in that kind of research. Before each race, I would announce that I was going to the paddock to look for "signals." Even though I wasn't all that methodical, my "signaling" horses often came into the money (including some long shots). Initially, Max scoffed at my system, but after a while he began asking me about my reconnaissance missions.

Back at the hotel, I spotted the mayor of Boston, John Collins, who had used a wheelchair since contracting polio in 1955. I told Genevieve that we ought to introduce ourselves since we were fellow Bay Staters. The mayor turned out to be quite friendly, and we got into a conversation. To Genevieve's horror, I told him about my system for picking horses and its apparent success. The next day at the races, we spotted the mayor. He was over by the paddock in his wheelchair, eyes peeled to the ground.

Max became involved in other ventures. He ran a sporting goods chain and, starting in 1961, Yoo-hoo beverages. Yankee and Mets great Yogi Berra was the corporate face of the chocolate milk drink, unusual for its time because it didn't have to be refrigerated. I sat with him on the board of directors, though I don't recall him contributing any of his famous sayings to our deliberations. Mostly, he got our clients autographed baseballs and VIP treatment at the ballpark. Our kids got in the act, too, appearing in several Yoo-hoo commercials.

A SNIFF OF SCANDAL

In the mid-'70s, Max sold Yoo-hoo to Iroquois Brands, an Upstate New York brewery that had expanded into malt liquor, caviar and vitamins. In return he received Iroquois stock, but was restricted from selling it for a specified period so as not to depress the price of the shares. As Max got older and his health deteriorated, he was no longer able to participate in Iroquois meetings. In the mid-1980s, he wanted to sell his stock. First, he had to get the permission of the company's chairman, Terence J. Fox, because the sales restriction hadn't expired. Fox dragged his feet. I became suspicious and offered to help. I took out an ad in *The Wall Street Journal* to see if other Iroquois shareholders were concerned about the company's management.

As a result, I received a call from Mario Joseph Gabelli, a prominent Wall Street investor and analyst who was actively following the Iroquois stock at the time. Apparently after learning that Gabelli and I were talking, Fox had second thoughts about having brushed Max and me off. He agreed to release the shares for sale, asking me to meet him at a Hartford hotel to seal the deal. I drove down from Boston, and Fox met me in the lobby. He seemed to have a very bad cold, which made me reluctant to go back to his room and talk. Fortunately, I didn't have to. To my surprise and relief, he settled the matter there and then.

Fox's stuffy nose apparently had to do more with powder than germs. A week later I read in *The New York Times* that the 47-year-old company president had been led away in handcuffs from the Hartford hotel along with a 38-year-old woman. Tipped off by a maid, police reported finding 17 grams of cocaine and various drug paraphernalia. I could only think how close I had come to having been in that room and, if not present during a bust, having my fingerprints turn up. That wouldn't have looked good for a former (and future) Brookline town moderator and Temple Israel president. Fox, by the way, got the charges dropped after agreeing to enter rehab.

WAITING FOR THE ELEVATOR

Not all of Max's businesses involved celebrity and intrigue. Yoo-hoo was offered a chance to acquire ABC Sample Card Company, which produced fabric display cards. I tried to talk Max out of buying the firm, as it seemed so far afield of Yoo-hoo's other investments. I pointed out that the institutional knowledge of the company would walk out the door with the sellers. And sure enough, that's what happened. Soon the Yoo-hoo board was told that the company was losing money.

Max asked me to visit the company, which was in a multistory garment manufacturing building in Lower Manhattan. The first thing I noticed was that production was on two floors, spaced several stories apart. Workers relied on a small freight elevator that also served many other businesses in the 12-story building. So, the company was paying its employees to spend a lot of time waiting for the elevator. Upstairs, I watched the workers in action; by then, I had become accustomed to doing time-and-motion studies with my wristwatch. After estimating production costs, I realized that the company was losing money on each piece it sent out the door to its biggest customer, JC Penney. When I asked one of the managers about raising the price, he said his hands were tied: JC Penney wouldn't stand for it. After further investigation, I learned that to retain this money-losing contract, the sample card company was paying off JC Penney's buyer.

I called Max and urged him to drop JC Penney and to force an immediate halt to the payoffs. In addition, I pointed out that without JC Penney as a customer, he could consolidate his operations onto one floor, thus saving on rent and the workers' time wasted waiting for the elevator. With those changes, the business was back in the black. Then we got a bonus: JC Penney wanted back in and was willing to pay substantially more – without a bribe-taking buyer. In the end, ABC, even with JC Penney's business, managed to operate on one floor. The company went from incurring substantial losses to turning a very respectable profit. Max was delighted and proud of what his son-in-law had accomplished in one visit to the site.

We always had a wonderful relationship. We talked about business and current events and were golfing friends as well. With his own son, Jack, living on the West Coast, I felt I received some of the love that would have gone to him – but from afar, there was still plenty left over for Jack.

THE WEEKEND THAT CHANGED OUR LIVES

Why I'm forever grateful Genevieve dragged me to Marriage Encounter

I LEARNED SOMETHING ABOUT love on the factory floor. As a byproduct of our research into fabric composites, we came up with a method of making imitation suede. It had the look and feel of the genuine article, but not the smell. After reading an article in the *New York Times* about Tuli-Latus, a company in Brooklyn that uncannily imitated famous perfumes, I decided to inquire if the firm could create the aroma of leather suede for embedding in our fabrics. It accepted the challenge and 30 days later sent me a small vial that I thought perfectly captured the smell. But when Ray Franks, our longtime associate, sampled a whiff, he pronounced that it smelled like garbage. I explained the problem to Tuli-Latus, which said it would take just a tweak in the formula to satisfy Ray. Indeed, the tweaked scent did please Ray, but to me it smelled like putrid chicken.

Since then, I've thought about how that episode relates to marriage. In our early years, I would fixate on things I had wished were different about Genevieve that I believed would have made our relationship better. But now I realize that Genevieve is like an intoxicating perfume. If I tried to make the slightest change, I risked ruining the magic formula that I loved so much. After all, each of us is the sum of countless traits, some pronounced, others subtle, many seemingly contradictory. Tinker with one, and you upset everything. Whenever I start thinking "If only Genevieve would be like such and such," I stop and remember how I spoiled the *eau de suede*.

I'm not sure I would have made that connection had it not been for a weekend Genevieve and I spent at an inn in New Hampshire shortly after the Blizzard of '78. The experience was so powerful that you could almost split my life into before and after. It changed the ways I thought and felt about things, how Genevieve and I related to each other, and – serendipitously – the future of Shawmut, as I recount in another chapter.

The trigger for that transformation: Marriage Encounter.

OK, I can imagine the skeptics rolling their eyes. "Marriage Encounter"? That sounds like some sort of psychobabble fad. I admit that was what I once thought, too. When Genevieve suggested attending a weekend retreat where we would share our feelings about ourselves and our relationship, I said no way. Remember, I had been raised by a mother who insisted that well-bred people kept their feelings to themselves. I saw this retreat as an invitation for trouble. Yes, our marriage had its ups and downs, but what marriage didn't? If it's not broke, why fix it? But, as Genevieve would point out, the purpose of Marriage Encounter wasn't to save bad marriages, but to enrich good ones (indeed, the name was later changed to Marriage Enrichment). I only agreed to go after seeing how much a weekend at Marriage Encounter had benefited Genevieve's sister Harriet and her husband, Michael Greenfield, whom I respected as a no-nonsense guy.

When we arrived at the inn, we were ushered into another world. Everything had been arranged to remove the distractions of our daily lives and put us at ease. A volunteer couple took our luggage to our room. We were told to remove our watches; had there been cell phones then, I'm sure we would have been asked to surrender them, too. To make certain we received no distracting calls, we were not even registered as guests. I discovered that fact when, after returning from an errand, I asked at the front desk for our room number, and the clerk had no idea.

Four couples conducted the weekend, including a rabbinic couple. Clearly having taken much care in preparing what they would say, they shared with us intimate feelings on almost every phase of life. After each session with the presenters, Genevieve and I and the other couples enrolled in the program returned to our rooms. We were assigned to write love letters to each other, describing our feelings in tender detail about the topic of the session. Then we read the letters to each other and talked about them. All of this was done in the privacy of our rooms. I found it reassuring that we were not expected to show our letters to the presenting couples. Their role was not to judge or correct us.

The topics ran the gamut. Recall how you felt about the death of a loved one. How do you describe the feeling of satisfaction? How do you feel about growing old with your spouse? What small courtesy do you wish your partner would display more often and how would it make you feel? How have you demonstrated confidence in your spouse?

Genevieve and I rediscovered each other through Marriage Encounter.

Having to sit down and put my feelings into words was not easy. Because the questions were specific, we couldn't brush them off with platitudes. Because we were expected to write at length, we couldn't get away with pat answers. Once I knocked down the wall that I had been erecting for years around my feelings, I surprised myself by how much I had to say. At the start, I never knew where I would end up. As with a Ouija board, I seemed to magically glide from one direction to another.

Because our writings took the form of love letters, we emphasized what we appreciated about each other. At the same time, by sharing our deepest feelings, we could help each other understand why our behavior at times might be perplexing or hurtful. Even the closest of couples don't perceive the world alike. Everyone is born with a distinct set of traits, and shaped by different family and social traditions and life experiences.

Seemingly little things can be the source of great frustration, such as a wife annoyed that her husband doesn't bother to look up from his newspaper when she asks him a question. Perhaps it makes her think he doesn't really care what's on her mind – that the paper matters more to him than she does. But if she were just to tell her husband she thinks he's shutting her out of his life, he'd probably be baffled. He might wonder why she was making such a big deal out of something seemingly innocuous. He might react by telling her she's wrong, which would only lead to an endless cycle of recriminations.

Marriage Encounter encourages empathy between couples by helping them reframe conversations to focus on feelings. That takes the discussion out of the realm of who is right and who is wrong. A basic tenet of Marriage Encounter is that there are no right feelings or wrong feelings. The more a husband and wife know about each other's feelings, the less likely they are to inadvertently inflict pain with their actions and words. And that same knowledge will help them bring out the best in each other, evoking feelings of satisfaction, pleasure and joy.

At the end of the weekend, we were not presented with a bill. We were told that the cost of everything, including the hotel and meals, had been covered by donations made by previous participants. We, in turn, were invited to contribute to the expenses of those who might follow us. Our gifts would be anonymous; no one would know who gave what, if anything at all.

MEMBERS OF A CLUB

I came out of that first Marriage Encounter weekend feeling as if I had just emerged from a long swim underwater to discover that I was in a new world. Those two days turned me from a skeptic into a proselytizer. Many times, I would hear others express the same reaction to Marriage Encounter.

One day, not long after, Genevieve was stopped in a grocery store parking lot by someone who had noticed the Marriage Encounter sticker on our car. She, too, had been on a weekend. It was as if we were all members of the same club. Through this chance encounter, we were invited to join a Marriage Encounter Havurah, a group of couples who met twice monthly in each other's homes to share the love letters that they had written on assigned questions.

I tend to be a private person, so I was afraid at first to expose my most personal feelings to relative strangers. But as I developed trust in the group, my wariness vanished. For years, the group continued to meet, though our numbers dwindled. We finally ran out of energy a few years back.

Having accustomed us to revealing our innermost selves, the Havurah experience emboldened us to train as presenting couples at Marriage Encounter weekends. It was a grueling process. We'd prepare our remarks in advance, only to have our designated critiquing couple challenge us at every turn. They forced us to dig deep into ourselves, to unearth and describe the unvarnished feelings at the roots of our thoughts. We learned how to express ourselves in ways that others could relate to. It was not enough for me to say that I felt unloved when my wife seemed to ignore me. I had to describe the physical feeling of being unloved. Metaphors helped. For example, I might have said, "Imagine you're luxuriating in a warm shower and suddenly the water turned ice cold. That is how I feel when you abruptly shut me out."

Being a presenting couple was exhausting work – each weekend a 44-hour commitment, often with little sleep. We engaged in the same writing and sharing exercises as the participants, and we met with them one-on-one if they asked to speak in private. But the compensation was incalculable. As the weekend progressed, we only needed to look at the joy in the eyes of the couples we helped.

BARING ALL

Marriage Encounter paid dividends in both our personal and public lives. Recognizing the futility of trying to argue with another's feelings helped me mediate business and civic disputes. I find that people are much more amenable to exploring solutions once they're satisfied that their feelings have been sincerely acknowledged.

Marriage Encounter inspired Genevieve and me to continue the practice of sharing our feelings through love letters almost daily for many years. One exchange led to our romance with the sea, which I'll get to later.

On a trip to what was then Yugoslavia, we had an experience of sharing or openness that reminded us of Marriage Encounter. We were strolling on an island off Dubrovnik when, unable to translate the posted signs, we wandered onto a sprawling nude bathing beach and recreation area. I said to Genevieve, "If we are going to continue to explore this beautiful area, we have to take our clothes off. We can't walk around here like a couple of voyeurs." After some hesitation, she agreed. It was a remarkable experience. As soon as we stripped down, we felt like part of the crowd. Not until the end of the day, when everyone started to put their clothes back on and leave the beach for their homes, did we think about the nudity. When it comes to baring feelings, there is comfort in company, too.

RENEWING OUR VOWS

At the end of that first Marriage Encounter weekend, all the couples gathered together to renew their vows. The tears in people's eyes showed that nobody was just going through the motions. The ceremony reinforced the decision Genevieve and I had made when we first married, the decision to love. Keeping that in mind during the inevitable squabbles of daily life makes it much easier to shake thoughts like "How did I ever get stuck with this person?" For me, it comes down to this: Genevieve is the woman I love, and I'm going to try to fix everything that stands in the way of our enjoying that love.

Genevieve and I continue to view the world in different ways. But I've come to realize what a good thing that is. When I look out the window I may see one view and Genevieve another. By sharing what we see, we double our pleasure.

THIS NEW HOUSE

How my life in a dream house ended in a nightmare

OUR SECOND HOUSE IN Brookline played the starring role for a season of the PBS series *This Old House,* though in this case it was really "This New House." Over 26 episodes, viewers watched each step of construction, from the site selection to the finished building. What happened afterward would have made for a sequel at turns informative, dramatic, heartbreaking and infuriating – one with its very own villain.

The saga starts in the early '80s with an elderly woman who lived near us in Brookline in a tumble-down house on the edge of a hill. It overlooked a vast tract of woodlands she owned that sprawled across the Newton border. Well into her 90s, she would tool around the neighborhood in her little red Fiat convertible with the top down. After she died, Boston Edison purchased the property from her heirs.

At first, I thought this would be a great suburban location for Temple Israel, but Rabbi Roland Gittelsohn – wisely, I think in retrospect – shot that idea down. The rabbi pointed out that the move would make us inaccessible to anyone who relied on the subway, among whom numbered the great majority of those who attended the religious school.

CALLING BOB VILA

All but five of the woman's 180 acres were in Newton. Boston Edison envisioned selling the land off to developers. Their plans called for chopping up the property into lots of 10,000 square feet. The resulting huge subdivision of comparatively modest homes would have altered the character of the neighborhood. On the Brookline side, the utility set aside a hilltop lot for the "Impact 2000 House," which would promote the latest environmentally friendly technology and building practices. WGBH agreed to film the construction for *This Old House.* Boston Edison's motivations weren't entirely altruistic; it needed some good publicity after management problems had forced the temporary shutdown of its Pilgrim nuclear power plant in Plymouth.

Some nine million viewers nationwide tuned in as host Bob Vila and his sidekick, carpenter Norm Abrams, provided the play-by-play for the series, redubbed that year as *The All-New This Old House.* After the house was finished, 30,000 people toured it. Genevieve and I were among the first, and we took home a detailed brochure.

After the "For Sale" sign was removed, rumors circulated that Boston Celtics star Larry Bird, a neighbor who at the time lived at the corner of Newton Street and Marthas Lane, had purchased the house. But complications off the basketball court led him to back out. Meanwhile, we had just backed out of buying a unit in the then-new Rowes Wharf development on Boston Harbor, because ownership did

132

not come with docking privileges for our sailboat. For a tech-geek like me, the Impact 2000 House was irresistible. When the "For Sale" sign popped back up, Genevieve and I took it as a good omen.

But I didn't want our dream house to overlook that planned subdivision of cookie-cutter homes. To create a buffer, I negotiated a deal with Boston Edison to buy the five acres that were in Brookline. A brook ran through the property, providing a natural boundary for us to keep two acres on our side. We divided the remainder into one-acre lots, which we sold with stipulations that the homes would be of high quality and designed in such a way as to block the view of the Newton subdivision.

We hired Carol Johnson Associates, an architectural firm that had laid out the grounds of Shawmut's West Bridgewater plant, to landscape our new home. We preserved as much of the woods as we could, reinforced a bridge over the brook, and created hiking trails and gardens. The grounds already had been enhanced with a small fish pond stocked with koi.

The 2,800-square-foot Impact 2000 house had been built into the hillside, taking advantage of the earth's moderating effect on temperature extremes. The south-facing back takes full advantage of sunlight with large expanses of window. The dining room looks over a two-story living room; the library, over a two-story sun space. Decks off the top two floors overlook the pond and gardens.

The sun heated the water and generated electricity for our house of the future, which was a star on PBS.

JERRY, THE HOUSE TUNER

The house used solar and geothermal energy to reduce heating and cooling costs. A 4,000-watt photovoltaic array on the roof generated electricity that we'd use in the house or, if not needed, feed into the utility's power grid, reducing our electric bills. The goal was to show that, with the right design and equipment, an all-electric house could operate more efficiently and economically than the customary one heated with natural gas or oil. I can testify that the house fulfilled its promise.

Steven Strong, who designed the house, featured it in his 1994 book, *The Solar Electric House: Energy for the Environmentally Responsive, Energy-Independent Home.* A museum-quality, large-scale model of the house was displayed at Logan Airport for two years. Afterward, as part of the purchase price of the house, the model went to us.

A geothermal heat pump kept the house toasty in the winter and cool in the summer. It extracted energy from water that circulated through a closed loop pipe that descended to the bottom of a 400-foot well. A computer in the cellar collected data from some 200 sensors distributed throughout the house to calculate the efficiency of the various energy-saving systems. In the winter, for example, a heat exchanger warmed fresh air from the outside with heat extracted from air exhausted from the interior. Based on the computer calculations, the cost of running the electric motor in the exchanger was just 30 percent of the cost of heating the incoming air by conventional means.

I allowed engineers at Boston Edison to continue monitoring the energy efficiency of this house of the future in return for sharing their findings. I would pore through an inch-thick printout of hourly sensor readings and energy calculations they sent me each month. In the middle of winter, I discovered that the heat pump would turn off at night. The system extracted so much energy in the form of heat from the water that its temperature dropped to the point that the water could freeze in the well. Before that happened, a monitor triggered the pump to shut down. Pointing to the performance specifications for the heat pump system in the Edison brochure, I told the company that it should have realized that the equipment and well were too small for the task.

The solution, as I saw it, was a larger pump and a deeper well. The company agreed to change the heat pump, but balked at further drilling. Its engineer said that the geothermal capacity could be increased in the winter by programming the system to occasionally discharge water into a nearby stream. As a result, the well would be recharged by warmer water from deeper underground. I responded that that would be wasting perfectly good water from the aquifer, which I believed ran counter to the house's environmental mission. In the end, Edison agreed to drill the well down to 600 feet.

The only other major problem we had was self-inflicted, and had nothing to do with the house itself. Since Genevieve had so proficiently carried on her family's tennis tradition, we decided to build a court. Potential sites were limited by the topography of the property. A consultant from Carol Johnson's group warned against the location we thought was best, saying the court would endanger a pair of 150-year-old sycamore trees. To level additional ground so that we could safeguard the trees, we had to blast through rocky ledge. The results looked great, but six weeks after the court was finished Genevieve was sidelined with knee problems. She had to undergo replacement surgery. To keep up appearances, we purchased a ball machine to play against me. After all, what would the neighbors think if we had this private court and never used it? The next blow came when a mild windstorm toppled the bigger of the two sycamores. Looking inside the trunk, we could see that its first 15 feet or so were nearly hollow. To think we had been so attentive to the tree. Not only had we preserved and faithfully fed it, we had called in an arborist to give it a checkup. Despite all that, no one had noticed that the tree was dying from the inside out. Had we felled it in the first place, we could have saved a fortune on the blasting.

A COSTLY PROMISE

In the '90s, after we had acquired a second home on the Vineyard, we decided that we didn't want the burden of maintaining two large yards. So, we started to look for a condo in the city. Before we put the house on the market, I visited my neighbors and told them we would do our best to sell the parcel to someone who would keep it intact. But if that were not possible, I requested their cooperation should a buyer want to subdivide it to allow for three more houses. I even had plans drawn up that would position any new homes as far from theirs as possible. From my many years in town government, I had learned that surprising the neighbors with a subdivision plan at Town Meeting was a sure way of having it shot down. My diplomacy paid off: The entire neighborhood supported us at the hearing on our subdivision plan.

Within a month, we received an offer of $2.6 million for the property. But the buyer was a developer who wanted to divvy up the land for the additional houses. I felt that to jump at the offer would show bad faith to my neighbors. Genevieve agreed. When we turned him down, the buyer warned we'd never get such a good offer again. Sadly, he was right.

Months went by without any significant interest in the property. Meanwhile, we had signed an agreement to buy a condo at Rowes Wharf. We no longer could afford to be choosy about buyers. The owner of a family-owned construction and development firm offered $2.2 million. We had known the man personally for many years. Although we knew he intended to subdivide the property, we signed a purchase and sale agreement. By this point, we felt that we had honored our commitment to our neighbors to try to find a buyer who would keep the property intact. Beyond that, we had as a fallback the subdivision plan already approved by the town.

Three months after putting down a 10 percent deposit of $220,000, my developer friend informed me that he wouldn't close on the property unless we knocked off another $300,000. Pointing to the P&S agreement, I said, "We made a deal; you gave me a deposit." He argued that since signing it, he had found out that he couldn't place five additional houses on the property. I responded that we had never presented the property with a potential other than the subdivision plan approved by the town for three additional houses. He told me that if I refused to accept his revised offer, he'd walk away from the deal. If that's the case, I told him, we'd keep the deposit. If I did that, he warned, he'd sue me. Exasperated, I said, "I just can't believe that I've known you all my life, and that's the way you do business."

Our lawyer said a court battle would be expensive and its outcome far from certain. Genevieve said we should just get on with our lives. I gave in, even though I suspected that he had intended to pull this stunt from the start. He knew my back was against the wall. I still shudder when I think of how much I had misjudged him. Passing up that initial offer had cost us $700,000, but at least I could live with myself. I had kept my word. You can't place a price on integrity.

Besides digging up our carefully planned and constructed nature preserve, he removed and junked the house's solar panels and geothermal system. "Nobody would understand it," he said. "I'd never be able to sell the house."

One last kick in the pants: the new owner managed to obtain permission to build five additional houses on the property after all.

AT THE HELM OF ROWES WHARF

And to think I thought my leadership days were over

WHEN GENEVIEVE WALKED INTO the condo at Rowes Wharf, she spotted a grand piano in the living room, its black lacquered surface set off by the deep white pile carpeting, and fell in love.

"This is just what I was looking for," she said to the owners of the fifth-floor corner unit. Well, that pulled the plug on any bargaining power I had. But Genevieve was right: This was the place for us.

I had first heard about Rowes Wharf in the 1980s while it was still in the planning stage. I ran into developer Ed Sidman at Belmont Country Club and asked him what he was up to. Ed told me that he and his father-in-law, Norman Leventhal, were building the hotel and condo complex on Boston's waterfront. At the time, with the kids getting older, Genevieve and I were thinking of moving out of our home on Marthas Lane in Newton. We toured a model condo, which was on display at a Broad Street building, and put down a deposit. But several years later, when the building was ready for occupancy, we learned that a change in city rules required that all the boat slips be available to the public; even as residents, we couldn't be assured a space. I didn't relish the idea of looking out my window at the boats, knowing that mine was docked blocks, if not miles, away.

We ended up buying the Impact 2000 house instead. It was not until the late 1990s that we again decided to exchange the suburbs for city living. Our real estate agent told us that a double-size condo had just come on the market at Rowes Wharf – and we could even get a boat slip. We moved in February 1998.

MEETING THE 'MAYOR'

At the time of our move, we really did not know what kind of a community we would find at Rowes Wharf. From our earlier years in Brookline, we were acquainted with three of our new neighbors: Rhoda and Bill Sapers (his brother Carl had succeeded me as town moderator in Brookline) and Ruth Kaufman. Rhoda had been extremely encouraging about our moving in.

The first new person we met was Paul Saperstein, who was introduced to us as the "mayor of Rowes Wharf." Paul was a former Dorchester boy who had built up a prosperous auction company. Although I didn't know much about him, Paul seemed to know everything about me. While his company deals in heirlooms and real estate, Paul specializes in people. Aside from seemingly every Jewish native of Boston, he knows community leaders and municipal workers ranging from the cop on the beat to the top brass at City Hall. Early on, we were invited to a birthday party for Paul at which Tom Menino, then mayor of Boston, was among the guests.

For the benefit of a charity, Paul's son (who works for the family business) auctioned off an evening for two at a Celtics game. As part of the package, he said his father would walk with the successful bidders from Rowes Wharf to the Boston Garden. As further incentive, he said if Paul couldn't introduce them to at least 50 people along the way, the winners would receive their bid money back. I never did hear the end of the story, but I'd be surprised if Paul didn't live up to his billing.

Not long after we moved in, I did something unusual for a resident: I attended a meeting of the condo association's board of managers. While it shouldn't come as a surprise to anyone who knows me, I asked a question. It had something to do with finances. The next thing I knew I was invited to sit on the finance committee. Not long after that, in May 1999, I was elected to the condo board. I had been urged to run by Rhoda Sapers, who was always one to overestimate my talents. Two years later, I was elected president – a position I held until May 2015, when we decided to move to NewBridge on the Charles in Dedham.

THE 'YES' POLICY

Serving as president was time-consuming, but never a burden. That was thanks to the goodwill of fellow board members, the gratitude of the residents and the devotion of the staff. I was particularly indebted to Katherine McCabe Scott, the property manager who came on board along with Barkan Management just as I assumed the presidency. A smart, delightful person, Katherine kept her composure even when trying to satisfy the demands of a handful of sometimes lovable but often difficult residents. I told Katherine that our goal should be to say "yes." In those infrequent cases where we couldn't, I would deliver the bad news. That way she wouldn't have to worry about disappointed residents threatening her job. If I said "no," they could always unseat me at the next election. With that guiding philosophy, we rarely had a problem.

The residents ranged widely in age, ethnicity (about 20 percent were Jewish) and financial status. None were judgmental, at least in public. At holiday gatherings and the annual meeting, people mixed and genuinely enjoyed one another's company. I had heard stories about times in the past when residents were roiled by disagreements. During my tenure, I encountered only a few residents who sought to undermine the board. My experiences with Marriage Encounter and with leading Temple Israel and Brookline Town Meeting had taught me the importance of listening and being empathetic. I like to think that residents felt the board would take their concerns seriously, rather than seeing voting us out of office as their only recourse.

But there were some aggravating challenges – from the four-legged variety to the seven-figure kind (namely, a complete interior renovation). As to the former, we had soiling dogs, fighting dogs, biting dogs, barking dogs, and – in one apartment – too many dogs. But through diplomacy, the board managed to work things out.

Sayed Saleh, during his first term on the board, contributed toward creating our cooperative spirit. He invited all the board members, their spouses and Katherine to a retreat at the Orchards, a resort hotel (I give it 10 stars) he then owned in Williamstown. That gave us an opportunity to think hard about ways to improve the experience of living at Rowes Wharf, inspired by the high caliber of service at Sayed's hotel.

FIGHTING CITY HALL

Boston was still in the throes of the Big Dig when I started out as condo president. Norman Leventhal, who lived in a penthouse at Rowes Wharf until his death in 2015, would give me advice from time to time. He warned me that, as board president, I needed to keep a close eye on plans for the Greenway, the wide band of open land above the newly built tunnel in front of Rowes Wharf. He urged me to use my influence to promote plans that would enable not just our district but the entire city to enjoy the waterfront area.

Following Norman's advice, I began attending neighborhood meetings sponsored variously by the city, the Turnpike Authority and the Boston Redevelopment Authority. It seemed as though everyone in the neighborhood came out to denounce ideas rather than propose or support them. I worked hard to shift the conversation to what we all could agree on, pointing out that being constantly negative would cost us credibility. Further, I said, if we succeeded in getting what we did want, there wouldn't be room for what we opposed.

As in other settings, I embraced the challenge of getting people who disagreed with one another to find a way to work together. When the focus is on common interests, conflicts tend to recede in importance. And that's what happened, as our informal neighborhood group became the Wharf District Task Force and then the Wharf District Council. Once a bunch of squabbling neighbors, we became a force that gained the full attention of City Hall. We had found common ground with not only other residents, but also the private sector (former Boston transportation commissioner Rick Dimino had formed the Artery Business Committee), the New England Aquarium (through its president, Bud Ris) and area hotels. Among the others who spearheaded efforts to shape the Greenway were Harbor Tower residents, notably Susanne Lavoie and Chris Fincham.

When the city's professional planners initially dismissed us as meddling amateurs, we hired a professional, Kathryn Madden, to present our ideas for landscaping the Greenway. We wouldn't have gotten anywhere without Madden, who was then a principal at Sasaki Associates and now has her own firm.

At that time plans for the Greenway were very much in flux. Boston was still mapping out the surface roads above the tunnel. One of them – Broad Street – nearly ended up right at our front door. "Why," I asked city planners, "extend Broad Street through the Greenway and break up a beautiful stretch of green into two traffic-bound islands?" Instead of a park, Rowes Wharf would have faced a traffic jam. The planners countered that merchants feared that without the extension drivers would pass right by Broad Street.

With the construction deadline just three weeks away, I enlisted architect Si Mintz, my then-Rowes Wharf neighbor, and Diane Rubin, the attorney for Harbor Towers. We met with every property owner on Broad Street. One of our fiercest foes owned a building located where Broad ends at State Street – you couldn't even see the Greenway from there. We managed to win over the other owners, though. We asked them, "Which would you rather see at the end of your street: a lot of traffic or a beautifully landscaped space?"

I didn't just argue aesthetics. I promised to join forces with the merchants and owners in their campaign to have the city spruce up Broad Street. Only days ahead of the bulldozer, we obtained the support of all the landlords except that one man at the far end of the street. The city canceled the extension. And later I delivered on the street improvements by pointing out their merits to the then-director of the BRA, Mark Maloney, who just happened to live at Rowes Wharf. A reinvigorated Broad Street became the starting point of his Crossroads Plan, connecting the city with the harbor. Everyone won – and, as a byproduct, I established a reputation in the area that would help in battles to come.

Another fight with City Hall involved our push for street parking in front of the Rowes Wharf entrance. Along with sidewalk spaces owned by the building, the curbside spots provide valets with sufficient room to accommodate owners who have requested in advance that their cars be fetched from the garage. Paul Saperstein deserves the credit for helping us cut through the red tape. He called someone he knew at the Boston Transportation Department, who then came up with a plan for Rowes Wharf to rent street parking. The proposal still had to survive a series of meetings, but I made sure to attend every one of them lest some bureaucrat shoot it down. Indeed, the agenda of every meeting included an item to scotch the parking agreement. I had a 102-degree fever at the final meeting that decided the matter once and for all. As far as I know, no other condo association has made such a deal with the city. The arrangement should last forever, provided no one forgets to pay the rent.

A SHOCK FROM THE ELECTRIC COMPANY

Early in my tenure as president, the electric company unwittingly helped me establish my credibility with the residents. One month, NStar, our service provider, sent us a bill for $56,000 for the cost of heating, cooling and lighting the front-lobby area. A typical bill would be $500 to $1,500 a month. When we protested, the utility responded that it had noticed a large surge in use about six months before, but just assumed a malfunctioning meter was to blame. Too busy to check out the meter, the company decided to bill based on average prior readings. After finally inspecting the meter and finding that it was working properly, NStar tallied up the cost based on the actual readings. When we investigated, we found that a thermostat had been mistakenly set to its highest level. As a result, the heating unit had been running all-out day and night. That in turn caused the air conditioning unit to kick in to keep the lobby at a comfortable temperature, further running up the bill. With one turn of the dial, we put everything back to normal.

I told Katherine to tell the company that we would not pay the bill. The company responded that we had no choice in the matter. It said that the charges were controlled by Department of Public Utilities, which did not allow for any adjustments. I countered that if the company had billed us correctly from the start, we would have rectified the problem immediately. I insisted that we were accountable for only the first month in question, plus the 10 days it normally took a bill to arrive. NStar wouldn't budge. Instead, the company held a hearing, at which it was represented by a young woman. The meeting got off to a bad start.

"Mr. Wyner, why are you so excited about these things?" the NStar attorney said, speaking to me as if I were a senile old man.

"I'm not excited," I said in as relaxed a voice as I could muster. "This is just wrong, and we're not going to accept a compromise of any kind. We'll take the matter to the DPU. If it insists that we pay you what you charged us, then I'll go to the Legislature and have a bill filed to change the law – even if it takes me years."

When she offered to split the difference, I said, "We're either right or wrong. This is the formula I have. You're either going to follow that formula or not. Compromise makes no sense."

The lawyer looked at me in amazement. Shortly after the meeting, NStar sent us a corrected bill for the exact amount that I had proposed.

My Segway and I became a familiar sight around town.

WIN SOME, LOSE SOME

Whenever I chair an organization, I try to avoid the appearance of pushing my own agenda. I see my role as helping others tease out the right decision. A good discussion helps people separate their feelings from the facts at hand. As I learned at Marriage Encounter, you can't argue with someone's feelings.

But there have been times when I wished I didn't have to bite my tongue. For example, while I was chair of the Wharf District Council, a city councilor came before us advocating a ban on Segways, the electric scooters designed for pedestrian areas. He was responding to complaints about Boston Segway Tours. The company, which was not connected with the makers of Segway, had failed to train its guides in common courtesy. Their tour parties zoomed along so fast that pedestrians felt intimidated.

As it happened, Genevieve and I were among the first owners of a Segway in Boston, a gift from our sons in January 2004. I was well known for using the Segway to go to meetings, taking it on the elevator at my bank and offering people rides all over the North End.

My fellow Wharf District Council members told me not to worry, that the ban would not apply to me. I said with some reticence that it seemed that it would indeed cover me. Still, I felt that I'd lose credibility as the chair if I engaged in the debate. Had I been simply a board member, I would have spoken up. In the end, promises were made – but not kept – to exempt private owners like myself. The tour operator, though, continued to run tours, amassing fines that so far as I know he never paid. Ever law-abiding, I put my Segway in storage. Oddly enough, Boston hasn't bothered to consider how Segway tours manage to operate successfully in 500 cities, from Paris to Shanghai.

In chairing boards, besides trying to remain impartial, I've sought to strike a balance between enforcing rules and not being straitjacketed by them. Once at Rowes Wharf we were asked to make an exception to a ban on renters having dogs. The prospective tenants had a 10-year-old dog with terminal cancer. They didn't want to abandon him in his final days. The wife sent me testimonials from neighbors about how the dog was wonderful and very quiet. I emailed all the members of the condo board about making an exception to the ban, attaching the testimonials. One trustee responded: "If only all of our residents were as well behaved and recommended." Another wrote: "Dog doesn't seem to be an issue, but do the renters bark?" The dog got a reprieve from the rules. Sadly, he died before the tenants moved in, but whenever I ran into them, they told me how grateful they were to be part of a community that showed it had a heart.

ONE LAST CHALLENGE

My last years of chairing the condo board were dominated by our efforts to keep Rowes Wharf looking fresh. We were concerned that our building was beginning to appear dowdy compared with all the new luxury condominiums sprouting up in Boston. As we had done for the makeover eight years before, I assembled a redecorating committee. Since this project was to be more extensive than the last, I was determined to appoint members who represented as wide a variety of viewpoints as possible. As I would learn, that was a mistake.

Committee members spent nearly a year just trying to agree on the selection of a design team. It took another year for them to present a consensus plan, which the owners then promptly and overwhelmingly rejected. At first, I was puzzled why the product of such a lengthy effort could be so far off the mark. But when I visited the committee co-chairs at their condos, I could see why. The decor of one home was highly traditional, and that of the other, modern minimalist. By that point I also realized that the problem wasn't just that their tastes were irreconcilable. With the real estate values of multimillion-dollar condos on the line, the job of redesigning the public face of Rowes Wharf was beyond the capabilities of a group of nonprofessionals, no matter how well-intentioned.

I needed to find a way to shift oversight to a small task force of the board without appearing to denigrate the committee's two years of study. When people invest so much of themselves in a project, they can't help but take personally how their ideas are received. I publicly thanked the committee for its work and stressed its success in setting the stage for the final design. With a much clearer idea of resident preferences, I formed an in-house team and engaged Jinnie Kim Design, a Boston-based company that had impressed us in a previous project at Rowes Wharf.

The other members of the in-house team were Sayed, whom as I already noted was a veteran of the hospitality industry; fellow owner Cynthia Carpenter, who chaired the previous redecorating project; and Katherine, who brought the same mix of diligence and diplomacy to the renovation effort that she displayed daily as our property manager.

While Jinnie and her staff managed the major design elements, our group took care of many of the smaller details. For example, while Jinnie a suggested a style for hallway sconces, we decided on the model and supplier. Since the four of us had different ideas about light levels, we used my hallway to put up various sconces on a trial basis. After two months, we settled on a fixture manufactured in China. But when Katherine and I took one last walk through the corridor, we noticed that the white plastic shades were turning yellow. When she touched one, it was so brittle that it cracked.

I consulted with an expert at a Shawmut division that makes similar materials for the US. lampshade industry. He explained that the traditional plastic used for shades did not stand up to the ultraviolet light emitted by low-wattage compact fluorescent bulbs that were quickly replacing incandescent bulbs to reduce power consumption. Although ultraviolet-resistant shades were coming onto the market, Cynthia had a better idea: Contact the California company that had made the sconces we had used in the previous redesign. The manufacture came up with a fixture much like the Chinese one, but with a glass shade. Not only was its product more elegant and durable, we would not be at the mercy of a supplier halfway around the world. Sometimes you just get lucky. If Katherine and I had not conducted that last inspection – and both been so fixated on details – we would have had the embarrassing and expensive job of replacing hundreds of sconces just a few months after completing the overall project.

In the end, while it had its inevitable detractors, the renovation was deemed a success. The residents felt they had been heard, and Jinnie Kim had fashioned a refreshing new look for Rowes Wharf that would secure its reputation as one of Boston's most desirable residences for many years to come.

The old man and the (icy) sea: I take my annual New Year's Day dip at Rowes Wharf.

HARBOR HIJINKS

While I noted earlier that it was rare for ordinary residents to show up at board meetings, they weren't shy about calling or emailing me about problems. I found that a prompt response was the best way to defuse tempers. In one case, the complaint concerned late-night booze cruises out of the Rowes Wharf public docks. To find out what the fuss was about, I stood by in the early morning hours when the boats returned. Sure enough, the crowds were rowdy and noisy. Many passengers were clearly drunk and possibly dangerous. I found a video on the Internet of the hell-raisers on one booze cruise. After I shared it with a contact at the BRA, he quietly arranged to put a stop to them – at least from our docks.

When it came to the harbor, I preferred more chilling experiences. Every New Year's, I would take a dip in the water at Rowes Wharf. Originally, I had intended to join the annual party at the L Street Bathhouse, but my pride changed my mind. I feared that if I chickened out at the last minute, my cowardice would have been preserved for posterity by the news photographers covering the event.

At first, I did my New Year's dips alone. In later years, the concierge on duty would show up on the pretense of snapping a photo – but I suspect that Katherine just wanted to make sure someone was looking out for me. Inevitably, the photo made the rounds among the residents. The fact of the matter is that braving the January waters isn't so hard; they were so frigid that my body quickly went numb. Indeed, I found those frigid dips easier than going into 65-degree water in the summer. I'll have to decide whether to keep up the tradition at our new home at NewBridge. It is on the Charles, after all.

BENCHED AT LAST

The decision to move to NewBridge was not easy. Genevieve and I loved living at Rowes Wharf. We loved waking up in the morning and looking out from our bed at a magnificent harbor view. We loved the people at Rowes Wharf. Though from many backgrounds, they formed a community united by mutual respect. We had none of the wild parties that plague other upscale places.

The staff members were like family. They spoiled us, such as the times when they would provide us with the amenities of room service from the hotel. I was energized by my workouts in the health club, encouraged by my long-time trainer, Sharon Donovan. And I've already spoken of the camaraderie of the condo board; the vigilance of Katherine McCabe Scott, the property manager; and the pleasure I took in forging strong working relationships on the Wharf District Council.

I doubted we would find such an array of experiences elsewhere. But it was time to move on. It had become increasingly difficult for Genevieve to get around the city. Dependent on a walker, she couldn't drive someplace, park and walk two blocks over curbs and such to her destination. I was happy and felt privileged to drive her, but in the back of our minds was the question of how we would manage if I developed mobility problems. We would then be prisoners in our wonderful Rowes Wharf home.

It was even more difficult, but heartwarming, when we announced that we were leaving. We received many sincere expressions of sadness. I knew I would be leaving the condo board in the good hands of Jim Shane, who had been vice president for nearly as long as I had been president. Behind my back, Jim and other condo board members, along with Katherine, ran a gauntlet of municipal red tape to obtain

HAVE I TOLD YOU ABOUT ...?

permission to erect a granite bench on a sun-splashed brick plaza that is part of the harbor walk. One day, I received a mysterious invitation to attend a ceremony. There, the bench was unveiled. On it is carved:

The Rowes Wharf community thanks Justin L. Wyner for his thoughtful and dedicated leadership.

I was never so moved. Every time I return to Rowes Wharf, I sneak out to just sit on that bench and think of the wonderful people who gave it to me.

My bench of honor at Rowes Wharf.

HOME AWAY FROM HOME

The Vineyard casts its spell on us, but even in paradise there can be trouble

IT TURNED OUT TO be a pivotal evening in our lives. After a day's sailing on Memorial Day weekend in 1997, we pulled into Martha's Vineyard and, as we often did, called Mary Ann and Stanley Snider about meeting us for dinner.

Stanley told us they were having a party that night and invited us to join them. In a sense, you might say we never left. We liked their house so much that Mary Ann offered to rent it to us the following summer for the two weeks they would be in Europe. They hadn't rented the house before, but were comfortable making an exception for us. That got us hooked on Vineyard living, especially after our kids told us they much preferred the house to being squeezed in on Seabiscuit, our sailboat. Since the Sniders' house would not be available again, we (after a lot of soul searching) bought one identical to theirs two doors down.

That party was also important because it introduced me to Dan Kaplan, a major figure in New York's legal, financial and Jewish organizational circles. He was president of the 92nd Street Y and of his condominium association at the Hampshire House overlooking Central Park. We instantly found much in common. He had known of me because of my work at the American Jewish Historical Society, and wasted no time telling me that as president I was going about things in the wrong way. He said the first thing I should do was not let anyone on the board who didn't contribute a minimum of $10,000 a year. "Why don't you come on the board and show me how it's done?" I challenged him. Not only did he join the board to prove his point, but he later became one of its greatest presidents. And the two of us became very good friends, as well as Vineyard neighbors.

Yen Chau tends to a Vietnamese ritual at the marriage of her daughter Giang to our son James.

Dan has a knack for coming up with a personal connection to everyone – and I mean everyone – he meets. He immediately came up with ties to Genevieve's father, Max, and her brother, Jack – and then found out that the parents of our brother-in-law Michael Greenfield used to play bridge with his parents. Just when we thought we'd never stump him, we introduced Dan to Yen Chau, the lovely mother of James' wife, Giang. Yen had escaped Vietnam with her husband, Dang Van Chau, and their family, settling in Paris in 1975. After just a brief conversation, Dan was certain that as a naval officer he had met Chau during the Vietnam War. Yen called her husband, who was in Texas visiting relatives. Chau confirmed that indeed he had met Dan. As harbormaster in Haiphong, Chau had come aboard Dan's ship to guide it upriver. Never again would I challenge Dan's gift for connection.

Both Dan and Stanley each figured in two major Vineyard institutions with which I became deeply involved: the Hebrew Center and Martha's Vineyard Hospital. Even on a vacation island, I would find myself, without seeking the role, playing Mr. Fix-It when problems arose at those institutions. And, in some cases, my good intentions would go awry.

Our drone's-eye view of our Vineyard home.

View of the back of our home.

SUMMERS AT THE TASHMOO

My first memories of the Vineyard are from 1939, when our family started spending about a month together each summer at the Tashmoo Inn at the corner of Tashmoo Avenue and Main Street in Vineyard Haven. The rambling building, which has since burned down, contained a huge dining room. Its facilities also included cottages and a little beach at the end of Owen Little Way.

We knew many if not most of the guests – Jewish families from Boston and Brockton. They included the Kivie Kaplan family; the Tarlows of the FootJoy shoe company in Brockton; Joe and Sadie Riesman and their sons, Bob and Gene; Dr. Charles Wilinsky (longtime Beth Israel Hospital director) and his family, including their son, Gene, and daughter Florence, who later married my mother's brother Harry (Goldberg) Gilbert; and Rabbi Beryl Cohon, who had recently formed Temple Sinai of Brookline after being passed over for the top job at Temple Israel.

One of the more unusual characters was Dr. William Liebman, an ophthalmologist. I'd see him at the beach every day reading *The New York Times* – not the current edition, but the one from the exact date of the year before. Each day he would select the appropriate paper from the trunk of his car to see, he said, "just how correct their reporting had been."

The innkeepers were Mr. and Mrs. Thomas Rabbitt. I got to know their children, Esther, and her younger brother, Tommy. Esther's future husband, Chester Cummings, used to ferry my father and me around the island in his small fishing boat when we competed in the annual striped bass derby, starting in 1945.

My favorite derby memory is of a midnight reconnaissance mission undertaken by my father, his business associate Ray Franks, and me. We drove around all the known fishing spots to see where the action was. When we stopped to chat with an old guy fishing off the Edgartown-Oak Bluffs bridge, Dad asked politely if he was catching anything. The old fellow ignored him. Hesitantly, my father repeated his question. The fellow jumped up and jerked on his rod. Then he turned to us in anger and said, "I have been fishing here for four hours without a strike, and you just distracted me from the only one I had all night."

My favorite seafood memory is of eating shellfish at the pier in Edgartown. We paid 15 cents a dozen for opened littleneck clams, 25 cents a dozen for cherrystone clams and 50 cents for a boiled lobster. (Yes, I know it wasn't kosher by traditional standards, but it was Wyner kosher.) It's amazing how in the past 75 years the price of a dozen opened raw clams has risen to $25. As I get older, I find it increasingly difficult to reconcile myself to current prices and resist recalling what they were when I was a boy. My first new Chevrolet in 1945 was $895!

UNITING THE JEWS

When I was 15 in the summer of 1940, Gene Wilinsky was 16 and had his driver's license. He took me on double dates with the Cronig girls, he with Shirley and I with June. The Cronigs were among the early Jewish settlers on the Vineyard, arriving before World War I. Their grocery story is still doing business. But as summer kids from Boston, I don't think we were totally trusted by the islanders. We had to take the girls' 11-year-old sister, Ruthie, along on our dates – an interesting variation on a chaperone. Decades later, when we were all in our 70s and 80s, I enjoyed renewing friendships with the Cronig sisters.

In those early days, most, if not all the social institutions on the island were deliberately or de facto restricted. Friends of my sister, Betty, from Beaver Country Day School invited us to dances at the Edgartown Yacht Club. When I accepted one of the invitations and escorted a girl from the Tashmoo Inn, I recall thinking that we might have been the first Jewish couple to grace the yacht club's dance floor.

Back then, the summertime Jews had limited interaction with the year-round Jewish families, the Cronigs, the Brickners, the Levines and the Issoksons. My family only knew them from shopping at their retail and grocery stores. But one large, united Jewish community emerged after 10 families, a mix of summer and year-round residents, purchased and modified a building to house the Martha's Vineyard Hebrew Center in 1940. Until then, Jews had worshipped as a minyan in the home of Samuel Cronig. The Hebrew Center hired Rabbi Maurice Zigmond – whom my family knew well from Harvard Hillel – as the Vineyard's first full-time summer rabbi.

After the Hebrew Center was established, everything began to change. With a prominent structure that everyone could see – in contrast with the minyan at Sam Cronig's that the non-Jews knew nothing about – relations with other clergy, churches and congregants began to flourish to the point where the Vineyard today has one of the strongest ecumenical communities that I have seen.

A COSTLY FAVOR

By the time Genevieve and I joined the Hebrew Center in 1998, the congregation had grown to 300 families, about half of whom lived on the island year-round. It had moved to new quarters three years before. Knowing my experience negotiating rabbinical contracts at Temple Israel in Boston, the then-president of the center, Herb Foster, asked me that year to help him work on a new contract for its rabbi, Joshua Platt, who would go from part time to full.

We had known Joshua before moving to the Vineyard. He had given the first talk in the lecture series that my family had endowed at Temple Israel, spending the night at our Brookline home. He was the son of a rabbi (Walter Plaut) and the nephew of another, W. Gunther Plaut, a prominent Torah scholar. When we moved into our Vineyard house, Joshua blessed our mezuzah and our home. We became friends with him and his wife, Laurie, an attorney, and their son, Jonas.

Joshua had been at the congregation for eight years, while also serving as chaplain at MIT. I had worked with him when I was among the organizers of the Hebrew Center's Summer Institute. I especially recall the program he created for us centered around a lecture on aging gracefully, presented by his Uncle Gunther, who had just written a book on the subject. Joshua invited clergy of various faiths from the Vineyard to attend the talk and bring along congregants whom they thought exemplified graceful aging. It was quite a moving experience. The ministers each introduced the couple or individual they had brought along, explaining why they had done so. Joshua presented each woman among the guests with a bouquet. It was an amazing example of the incomparable interfaith community of Martha's Vineyard.

For another program, Joshua invited Alan Dershowitz to speak about his 1999 novel *Just Revenge*, in which a Holocaust survivor decides to take the law into his own hands. The book was controversial, and some in the audience – who clearly hadn't read the book – spoke out against it. I had read it, and from the back of the floor rose to defend the famous lawyer. He responded with a laugh, "Thank you, Uncle Arthur," kiddingly implying I had been planted in the crowd.

Joshua had both ardent fans and foes among the congregation. When the Hebrew Center president asked me to negotiate the new contract, I suggested that he first make sure the board of trustees agreed with extending Joshua's term and converting his job to full-time. After consulting with the board, the president assured me of unanimous support. I still was skeptical, because the president who had originally hired Joshua was said to have called the decision the worst thing he'd ever done. But the new president insisted that his predecessor had changed his mind.

When I first talked with Joshua, he said, "I'd really like to stay here. We have just built a new house. We want to bring up our son here." He added that he wanted to go full-time, instead of coming in just once a month during the winter. Joshua, who was then paid $65,000 a year, pointed to colleagues of his with similar experience who were earning much more. Having served as a rabbi for 10 years, Joshua was eligible to take a pulpit at a large congregation off island where, under the guidelines of the Central Conference of American Rabbis, he could have earned $175,000 or more. He asked the Hebrew Center for $125,000, which I felt was quite reasonable. But when I presented his case to the leadership, I met with opposition. "That's offensive to ask for such a large salary," one of the leaders was said to have fumed. I later learned that this fellow hadn't really wanted to renew the contract in the first place, but had not wanted to be the lone opponent. Now he seized on the salary issue. He worked others up into such a lather that they essentially said of the rabbi: "We're so angry that he would ask for that amount of money, that we don't want to negotiate with him anymore. He's through."

When I reported back to Joshua, he said he was extremely anxious to stay. He said that if he could continue to work at MIT, he could accept $75,000. But the leaders wouldn't budge. Not only that, they weren't willing to pay any severance. A highly respected congregant, Sam Feldman, asked the leaders if they would at least give the rabbi a year's severance. He offered to come up with $30,000 from concerned congregants, provided the board authorized the rest. He then told me about the arrangement. I agreed to help. We figured we needed to find 15 people to donate $2,000 each. But then Sam said, "Here's my $2,000," and I was left to take things from there. Thus, what started out as my negotiating the rabbi's salary as a favor to the temple's president turned into the task of raising money for the severance package. I did manage to get 13 others to join us with $2,000 each. I think Joshua ended up getting $50,000, with the congregation as a whole chipping in $20,000 of it.

After a stint as executive director at the Center for Jewish History in New York, Joshua is now serving with tremendous success as executive director of the American Friends of the Rabin Medical Center. Fluent in Hebrew, he shuttles back and forth to Israel. He has enlisted such celebrities as Larry King to tout the hospital.

Martha's Vineyard Hebrew Center president Sally Cohn wraps me in a tallit as I receive a blessing for my 90th birthday from Rabbi Caryn B. Broitman at the congregation's Shabbat service on the beach.

For all its penny-pinching with Joshua, the Hebrew Center board found it had to pay his successor, Rabbi Caryn B. Broitman, $100,000 a year to start.

The Summer Institute I mentioned earlier grew out of a discussion organized by Stanley Snider. He invited a small group of our friends, including Dan Kaplan, to come up with a way to engage the large number of Jews, many of them prominent, who summer on the Vineyard. By tapping into this rich resource, Stanley pointed out, the Hebrew Center could contribute to the overall Vineyard community. He started out by sponsoring a Fourth of July celebration outside the Hebrew Center, and personally paid to have the grounds groomed and a tent erected.

Building on that program, Stanley and the rest of our group – four couples in all – launched a summer lecture series. Kate Feiffer, daughter of the cartoonist, did the PR. Billed as the Summer Institute, the Thursday night lectures packed the synagogue. Between sponsor contributions and the $10 donations at the door, the series proved to be a significant fundraiser for the Hebrew Center. Besides eight talks, it featured movies on Sunday nights in conjunction with the Boston Jewish Film Festival.

As we expanded to include speakers from off the island, we sought additional sponsors. As an incentive, we offered reserved seating in a special section to those who donated at least $1,000 toward the series. Many people became contributors just to make sure they'd get a seat.

But we had our growing pains. Some people who didn't like the rabbi objected that all the proceeds were going to the synagogue. Year-round members of the synagogue were upset that they weren't guaranteed admission, which exacerbated tensions between the locals and the more affluent summer residents. Several times I discreetly helped to curb emotions and forge compromises. For example, we agreed that the money from the gate would only go toward capital expenditures at the temple.

A HOSPITAL ON LIFE SUPPORT

The controversies at the synagogue pale when compared with those at the Martha's Vineyard Hospital. By the mid-'90s, the hospital was burning through its endowment to pay operating expenses and interest on bonds it had taken out to build the Windemere Nursing Home next door. William (Bill) Graham, son of the late *Washington Post* publisher Katharine Graham, helmed an emergency board charged with rescuing the hospital. After declaring bankruptcy and slashing costs, the hospital briefly returned to solvency. But then in 1999, contending that the hospital was veering off course, Graham jumped ship and predicted its sinking was imminent.

That's when Dan Kaplan recruited me to join an exceptional group of people on the hospital board of trustees. They included Sandy Ray, an insurance broker; Charlie Harff, a lawyer from Chicago who spearheaded the creation of Farm Neck Golf Club, an unusual public-private venture; a true World War II hero, Edgartown's selectmen chairman, Ted Morgan, who as a medic with the 82nd Airborne Division jumped into Normandy and under fire saved a wounded soldier; Arthur Smadbeck, also an Edgartown selectman and later board chairman; and Tim Sweet, who at the time was CEO of Farm Neck.

I don't have much competition in my age class in the annual MV 5K Walk/Run Race.

The most prominent member of the board was Dr. Louis Sullivan, secretary of Health and Human Services under the first President Bush. Lou came up with the idea of the annual MV 5K Walk/Run Race (it's now named for him) to inspire people to exercise more and to raise money for the hospital. I've entered the walk division for the last 15 years. While my golf drives may have gotten shorter, I have pushed myself so that I still maintain the same walking speed and finish in the top fifth. One fellow accused me of secretly running.

I served on the board for its three most critical years, 1999 to 2002. Previous boards had been hamstrung by grandstanding and finger pointing. Not so with our group. Despite all the turmoil, I enjoyed the experience. This may have been the only board of the many on which I've served where everyone hung in there and did their job.

Like its counterparts in other resort communities, the Vineyard hospital confronts a thorny staffing situation. It serves a population of 13,000 in the winter, 125,000 in the summer. Its union contract required that nurses be kept on staff year-round. We found that many of the nurses – who have little to do in the off-season – elected to take their vacations in the summer. Some of them took off as many as eight weeks. As a result, the hospital was spending more than $1 million on fill-in coverage. After bitter negotiations, we worked out a deal that limited nurses to two weeks' vacation and gave them a $1,000 bonus if they took all their vacation time in the off-season.

Personnel matters dominated many of our board meetings. Given how deeply disgruntled the staff had become, we could have easily dismissed a lot of the complaints as bellyaching. But we recognized that if we were going to make any progress, we had to have an open mind. So, we did a lot of listening. Having been brushed off by hospital leaders in the past, some of the doctors came to us with indignation burning in their eyes. They complained about inconsistent policies and standards of care; they said that the workload was unfairly distributed. Many of their complaints were justified. For example, we withdrew the privileges of one obstetrician who on many occasions had mishandled his duties.

There was one doctor on staff who was so embittered that some of my colleagues simply wanted to show him the door. I thought that would be mistake. I believed if I could peel away his resentment, I could not only win him over but also help him make his case. It was a matter of listening, which, ironically, was a big part of this doctor's specialty. Charles Silberstein is a psychiatrist whose practice included many patients struggling with drug and alcohol dependency. I spent hours with Charlie. He was cynical at first, but eventually came to see me as an ally. I addressed many of his concerns and persuaded board members to curb their criticism. But what I think mattered most to Charlie was feeling at last that someone cared about what he thought. Over the years, I have been pleased to see how both the hospital and the community have come to appreciate his dedication to treating addiction.

PASS THE SCALPEL

Much of the credit for the hospital's turnaround should go to Kevin Burchill, a veteran administrator whom we hired as CEO in 1999. The messy situation called for a hard-nosed, thick-skinned leader. Used to malleable directors, some people complained that Kevin was too abrasive. At times, I agreed – and I would tell him to be nicer.

Ultimately, the traits that served Kevin well in restoring the hospital to health set the stage for his departure, as the personnel disputes went public. The nastiest battle involved a surgeon widely admired by his patients, but considered a prima donna by many of his colleagues. Everything had to be his way. He'd refuse to take on-call assignments and limited his availability. His wife, who was on the hospital board, was caught in the middle. She found it hard to accept that her husband was so difficult. I used to give her a ride home from meetings, and she'd be in tears. Eventually, the doctor, rejecting our conditions, left the hospital to practice on the mainland. That triggered an uproar, and Kevin resigned not long afterward. The surgeon, by the way, returned to the hospital – by then having divorced his wife.

It didn't help matters that the hospital already had been battered by hostile coverage from the *Vineyard Gazette*. Every week, it seemed, the *Gazette* carried a story about the board's supposed mismanagement of the hospital and how it was teetering on bankruptcy. The only times we got a reprieve were when the ferry had mishaps, crowding us out of the news. Several of us attributed the bad press to the close friendship between *Gazette* editor Julia Wells and Bill Graham. Our board had pulled the hospital out of bankruptcy, despite Bill's declaration that it was beyond saving. Perhaps Julia, sensitive to Bill's feelings, thought that positive news about the hospital would reflect badly on her friend.

Since the hospital was so misrepresented in the press, I suggested to my board colleagues that we hold regular public meetings to listen to complaints. The board wisely decided to hold them at different venues around the island. Genevieve and I would go down to the Vineyard every month for them. Those visits led to us becoming even more involved in the community.

Besides getting grief from the *Gazette,* we had to contend with the wrath of Massachusetts General Hospital. The Vineyard hospital worked closely with MGH, sending serious emergency cases to the Boston hospital unless patients requested otherwise. An MGH staff radiologist worked full-time at the Vineyard hospital X-ray room. For the arrangement, MGH received $250,000 a year from the hospital and all the radiologist's charges to the patients.

When the MGH sought a steep increase in our annual payment, I suggested that the hospital look at alternatives. I talked with Paul Levy, who was then head of Beth Israel Hospital, about putting digital equipment in the Vineyard hospital that would allow BI doctors to read X-rays remotely any time day or night. It would have been a win-win, opening the way for Beth Israel to get many of the referrals then going to MGH. Beth Israel was prepared to buy all the necessary equipment, without any charge to us. Since we'd no longer have to rent a radiologist, we'd save a quarter of a million dollars a year. It proved too good to be true.

At the last minute, MGH chief Peter Slavin got wind of the deal. Slavin threatened that if the Vineyard hospital didn't renew its contract immediately, at an increased cost, MGH would abruptly pull out its radiologist. A hospital can make do temporarily without some of its specialists, but not without a radiologist. No one can predict when the next emergency patient will arrive. So MGH got its way. Not that we should have been surprised; the hospital has a reputation for playing hardball. But on the upside, the MGH connection has enabled the hospital to provide the community with a full array of services. In addition, the partnership helped us to go on as planned to build a state-of-the-art building. (Today, both hospitals are owned by Partners HealthCare.)

Charlie Harff and Dan Kaplan banished the last big cloud over the hospital's finances. In renegotiating the bonds on Windemere Nursing Home, they exceeded everyone's expectations by reducing our debt burden to an almost inconsequential amount.

I left the hospital board in 2002 after we voted to make Tim Walsh the CEO. We had originally brought him to the hospital as its first truly competent CFO. Just as Kevin was suited to righting the ship, Tim has been the perfect person to keep it on an even keel. He has made the finances transparent and repaired relations with the staff. He reached out, and people loved him for it.

'MR. WYNER, DON'T YOU WORRY'

I have one more story relating to the hospital – and this time it's from the perspective of the emergency room, not the boardroom.

In summer 2004, Genevieve tripped in the living room of our Vineyard house and conked her head against a coffee table. The next morning, she felt her balance was off and fell out of bed. I took her to the hospital ER. After viewing her X-rays, the doctors reported that she had broken her neck and required treatment in Boston ASAP. I wanted to join her in the Oak Bluffs Fire Department ambulance for the ride to the city, but the rescue squad said regulations wouldn't allow that. Seeing my distress, an EMS squad member approached me and said, "Mr. Wyner, don't you worry. When I was at Stoughton High School, your father gave me a job and everyone else in my class who wanted one. I will never forget it. I'll take care of your wife. I'll be with her the whole time." Hearing that confirmed the credo that I have followed all my life: If you follow your own heart and do the right thing, things will work out for you in the end.

In Boston, surgeons fused several of Genevieve's vertebrae and inserted two rods between the back of her head and her vertebrae. That limited how much she could move her head. Six months later, she found that she could turn her head more widely. But when she did so, we heard a clicking sound. Her doctor said that the rods had broken. He wasn't worried, though. He said the clicking sound would eventually stop, and that the rods would stay in place without need for further surgery. So far, so good.

UNWELCOME ADVICE

One place where I – or at least my advice – was not welcome was Edgartown Town Meeting. Because Boston politics are such a mess, I decided to register to vote on the Vineyard. Edgartown has an open Town Meeting, which means any registered voter can participate.

At my first Town Meeting, the big controversy was over renovating and expanding the library. As I recall, the state was willing to reimburse 85 percent of the first $5 million and something like 40 percent of the next $5 million. The library board favored the plan, but some town officials opposed it. In presenting the proposal at Town Meeting, those officials led residents to believe that if the project exceeded $5 million, the reimbursement would revert to 40 percent of the *entire* cost.

When the moderator failed to correct this misinterpretation, I stood up and suggested that town counsel be consulted. No one there knew my background in Brookline. And since I was not known to many year-round residents, I was pretty much disregarded.

I suspect that opponents of the building plan had no interest in clearing up the confusion. Voters rejected the project, and I have yet to return to Town Meeting. It wasn't worth the frustration or the special trip in spring from Boston.

But there is a happy ending to the library story: Several years later Town Meeting voted to build a library at a location that allowed for more parking and was near a public school. Today, it's a bustling community hub.

I'm now involved with many more organizations on the Vineyard than I am in Boston. We've joined two clubs: the Boathouse, which has a workout facility, spa, tennis courts, lap pool and two restaurants; and the Farm Neck Golf Club, which is mixed both ethnically and economically. Membership is heavily discounted for year-round residents.

Stanley Snider organized a Wednesday morning men's discussion group at Farm Neck. As many as 35 of us attend, including Harvard Business School professors, the former head of Merck pharmaceuticals and a world-renowned expert on earthquakes. One of us prepares a talk for each meeting. I once spoke about the fence and wall separating Israel from the West Bank.

Inspired by the men's group, the women – including Genevieve – formed their own. Its members, too, are professors, doctors and other high achievers. Sometimes, their meetings sound more interesting than ours. Why we don't just combine our groups is beyond me.

EEE-I-EE-I-O

Surprisingly for a suburban gal from New Rochelle, New York, Genevieve has taken a special interest in the Farm Institute, which was founded to keep the Vineyard's agricultural tradition alive. Originally, the institute leased land near Edgartown. Then a larger plot next to the Katama Airport became open after several farmers in succession failed to make a go of it on the town-owned land. When the institute announced its interest in moving to the property, some neighbors became very vocal in their opposition. They thought the land should be used only for recreation. Genevieve, who knew some of the players, brought everyone together for a powwow on our front porch. She encouraged the neighbors to talk about their concerns, such as traffic and public access, and helped the institute representatives come up with possible solutions. In the end, everyone went home happy, and shortly later Genevieve joined the institute board.

The Farm Institute, which leases its land from the Conservation Commission, has become a popular addition to the community. In summer, the institute hosts 1,000 kids at a day camp. Our grandchildren, who occasionally stay with us for several weeks during the summer, have attended. Several years ago, our then 10-year-old granddaughter, Lam An, signed up for a program called From Farm to Table. She had to get her parents' permission, because some children find part of the process to be a bit gruesome. We worried about how Lam An would react. But afterward she put our minds at ease, speaking thoughtfully about her assignment to calm the chicken before it was carefully slaughtered.

As I write this chapter, the future of the Farm Institute is being secured. Genevieve and the other institute leaders have agreed to step down and turn the farm over to the Trustees of Reservations, a state-wide conservation organization.

WE BECOME CHARACTERS

Looking back on what I've written, I fear I may have left the impression that life on Martha's Vineyard is full of rancor. Yes, passions can run high, as in any other small community, but day to day what strikes me is the island's spell over its residents and visitors. All over, people smile and open their doors to visitors. While there certainly is a great span economically between the year-round residents and the well-heeled summer folks, few flaunt their wealth or celebrity. No one makes a fuss when they see a famous face at the grocery store or a restaurant. Once when we were in our dinghy pulling up to the public dock in Vineyard Haven, a fellow offered to grab our line. It was Mike Wallace.

The one time of year when the rich and famous stand out is at the annual auction to support MV Community Services, which helps elderly and low-income people. For a $25 entry fee, anyone can watch the spectacle of icons like the late Walter Cronkite and Carly Simon trying to outbid each other. And if Carly wasn't bidding, she was offering to serenade you while strolling the beach – that opportunity went for something like $85,000. For many years, the humor columnist Art Buchwald was the auctioneer, saving one of his zany hats as the last item. After his death, the auction was never quite the same.

When a friend of ours, Jim Shane, served as chairman of the auction, I felt we should join in to support his efforts. With a bid of $3,500, we won the chance to be characters in the next mystery by the prolific local mystery writer Philip R. Craig. The prize also included lunch with the author, but he died before we could meet him. Instead, we went for tea with his wife and son. She told us that they were just finishing up one of her husband's books and hadn't yet decided which characters would take our names. I said I'd rather not be a dog or a murderer. In *Vineyard Chill,* Genevieve and Justin Wyner are avid conservationists who live next door to the scene of the crime. Someone called me a while back to say, "I just read this book by Philip Craig and you're in it!"

Gathering on Martha's Vineyard for our 50th wedding anniversary. Clockwise from Genevieve and me are our sons' families: James and Giang, with their children, Oliver and Lam An: Daniel and Lorna, with their daughter, Madelyn; and George and Barbara, with their children, Samuel and Hannah.

PART IV: BUSINESS WORLD

- **University of Shawmut:** Learning the hard way, on the job

- **My underwear is showing:** Running my first factory

- **Going South:** Expanding Vanta to Georgia, the Caribbean

- **The ugly side of the South:** Trying to sidestep segregation

- **Justin's ark:** My sideline in unsinkable sailboats

- **Shawmut transformed:** Perfecting lamination

- **A close call:** Nearly going down with Duplan's ship

- **The car guys:** The road to our future goes through Detroit

- **Our oasis in West Bridgewater:** A factory in the woods

- **Funny business:** Furniture fraud, shifty pols

UNIVERSITY OF SHAWMUT

Tossed into the deep water, I avoid a $100,000 soaking

TARGET PRACTICE WITH B-29 gun turrets or work in a textile mill?

That was the choice I faced when I graduated from Tufts in June 1945. The Nazis had surrendered just a few months before, and the war with Japan was nearing its climax, rendering my previous plan to enlist as an officer obsolete. By the time I finished training, America would likely be at peace.

Meanwhile, the war had come to Tufts. The Army had commissioned the psychology department to evaluate a projection system that simulated air-to-air gunfights. How well did people trained through the simulator stack up against seasoned combat pilots? During my last semester at Tufts, I had worked part-time on the planning stage of the simulator. After I graduated, I was offered a full-time job. It was tempting: I could have target-practiced with an actual B-29 gun turret.

But I never did have my "12 O'Clock High" moment. My father talked me into a full-time job at the plant. He offered me $100 a month, compared with the $65 I could earn at Tufts. And, appealing to my patriotism, he said, "We're doing more important stuff for the war effort at the factory."

What the important stuff was I still can't say for sure. As I've described earlier, one of my jobs as a teenager was the laborious task of tying parachute cords used for bombs. After the atomic bombs were dropped on Hiroshima and Nagasaki in August 1945, rumors circulated that they drifted to earth beneath parachutes Shawmut had manufactured. But I must emphasize that those were rumors.

I'm now officially in business, as captured in this Bachrach studio portrait.

BATTLES ON THE HOMEFRONT

The military virtually commandeered Shawmut for war production, allowing us to continue only limited manufacturing for the civilian market. Besides parachutes, we made knitted wool blankets for the Army and Navy, and Army field jackets.

With the Japanese surrender, the military abruptly switched off the nation's gigantic war machine. My job was to wrap up contracts with our wartime suppliers. Some of them put profits ahead of patriotism. As soon as they received cancellation notices, the dyers threw all the fabric into the dye kettles, and other suppliers did whatever they could to show that our orders were already in production. That way they could demand payment for the finished products, not just the cost of their raw materials. Most galling was the company that had provided us specialized sewing machines for making parachutes. Squeezed by wartime deadlines, we had been forced into a three-year lease. The total amount we were due to pay exceeded by several times the actual value of the equipment. By the time we were about to put the machines on line, the Japanese had surrendered. The company refused to suspend the lease, demanding that we pay the full three-year lease amount. In effect, the company exploited our failure to anticipate Hiroshima.

Meanwhile, the government was dragging its feet in paying our bills. After waiting months, my father hired a politically wired attorney, Joe Mulhern. Together, they went down to the Pentagon to see the officer in charge of supply. As my father tells the story, Mulhern wasn't the least bit intimidated by the guy's giant office. "Listen, general, you goddam son of a bitch, you've got to take care of my client. He's been left hanging here," Mulhern said. Stunned by the lawyer's language, my father pulled him aside and said, "You can't talk to a general that way." Mulhern responded: "He's a general, isn't he? He can take it. And he's the one to make the decision. You hired me to straighten this out, and I'll talk to him any way I have to."

The lawyer's tactics worked; the general guaranteed payment in full. My father and I were both surprised that the general hadn't tossed the lawyer out on his ear. But, then again, he did get results. We were out of our league with the Pentagon brass, but Mulhern knew how to play the game. Perhaps the general had dealt with Mulhern before and was accustomed to his coarse language. Fortunately, we were never in a position where we needed to consider hiring Mulhern or someone like him again. I'm sure we wouldn't have, though. We wanted the people who represented us to reflect our manner of doing business.

I suppose in retrospect I appear naïve to have been astonished by unscrupulous behavior in business. But remember where and how I was educated. I'm not talking about the classrooms of Tufts or Harvard, but the factory floor and offices at Shawmut – and the mobile classroom that was our car when my father and I commuted together from home for the decade before I got married and moved out. While business school graduates today covet Wall Street jobs where they can earn millions by making nothing, I was motivated by my father's pride in raising industry standards with the quality of our products and making it possible for hundreds of employees to lead comfortable lives. RH – as we all called him on the factory floor – was not just my dad, but my pal and my lifelong professor. His most important lesson: Your word is your bond. If you break it once, you will never be able to piece it back together.

ROOTING OUT RIPOFFS

The University of Shawmut had no formal curriculum. Far from it. My father basically set me loose in the factory to find my own role. He wanted me to learn the business from the ground up, just as he did. And he made clear to all the factory workers that I was to receive no special treatment. But I wasn't one to just wander around. I needed a purpose, a sense of making a concrete contribution. What first caught my attention was that while the company was systematic in the way it procured the raw materials for fabric, it was lax about purchasing other supplies. As a result, some suppliers would ship us three times as much as we had ordered – and we'd pay for it all. I stopped doing business with the worst offenders, finding that they were little better than thieves. I looked at quality as well as quantity. Was the shipping paper we used to wrap fabric the appropriate weight and grade? I checked around to see what others in the industry used. I scrutinized even routine purchases, from twine and tape to cleaning supplies.

But I had enough sense to realize that I couldn't just waltz in and change everything. When I set out to buy parts for the knitting machines, I asked the operators what they needed. They reminded me of what my father had said: that I had to learn the equipment for myself. I started up one of the machines and smashed a bunch of needles, but I eventually got the hang of it.

One of the first big challenges my father handed me was scouting out equipment, such as this multiple-feed, high-speed circular knitting machine.

I had much to learn about people as well as machines. For instance, the quality and size of thread was traditionally indicated by the color on top of the cone. Once one of our suppliers inexplicably decided to change the color coding. Our workers insisted that the thread was inferior. Understandably, they were wary of the slightest change in procedures that had been honed over decades. They refused to believe the supplier's claims that only the coding, not the thread, was different. Perhaps it was a case of mind over matter, but the machine operators could not adjust to the new color scheme. I finally insisted that the supplier take back the cones and rewind the thread onto cones with tips that matched the previous color coding. After that, lo and behold, the thread met with the workers' approval. The new coding system may have made sense to the supplier, but it didn't to the customer, namely our machine operators. That experience taught me an important lesson: You can't ignore people's feelings, no matter how irrational they may seem. People aren't machines, after all.

Greed thwarted one change I tried to implement. From talking with dye manufacturers, I realized we were vastly overpaying for supplies. Our dyers were receiving kickbacks from dyestuff jobbers who would use salt to dilute the expensive powder that they purchased in bulk from the manufacturers and resold to local dye rooms. To get the color depths we wanted, we had to use twice as much dye as would have been necessary if it had been pure. I tried to circumvent the middlemen by buying dyes directly from the manufacturer. However, our chief dyer had a vested interest in undermining my efforts; after all, he was losing out on kickbacks. He manipulated the dyeing process so that we ended up with mounds of streaky cloth. He told my father it was my fault because he had to use the dyestuffs that I had insisted on purchasing. My father and I decided that while we might be able to win this battle, we'd risk losing a very expensive war. We'd be hard-pressed to stop the dyer from continuing to sabotage the process. Almost every dyer in the industry was accustomed to receiving large gifts from jobbers. Later, though, when we set up a plant in Georgia, I found a head dyer who wasn't in on the scam.

An impromptu gathering of Shawmut office staff before the December 1945 holiday break: I'm in the back row at the far left. To my immediate right are Joseph Epstein, the production manager, with whom I shared (and fought over) a double desk; and my father, Rudolph Wyner.

DESKTOP DIPLOMACY

I had better luck in one of my other early games of office politics. I shared an old-fashioned double lawyer's desk with Joe Epstein, one of the sons of the owner of a contract garment plant that Shawmut had bought out in the 1930s. We sat opposite each other, a huge expanse of desktop in between. Joe, a graduate of Harvard Business School who was about 10 years my senior, excelled at managing the garment manufacturing, but not at managing the paperwork that piled up on his desk. Since he never seemed to file anything, the stacks inevitably spilled over to my side of the desk. When I protested, he insisted that he needed every scrap at his fingertips. Surreptitiously, I kept track of what he bothered to touch in the piles nearest me. Discovering that he never bothered with many of the papers, I began to remove them, one pile a week. I stashed them in a file cabinet. If he had ever asked about a missing paper, I could have found it for him – but he never did. After six months, I had pretty much straightened up the desk. The quiet approach worked. Joe just didn't like being told what to do.

My father put a surprising amount of trust in me as his novice purchasing agent – and it nearly cost us $100,000. A New York company announced that it had developed a knitting machine that would dramatically boost production by increasing the number of yarns feeding into it. If, say, you have 16 feeds, a machine will make 16 stitches – an inch of cloth – every revolution. If the machine has 64 feeds – as many of ours did – it will produce four inches per revolution. This breakthrough machine was advertised as handling 128 feeds.

I went down to New York to check it out. After answering a couple of questions, the company owner decided that I wasn't worth his time. "Why should I talk to you? You don't know anything about knitting machines," he told me. "You're still wet behind your ears. Send your father down." He was riding high on favorable notices in the trade press.

Trying to conceal my nerves, I said if he wanted to do business with us, it would have to be with me. I told him that I was authorized to buy the machine if I found it satisfactory. Getting nowhere, I asked to borrow a phone. I called Sidney Mishkin at Supreme Knitting Machine Company in Brooklyn. Supreme had supplied all our 64-feed machines over the years. After I explained the situation, Sidney said he'd pick me up and show me what his company was developing. He, too, had a 128-feed machine, but it wouldn't be ready for another six months. It was worth the wait. I later learned that the other company had to take back just about every machine it had sold because the needles kept smashing together.

MY FIRST COMPANY

On the spur of the moment, my father devised another crash course for me. Just after I completed business school, he presented me the opportunity to put theory into practice. He hatched the plan as we were making our monthly Saturday visit to the cutters and dressmakers who bought our fabrics. Most had offices at 600 Washington Street in Boston, just north of Chinatown. Justin Nevins, who specialized in making coats and women's suits, told us he wanted to buy a particular type of flannel. "Why don't we let Jerry form a company and get someone to weave and finish it," my father suggested. And suddenly I was in business.

The first step was obtaining the wool yarns. After the sheep is sheared, experts sort out the various grades. Most valuable are the long, soft and very fine diameter fibers from the belly area. They go into worsted yarns, such as for men's tailored suits. The shorter, coarser fibers are used to make woolen yarns, such as for a Harris Tweed jacket. Flannel was made from worsted yarn. Phil Brauer, Shawmut's wool buyer, helped me buy yarn made out of the correct grade of wool and contract with a weaver in Connecticut to make the cloth. I had the cloth dyed and finished at Morschner Dye Works in Needham. I then inspected the final product before shipping it off to Nevins, with whom I kept in regular contact to make sure he was satisfied. The little business, which lasted for a year and a half, didn't make a lot of money, but it gave me valuable experience in smoothing out production problems, limiting waste, managing inventory, overseeing quality control and handling customer relations.

I didn't have long to wait before I was faced with my first big challenge.

MY UNDERWEAR IS SHOWING

In which I run my first factory, get our photo in Life and fall in love with Lucy

A GRADUATE OF BOSTON LATIN, the public school rival to my Roxbury Latin, paved the way for a pivotal stage of my career – 14 years before I was born.

George Frederick Earnshaw founded the Earnshaw Knitting Company in 1911. The father of six, he undoubtedly had more than a professional interest in infant wear. At the time, shirts were designed so that toddlers put their arms through holes, and the garments were secured with buttons or safety pins in the back. They were not very comfortable, but pullover shirts present a problem for tots. Since babies' heads are disproportionately large, a neck opening would have to be so wide that the shirt would fall off. Earnshaw introduced a double-breasted knit shirt for infants that was fastened by tying tape in the back into cute little bows. No more risk that baby would swallow buttons or be stabbed by pins.

When he started hearing complaints that the tape curled up after being washed, Earnshaw patented a "twistless tape." He incorporated his innovations into a variety of infants' garments that he sold under the Vanta label. Legend has it that the name came from his overhearing an immigrant woman say, "I vanta best clothes for my bambino." Another story has it that Earnshaw got the name from an immigrant store owner who pointed to the success of the brand Uneeda Biscuit and suggested playing off the phrase "I vant a vest."

OK, so what does this have to do with me? After World War II, Shawmut salesmen convinced my father that the company could capture a larger share of the children's clothing market – both in department stores and in the 10,000 or so independent infant clothing shops – if we were to add a line of children's knit underwear. They wanted to take on the giant in the field, Needham-based William Carter Company. Shawmut's McKem line had already earned an outstanding reputation for its polo shirts, rib-neck pullovers, knit shorts and snowsuits. In fact, our snowsuits, which were made from our own knitted wool Melton fabric, were so durable that large families would hand the garments down from one child to the next. Customers would send us snowsuits that had already been passed down twice, requesting that we add a gusset so that they would fit a third, chubbier child. We'd proudly do so at no cost, though we drew the line when the garments came in soiled.

The quickest way for us to enter the underwear business was to buy an existing company. Since the death of its owner, Earnshaw Knitting Mills had been struggling. Its Vanta plant in Newton was kept on life support by Brookline Savings Bank, which was overseeing Earnshaw's estate. Recognizing its potential, my father arranged for Shawmut to purchase Vanta in 1948 to create McKem-Vanta. My Uncle Murray Wyner of McKem was placed in charge of sales, and shortly after I graduated from business school, my father assigned me to run the factory.

HUMAN NATURE AND THE HIJACKED CRANE

The passenger sitting next to me on the flight to Washington was shaking his head in amazement.

He just couldn't believe what had just happened in his construction business. A piece of equipment had gone missing: a giant crane worth $750,000. It had been sitting at a building site when a flatbed trailer-truck drove up. A man in a business suit hopped out and directed the site superintendent to have the crane loaded onto the trailer. The man said that he had orders to take the crane to another site. Impressed by the man's official demeanor and executive-style dress, the superintendent did as he was asked. The crane hasn't been seen since.

My seatmate said that his superintendent admitted he was duped because the man looked to be important and spoke with authority. "Now my crane is gone forever," he said.

The saga of the hijacked crane got me thinking. Would my employees be so easily fooled? When I returned to our Brockton factory, where I was based for a time in the '50s, I decided to conduct a little experiment. I had a corner office with its own outside entrance. Seeing two new McKem-Vanta salesmen approaching the building, I waved them over. Since no one else in the building had yet met them, they were perfect for the job I had in mind. I gave them these instructions: Go through the main entrance, breeze past the receptionist and stride through the plant as if you own the place. Climb up to the shipping area on the second floor, and instruct the workers that you've come to collect 10 boxes of this and 10 of that.

Shortly later, the two salesmen returned to my office with all the boxes. My little con had gone off without a hitch – sad to say.

Afterward, I stopped by the shipping room and asked the workers how they could just give away our merchandise to a pair of strangers. Just as with that building-site superintendent, they had done as they were asked because the visitors had acted as if they knew what they were doing.

It just goes to show how much you can get away with if you just behave in an authoritative way. I've resorted to this tactic myself at a hotel or restaurant when something goes awry and the staff reacts with indifference. Once when dining out, I noticed spilled food congealing on the floor. I went up to a waiter and told him to get three people over to clean the mess up. "Yes, sir," he said without hesitation. I guess he just needed somebody to take charge.

GETTING MY FEET WET – AND BURNT

So far as Vanta's workforce was concerned, I was in charge. I don't believe my father visited the plant more than once. He didn't want to undermine my authority. He felt confident enough to let me make my own mistakes and learn from them. Along with representatives of other Shawmut affiliates, I updated my father each week at a Monday morning conference in Stoughton.

When we took over, the Vanta factory was located on California Street, not far from Watertown Square. It was run by a bank representative, Benjamin Boynton, who knew little if anything about the apparel business. Among the first things I did was to meet individually with each of the 50 or so front-office workers to find out what they did. A typical exchange would go like this: The employee would say he was responsible for keeping such-and-such report. "Really," I'd say. "I haven't seen that report. When was the last time anybody looked at it?" And he'd reply, "Mr. Boynton looked at it two years ago at Christmas time." I got the impression, sadly, that we could clear out almost the entire front office, and the factory would keep humming.

One of the first steps we took was closing the Newton plant. We moved all the employees in the cutting and sewing operations to smaller quarters on River Street in Waltham, less than a mile away. We relocated the accounting and shipping departments to spare space at our Robison Rayon plant in Pawtucket. We moved the knitting machines to our Stoughton knitting plant and accommodated Vanta's dyeing and bleaching operations with the existing equipment at our Stoughton dye house. The finished fabric was then trucked up to Waltham for cutting and sewing.

At Shawmut, many of the workers had watched me grow up; I was a known quantity. But at Vanta I had to prove myself. I made it a priority to win the trust of the workers, most of whom were of Italian background and had been with Vanta for decades. Women ran the sewing machines; men cut the material. I spent a lot of time on the floor getting to know them all. When introducing industrial engineering techniques that we had honed at Shawmut, I made it a point to stress that no one would be laid off. While I didn't expect them to work harder, I told them, I did want to find ways to make production more efficient. I wanted them to understand that everyone would benefit. They could see the pressure we were under. We had to become more competitive just to stay in business, not to mention expand our market share.

My father had taught me that a factory makes its money out on the floor, not in the office. I didn't just poke my head around; I learned how to operate both the cutting and the sewing machines. I can't claim to have become an expert – that takes years of practice – but I was proficient enough to teach new employees when we opened other factories. I also got to know the other jobs at the plant and on occasion worked the evening shift.

One frigid night, after we had consolidated production at a plant on Clifton Avenue in Brockton, I drove the snowplow to clear the parking lot. Back inside, after about two hours out in the truck in freezing weather, I put my feet up on the radiator. "Watch out! You'll burn your feet," the foreman barked. It was a good thing he warned me. The cold had numbed my feet; I could have roasted my heels to a crisp. The evening shift would sometimes find me down on my knees on the factory floor trying to fix a jammed machine. I pretty much taught myself how to repair all the equipment.

I was always looking for ways to save money, such as the time I purchased a surplus army truck sight unseen at an auction. I had gone up to Fort Devens beforehand and picked out 15 potential trucks. I figured that I didn't need to check out any others, but was surprised when auto dealers at the auction quickly outbid me on my entire list. Not wanting to pass up a potential bargain, I bid on a truck I hadn't inspected – and won. When I went to pick it up, I didn't take any chances. I took along a mechanic with a tow truck and an Army major, the brother of one of our executives, Phil Brauer. To my great relief, we found that the truck was in working order and good condition. However, it was missing its cover and all the supporting ribs, among other parts. The major – who had no official authority at Fort Devens – ordered soldiers at the base to scavenge other trucks for parts. Nobody questioned his command, and we left with a complete truck.

OUR STUDENT BRAIN TRUST

Shortly after we took over Vanta, Northeastern University approached me about hiring co-op students from its engineering department. It was at the dawn of the co-op program that has become the hallmark of the university. At first, I was reluctant, because the students would cycle in and out every three months. But school officials persuaded me that the program would work if two students alternated over a year in the same full-time position. In the end, we had two or three co-op students working for us at a time. We paid them 75 cents an hour, the same as for a filing clerk. But they quickly proved they were worth much more than that.

Most of them were about 19, but one of the first, Bernie Kaufman, was a former Army captain who had left the service when he was in his 30s to get a degree. I started him out filing, but the next thing I knew he was out on the factory floor making suggestions. Bernie exemplified one of my father's maxims: If you put your shoulder out to take on a job, people will always be around to offload something onto it – and if you do a good job, people will keep dropping more on your shoulder. You don't need a title. People will let you do what you want; after all, it means less work for them.

The Waltham plant, in effect, became a lab for me to try out lessons that I had learned at Harvard and that Bernie and his fellow interns were then studying at Northeastern. We were particularly interested in conducting time, motion and method studies. Attaching three stopwatches to a clipboard, we broke down the workers' routines into their component steps and timed them. We identified which employees had hit upon the most efficient ways of performing each particular element of a given task. In effect, we compiled a manual of best practices. Slower workers could then learn from faster ones. We also sought ways to position the material and the machines more efficiently, both for the operators' comfort and to streamline the work flow. For example, if a woman could sew 1,200 bottom hems a day, we had her feed her work to two operators who could each finish 600 collars a day. That approach later became common in sewing factories elsewhere, but for its time our thinking was on the cutting edge.

From reading business journals, I got the idea of using music to smooth out the work flow. Researchers had observed that productivity tended to slow down during the hour or so before lunch, then rise in the early afternoon before falling once again. They suggested that playing music for brief periods would have the same invigorating effect as giving employees an actual break. Muzak had been in business for several decades, but it had yet to become as ubiquitous as it is today. I dove into my own record collection, seeking to strike the right balance between music that was so soothing it would lull people to sleep and selections that were so rhythmic that they would disrupt work routines. For about 20 minutes, at 11 a.m. and then again at 2 p.m., I'd spin records by Benny Goodman and other Big Band leaders. You can add disc jockey to my resume. And the music really did improve productivity.

Our workers were paid on a piece basis, meaning the more they produced, the more money they took home. In devising an incentive pay system, we had to take account of the fact that workers varied in their abilities, and that some tasks were simply more time-consuming than others. We found that for workers to respond to an incentive program, they had to see an opportunity to earn at least 15 percent more. The most motivated workers would earn up to 25 percent more. Setting the incentives required fine tuning. If they were too liberal, some workers would earn so much that everyone else would feel the system was stacked against them. We had to build in rewards for the person of average dexterity, but still recognize the exceptional operators. One woman achieved double the output of anyone else doing the same task. Her job was to put labels on two sides of a garment. Normally, the procedure required stopping the machine, but she had developed a fluid rhythm that allowed her to manipulate the material without taking her foot off the pedal. She was such a marvel that a major Boston sewing machine maker, the Reece Buttonhole Machine Company, would send over employees to study how she operated its equipment in a way they hadn't known was possible.

But while many of the tasks were repetitive, the factory was nothing like the frenetic operation depicted in Charlie Chaplin's *Modern Times*. The work required skill, precision and the flexibility to adjust to different materials and clothing styles. Next time you see a striped shirt, look at how well the patterns match up.

Streamlining doesn't work for everything. We had opened a mill store at the Waltham factory to sell seconds and quality rejects. It did phenomenal business, but the place was a mess. It made the closet of a typical teenager look organized. I figured we could boost sales even more by making it easier for people to find what they wanted. The result: People stopped coming. Shoppers apparently equated mess with bargains. They took delight in picking through mounds of clothes for what they thought were unintentional discounts. By giving the store some semblance of order, we gave the impression that we had wised up and there were no longer any steals among the deals. In fact, we hadn't changed the prices at all. Realizing the error of my compulsive ways, I systematically went about making the place a mess again – and business boomed.

Credit: Yale Joel/Life Magazine Collection/Getty Images

Life magazine ran this photo of a Vanta worker modeling the long underwear we made for the Korean War. The worker was a co-op student from Northeastern, majoring in industrial engineering.

VANTA GOES TO WAR

It was thanks to his body, not his mind, that a Northeastern intern helped Vanta score a publicity coup during the Korean War. We were one of the military's major suppliers of long underwear for the frigid Korean winters. A *Life* magazine writer wandered into the factory one day after visiting nearby Raytheon, which manufactured heavy combat equipment. "I see you guys got an $8 million contract," he said to me. "What is it that you make here?" I told him that I wasn't authorized to disclose any details. The reporter could see for himself that we were making skivvies. "What do you mean?" he asked. I explained that I would have to check with the quartermaster before I talked with the press. That whetted the journalist's appetite. "I don't think we are actually going to run a story on Raytheon, but this will get my editor so mad, that this *will* be a story," he said, referring to my insistence on getting clearance. With the quartermaster's OK, we went to town. I had this strapping student model our two-piece military long johns by standing astride a sewing machine. His photo made the magazine, March 12, 1951, but Raytheon didn't.

The editors at *Life* may have found our long underwear to be picture-perfect, but it literally didn't sit well with one government inspector. Everything on the garment could be precisely measured except for the seat. The specifications called for minimum and maximum dimensions, as the material had to be flexible. To properly determine the maximum, the inspector was expected to apply a reasonable amount of pressure to spread out the material. This guy, though, had it in for us. He would hardly stretch the seat at all and then reject the garment as too small. He put us to the considerable expense of repeatedly resubmitting samples.

One morning, my superintendent hurried in to tell me of a conversation he had just had with the inspector. "I bet you $200 I can pass 10,000 garments today," the inspector had said. The superintendent asked me what he should do. "We cannot have anything to do with this," I responded. "If you say 'no,' then he's clearly going to reject everything. And we're not going to say 'yes.'" In effect, the inspector was soliciting a bribe. I consulted with my father, who suggested that I go up the chain of command. I called the chief buyer at the quartermaster's office, with whom we had negotiated our contract. "You've got to take my word; you've got to take this inspector out today," I told him, after explaining the problem. "We don't ever want to have him here again."

I was taking a big risk. My demand could have been met with outrage and cost us the contract – possibly sinking our business. Fortunately, the risk paid off. The crooked inspector was gone in a flash. We never heard a word about under-sized seats again. But the incident showed the danger of putting a lot of power into the hands of petty bureaucrats. How many of them are tempted to look at a company and think, "You're making plenty of money; why shouldn't I get some of it?"

That's not to say I'm against regulators. Our military contract specified that the material be 50 percent wool, 50 percent cotton. Wool prices soared because of war demand, and one unscrupulous competitor found a way to cut corners. He discovered a vulnerability in the process inspectors used to test wool content. The sample size specified for testing was larger than could be cut from a sleeve. So, this manufacturer cut costs by cutting the wool content of his sleeves to just 20 percent – never mind the shivering arms of our boys in South Korea. Somehow, the military caught on to his scheme. A judge transferred him from his factory to a prison.

THE SHRINK PATROL

Please pardon the personal nature of this comment, but you can thank me that your underwear is not chafing. Well, at least give me some credit.

Like my father, I became involved in industry associations. While its name may sound a bit grandiose considering its purpose, the Underwear Institute served as the trade association for makers of garden-variety cotton-knit underwear. The makers of lingerie had their own association. While the lingerie manufacturers were primarily Jewish, the rest of the underwear market was dominated by Christians. So long as William Carter, Standard Knitting Mills, Munsingwear and Jockey belonged to the Underwear Institute, I felt Vanta should, too. I approached the paid director of the association, an old Yankee by the name of Roy Cheney. He sort of stuck his nose up in the air and said that of course I could join, but I would have to be elected first. I did get elected – becoming, I believe, the first Jewish member.

As I have said elsewhere, I don't join groups just for the sake of adding to my resumé. I went to my first meeting as a man with a mission. Increasingly, people were using washing machines. That caused many clothes to shrink, especially underwear, which is often washed in hot water. Shawmut and the William Carter Company had worked with Tubular Textile, a manufacturer of finishing machines for knitted fabrics, to pioneer a process to reduce shrinkage. But other manufacturers were advertising that their underwear didn't shrink when in fact it did. After I pointed out that that practice was giving us all a bad name, my fellow members of the Underwear Institute named me to head its shrinkage committee. To regain the public's trust, the institute established standards that prohibited advertising that a garment does not shrink; instead, a manufacturer could say "shrinkage-controlled," provided that the clothing shrunk by no more than 3 percent after being machine-washed and tumble-dried. All the major mills adopted this policy.

A PATENT FOR THE PINT-SIZE SET

Despite Earnshaw's innovations in fasteners, squirming infants continued to challenge parents' efforts to dress and undress them. We refined the double-breasted shirt by having the strands of tape snap together, rather than being tied. That made the fastener more secure and reduced the strands to just an inch long from 6-plus inches, eliminating the chance they would get in the baby's mouth. But we started getting complaints that the garments weren't flexible enough to accommodate an infant's rapid growth. Ruth Scharf, a New York sales manager for McKem-Vanta, suggested adding a second snap to the tape strand. In the end, Ruth and I came up with the idea of stitching a pleat into the tape. When the baby grew larger, parents simply had to snip a stitch to let out the garment. Now, a garment sized for, say, a 3-month-old baby could be expanded to the 6-month size. The new shirt was a big hit. Ruth and I patented it in 1953.

William Carter Company felt compelled to come out with a shirt just like ours. Despite our rivalry and his being twice my age, I had become friends with Lyndall Carter, grandson of the founder. I called to tell him that his company was infringing on our patent. "Jerry," he said, "*you* don't think that we're going to give up our position to you upstairs in the department stores just because we are unable to offer this shirt?" He then added, "You can either give us a license or sue us." In the end, he agreed to a license, paying us 3 percent of the proceeds from each shirt for the life of the patent. But he made an important stipulation: The agreement would be null if we failed to enforce the patent with other competitors.

Soon, Carter was paying us something like $25,000 to $30,000 a year. When Hanes started copying us, Lyndall wrote me inquiring what we were going to do about it. I called up Hubert Hanes and explained my arrangement with Carter. I said – in a friendly way, of course – that if he didn't take out a license, we'd sue. Going to court, I told him, would cost us far less than forfeiting years of royalties from Carter. Hanes caved in, and from then on it was easier to get others to fall in line. Eventually we had more than 10 licensees, paying us a total of $250,000 a year. That patent was a gift that would keep giving – and, to the chagrin of Vanta's next owner, taking.

Our McKem-Vanta line emphasized durability as seen in this ad from around 1950.

WE LOVE LUCY

Marketing, of course, is just as important – if not more so – than innovation. Shawmut had learned that almost from its beginning with the success of a swimsuit named for the aquatic sensation Annette Kellermann, and later, through subsidiary McKem, the Winnie the Pooh and Shirley Temple clothing lines. In January 1953, nearly three out of four homes with televisions – translating to 44 million viewers, including me – tuned in to see Lucy give birth to Little Ricky. It so happened that at the time I had been trying to figure out what to do with the material that landed on our cutting-room floor. Lucy gave me the answer: clothes for a Little Ricky doll.

Using a doll supplied by Mattel, we assembled a package that included a miniature nightgown, undershirt, diaper, towel and sheet – basically a micro-layette. I priced it very reasonably because I figured that we could obtain all the raw materials we needed from waste fabric left over from making the full-size garments. But the product was such a success that we ran out of scrap cuttings and had to draw from our regular material. Once we figured in the labor costs – which were about the same as for full-size garments – we found that the doll sets weren't all that profitable, but our line of "Lucy"-themed clothes for actual babies was.

Indeed, acquiring the rights to television characters – such as Smokey Bear and Davy Crockett – proved quite lucrative. We could take any shirt, decorate it with a patch of Davy wearing his trademark coonskin cap, and it would fly off the shelves.

Speaking of the layettes, I sent a full-size one to Queen Elizabeth in 1948 after the birth of Prince Charles. I seem to recall receiving thanks from Buckingham Palace, though I have no idea if the little prince wore Vanta. We do have a letter from Princess Grace of Monaco thanking us for the layette we sent for her newborn.

NO TEARS

Besides continuing and expanding Vanta's clothing line, we also bolstered its toiletries for tots. We contracted with other companies to make soap, baby powder and shampoo under the Vanta name. One of the suppliers was Henry Thayer Co., founded a century earlier in Cambridge and famous for its Slippery Elm Lozenges (a favorite of spitball pitchers). When I contracted with the company, it was co-owned by James J. Storrow, grandson of the philanthropist for whom Boston's Storrow Drive is named. It manufactured Vanta Nionic Shampoo, which was touted as less irritating because the soap was not ionized. "No Eye Sting! Children Will Love It!" promises a 1949 ad for the shampoo in the *Globe*. This was four years before Johnson's came out with its "No More Tears" baby shampoo.

That same *Globe* ad touts an upcoming visit to Jordan Marsh by Miss Helena King, "consultant for Vanta Nionic Shampoo." We carried on a tradition of sending uniformed "Vanta nurses" out to department stores to give talks and advice on baby care. They also taught a seminar to saleswomen under the auspices of Vanta's Institute of Mothercraft. Graduates would proudly wear emblems signifying they had received the institute's certificate and were qualified to give talks on babies. Genevieve, by the way, received a certificate. Vanta also distributed a 70-page guide "Your Baby and You," with detailed advice on diet, health, hygiene, exercise and, of course, wardrobe needs. By 1956, it was in its ninth edition and boasting seven million reprints.

From the start, my father knew that if Vanta were to make a serious run at the William Carter Company, it needed to expand its production facilities. Shawmut's future, he decided, was in the South.

GOING SOUTH

Teaching workers to spend, surviving no-see-ums, and a taking a crash course in Spanish

IN 1854, EIGHT YEARS before my grandfather George was born in Vilna, Montezuma, Georgia, was formerly incorporated. Its founders included veterans of the Mexican-American War, who named the south-central Georgia city for the legendary Aztec leader.

Flash forward about a century, and the city and its surroundings were home to 3,000, many of whom farmed peaches, cotton, peanuts and tomatoes. The city served as a magnet for residents within a 15-mile radius because of its hospital and shops.

In the late 1940s, my father visited Montezuma as a guest of Southern Railroad, which hoped he would build a factory there and use its rail line for shipping. He picked a site that bordered a small airfield. Governor Herman Talmadge helped cut through the red tape. Although Montezuma was small, Georgia's political structure gave disproportionate electoral power to rural areas. As a result, the governor would often pay more attention to struggling tiny municipalities than he would to Atlanta. Talmadge even attended the groundbreaking for Vanta. It happened to be a rainy day, turning the access road into a muddy mess. Soon after his visit, Talmadge sent down a chain gang to pave the road – much to my mother's horror.

MEET THE WYNERS

As head of a northern company expanding into the Deep South, my father wanted to win the goodwill of the community. He appeared at an open meeting to lay out the company's plans and to express its concerns. Pointing out that Shawmut was owned by people of the Jewish faith and that many of its managers were Irish Catholics, he said he was worried about the Ku Klux Klan. The residents tried to put his fears to rest. One older fellow got up and said, "Yeah, they've been around, but they want $5 a month in dues; who's going to pay them for that?"

Although we didn't need the extra financing, Shawmut offered residents the opportunity to buy company bonds. My father believed that by giving them even a small investment in the company, they would be sympathetic to its future needs. Located outside Montezuma's borders and under Oglethorpe County jurisdiction, the factory was not subject to city taxes. So many residents had invested in Shawmut that when Montezuma later expanded its borders within the county, the city found it politically expedient not to include our property.

Montezuma was one of those places where everyone seemed to know everyone else's business. When I first visited, I found only one public phone. It was at a restaurant called Betty's Chicken Coop. There were no phone numbers – residents just gave the operator a name, and she put through the call. I wanted to speak to John McKenzie, a prominent local businessman who had spearheaded the effort to entice us to Montezuma and who was to be my contact. When I told the operator, she said, "I just heard him tell his wife that he has gone to the golf club. Is this Mr. Wyner?" Although I had only just arrived in town, she either guessed who I was by my northern accent or she already knew my name from listening in on phone conversations. It was not exactly the National Security Agency, just small-town America.

We applied the lessons we had learned at the Waltham plant when we designed and organized the Montezuma operation. I sent Bernie Kaufman – the Northeastern University co-op student who had so impressed us that we had hired him after he graduated – to help get the plant up and running. But we quickly discovered that we had to adapt to a different work culture. When we opened our plant, peach packers were the major employers. Hundreds of women – all white, by the way – sorted the fruit, making sure to put the pick of the crop at the top of the baskets. It was a seasonal job, about three months a year, paying 50 cents an hour.

We offered 65 cents an hour to start, with a 10-cent raise soon to follow. After six months working for us, these women had earned more than double what they had previously taken home in a year. At that point, many of them quit – not because they were unhappy, but because they didn't see the need for more money. People here lived a simple life and had simple needs. There was no middle class to envy, and the wealthy lived in another world. For many, home was a shack with an outhouse in the backyard. If there was electricity, it was just enough to plug in a few lamps.

My father and I realized that we had to show people how they could use their dollars to buy more than just groceries. We arranged for exhibits of washing machines, stoves and other appliances. We talked about how big-ticket items could be bought on the installment plan. We urged residents to press the electric utility to upgrade their service. From today's perspective, I suppose that what we did might seem insidious; after all, who were we to shake up their lifestyles? But back then no one was talking about the evils of materialism. We saw ourselves as instilling ambition and raising the standard of living. In the end, our efforts had the desired effect, and our problems with high turnover faded away.

FLIGHT OF THE MANAGERS

If employee turnover was one problem, keeping the manager was another – this, despite our providing a beautiful ranch-style house that had won a prize from *Good Housekeeping* magazine. The first man we sent down was a former plant manager of Munsingwear, a Minnesota-based underwear manufacturer. His wife was looking forward to being queen of Montezuma high society, which gathered at the clubhouse of the local golf course. Though the course had been constructed as part of the Depression-era Works Progress Administration, only the city's white elite could enjoy it. No "white trash," and certainly no blacks were allowed – except to serve the drinks and tend to the grounds. When the club members failed to roll out the red carpet for the newcomers from the North, the manager's wife told her husband, "If you ever want to see me again, I'll be back in Minnesota." He followed her.

Next, we sent down Herb Robison, the brother-in-law of Ray Franks, head of Shawmut's Robison Rayon subsidiary. Herb liked the job, but once again we had a spouse problem. His wife, Mona, didn't take to Montezuma, the laid-back Southern lifestyle or the *Good Housekeeping* house. I had hoped to win Mona over by making a trip down to see the Robisons. Before I went, my father and Ray warned me that of late she had been on a tear about no-see-ums, tiny biting bugs that emerged at dinnertime with a ferocious appetite for humans. My dad and Ray said the best way to handle Mona was to no-notice-um. When the Robisons greeted me outside the house, I pretended to be oblivious to the carnivorous critters swarming around my face and crawling up my nose. Finally, Mona said, "I can't stand it, Jerry, they're crawling all over you, and you haven't said a word. They don't bother you at all?" I probably only succeeded in making Mona more determined to leave.

In the end, it was Dennis Shea, an Irish Catholic from Newton, who put down roots in Montezuma. In fact, those roots would run so deep that his two children ended up with Southern accents and he on the city council. Denny, who had been a superintendent at my Waltham plant, had such a winning way about him that he emboldened Montezuma's few Catholics to hold weekly services. They gathered at first in the small office building of a lumber yard. Denny arranged for a priest to visit monthly and for the Methodist church to donate a few pews. When the town fathers heard about Denny's group, they offered to help him build a church. "You know, we're proud of our little town. We have this Methodist Church on our main street, and this Episcopalian Church, too," they told him. One of them said that if the Catholics built their church on the main street, he would donate $5,000. That was a great deal of money in those days. Other Protestants chipped in as well. Today, St. Michael Mission Catholic Church still stands just a few minutes' drive up the street from City Hall.

COOL AND NOT-SO-COOL IDEAS

Besides bringing jobs to Montezuma, we brought something that was as much appreciated, if not more so: air conditioning. Today's air-conditioning systems had yet to be invented, but for several decades movie theaters had cooled their auditoriums by about 15 degrees using a large fan to evaporate water from the absorbent surface of a large drum that rotated into a storage tank. We installed this system and augmented it with a new evaporative cooling process called April Showers. The setup continuously sprinkled water on the flat roof of our factory. In the hot summer months of southern Georgia, we were so successful at making the factory comfortable, that we became a threat to the other local factory. While its workers had never complained before, now they wanted to flee Montezuma Knitting Mills and its "hot" interior. We didn't want the other company to think we were deliberating trying to steal their most experienced employees, so we had to be politic about whom we hired.

Not everything worked out in Montezuma. For example, there was our foray into ranching. At about the same time we set up the new plant, James Norris – the sports mogul perhaps best known for his scandal-ridden tenure as head of the International Boxing Club of New York – was making headlines with his experiment raising cattle in the South. Since we had plenty of extra space on our 150-acre property, my father and I bought a herd of Florida scrub cattle. The business plan seemed simple enough: Buy the cattle at 10 cents a pound on the hoof, fatten them up until they weighed 50 percent more, and then

LOSING MY COOL – AND NEARLY MY LIFE

It was the most humbling experience of my life.

The date was November 1, 1949, a Tuesday. I had rushed to Logan Airport, anxious to start a whirl-wind trip to the Vanta plant in Georgia followed by a weekend in Cuba. I was looking forward to staying with my good friends Phil and Lilly Richards in Havana and going on a date with their lovely Cuban neighbor, Maria Louisa Fonz.

While I was standing on the tarmac waiting to board my flight, the Eastern Airlines crew announced that the flight had been oversold and there were no more seats. The flight was to Washington, D.C., the first link in my tight schedule. The next plane was in four hours. The delay meant I wouldn't be able to conclude my business in Georgia in time to go to Cuba.

Furious, I placed my foot at the bottom of the airplane stairs and said, "Don't you dare push off!" After a long argument, I relented, and the plane took off without me.

I finally arrived at the Shawmut-owned house in Georgia at 6:30 in the evening. I was greeted by a ringing phone. It was my dad. "Thank God, you're there," he told me. The DC-4 I had originally planned to take had collided mid-air with a surplus fighter that had been purchased by Bolivia. The accident occurred just outside National Airport. All 55 people aboard the Eastern flight were killed.

I vowed to myself I would never again behave as boorishly as I had back at Logan. I also swore off air travel, but that didn't last long. Six months later I was traveling by train to Mexico City when at a stopover in Houston I met a couple of American Airline stewardesses. They managed to persuade me to take their flight the rest of the way.

sell them. Proceeds from those extra pounds – minus grazing costs – would be our profit. But we wound up losing nearly half our herd to disease. We were lucky to recover most of our original investment. After that, we stuck to our knitting.

And then there was my brainstorm. We were having trouble finding people with the highly specialized skills required to repair sewing machines. So, I approached the state about providing early release to convicts who had worked as mechanics in the penitentiary's sewing operations. I figured that they must have obtained plenty of experience from fixing machines sabotaged by inmates who didn't feel like working. I specified I didn't want crooks, but rather prisoners who had committed crimes of passion. I figured they were not as likely to reoffend. The state officials weighed my request, but never came through with any workers. They probably realized that if they let anyone go, they'd have their own mechanic shortage. So much for Jerry's prisoner rehabilitation program.

A GRINGO IN PUERTO RICO

Even with the Montezuma plant, we were looking for more capacity. McKem-Vanta wanted to expand its sportswear line. This time, it was Puerto Rico that was offering incentives to companies like ours. We moved into a 10,000-square-foot building in Yauco, located in the southern part of the island. It was one of many buildings throughout the commonwealth that the Puerto Rican Industry Development Corp. had built to house factories.

We chose the location because immediately next door was a similar building that housed a successful embroidery factory. Impressed by its operations, my father arranged a partnership with the plant's Puerto Rican owners. In exchange for 75 percent of our manufacturing profits there, they provided all the management functions that we needed along with sewing-machine mechanics and a superintendent. The factory turned out to be trouble-free and the employees reliable, accustomed as they were to seasonal swings in production. The plant had none of the employee relations issues that had arisen in Montezuma when we had managers who did not understand the local culture.

I helped launch operations with frequent 10-day visits to Puerto Rico. I learned Spanish by immersing myself in the community, staying at a small hotel where no one spoke English. At night, I would cruise the bars – not for women but for people to chat with in Spanish. Sometimes I'd crack the locals up with my feeble attempts to piece together words from my Spanish-English dictionary or adapt words I knew from French and Latin. They'd say they understood what I was trying to say, but that I was using language they hadn't heard since their grandparents died. I also went to a lot of movies to study the Spanish or English subtitles. Whenever I had extra time, say while waiting for a traffic light to change, I'd whip out flash cards I had made to memorize words. I got very good at manufacturing my own version of Spanish, at least good enough to teach our workers how to operate the sewing machines.

Originally, we had planned to offer employees an incentive pay plan like the one we had in the States. When I told our Puerto Rican partner, he thought I was crazy. Pointing to the job seekers lined up outside his factory, he said, "That's incentive." Then, in Spanish, he shouted at his workers: "If you don't pick up the speed, you're all fired." Stunned, I asked, "How can you talk to them that way?" And he responded, "That's what people understand." And indeed, when he bellowed, you could hear the sewing machines rev up.

Nearby, another company from the mainland had set up shop. It offered incentive pay and something else then unheard of in Puerto Rico: paid holidays. But the company eventually closed because it couldn't find enough workers. They wanted to stick with the work culture they knew. My father was right about the importance of learning local ways.

WHO WANTS A JOB?

Meanwhile, we decided to consolidate the Vanta operations in Massachusetts by moving the Waltham operations to our plant in Brockton. We chartered buses for all the Waltham employees willing to make the longer commute. But when workers retired, we found it increasingly hard to replace them. For one thing, high school graduates were opting to go to college or enter the building trades. For another, we couldn't keep all our workers employed year-round because of the seasonal demand for our products.

We turned to the unemployment office in Brockton for help. But although the bureau pointed potential workers to our factory, hardly anyone showed up. Instead, to continue collecting benefits, they would concoct some reason why they couldn't get a job with us. So, I obtained permission to set up a desk in the bureau itself. Officials sent claimants directly to me, and I would hire them on the spot. If they didn't come to work the next day, they'd lose their jobless benefits. Of the people I hired that way, many stayed on to become regular employees. Still, about half of them did all they could do to get dismissed right away and resume collecting unemployment checks.

We did, however, have great success recruiting recent immigrants from the Azores. Once we hired a few, we subsidized car pools from their homes in Fall River and New Bedford. Over the years, the immigrants and their children and grandchildren would make up the largest share of our employees.

MACHINE POLITICS

Closing the Waltham plant furthered my education in human nature. When we sold off machinery that duplicated what we already had in Brockton, I recalled my own experiences buying used machines. Around the same time we had moved to Waltham, Boston Knitting Mills was closing its plant down the street and auctioning off its equipment. When I inspected the machines before the sale, I was approached by a secondhand sewing machine dealer whom I knew well. "What are you doing here?" he asked me. After I rattled off my shopping list, he told me to hold off. Taking me into his confidence, he explained that he and other dealers had agreed on low-ball prices for the machinery. After the Boston Knitting Mills auction, they would hold their own auction and split the profits. Their scheme, of course, would only work if they were the only bidders at the first auction. "We don't want you to bid," my dealer colleague told me. "We'll give you a good price on what you want."

Such collusion didn't sit well with me. The factory owner was a friend, and I knew that his equipment had been well-maintained. "You guys can do what you want; you can bid me up," I told the secondhand dealer. "I'm prepared to pay full retail price if necessary." By bidding at the auction, I forced the dealers to compete not just with me but with each other. I bought what I needed at a fair price, and the owner was spared a fleecing.

Much later, holding my own equipment auction, I thought I was prepared for the secondhand dealers' games. I put them on notice that an out-of-state dealer whom they didn't know would be bidding. In effect, I was taking a page from their playbook. One of the dealers' ploys was to bring in a crony to make ridiculously low bids that would make their own look reasonable. The buyer I invited was from Upstate New York. I knew from past dealings that I could count on him to make fair offers. But after inspecting the machines, he reported that they were all missing very small but essential and expensive parts. Evidently, some local dealers had surreptitiously pocketed them at a sales preview when they were given free rein to inspect and even handle each machine. Without those key parts, the machines were much less valuable. Perhaps it was more than a coincidence that a couple of those dealers also happened to be locally popular amateur magicians.

A ROYALTY SCREW-UP

My friend from Upstate New York proved helpful again nearly 20 years later when we sold Vanta's Georgia plant. That was at the time when we needed to raise capital to buy out the Shawmut interests held by the families of my father's brothers. Fortunately, the factory was doing well and drew many potential buyers. It was particularly coveted by the owners of another knitting mill in town, the Flagg Utica subsidiary of Genesco, a large shoe and apparel company. I suspect that our competitor was less interested in acquiring the Vanta brand than in seeing us exit the local labor market. Its plant was always losing workers to our factory, which offered much better working conditions.

As part of the purchase agreement, Flagg Utica was to buy our equipment at a price that accorded with its value on the used market. Touring the factory with the Flagg Utica people, the New York dealer announced what he would pay for each piece of equipment. His valuations helped us get a fair price from Flagg Utica. Although he was mainly doing us a favor, my friend was prepared to back up his quotes and even buy the machinery if it had come to that.

Sealing the overall deal, however, was not so easy. Our frontline contact was Jewett Flagg, executive vice president of the Flagg Utica division. Flagg, whom I had known for a decade, had come over to Genesco after it bought his family's business. Just as I thought we had negotiated a fair price, he said he had to consult with his boss: W. Maxey Jarman, the much feared chairman of Genesco. Flagg next told us that Jarman wanted to see us in New York. Expecting a tough fight, my father and I brought along Irving Hellman, our $500-an-hour (a huge fee in those days) lawyer from Nutter McLennan & Fish, the Boston firm founded by Justice Louis Brandeis.

A strict Methodist, Jarman refused to allow smoking in his office. His one concession to visitors was a tray of jelly beans. After the introductions, Jarman's first move was to dismiss Flagg from the meeting. The fewer people in the room, the fewer complications, he said. That was fine with me: Flagg could be a pretty officious guy. Then our attorney asked Jarman, "Don't you want to have your lawyer here?" The CEO responded that the deal – which was in the $3 million to $4 million range (a tenth of what it would be in today's prices) – wasn't big enough to warrant the presence of another attorney. "Sit down and tell me what the problem is," he said. When I quoted the same price and terms I had given Flagg, Jarman simply said, "That's fine," adding that he'd sign as soon as Hellman drew up the agreement. Typically, such deals involve so much nitpicking that the contracts are as thick as a book. Not in this case. After half an hour, Hellman came back with a five-page document that he had written out by hand. Jarman signed. And that was that.

Or so we thought. As part of the deal, Genesco was to continue to collect the royalties on that Vanta patent for snaps I described earlier and then pass along a sizable chunk of the proceeds to us. In time, Genesco sold Vanta to Glendale, the company that made Nitey Nite, the famous one-piece sleeping garments. Somehow, Genesco overlooked the provisions of the Vanta patent. As a result, Glendale pocketed all the royalties, but Genesco was still responsible for making sure we got our share. Without acknowledging the bind it had gotten itself into, Genesco tried to buy us off by offering a lump sum of two years' worth of royalties. I said, "Why would we do that? There are 10 years left on the patent." In the end, I took mercy on Genesco and accepted five years' worth of payments.

THE UGLY SIDE OF THE SOUTH

*Why my Harvard friend had to carry my bags and some
of my best workers in Georgia had to eat outside*

AMONG MY CLASSMATES AT Harvard Business School was one with whom I couldn't be seen dining in his hometown.

He was one of three black students then at the school. The other two attended on scholarships from the Pullman car porters' union. My friend's father owned a business school in New Orleans. Sometime after we both had graduated, I arranged to meet him when I was on business in New Orleans. We ate dinner in a restaurant well out of town. Had we shared a meal at a restaurant in the city we could have been arrested. Such were the depths of discrimination in the South just 65 years ago.

When my friend saw me off at the train station, he carried my bags to my rail car. He told me he had to carry both of them so that he would appear to be a porter; otherwise, he wouldn't have been allowed in that part of the station. This was a guy who had been showing me around the city in his family's chauffeur-driven car.

THE CHAIN GANG

New Orleans, of course, wasn't the only place to practice a peculiar form of Southern hospitality when it came to blacks. I discovered that quickly when I first visited Montezuma, Georgia. Strolling around the town, I was about to take a sip from a water fountain when someone rushed up to me. "You're drinking out of the wrong side," he told me. "That's the nigger side of the fountain."

That was just one of the indignities experienced by blacks, who made up at least half of the town's residents. They were only allowed to shop on Saturdays. They had to step off the sidewalk if a white person walked toward them. Betty's Chicken Coop was happy to sell blacks dinner, but they had to buy it from a window that opened onto the street; they could not enter the restaurant itself and had to eat outside. At the movies, blacks were restricted to the balcony, which was known as "nigger heaven."

When my mother visited our plant on its opening day, she was shocked to see the chain gang of black prisoners that then-governor Herman Talmadge had sent down to build a road to our factory site. At night, the inmates slept manacled at a makeshift camp. While they were in town, they also built streets for a subdivision that happened to be owned by a member of the Governor's Council. Nobody in town seemed to be the least perturbed that prisoners were put to work on a private development. And nobody was worried about the prisoners escaping. Uniformed guards with shotguns watched over the gangs, just as in the movie *Cool Hand Luke*.

Talmadge, who liked to boast about his efforts to attract industry to Georgia, attended the opening of the factory. But while he might have been enlightened economically, he was a staunch segregationist. At the time, we didn't feel we could do much to buck the status quo. The civil rights movement was still in its infancy. We were told we could only hire blacks as porters, meaning they could carry things but not make them. Had we placed them in higher-paid positions, we would have faced a revolt from the white workforce.

OUTSMARTED BY WILLY

Sometimes, though, we managed to work around the system. For example, the shipping room was manned by a bunch of less-than-enlightened whites. They were basically a lazy bunch. When boxes came in from the production line, they'd just leave them on the floor. A "porter" by the name of Willy shelved the packages. He created a system for marking each to identify its destination. The whites looked down on Willy, dismissing his duties as straightening up their mess. But when it came time to load the shipments, they had to go to Willy to find out where everything was. Willy had become the de facto manager. Eventually, he was sitting at a desk recording the orders and telling the white workers which packages to put where. Very quietly, but gleefully, we paid him a shipping-room manager's wage, because if the others had realized they were actually working for him, they would have quit.

Still, when Willy bought his lunch at the cafeteria, he couldn't sit down there. Like the other blacks, he had to eat his meals on benches outside. And when he went to the restroom, he had to use the ones designated "colored."

I faced another racial dilemma when our trade organization notified us that we risked losing government contracts if we failed to post copies in the restrooms and the office of the federal Walsh-Healey Act, Depression-era fair employment legislation. How could I post an equal opportunity notice in a segregated bathroom? I called the local chapter of the NAACP. "I'm sick about this," I told a representative. "If I integrate the toilets, I'll go to jail." He responded: "If you post that notice and truly give equal opportunity, yours will be the first company that ever did it in Georgia. We'll worry about the toilets years from now."

I posted the fair employment notice in the executive washroom and on the company's main bulletin board. The only complaint I got was from the woman who was foreman in the stitching room; she quit in protest – no great loss. We did dent the color barrier by hiring a few blacks as stitchers. We might have hired more, but few dared risk the wrath of the whites.

Over time, I found two kinds of prejudice in Georgia. The landed gentry who lived off their peach crops had basically been raised by black mammies. They may have been patronizing, but I don't think they were truly prejudiced. Segregation, though, served their interests by maintaining the social order. With blacks to look down on, the poor whites weren't as likely to challenge the affluent ones.

One other observation: I occasionally would visit our workers' homes. While I hate to generalize, it struck me that blacks took greater pride in what little they had than did the whites. And the atmosphere in their homes was more gracious and hospitable.

CROSSING BOSTON'S COLOR LINE

In Boston back in the '40s, races didn't mix much, either – not because of the law, but because of social and economic forces. At that time, many blacks lived in the South End, while Roxbury and Mattapan were still Jewish "ghettos." I was a fan of the South End jazz clubs and would take dates to them. Often, my companion would be startled to find that we were the only two whites there. But we always felt welcome. If I had to go to the men's room, I would turn to the fellows and gals at the next table and ask them to keep an eye on my date.

One of my favorite spots was the Savoy. Or I'd go across Mass. Ave. to Wally's Paradise, a much less flashy place where the beer was half the price. I saw such black greats as Sabby Lewis, Sarah Vaughan and Sidney Bechet.

On Saturday nights, liquor couldn't be served after midnight, but I was allowed into several after-hours joints. One of them, the Pioneer Club, was enormous, with a band on the second floor and card games on the third. Around the corner from the Savoy, the Pioneer had a peephole in the door. But from time to time, you'd see a policeman inside, perhaps getting a payoff. Another popular spot, but smaller, was Rick Johnson's. Located in an apartment on St. Botolph Street, it was run by a woman who called herself Mrs. Johnson. She didn't charge an entrance fee and let customers get their own drinks. On leaving, they'd ask her how much they owed, and she'd say, "Oh, I guess you drank about so much" and charge accordingly. People were well behaved in these after-hours clubs. Most of the customers were local entertainers who had just gotten off work, and a few were people like me.

A footnote: In 2007, when Wally's Paradise marked its 60th anniversary, I stopped by. I was interviewed by a reporter because I was the only one there, besides his daughter, who had known Wally.

JUSTIN'S ARK

Well, it was just a sailboat – and, for a time, a lucrative sideline

We had our babysitter, Patty Mallin, and our dog, Wendy, pose in half a sailboat for this promotional photo for the unsinkable Squall.

IN MY PHOTO COLLECTION, there's a picture of Wendy, our English sheepdog, sailing with our babysitter, Patty Mallin, in half a sailboat. I believe it was taken in 1962.

My little outfit, the Chestnut Hill Boat Company, used that stunt to sell our unsinkable sailboat, the Squall. You could cut it lengthwise, leaving just enough space for the daggerboard, and it would still float. You could even sail it, but maneuverability was limited since the boat could only heel on its remaining side. Besides being practically unsinkable, the Squall was an attractive, high-quality yacht tender.

My shipbuilding career was unintentional. I had seen so many people having fun out in their new Alcort Sailfish boats that I decided to buy one myself when it became available as a kit. Simply designed, the boat was essentially a surfboard with a rudder, a daggerboard (centerboard) and a lateen-rigged sail (a triangular sail set at a 45-degree angle to the mast). The kit consisted of several sheets of plywood, a few oak boards, and a pattern for cutting the sail and mast. Pretty basic, considering the price tag. My nautical and entrepreneurial instincts combined to get me thinking: I love boats, so why not go into the boat-building business?

By this time, 1958, we had sold off much of Shawmut to provide the funds to buy out the interests of the families of my father's brothers, IA and Murray Wyner. We were basically down to a small laminating business that we were operating out of our original Canton Street plant in Stoughton. I had both the time and the space to try something new.

Relaxing with my friend Stanley Snider after tennis at Belmont Country Club, I brought up the idea of us going into the boat-building business together. Stanley was then in the lumber business, so I figured he'd be the perfect partner. I invited him over to the house in Brookline, where we began to build the first model in my garage workshop. It was a hot August day. The garage was not air-conditioned. After spending five minutes at his turn with the sawing – and sweating – Stanley stopped and announced the boat-building business was not for him. He said his wife, Mary Ann, had been trying to get him to leave the family lumber business and form a company to construct vacation homes. He said this little experience in my garage had convinced him that she was right. In the decades since, Stanley's company, Stanmar, has made a big name for itself building recreational centers for Harvard, Yale and a variety of other institutions. Its more ambitious projects have included the Mattakesett vacation community on Martha's Vineyard and the Smugglers' Notch ski resort in Vermont.

MY OWN LITTLE FACTORY

Encouraged by my father, I started off by building my own version of the Sailfish. I got it up and running quickly by buying out a modest-sized manufacturer of wooden boats in Stoughton. With a small crew, the owner built amazingly high-quality 8-foot skiffs and prams. The sturdy crafts were constructed with oak chines, marine plywood and bronze boat nails. He marketed them unpainted through gas stations, receiving $14 for the skiffs and $18 for the prams. The price was so low that if the cost of a square foot of plywood went up by a dime, he'd lose money.

We moved the business, complete with former owner and crew, into a corner of Shawmut. At first, I continued to sell the unpainted boats, delivering them to gas stations by the truckload. I added a painted and finished "Sailbird" (our version of the Sailfish) along with a painted sail version of our pram, which we called "Sunbird." We boxed them up and sold them through retail stores, beginning with the well-respected old Jordan Marsh department store. The Sailbird retailed for $199, and the Sunbird for $99; Jordan's kept 35 percent. The boats were equipped with nylon sails and aluminum masts and booms.

When the New York boat show refused to let us exhibit, we rented window space
from the Pontiac dealership across the street from the expo.

Thinking big, I tried to enter my boats into the New York boat show in 1958. At the time, before the Arab oil boycott, gas and diesel were cheap and power boats still all the rage. Only two lines of sailboats were in the entire show. My little unknown company didn't stand a chance of being accepted. So, I exhibited our boats out of a window space I rented from the Don Allen Pontiac dealer across the street from the boat show, which was held at the New York Coliseum. We sold enough boats to cover our expenses and make a small profit, but I realized that a business model built only on undercutting competitors' prices was bound to fail. It certainly wasn't the philosophy we had at Shawmut. Once others found cheaper ways to make the same boats, we'd be – well – sunk. And undoubtedly some poor fool would keep cutting his prices without realizing he wasn't making back his costs. I started looking for a model that would appeal to the high end of the market, a boat that stood out for its unusual features and construction.

My search ended with a news article about the arrest of a boat builder for being a public nuisance. He had stopped boat traffic in the Charles River while demonstrating that his sailboat still floated after being cut in half. I purchased his business, which primarily consisted of the molds for the boat's fiberglass hull and a process (yet to be perfected, I later discovered) to inject foam in place. The hull of the sailboat itself had been designed as a dinghy by a prominent maritime architect and curator of maritime history at the Smithsonian Institution, Howard Chappelle. The lines of this 9-by-3-foot dinghy were truly beautiful. The seller of the boat business hadn't obtained Chappelle's permission to use his design, so I contacted him. Chappelle graciously agreed to let me use his design, saying he only wanted a credit line but not royalties.

The double-hull construction was similar in concept to that of the increasingly popular Boston Whaler boats. It consisted of two thin fiberglass skins bonded together by a layer of rigid foam. After moving the operation to our corner of the Shawmut factory, I discovered that like so many other efforts to copy the Boston Whaler foam-injection process, this one flunked the durability test.

Using my lamination experience from Shawmut, I practically reinvented the process to strengthen the bonding of the rigid foam to the thin exterior fiberglass shells. That provided long-term stability. The bonding process was my secret edge – and if I hadn't been so certain of its success, I wouldn't have put Wendy (or our babysitter, Patty) at risk on the Charles.

But I shouldn't sound too boastful. In the process of trying out different bonding materials, I managed to inhale a very nasty chemical, reactive isocyanate. I stupidly was looking in a vent hole in the molds when suddenly I felt something funny in my lungs. My voice became hoarse, and I worried that I had permanently damaged it. After a few weeks, I recovered, but I wonder if that mishap years ago contributed to the vocal cord cancer that showed up some 50 years later.

WYNER'S LAST STAND

Now my challenge was to build sales, and that's where Genevieve was a big help. Drawing on the experience she had picked up working for a public relations firm before we got married, she suggested that every time I went to New York on business for Shawmut, I also call upon the editor of one of the boating magazines to tout the unsinkable Squall. They were all based in New York City.

At first, I got no results. But then the sailing editor for *MotorBoating* magazine called. She said she was planning to go to Newport, Rhode Island, to demonstrate two well-known New England sailing dinghies, Dyer and O'Day, and her editor-in-chief – recalling that I had stopped by his office – suggested that the Squall be included in the trials. I could tell from the disdain in her voice that the sailing editor wasn't particularly crazy about including an unknown boat maker. But that didn't put me off.

Genevieve and I went to Newport accompanied by Duncan Scott, whose South Dartmouth company, Glasstronics, made the Squall's fiberglass skins for us. Scott, the son of a boat builder, was also a famed competitive sailor. Duncan manned the Squall as the three boats engaged in a token race for the benefit of a camera boat. When the wind suddenly came up, the O'Day boat lost its rudder, and the Dyer boat swamped and foundered. Meanwhile, Duncan sailed circles around the camera boat, where I was stationed. Since the magazine had reserved its cover for a color shot of the demonstration, it had no choice but to feature our Squall all by itself. Genevieve's push had pushed us into the big time.

The New York boat show, which had brushed us off the previous year, deigned to rent us a small booth. I had a plywood holder custom-made to allow the boat to be displayed vertically – with the bow pointed down – so that it would not take up the entire booth. By show's end, we had lined up dealers all over the country. We even sold our exhibit model. Rather than tossing the stand, I decided to take it back to Boston. After all, it had been specially made. Dumb move.

First, we managed to shoehorn the stand into one of those boxlike Checker cabs for the ride to the airport. In those days, before all the worries about airplane hijackings, you could walk directly onto the tarmac. So, we marched right through the gate with our plywood base and gave it to the baggage loader at the nearest plane. The loader went through all sorts of gyrations before finally figuring out that he would have to unscrew a hinge on the baggage door to stow the unwieldy platform inside. I then boarded the plane, only to learn it was headed for Washington. So, the poor baggage attendant had to repeat the whole process in reverse to retrieve my stand. At least I now knew how to get the platform on the Boston-bound plane.

When I arrived in Boston, I thought I'd head off problems by telling the baggage handler there about how he would need to unscrew the door to remove the platform. He wasn't interested in my advice. "We know what we're doing," he told me. "Go inside and wait for your luggage." We waited. And waited. And waited. Not a stick of luggage appeared. After about 20 minutes, that baggage handler popped in and asked for that fellow with the platform, namely me. "You better tell us how to get it out," he said. "It's blocking all the luggage." All that trouble for $5 worth of plywood.

THE CUSTOMER IS ALWAYS RIGHT

After the Chestnut Hill Boat Company had sold about 100 vessels across the country, I received an angry call from a customer in Virginia. He and a companion had capsized the boat while sailing it across Hampton Roads, a body of water with some of the highest boat traffic in the East. In their effort to tip the boat upright, they both stood on the exposed daggerboard, grabbed the edge of the hull and leaned back. That would have worked were it not for the design of the lateen rigged sail. It included a triangular area forward of the mast that trapped water if the sail was submerged. Before trying to right the boat, the men should have punched out that water because it weighed nearly as much as the two of them combined. As they tugged the hull, they strained the mast to the point that it tore away from the boat. That, in turn, pulled up much of the foam and deck. The boat was ruined.

My initial reaction was that the fellow had to be pretty dumb to try to right the boat without first emptying the water out of the pocket. But I knew that I wouldn't stay in business long if I lectured my customers or made them pass a test before they could buy a boat. I realized that this customer had in fact done me a great favor. Undoubtedly, others would make the same mistake. I felt obligated to redesign the boat to be as trouble-free as possible – even in the hands of dummies. After a lot of experimenting, I came up with a $3.50 fix that involved driving a stainless-steel pin up through the keel into the bottom of the mast step to reinforce it. That way, the mast would bend and break away without damaging the rest of the boat. I then tried to contact customers, using the registration forms I had asked them to fill out upon purchase. I had arranged for them to have the repair done free at their closest dealer. I succeeded in tracking down all but one buyer; unfortunately, he had not submitted a registration form.

But I eventually did hear from him. He lived in California and had managed to wreck his boat in much the same way as did the customer in Virginia. He wrote me a very angry letter. I wrote him back and told him how glad I was to have finally made contact. I explained that everyone who had registered the boat had obtained a $3.50 fix. But I didn't want to put the onus on him because he had failed to fill out a form. I took full responsibility, offering to send him a new boat, freight prepaid, if he would send me a picture of his damaged one after he had cut it in half. I made that request so that he couldn't make a cosmetic repair to the old boat and sell it to someone else who would then hit me with the same damage claim.

I completely disarmed the man. He had anticipated that I would put up a big fight. He was so pleased with the outcome that he went up and down the West Coast touting the virtues of the boat. Thanks to him, I signed up seven or eight new dealers. I figured if just one in 100 boats had to be replaced, that was a 1 percent cost of doing business. If a much higher percentage of boats had to be replaced, I deserved to go out of business. But in any case, the customer shouldn't have to pay the price for my mistakes.

TEDDY DELIVERS

Sales of the boat got another boost thanks to a suggestion from my father. "You should write your senators and tell them about your little company and its boat and ask how they might help it grow," he said. "Maybe they can help you out." I wrote to Ed Brooke and Ted Kennedy. As a member of Brookline's Republican Town Committee, I had expected that I'd at least hear from Brooke. But all I got from him was a form letter saying, "The senator appreciated your comments. Thank you very much." A week or two later, I received a letter from Kennedy's office. The senator's team had arranged for the Navy to recognize our boat as a recreational sailboat for use at the naval base at Okinawa. Kennedy's office had also arranged for the Department of Commerce to exhibit the boat in a show it was mounting in Brazil. Besides covering all the expenses, the government took sales orders and relayed them to us. Thus, I saw firsthand why Kennedy earned such a great reputation for constituent services.

My boat was popular with Boston Whaler dealers because it filled out their line. Boston Whaler's smallest boat was 11 feet and not as stylish as our 9-foot sail, outboard or rowing dinghy. Many customers purchased our boat to use as a dinghy to row to shore when they were anchored in the harbor. They could tow it behind their large cruising sailboats or haul it aboard – Boston Whaler's 11-foot models were too heavy to be used that way.

Eventually Boston Whaler's founder and owner, Dick Fisher, asked to visit our factory. In itself, that was an honor; Dick had conceived the first foamed-in-place hull. Many other builders had tried to copy it, but failed to obtain the strength that he – and we – had. Dick hadn't patented his process because he thought that would have made it too easy for competitors to develop alternatives. When I showed him how we did it, he gasped. He had assumed that our way would be much like his. It was so different that had he held a patent, he wouldn't have been able to sue us for infringement. Right then, he proposed to buy me out, presenting an offer I couldn't refuse. I would get a royalty on every Squall he produced. I realized that what was most important to him was my signature on an agreement not to disclose our process to his competition.

After taking over the business in 1965, Dick more than tripled the price of the Squall, from $900 to $2,900. With the 5 percent royalty, I cleared more per boat than I had when I was building them. After about 15 years, Dick's company, Fisher-Pierce, was bought out by a public conglomerate, and the Squall was discontinued – as was my royalty stream.

SHAWMUT TRANSFORMED

A-line skirts, shoe linings and college chemistry change the company

WHEN MY DAD JOINED the Navy in 1917, he made a deal with his father that over the decades turned out to be fraught with problems. My grandfather agreed to watch over Shawmut if my dad would promise to take his brothers into the business after they were discharged from the armed forces.

And so, my uncles Murray and IA wound up in the family business, representing Shawmut out of offices in New York City. Eddie, as I discuss in an earlier chapter, took over the Ritz from my grandfather.

Along with Horace McCormack, Murray ran the sales operation for McKem, Shawmut's children's clothing line. The problem with Murray was his devotion to his wife, Dolly. They were inseparable. When Dolly accompanied her husband to Shawmut to review the designs for the next year, she succeeded in alienating just about everyone with her outspoken pronouncements.

Receiving the brunt of Dolly's barrage was a lovely and gentle man who managed cutting and sewing, Louis Epstein. He had been with Shawmut since we had merged with his company years before. By the time Dolly was through with him, he would usually be in tears. Dolly, who could be most charming outside of business, appeared oblivious to how she devastated this man with a few minutes' comments about work on which he had spent three months. But Murray couldn't be persuaded to leave his wife at home.

High-fashion magazines in the 1950s feature ads of outfits made from Sag-No-Mor worsted wool by Wyner.

Meanwhile, IA was the public face of Shawmut's trademark Sag-No-Mor wool jersey. Especially as he got on in years, IA was prone to impulsive decisions that would drive my father crazy. Without consulting anyone else in the company or obtaining sales commitments for the equivalent in finished jersey cloth, he would take out contracts in the volatile wool market. With similar lack of foresight, he would commit the company to future deliveries of jersey cloth at a price he had not covered with a future contract for buying the raw material. Over a matter of months, the price of raw wool could soar or plummet, much like oil prices today.

By the 1950s, a new and larger generation of Wyners was coming of age and expecting good jobs in the family business. That presented a dilemma. Even if we had open positions and our relatives were qualified, we would risk discouraging non-family members who were working hard to move up the ladder based on their merits. My father and I decided the best way to maintain harmony within the family was to buy out the brothers or, in the case of IA, give him a division to own and operate. To raise the money, we sold Vanta to Flagg Utica and McKem to BVD, thus disposing of our plants in Georgia and Puerto Rico. I've never forgotten what BVD's Sol Kittay told me about acquisitions: "I can gobble up a lot of companies, but if they do not come with management, I will get a severe case of indigestion."

By mid-decade, Shawmut itself was reduced to the original Canton Street plant in Stoughton, where we manufactured Sag-No-Mor wool jersey for IA's company. Unfortunately, but not surprisingly, IA was struggling within a year to stay afloat.

To save his brother from financial failure, my father partnered with Ames Textile Corp. – the historic Merrimack Valley-based mill firm – to buy out IA. We leased Ames our dye and finishing house on Porter Street in Stoughton, and we continued to knit the jersey cloth on Canton Street.

At the same time, the fabric industry was being upended by advances in lamination: the process by which different materials are sandwiched together. Again partnering with Ames, we bought a lamination machine, which we set up on Canton Street. We didn't realize it at the time, but we had just taken the first step that would lead us into the 21st century.

THE YANKEE CONNECTION

It might seem an unlikely partnership: the Yankee grandson of a Lowell textile dynasty and the Jewish grandson of a Lithuanian lumber dealer. But both shared a commitment to quality and integrity, which formed the basis for strong mutual respect. Ames Stevens Sr. ran the business with his brother, Brooks, and their sons. (Their cousins owned the J.P. Stevens Company.) They were true gentlemen, who didn't put on airs, even with all their wealth.

I became particularly close to Ames Stevens Jr. We would occasionally travel to New York together to make sales calls. I recall once after we had shared a cab in Manhattan, he paid the $2.50 tab and then put 15 cents in the driver's hand. The cabbie looked at him and said, "What's this?" Young Ames paused, then took back the change and put it in his pocket. Maybe he was unfamiliar with tipping etiquette. I don't think he was being cheap, just frugal. It was at his suggestion that I joined the Harvard Club in New York, where we could stay in the dorm for $6 a night as opposed to paying $20 for a private room upstairs.

I learned a lesson from our dealings with the Ames family. Ames Sr. would never immediately make a commitment. He would say he wanted to consult first with his brother. He wasn't being devious; indeed, he was a very nice fellow. But intentionally or not, he was employing a smart negotiating strategy. By saying you must consult with someone else – be it your brother or your board – you avoid making the discussion too personal. You also avoid becoming viewed as the obstacle. If you simply respond by saying, "No," the other party might get angry at you; before you know it, what should be a business transaction becomes a matter of egos.

The stage had been set for our leap into the lamination business earlier in the decade at a company famous for building much of America's World War II air fleet.

IT ALL STARTED WITH CARPET

In the mid-1950s, the Curtiss-Wright Corp. was grappling with a more down-to-earth challenge: creating a better carpet pad. Having diversified into the consumer market, the company had developed a carpet underlay made of polyurethane foam. But the foam, being somewhat tacky, would bunch up and tear when the carpet was rolled over it. Placing muslin over the foam addressed that problem, but introduced another one: how to secure the cloth to the foam. Assigned to the task, a chemical engineer, John W. Dickey, discovered that when he passed foam over the flame of a Bunsen burner, it become sticky. If cloth were then pressed against it, the combined materials would bond after cooling. Eventually, Dickey came up with a way to mass-produce the laminated material: a flatbed conveyor that pushed the foam underneath a flame and then onto a roller that was simultaneously fed with fabric.

Reeves Bros., a textile manufacturing and finishing concern, bought the patent on the flame technology. Besides marketing its own laminated fabric, Reeves licensed other manufacturers to use its machine design and flame laminating process in return for a royalty per yard of laminated fabric. The timing was perfect: Women's A-line skirts had just come into fashion, and foam-backed fabric was ideal for keeping their flared shape. For men, laminates proved an inexpensive way to make double-knit suits. The bonded material was like a sandwich. Typical would be a lining of acetate tricot on the inside; foam in the middle; and a thin layer of wool on the outside. It was the textile counterpart to wood veneer furniture.

Since there was no room in the dye house, we installed our new laminating operation on Canton Street. Just as we had with knitting equipment, we found many ways to refine the machinery. Besides boosting output, we produced a more consistent and durable laminated fabric. We kept our improvements under wraps for fear of losing our competitive advantage. We didn't want the manufacturer of the machines to incorporate our changes for the benefit of other customers.

Working with knitted materials presented its own set of problems. Unlike woven fabrics, knitted ones are prone to stretching out of shape. That's because they are essentially made up of loops within loops. Say you have a roll of knitted wool that is 100 yards long and 54 inches wide. If you stretch the width to 64 inches, the roll will get shorter, perhaps by as much as 8 yards. In the knitting process, you have to strike a balance. The material must be placed under sufficient tension to remove wrinkles and prevent sagging, but not be stretched so much that the final garment starts to shrink the minute the customer puts it on.

The success of Sag-No-More wool jersey reflected our expertise in producing knitted fabrics. That same knowledge base helped us become industry leaders in laminating a full range of knitted fabrics.

Belmont Country Club played a role in our success as well. Several friends and acquaintances at the club were shoe industry suppliers. They helped Shawmut early on to become the major source of laminated linings for women's shoes. In the middle of the last century, the shoe-finding capital of the United States was located in a several-block area near Boston's Chinatown. About 10 companies along Lincoln and South streets supplied nearly all the materials that went into shoes besides the leather. The term "shoe finders" is believed to have come from the days when itinerant shoemakers commissioned people to find them buttons, bows, laces, eyelets and such. You know the tricot linings in women's shoes? They're laminated to foam. At one point, more than 90 percent of the women's shoes sold in America contained Shawmut-made linings.

The machine we had bought from Reeves laminated only one surface at a time. Since many of our orders from garment manufacturers were for three-layer laminates, we designed a machine that would do two sides at once. We had it built by a company in New Jersey. When that firm started selling what was essentially our machine to others, we decided to build and assemble future equipment in house. After all, we had been tearing down and rebuilding machines for decades.

At the start, lamination was just a sideline that paid for our lunches; in just a few years, it was buying our dinners, too.

LAM-SCAM

As dresses made with laminated fabrics became more popular, the dry cleaners literally began to feel as if they were being taken to the cleaners – and by their own customers. The problem: Garments that had been poorly laminated would delaminate after a single cleaning. Some unscrupulous customers took advantage of the flaw. If they had second thoughts about a dress after wearing it once, they would have it dry cleaned in hopes that the bonding would peel apart and they would be compensated for their loss. They would then use the money to buy another style. In response to all the claims for reimbursement, the dry cleaners' association had its members post signs refusing to accept laminated garments. Slipshod laminators were giving the entire industry a bad name.

We found ourselves in a situation like the one Vanta had encountered when competitors made false claims about shrink-proof underwear. That was remedied when I persuaded the underwear association to establish industrywide standards. Since laminators had no such association, I contacted quality-conscious competitors I had met on my selling trips to New York. We founded the National Fabric Laminators Association in 1960 and agreed on a standard tag specifying how a garment should be cleaned. In addition, we established quality standards for laminate manufacturers and their suppliers, designating who would be responsible for particular defects.

Unfortunately, some members of the group wanted to set prices along with standards. Whenever talk at our monthly meetings at Rumpelmayer's restaurant in New York's Hotel St. Moritz veered in that direction, I grabbed my hat and threatened to head for the door. The subject always would be dropped.

SPLIT PANTS SEAL A DEAL

There's an old saying that clothes make the man. This is a tale of how ripped clothes made the sale.

When I went on business trips in the 1950s – before the proliferation of wash-and-wear clothes – I devised my own way to travel light. In the summer, I'd wear the same seersucker suit every day. At night at the hotel, I'd take off my underwear and put on just the suit. I'd then take a shower and soap up the suit. After rinsing it off, I'd hang it up to dry. By morning, I had a fresh suit to wear.

Seersucker is made from cotton woven in such a way that it puckers up. That has two advantages for hot-weather traveling: The material doesn't cling, so air circulates under it, and it's supposed to look wrinkled, so you don't have to worry about ironing. Well, my seersucker system worked very well until one day when I had an important meeting in New York with the president of a major outerwear company, Bill Doniger of McGregor-Doniger. We had a factory in Puerto Rico and were looking for contract business to keep it busy during the off-season.

The saga began when my plane out of Boston came in for a landing in New York. Just as we were about to land, the plane took to the skies again. From my window, I could see officials gathered below looking up at us. Then they covered the runway with foam. Evidently, they were concerned that the landing gear had not fully extended. As the plane again dropped for a landing, I bent over in crash position. The tension was agonizing. Fortunately, though, it was a cockpit indicator light that had malfunctioned, not the landing gear. But the scare led to another malfunction, of the wardrobe variety.

Late because of the plane, I bolted out of the cab when I arrived at McGregor-Doniger. As I headed into the building, I felt a breeze on my rear end. I discovered that my pants were split, all the way from the crotch to the back. The pants must have started to unravel when I was bracing for the landing. Back then seersucker makers didn't expect their suits to be washed; they certainly didn't anticipate my shower system.

Since it was summer, I didn't have an overcoat. I had to move gingerly to keep the hem of my suit jacket from rising above the widening gap in my trousers. I was shown upstairs to a big open office. Doniger walked in from the other end. I stood stock still, risking discourtesy for the sake of my precarious dignity. The president strolled over to me and lit up a cigarette. He fumbled with his lighter, and it fell. It rolled along the floor, stopping right by me. I froze. I couldn't bend over. Finally, I said, "You know this may seem odd, but I have split my pants."

The president took me into his office and sent my pants out to be sewn up. Had it not been for my wardrobe malfunction, he would have been rid of me in two minutes. Instead, he was stuck with me for an hour and a half – and I got the order.

A STICKY PROBLEM

Our do-it-yourself approach to building equipment extended to research and development. In those days, we didn't have a team of college-educated engineers. My father and I explored new technologies, while tapping the deep well of experience of our machine operators and mechanics. At last I could put my college degree in organic chemistry to use. Since I understood the language of the scientists at adhesive manufacturers, I could recognize the most promising routes for overcoming technical challenges.

After the A-line dress went out of style, we had to devise methods to adhere a lining to an outer cloth without foam in the middle. We modified the flame lamination process to all but eliminate the foam. But the thin layer that remained prevented the fabric from draping over the body as gracefully as single-layer material.

We experimented with alternatives to flame laminating. Some laminators obtained quite good draping effects with a water-based acrylic adhesive. But the process required heat for the adhesive to cure for maximum durability, which had the unwanted side effect of stiffening the fibers in the fabric. We wanted a process that would cure at room temperature and, if possible, cross-link with the fabrics that we were bonding.

Besides finding an appropriate adhesive, we wrestled with various approaches for applying it. Think about what happens when you get taffy on your hands. You find all sorts of things sticking to your fingers. Now imagine if you were working with filmy material like the lining for a dress. One technique was to print dots of adhesive on a fabric and then join it with another material. We had to make sure that the dots themselves didn't leave an imprint on the final product. Additionally, since we were using nonflammable compounds, we had to heat the laminated materials to drive away the solvent. Until the solvent dries out, the adhesive creeps like molasses, preventing the fabrics from properly bonding (or curing).

SAVED BY THE BRITS

Across the Atlantic, a textile manufacturer with a passion for sports cars had developed a process that was the answer to our needs. I learned about him through his adhesive supplier, Imperial Chemical Industries (ICI), the British counterpart to Du Pont. An ICI representative based in Rhode Island accompanied me to Manchester, England, to see this innovative operation.

I took an instant liking to Rex Normington, a slim, tall, balding fellow who shared my love for tinkering. As Rex drove us from the airport to his family's factory, Minting Machines, he regaled us with stories about his automotive sideline. Britain taxed cars purchased in kit form at a much lower rate than it did those bought off the showroom floor. Rex would assemble the cars and sell them privately. He later took me for a test drive along one of England's notoriously narrow, winding lanes; I was left with my heart in my mouth. Less exhilarating but just as impressive was the treat that his brother gave Genevieve and me on another trip to England. A member of Parliament, Tom Normington, took us to lunch at the Westminster terrace restaurant.

But let's get back to laminating. Rex had devised an assembly-line system that began with a furnishing roll engraved with V-shaped grooves set in a corkscrew pattern. Beneath the roll was a tray of adhesive compound. As the roll spun through the tray, the grooves would pick up the adhesive. A sharp blade spanning the roll skimmed off any excess. Fabric fed by an adjoining roll would then "kiss" the adhesive roll, with fibers pulling out strings of glue. As the strings stretched farther and farther, more of the adhesive was exposed to air, accelerating the evaporation of the solvent. Eventually, the strings would snap, leaving a sticky, hair-like residue on the fabric. At the next stage, the treated fabric was married with another fabric as they were simultaneously squeezed between a pair of rollers.

Although Rex used a flammable adhesive compound, ICI assured us it could provide a nonflammable substitute that would work just as well. While that proved easier said than done, the company did come up with a self-curing urethane adhesive. I had studied urethane in that MIT course that I barely passed; I had never imagined the course would prove so useful. To fully explain how the process worked would require a mind-numbing chemistry lesson. Suffice it to say, after curing for 24 hours, the laminated fabrics were permanently joined by the cross-linking of their molecules.

We bought one of Rex's machines and modified it in Stoughton. My mother named the process Twin-Set because it permanently bonded two fabrics. In advertisements, we touted the Twin-Set bond as "guaranteed for the life of the fabric – can be washed or dry cleaned 100 times or more."

We arranged with Rex to market the machines around the world. Our territory was the Western Hemisphere. Customers rented the equipment, giving us a down payment equal to what it had cost us to build it. They then paid a minimum rental payment that rose with their annual production. In addition, we profited by supplying the adhesive for the machine.

We publicized our innovations by writing scientific papers for journals or presenting them at international conferences. In 1966, I presented one in Israel that was translated into 20 languages. Rex appeared at a conference in Moscow.

Shawmut employees in 2018 laminate the foam and fabric lining material to be used in the upper part of a leading athletic shoe brand.

I kept the personal touch, getting to know many of our customers well. Among them was U.S. Laminators, based in Long Island, New York. The owner had twin sons, whom he had photographed back to back for a Twin-Set advertisement. One day I got a desperate call from the owner. His plant had burned down. "I won't be able to rebuild for six months," he told me. "If I'm going to keep my business, then I have to ask your help. I'll run trucks with my customers' goods up every day. I'll be up there; other people from my plant will be up there; and if you'll run all the stuff, I'll just have to rely on you not to keep any of my customers after we get the plant operating again." For six months, we shifted around our production schedule to accommodate him. I didn't want to take advantage of another company's misfortune. As it happened, several of his customers, including one in Boston, did want to stay with us, but we turned them down.

Today, those twin sons run the Long Island business. A copy of the photo of them from the 50-year-old ad still hangs in Shawmut's offices.

We didn't patent the Twin-Set process. That would have provided our competitors with a roadmap for creating their own variations. And we required potential buyers to sign a nondisclosure letter before observing the machine in operation. Our restrictive policy turned out to be an effective sales tool. The veil of secrecy piqued our customers' curiosity, making them much more attentive than they might have been otherwise. Our insistence on confidentiality also played a central role in our most dramatic deal.

TOE-TO-TOE WITH A TITAN

When Roger Milliken took over his family's textile firm in 1949, it had just a handful of plants. When he died in 2010, Milliken & Company had 50 factories in seven countries, producing everything from the material in the balloons at Macy's Thanksgiving Day parade to the ingredient that makes Jell-O pudding smooth. His *New York Times* obituary credits the billionaire with building his company's home state, South Carolina, into a "bastion of the Republican Party." He was not a man to be trifled with. In the eyes of his employees, I did just that when I refused to exempt him from our nondisclosure policy.

It all started when one of my technical papers came to the attention of Milliken's R&D team in 1971. Excited by the advantages of purchasing the Twin-Set process, the team asked to inspect the equipment at our Stoughton plant. Informed of the nondisclosure policy, the Milliken representatives said they didn't think it would be a problem, but still wanted to check with headquarters. The company lawyer, however, told them that under no circumstances could they sign such an agreement in advance. However, if they liked what they saw and Milliken approved the deal, then they could sign the nondisclosure.

I came up with an alternative that I felt served the interests of both companies. I invited the Milliken people to write down their specifications for a test run of a batch of fabric, from the barrels of adhesive required to the number of workers on the line to the quality of the final product. I said they could see exactly what went in and what came out, but I would curtain off the machinery during the demonstration. If all went as specified, they would sign the sales form and nondisclosure agreement, and I would show them what they had just acquired.

The first reaction I got was: "Mr. Milliken is not going to like this!" But after some discussion back and forth, we came up with a plan. The International Textile Machinery Association (ITMA) was holding its exposition the following month in Paris, and Milliken would be attending with a team of his technicians. If after touring the entire show, he hadn't found anything that he thought was equal to our process, he would agree to my terms for viewing it.

Held every four years at different locations in Europe, the ITMA expo draws as many as 3,000 machinery manufacturers from around the world. They exhibit their equipment, often in full operation, to the more than 100,000 textile manufacturers in attendance. The temporary industrial park at the time of our visit consisted of some 30 buildings. The largest seemed to be the size of six football fields: With all the machinery inside clattering at once, the sound could be deafening.

I attended the expo not just to show our equipment and check out the competitors, but to seek out innovators with products or ideas that could benefit Shawmut. Joined in later years by one of my sons, I would walk the entire exhibit, darting in and out of every booth whether in my field or not. Anything that looked promising I would check off in the expo catalog. After my initial survey, which took two days, I would revisit booths I had flagged for more details about their products.

Like me, Milliken was systematic about viewing the expo. He hired a bus for his company's large contingent to make the rounds of the sprawling site. But I didn't have a chance to say more than hello to him when he and his retinue paraded past our exhibit. After he completed his grand tour, Milliken returned to us for a demonstration. Everything worked out as I had hoped, and we had a deal.

Milliken's purchase in effect gave Twin-Set an industry seal of approval. But while machine sales rose, we kept the price down to discourage competitors. Besides, we had that second profit stream: All those machines required our specially formulated urethane adhesive.

PITCHING KING ARTHUR

Even with the success of our machine sales, most of our earnings still came from the laminating work we did in Stoughton.

I set my sights on one of the biggest players in the garment industry, Arthur M. Gottlieb, president of Knitbrook Mills in New York City. Gruff, shrewd and heavyset, Arthur was an intimidating presence. And that's if you managed to be granted an audience. Tipped off that he ate his lunch at his desk, I bought a sandwich off the hallway food cart and joined him. To my delight, we hit if off right from the start. It didn't hurt that he was already a big fan of Wyner fabrics. He readily agreed to farm out his lamination work to us, but only if we could meet his strict deadlines.

Arthur had grabbed a lion's share of the fabric business by turning around orders in a matter of days, while his competitors would take weeks. He had everything down to a system so efficient that not a yard of fabric or a minute of time went to waste. If he received an order Monday for 25,000 yards in assorted colors, he could have it on the client's cutting tables in New York City first thing Wednesday – a previously unheard-of feat of logistics in the industry.

We, in effect, became a key cog in Arthur's interstate assembly line. He would have the raw material commission knit, dyed and finished at mills in Brooklyn. Orders placed that day by the garment manufacturers had to be finished by the dye house and loaded onto trucks by midnight for shipment to Shawmut. Like clockwork, the material would arrive at our docks at 6 a.m. the next day. By early evening we would have it laminated with foam and tricot lining, and loaded onto trucks bound for inside delivery in New York City. The completed order would be in the customer's hands by 6 the following morning.

In effect, Arthur had mastered "just-in-time" manufacturing a decade before it became a catch-phrase in America. And what we learned from him about logistics would later give us a leg up on competitors in the auto industry.

By the late '60s, Arthur accounted for 60 percent of our business. That put us in a precarious position, especially as we had doubts about the future of the lamination market. I went down to New York and told Arthur our concerns. "You have to buy us out," I said. "We depend too much on you."

Arthur said that he had already closed his own laminating plant, Laminac, because he preferred our work, but acquiring Shawmut might just fit into another business move he was making. He and a close friend, Bob Levinson, had just bought control of Duplan, a publicly traded company that made synthetic yarn. Arthur said the pair intended to transform Duplan into a textile conglomerate and were setting about buying up companies. They weren't particularly interested in the businesses themselves, but rather in how the acquisitions could boost Duplan's stock value. Duplan stock was selling at a multiple of profits of 12. They were seeking companies at multiples of 5 or 6. After the merger, Duplan's higher multiple raised the value of the acquisitions – at least that was the theory behind the strategy.

Besides Shawmut, Duplan acquired a hodgepodge of textile-related firms – from makers of products from apparel to yarn to buttons. As would eventually become apparent, by focusing on just the financials, Gottlieb and Levinson missed out on potential synergies. In other words, the total value of their acquisitions could have exceeded the sum of their parts had the companies provided each other supply and sales opportunities or economies of scale. As we'll see in the next chapter, Duplan didn't even bother to take advantage of the opportunities that serendipitously presented themselves.

But the game plan worked in the short run, principally because Duplan provided incentives for existing ownership and management teams to stick with the companies for at least the first five years.

Duplan made us a very appealing offer that included the opportunity for doing even better. However, we had to agree to stay on as the managers for at least 10 years. When I suggested that company officials might want to inspect the Stoughton plant first, Levinson said, "I'm looking at the factory now. I'm buying you and the factory comes along with it."

After more than half a century, Shawmut Inc. was no longer Wyner-owned. But it was still Wyner-run. A lot would happen over the next decade.

A CLOSE CALL

In which we manage to avoid going down with Duplan's ship

AS FAR AS OUR employees and customers were concerned, nothing changed when Shawmut became a subsidiary of the textile conglomerate Duplan Corp. in 1967.

Personally, I benefited. Up until then, my father had capped my salary at what my sister's husband, Melvin Mark, earned as a professor at Northeastern University. In the long run, Dad knew I would reap the rewards for my service to the company, but in the short run, he didn't want to see my standard of living exceed that of my sister's. It was a family-owned company. Had feminism emerged a half century earlier, my sister might well have entered the business alongside me.

But aside from getting a nice raise, my responsibilities remained the same, and Shawmut's continued success kept Duplan executives out of my hair.

Duplan settled on a purchase price for Shawmut by asking us to estimate our earnings over the next five years. Based on that figure, they valued us at five times our average annual earnings. That seemed fair enough.

Rather than paying us outright, the conglomerate gave us one-third of the amount up front, which covered our capital gains taxes. For the remainder, we received bonds that could be converted to stock. That way, if the company grew in value, we could share in the gains. As further incentive to keep us onboard, Duplan offered us an unusual bonus in the form of additional convertible bonds with a face value equal to the amount our annual earnings exceeded our estimates. Indeed, over the next five years our Duplan holdings on paper increased by several times the original purchase price. However, we couldn't cash in on the gains until the company issued a new stock offering.

Addressing the National Knitted Outerwear Association in 1968 for the last time as chairman of its Standards Committee – a post I had held for 18 years.

CALL IT DUDPLAN

That offering never came. After its initial success, the company began to falter as the five-year agreements with the owners of other acquired companies expired. Duplan's owners paid little heed as management deteriorated at their subsidiary companies. Further, Duplan failed to take advantage of potential synergies among their divisions. For example, headquarters rejected my suggestion that a sister company send 30 million yards of laminating my way rather than to one of my competitors. Compounding Duplan's woes was a sagging national economy, hit hard by the Arab oil embargo of 1973. Ultimately, the company was forced into bankruptcy.

Meanwhile, as I discuss in another chapter, we were hedging our bets by entering other businesses. We purchased a furniture distributor and later started a tennis and ice skating club. In addition, our laminating business with shoemakers remained strong, although it had slackened with garment makers.

We pinned our long-run hopes on supplying laminated materials for car interiors. In the late 1960s, Buick flirted with doing business with us. A decade later, we again saw an opening in Detroit, but feared that we would go under along with Duplan.

Duplan agreed to sell Shawmut back to us in return for what the conglomerate had originally paid in cash and its by-then nearly worthless convertible bonds. It seemed like more than a fair deal for Duplan, considering that the company had made no substantial improvements to Shawmut. Our equipment had suffered a decade's wear and tear, and, in some cases, was obsolete. But just as we were about to close on the deal, Duplan went into bankruptcy.

Making matters worse for us was that Duplan's collapse came at a time when bankruptcies were subject to heightened federal scrutiny. After the W.T. Grant chain of stores had gone belly up the year before – in one of the biggest bankruptcies in U.S. history up until then – the bankruptcy trustees were assailed for failing to get the most they could for the company's assets.

GRILLED BY A JUDGE

Officials at the Securities and Exchange Commission, which reviews bankruptcy filings, questioned whether we were paying Duplan enough for our repurchase of Shawmut. The bankruptcy court judge asked me how we expected to fare from the deal. "I hope we're going to make money. That is why we are offering to buy it, but there's no guarantee," I told him, adding that I hoped our customers would stay with us. "If they don't, we will lose a tremendous amount of money."

Noting that the laminating business was in decline, I cited a New Jersey company that was willing to unload its plant to us for just $1. It wanted to shed the cost of taxes and maintenance, and avoid the unknown costs of closing and liquidating. I also pointed out that we had to be independent of Duplan if we were to have any hope of securing business with auto manufacturers.

As I said earlier, many of our customers and suppliers hadn't even realized that Shawmut had become a Duplan subsidiary, because after the takeover their contacts continued to be my father, me, and a few long-time Wyner employees. Understandably, those suppliers were startled to receive notice from Duplan stating that the bankruptcy could leave them with just 10 cents on the dollar on outstanding invoices for material that had been shipped to us. When my father and I learned about their distress, we decided to pay off the accounts ourselves, taking the chance that we would be at least partially reimbursed out of settlement payments from the bankruptcy trustees. We didn't feel that our suppliers should suffer for Duplan's failings. But sometimes when you try to do the right thing, expecting little or no reward, you get one anyway. The bankruptcy liquidation raised more money than expected, and over several years we were reimbursed for almost all of what we had paid out to the creditors.

In 1977, after a decade's hiatus, the Wyners again owned Shawmut. Within the next couple of years, we recouped what we had paid Duplan. Now, we were set to penetrate the exclusive world of automobile suppliers.

THE CAR GUYS

In which we arrive in Detroit and get squeezed in traffic

I WAS STILL ON a high from that first weekend Marriage Encounter retreat in early 1978 when I arrived at the office the following Monday morning. I never was one to share my private feelings with work colleagues, but that morning I could not contain myself from saying to several of them, "I've just had one of the most remarkable experiences of my life!"

At lunch I was due to meet with executives of Inmont, a Port Huron, Michigan company that supplied molded headliners – the interior ceiling of automobiles – to original equipment manufacturers for the auto industry. I kept telling myself that if I didn't stop raving about the weekend, the executives would think I was crazy, and I'd blow our first shot in a decade at cracking this giant market. But at lunch, I couldn't resist bringing up Marriage Encounter.

To my astonishment, the two visiting executives, Stu Boyd, director of product development, and Ron Plant, chief of purchasing, were both veterans of Marriage Encounter. Suddenly, as we sang the program's praises, we became like longtime close friends. I can't say that Marriage Encounter alone made the difference, but that lunch put us on the road to Detroit.

A SECOND CHANCE

It's very difficult to break into the auto business. The Big Four manufacturers of the time – General Motors, Ford, Chrysler and American Motors – required subcontractors to go through all sorts of hoops to become qualified suppliers. As in other concentrated industries, who you know can be as important as the quality of what you make. Stu and Ron helped us break into the exclusive club. Our future competitors were represented by Detroit sales agencies with longtime connections to the auto companies.

In 1968, I had received a call from an executive at Buick who said his colleagues had read a paper I had written about lamination. The automaker was one of the first to use a molded headliner for the interior ceiling. Previously, fabric – usually mohair – was stretched over a frame, with no filling behind it for soundproofing and insulation. Stitched at various points, the material was vulnerable to holes and laborious to install. Buick's innovative headliner consisted of a fabric-covered moldable board that was popped into place and secured with screws. Initially, the fabric was backed with half-inch foam, but that tended to break and wrinkle when it was stretched over curves and bends.

Reeves, the company from which we had licensed our first laminating process, supplied Buick with foam-backed fabric. But because the foam didn't always adhere properly, some of the headliners fell apart in the cars after only a short time and had to be replaced in the field. Buick wanted to see if we could do a better job, and we showed them we could. Unfortunately, just as we were set to go into full production, Buick was hit by a wildcat strike. That gave Reeves the time it needed to remedy its quality problems.

This new shot at the auto industry a decade later came because of another case of shoddy workmanship. Inmont, which supplied General Motors, was unhappy with both the cost and the quality of laminated materials from its supplier. Stu believed Inmont would save a lot of money if it bought one of our machines and laminated in-house. With the stakes high for both Inmont and Shawmut, I cautioned Stu against rushing into things. He agreed to my suggestion that we run a few thousand yards of the fabric at our plant and ship it to them so that they could be sure it satisfied their needs. I charged the same price we set for other industries. A few days after Inmont had received the shipment, Stu called me. "We had a chance to run it through our process," he told me. "Now we think we have to change our plans."

For a moment, I wondered what could have possibly gone wrong with our material. Had we struck out again with the auto industry? Quite the opposite. It turned out we had hit a home run.

Stu said that because our price was so low, Inmont had decided to abandon the idea of laminating in-house. He went on to praise our fabric for its consistent quality and its compatibility with his equipment. Then he said the magic words: "We want to work with you to qualify you with General Motors to be our supplier." This came as a total and very welcome surprise.

When I was invited to Port Huron to complete the deal, Stu and Ron suggested that I bring along Genevieve and come a day early so that we could attend one of their Marriage Encounter sessions. It was an unusual beginning to what turned out to be a long partnership or, you could say, business marriage. Whenever I visited Inmont, I was greeted with hugs; I doubt any of the company's other vendors could have made that claim.

THE BLAME GAME

At last we were in that rarefied realm of Detroit suppliers – but to stay in, we pretty much had to be perfect. The automobile companies had no tolerance for defects. I realized why the first time I visited an assembly line. The factory didn't simply turn out a batch of the same color and make of car in a single day's run. A black sedan might be followed by a blue station wagon. Parts were arranged by the varying types of cars slotted to come down the line. If a worker noticed a defective headliner, he couldn't just grab the next one in the stack. At the end of the line, cars with defects were sent to a holding area to await replacement parts. The automaker would then assess a charge of $300 for swapping out the defective unit.

If problems with a supplier were so severe as to force the line to be shut down, the automaker would assess a penalty of up to $9,000 a minute. For us, that would have been a huge loss, given that our profit margin was just pennies per part. We've devoted considerable resources to improving the reliability and precision of our production process. Today, we use sophisticated imaging machines that enable us to adjust for defects on the spot, averting hundreds, if not thousands, of yards of spoiled material.

Over the years, we had our share of battles with the automakers over defects. In retrospect, some tiffs were almost comical, but at the time no one was laughing. Hundreds of thousands of dollars could be at stake. For us, it was usually a case of guilty until proven innocent.

J. L. WYNER, PRIVATE EYE

At times, we had to help customers save themselves from their own mistakes. Two such cases occurred with Ford. In the first, a plant manager claimed that 20 percent of our fabric was defective. Ours was one of two companies supplying fabric for headliners, and I felt like we were being singled out for blame. Ford allowed us to visit the plant floor to observe the assembly process. I noticed that the workers were using a different process from that which I had seen in other plants for applying the fabric. They molded the board first, sprayed it with adhesive and then pressed on the fabric. The mold contained two cavities to accommodate the sun visors.

Our fabric composite had to have a certain amount of stretch; otherwise it wouldn't stay put in the depths of the cavities. At first, I thought if indeed the problem was with our fabric, it might be because it wasn't sufficiently pliable or stretchable to conform to the cavity. But then as I walked around the factory, I noticed another pallet of headliners that had been rejected for the same reason ours had been. The headliners, which were of a different color than ours, had clearly been supplied by our competitor. That suggested that the problem was more likely with Ford's application method than with the fabric material.

I returned to the assembly line to watch the operators more closely. The fellow who was spraying on the adhesive was standing in one position. As a result, he was covering only one side of the cavities, leaving the other side uncoated. It came as no surprise to see rejects piling up at the end of the assembly line. But when I pointed out to a supervisor that it wasn't just our fabric that was being rejected, he refused to believe me. He told me to mind my own business or he would ask me to leave. I responded that he could throw me out, but that wouldn't solve the problem. The plant manager refused to hear me out.

Fortunately, our sales representative managed to persuade the plant's quality control supervisor to look into the matter. Sure enough, an investigation determined that the defects occurred only on the second shift, which just happened to be when the poorly trained operator was on duty. While Ford never acknowledged it had been wrong, the company did back off threats to reduce our share of its business.

Then, in a scene out of Kafka, I and several others from our plant were called before a quality control meeting at a Ford truck assembly plant. We were among a number of suppliers to be grilled by a panel of executives and an audience of 150. It was supposed to be a hearing, but it was more of a kangaroo court. Shawmut had been summoned because of occasional oil spots on the fabric.

We were told to report at 6 a.m. First off, we were given a tour of the plant. Fortunately, it was a very thorough tour. It included the room where our material was stored. I spotted a pipe that was dripping onto the pile. When I went before the investigative panel, I reported what I saw. The panelists told me that the drip was none of my concern – that I was there to tell them how we planned to solve our problems, not to point out theirs. Realizing I was in no position to argue further, I blathered on about procedures we'd implement to prevent any more stains. That appeared to satisfy them for the moment, but not me. After all, we couldn't control what happened to our fabric after it left our factory. But somebody at Ford must have been listening to me that day; we never heard a word again about oil stains.

Not all automakers take such a confrontational approach. Honda, for example, has the courage and wisdom to recognize that focusing on blame is counterproductive. The Japanese company treats us as strategic partners, teaming with our employees to identify mutually beneficial improvements.

My sons James and Daniel in the Shawmut booth at the Detroit Auto Show in 2000.

THE 'JUST IN TIME' EDGE

Speaking of the Japanese, their entry into the U.S. auto market forced Detroit to finally adopt the "just in time" assembly operation, popularized by W. Edwards Deming, among others. Instead of stocking up on parts, automakers ordered them to arrive within hours of their being fed to the assembly line. "Just in time" offers two key advantages. The obvious one is that it reduces the amount of money tied up in parts and inventory. But more important – and Deming's reason for advocating it – is that the process immediately reveals defective components.

Even before entering the auto sector, Shawmut had adopted just in time production. Thus, we already had the flexibility to respond to fluctuations in demand. And in those rare cases where defective material slipped through quality control, we could address problems within hours of receiving customer feedback. Unlike our competitors, who would keep a two-week stockpile, we didn't have to worry about tossing out mounds of flawed material.

Earlier in this chapter I stressed the importance of relationships in securing business in the auto industry. That became a more complex challenge in later years as the automakers divested themselves of their various parts divisions. That meant we became Tier 2 suppliers, dealing with the spinoffs, rather than Tier 1 suppliers selling directly to the automakers. Shawmut was lucky that by that time my son Daniel was onboard. Blessed with amazing people skills, he forged bonds with the Tier 1 companies that we still have today.

After graduating from Harvard Business School and putting in a stint at McKinsey & Company, my son James joined the firm and instituted an organizational structure that set the stage for us to become the largest independent Tier 2 supplier of headliners, capable of serving the increasingly global market. Shawmut has gained the reputation as the industry leader in quality, engineering and innovation. But those are stories for my sons to tell you.

OUR OASIS IN WEST BRIDGEWATER

We seek a new headquarters – and create a nature preserve

My father and the daughter of a Shawmut employee at a picnic in 1983 on the grounds of our West Bridgewater plant, which opened the following year.

NOW THAT SHAWMUT HAD entered the elite world of auto suppliers, we couldn't continue to operate out of our cramped and scattered buildings in Stoughton. It wasn't just that we were running out of space. If our customers in Detroit paid us a visit, they'd wonder what kind of an outfit they were dealing with. We wanted to build a plant that was both efficient in its layout and representative of the innovative supplier that we had become.

Looking to move closer to our workers, who mainly came from around Fall River and New Bedford, we zeroed in on West Bridgewater in the early 1980s. After viewing a number of sites in the area, we decided on the purchase of four undeveloped lots off Manley Street, near Route 24, the main highway to Fall River and New Bedford. Twenty acres in all, it was much more property than we needed, but we wanted to be surrounded by nature, not by other businesses, and to have room to expand. Besides, my father's philosophy was that you should never pass up an opportunity to buy land next door. Much of the site had been bulldozed for fill dirt decades before when Route 24 was built. What remained were high hills covered with new trees and deep, wet valleys.

A BUMP IN A DIRT ROAD

But to consolidate the four lots so we could build the factory in the center, we had to remove a dirt road that snaked through the property. Since that road was a right-of-way and the only access to a 38-acre farm, we had to buy the farm. It was touch-and-go for a while. We couldn't commit to the land in front unless we could buy the farm in back. It was owned by three sisters who lived out of town. Fortunately, William Bearce, our real estate agent and longtime friend, managed to track them down and obtain their agreement to sell.

Now we had a 58-acre campus on which to place our new headquarters. We hired internationally renowned landscape architect Carol R. Johnson – a friend of Genevieve's since they had lived in the same dorm at Wellesley College – to lay out the site. Carol, who would later help landscape our second Brookline property, wasn't daunted by the topographical hodgepodge. "Let's make the most of what we have," she said. Together, we created a network of wooded trails with several bridges.

The plans were well received by the town's Conservation Commission. With its blessing, we transformed the wetland into two ponds, which I stocked with fish. I had hoped that the employees – many of whose families had been Portuguese fishermen – would enjoy angling in their off hours. It turned out, though, that the Portuguese didn't have a taste for freshwater fish. And I decided it wouldn't look good for me to be out fishing while everyone else was working, so I limited my angling.

One day I noticed a stranger fishing at the upper pond, which I had stocked with rainbow trout. After telling him that he could not fish there without our permission, I noticed he was using worms for bait. "You'll never get any of those trout with worms," I said. He responded that he was catching bass. I had stocked the lower pond with bass. Although the ponds weren't connected, bass must have taken advantage of flooding during a rainstorm to migrate upward. I was amazed at the large size of the fish. Without anyone fishing for them for several years, the migrating bass had feasted on the smaller trout for which I had paid a hatchery good money.

PARADISE LOST

After all our efforts to create a natural sanctuary around our new factory, a less-than-scrupulous businessman grabbed up the parcel opposite our entrance; chopped down the stately, town-owned trees that lined Manley Road; and opened a lot with hundreds of trailers that he leased to truckers. I had passed up an opportunity to buy the land early on because I couldn't see how anyone could possibly build on what was mostly wetland. When I complained to the Conservation Commission about our neighbor violating environmental rules, town officials merely shrugged. Evidently, they had been just as bulldozed as the wetland they were supposed to protect.

Given the carefully landscaped surroundings, we didn't feel that the exterior architecture of the new building needed to be anything special. But I did enlist Genevieve to take on the task of designing and furnishing the office areas. She did a wonderful job with the layout of the two stories of offices, conference areas and lab space, creating a welcoming atmosphere for visiting customers. Her job was to have been temporary; she had planned to launch a career in counseling after earning a master's degree in education from Harvard in 1982. Instead, she accepted my offer to continue at Shawmut as vice president of human resources, applying her newly acquired skills to helping our employees.

When it opened in 1984, the West Bridgewater plant was running several shifts. Today, the once-packed parking lot is often less than half filled. That's because in the decades since, Shawmut has opened plants in Michigan, Tennessee, South Carolina and New York, and worldwide in Mexico, the Czech Republic and China. In almost every instance, we were compelled to do so. As our major automotive customers became more global, they required their suppliers to become more global. They did not want to have a different supplier for the same item in each area of the world where they had a factory. Plenty of competitors were ready to take our place.

And thus a company launched a century ago in the second oldest woolen mill in America is spreading its state-of-the-art technology across the globe.

FUNNY BUSINESS

Tangling with furniture fraud, crooked pols and the legendary Anthony

NO GOOD DEED GOES unpunished – at least so it has seemed many times in my life. But none no more so than when it appeared we would have to close up shop at Shawmut.

It was around 1970. Although the laminating business was running well, we lacked a diversified customer base. We had yet to find an on-ramp to the automobile industry. We had decided to sell out while business was good and found a buyer in the Duplan Corporation.

Meanwhile, we felt obligated to secure the future of the people who had devoted their careers to Shawmut. My father believed that finding comparably paying jobs would be toughest for the middle managers. "They're the ones who would take it on the neck," Dad said. So, we set out to find small businesses that we could eventually turn over to them.

As a result, over the next 15 years, I would root out fraud in the furniture industry, butt heads with Penn Central, threaten (sort of) to punch out a petty politician, and nearly find myself sucked into a Beacon Hill shakedown. Oh, and I mustn't forget the lunch at the legendary Pier 4 restaurant that left me with a bloody mouth and owner Anthony Athanas accusing me of planting glass shards in bouillabaisse.

Now I must warn you to be patient as I recount these stories. None follows a straight line. It seemed as if every time we made a move we would open a new Pandora's box.

SIDING SIDELINE

We ran small ads in *The Wall Street Journal* and *The Journal of Commerce* stating that we were looking to buy small manufacturing or service businesses. Out of many replies, we chose to acquire a Charlestown-based furniture warehousing and delivery company. It was called RADIN (Receivers and Distributors in New England). Cleverly enough, that acronym also happened to be the last name of the owner, Michael Radin. Located on a siding in the Charlestown yards of the Boston and Maine Railroad, the company annually unloaded 1,500 boxcars of furniture shipped from Southern manufacturers. While stockpiling some furniture in anticipation of future demand, RADIN delivered most of the merchandise to major New England retailers to fulfill existing orders. The company's books were sketchy, but seemed to show a profitable business.

Before making the purchase, we asked Dud Grant – then Shawmut's comptroller and the man whom we had tapped to run RADIN – to observe operations and determine whether everything was kosher. After he gave his thumbs up, we were ready to proceed with the purchase. But then the Boston Redevelopment Authority announced it was taking over the Charlestown rail yards.

Scrambling to relocate, RADIN leased a long freight building on Fan Pier in South Boston. Now this was not today's glittering South Boston, with its convention center, art museum, courthouse, office and apartment buildings, and hotels. The only retail business on Fan Pier at that time was an Italian deli. But the freight building suited us just fine. It sat next to a double siding off the New York, New Haven and Hartford Railroad, and its loading docks could accommodate some 50 trailers. With this move, RADIN was an even more attractive deal, so we went ahead with it.

RAILROADED BY A COUSIN

Long after we had left RADIN behind us, we found that we hadn't fully escaped the business.

In its never-ending search for revenue, Penn Central went after unpaid fines, called demurrage charges, that are imposed if a company takes too long unloading or loading a rail car. When we received a rail car, we had to turn it around within 10 days or pay a daily penalty. The railroad had checkpoints to scan barcodes on cars, recording the date they arrived in the Boston rail yards. The problem with this system, however, was that rail cars often had a tendency to get lost – sometimes for weeks – as they were shuffled around to their final destinations. But the railroad accounting system assumed that the cars were on the proper siding within three days after passing the checkpoint. We made sure to record exactly when each car arrived and departed RADIN. In fact, we kept the data in a specially bound ledger for tracking the cars. In many cases, we had records of tracer orders on cars that had not shown up for weeks. But our meticulous bookkeeping didn't stop Penn Central from going after us.

The railroad hired a lawyer to comb through the books for unpaid demurrage charges. The lawyer happened to be a distant cousin of mine, but that didn't stop him from badgering us without bothering to check if the railroad records were indeed correct. Even more infuriating was the way he went about collecting the money. Rather than making a single demand for the total amount he claimed we owed for the years in question, he sent out bills for separate incidents. He knew what he was doing, because each time I protested, our attorney would say the amount at issue was less than the cost of fighting it in court.

Then one day, my cousin slipped up. He sent us two demurrage charges at once. Now it was worth our while to contest the claims. When the case came before Framingham District Court, I arrived armed with my record books. My cousin put a Penn Central representative from Philadelphia on the stand. My lawyer asked him if based on his personal experience, he could flatly state my records were wrong. He could not.

After two hours of legal sparring, the judge said to me, "Mr. Wyner, would you pay anything to let this go?" I said, "Your honor, my son has a swimming match at 1 p.m.; it's worth $200 to me if I can leave now." That outraged my cousin, because he had been demanding $3,500. After he rejected my offer, the battle continued until 4 p.m. At that point, my cousin announced, "OK, I'll take the $200." No way, I responded. I'd missed my son's match. I wasn't about to pay anything, despite my lawyer's warning that the judge might not appreciate my stubbornness. The judge, however, turned out to be sympathetic, and my cousin went home with nothing. He never bothered us again.

BREAKING LEGS

Shortly after we took over the business, Dud was walking about the plant when he noticed something odd: a special stash of furniture in the corner. "That was Michael Radin's profit," a longtime employee told him. He went on to explain that shipments often included pieces that weren't listed on the manifest. Instead of telling the manufacturer of the overages, RADIN workers would set them aside and eventually break a leg or otherwise damage the pieces. They would then add the pieces to concealed damage claims that RADIN filed with the railroad on behalf of retailers who reported flawed furniture that they (ostensibly) found after unpacking crates. The railroad would pay those claims and send the damaged merchandise to a salvage facility.

When Dud asked me how to handle the situation, I ordered an immediate end to the practice. I told him that when new rail shipments came in, we should report all unordered pieces. Further, I said we should report all the overages that we found accumulated by the previous owner. The manufacturers and railroads didn't notice that we were doing anything differently, but doing the right thing showed up on our bottom line. Profits dropped dramatically.

As time went on, we learned that such deceit occurred at all levels of the furniture business. The retailers participated, too, especially when customers canceled special orders at the last minute. We suspected that many stores, rather than incur factory restocking fees and costly shipping charges, would, say, gouge the top of a table and claim it as "hidden damage" discovered when they uncrated the furniture. Such "hidden damages" were the railroad's responsibility, as it was assumed they occurred in transit. The giveaway to us was when the retailer didn't order a replacement.

I suggested a way for the railways to cut their losses: We would hire craftsmen to restore any furniture we or the retailer found to be damaged, and bill the railroad the actual cost of the repair. The railroad loved the idea, and RADIN's blue-ribbon service set a new standard among distribution services. We guaranteed damage-free delivery to the retailer. The amount of "damaged" furniture dwindled when retailers realized they no longer could game the system.

Soon, we had the business humming, with the capacity to handle well over 1,500 freight cars a year. RADIN had begun to develop a reputation as a progressive addition to the furniture scene. Our building was still the only structure on Fan Pier except for that corner deli. The location had a beautiful harbor view, and I was looking into buying a boat to tie up to the pier.

Then a decision made in corporate boardrooms hundreds of miles away literally threatened to derail us. In 1968, the federal government ordered Penn Central to take over the New York-New Haven line when it went into bankruptcy. Penn Central then sought to squeeze whatever money it could from the acquisition.

SHOVED OFF A PIER

To generate cash, the railroad looked to liquidate some of its properties, including the Fan Pier. Anxious to avoid another move, we approached Penn Central about buying the parcel. A railroad executive told us that only one other party was interested – Anthony Athanas of Pier 4 restaurant, who had designs on filling in the water between piers. The executive suggested that we meet with Athanas to consider partnering on the acquisition and sharing use of the property. We met at Pier 4, and I thought we really hit it off. Everything was "Anthony that" and "Jerry this," as if we were great friends. He told me that he planned to build a hotel complex. We worked out a plan to buy the Penn Central parcel together, setting aside an area for RADIN to continue business. We figured we would bid $1.5 million.

I felt pretty good about the outcome of our discussions until I started hearing people tell me I would be crazy to do business with Athanas. "He's the worst man you could ever meet," one person said, referring to him in saltier terms. I looked deeper into the matter and discovered that his sons had a similar reputation. My father and I decided that it would not be wise to partner with the Athanas family.

Still, we were wary of becoming embroiled in a bidding war with Athanas. Having obtained the rights to fill the area between his restaurant and Fan Pier, he had a greater incentive to pay a higher price. So, I met again with the restaurateur. I suggested that he purchase the property and then lease us the land we needed for our business. Athanas agreed and made a successful $1.5 million bid.

The next day we received a shock in the form of a letter from Athanas. It began with a misspelling: "Dear Mr. Weiner" and rapidly went downhill from there. The gist was that we were now considered trespassers. Athanas said that while we had the right to the property immediately along the tracks, our trucks could not use the driveway to our building. He stated he intended to bulldoze the truck's access road.

Athanas then proceeded to sue for trespass and damages both RADIN and its parent business, R. H. Wyner Associates (the name we went under after selling Shawmut to Duplan). Further, he added us personally to the suit, placing attachments on both my father's house and mine. Our lawyers called that tactic an unheard-of abuse of process.

In response, we instructed our law firm, Nutter McClennen & Fish, to file a countersuit and attach Pier 4 restaurant. To remove the liens on our homes, my father and I posted cash in escrow. Years later, Wursthaus owner Frank Cardullo – who was friends with both Athanas and our family – brought us together to settle the matter. We were surprised to learn that our attorneys had never actually attached Pier 4. Thus, we didn't have much bargaining power. But by that time, with accumulated interest, the escrow account had doubled. We agreed to split the money with Athanas just to get rid of him, and ended up with our original deposit.

WAREHOUSE MASTERPIECE

Meanwhile, I found a new site for RADIN on 56 acres in Sudbury, located at the crossroads of two railroads, the Boston and Albany and the Penn Central. We built a big and unusually attractive building for a warehouse and trucking company. At Genevieve's initiative, we became corporate sponsors of the Institute of Contemporary Art, which in turn helped us with the design of the structure. The ICA selected eye-catching, extra-large brick for the exterior, incorporating a large abstract welded steel sculpture. We equipped the interior with automated carts to shuttle the furniture. Together with the ICA, Genevieve came up with the idea of painting each cart a different color. Proud of the collaboration, the ICA touted the project as its first entry into the field of industrial art.

So once again we seemed to be sitting pretty: an artistically ambitious new building, rail access and the bonus of developable land fronting Route 20. What we didn't anticipate was the mischief of small-town politics.

Sudbury was an example of a town where apathetic citizens had relinquished control to a bunch of old cronies. The trouble started with an approach from the owner of a neighboring property, Milton Bartlett, who wanted an easement that would provide access to Route 20. Bartlett proposed a 60-foot-wide swath that would have crossed the railroad tracks and cut our property in two.

I explained to him that granting the easement would upend our plans for the property. It turned out that Bartlett was chairman of the local water authority. He said if we didn't provide the easement, he would block us from turning on our hookup to the town's water supply. We couldn't open without a functioning sprinkler system. I called up our less-than-neighborly neighbor and told him, "The water line is finished. I'm coming with a photographer and opening the valve myself." I then added, half-jokingly but to emphasize my determination: "If you try to physically prevent me from doing so, he might just get a picture of me punching you right in the nose."

As it wasn't my style to get physical, I was fortunate that the water czar didn't try to call my bluff. Without incident, I turned on the water valve, and we were in business.

But Bartlett wasn't finished. His brother John Bartlett happened to be chairman of the board of assessors. Suddenly, we found that the assessment for our 56 acres had soared to $20,000 an acre from just $500. I sent our attorney, Steve Comen, to meet with the assessors. Comen reported back that the chairman – evidently not realizing that our lawyer was Jewish – had made a reference to that "Jew Wyner." I might mention that the chairman had been a classmate of mine at Tufts – although we hardly knew each other then.

When Comen asked me what to do next, I said that I wasn't sure of anything except that we would never dignify that board by ever coming before it again. Then events finally broke our way. The Sudbury town counsel, David Turner, had somehow learned about the ethnic slur. Disgusted that such behavior could still occur, Turner quickly called for a meeting of the Sudbury Board of Selectmen. With the selectmen's backing, he then assembled the assessors. The chairman happened to be out of town; he returned to discover he'd been dethroned. Our property assessment was reduced to its previous level, and I never had any other issues on that score. I would later become good friends with Turner when he served as Brookline's town counsel while I was moderator. Eventually, he went from writing briefs to composing symphonies.

THOSE IMMORAL MOVIE HOUSES

With RADIN up and running, I turned my attention to the front part of the property. A developer proposed building a shopping center there that would include a Jerry Lewis Twin Cinemas, a Stop & Shop, a Medimart and a W.T. Grant. When I went before Town Meeting in 1971, I spoke of how we had contacted other retailers in town and spoke of our efforts to be a good neighbor. The planning board and finance committee endorsed our plans, citing the additional tax revenues and the possibility that the development would spur the state into making much-needed improvements to Route 20.

Other boards, including the selectmen, objected to the shopping center. They said it would draw traffic from out of town and undermine Sudbury's small-town atmosphere. You won't read it in the town's annual report for 1971, but what I think doomed the plan was a local druggist who didn't want the competition from a chain pharmacy. I suspect he may have been behind an anonymous mailing that went out to residents warning of the threat the movie theater posed to their children's morals. It sounded far-fetched, considering that Jerry Lewis Cinemas didn't show anything racier than PG films, but the campaign apparently worked. Sudbury has an open Town Meeting, which means all residents are eligible to vote. The letter brought out one of the largest turnouts for a Town Meeting in memory. Our plan was rejected by a vote of 120 in favor, 453 opposed.

The shopping center quashed, we came up with a new plan, one that tapped into Genevieve's favorite sport. We built Sudbury Skating and Tennis, featuring a full-size indoor hockey rink and four indoor tennis courts. We were confident that the demand for these sports was not only strong, but growing. Once again, though, we found our path strewn with unexpected obstacles.

At the request of the high school, we built a 500-seat stadium for the rink. School officials said they needed a venue of that size to accommodate all the fans of the very popular sport. We agreed, although seating for 500 meant additional costs for fire insulation and other features to meet stricter building codes. By the time we opened, the Metropolitan District Commission had finished its own rink in Marlborough. The MDC rink charged a quarter of what we did for renting the ice. The high school went with the Marlborough rink, and our extra expenditures went for naught. We never hosted a single game.

BARROOM POLITICS

Competing with a public facility is difficult under the best of circumstances, but the MDC rink enjoyed an advantage that we could never hope to counter. The Department of Public Utilities set an electric rate for the MDC that was below the power company's cost. This was at the time of the Arab oil boycott, when energy costs were skyrocketing. Our electric bill to run the compressors for making and maintaining the ice jumped from our original estimate of $25,000 a year to $175,000. I appealed to the state, arguing that since we shared the same customer base with the MDC, we should be charged the same electric rate. After making repeated requests, I finally was able to schedule a hearing with the DPU. When I arrived, I learned the hearing had been canceled. I also learned that I would not get anywhere unless I hired a lobbyist. I could sympathize with Dorothy when she arrived in Oz and pronounced, "Toto, I've a feeling we're not in Kansas anymore." Beacon Hill was not Brookline.

I hired a lobbyist, who made an appointment for me to meet with the head of the legislative committee that oversaw the DPU. My first clue of something fishy was the meeting's location: a bar on Cambridge Street. When I went inside, I was directed to a table with a phone on it and told to wait. This apparently was the lawmaker's unofficial office. When he arrived and got down to business, the conversation began veering in a direction that made me very uncomfortable. As he talked about calling this guy and that guy, I worried that he was going to ask me for money. Feeling my hair standing on end, I excused myself and left.

Meanwhile, the club was flourishing – from the standpoint of patronage, that is. Genevieve did a terrific job managing it. She earned a certificate to become a tennis pro and enlisted our brother-in-law Walter Levitan, a retired jeweler and terrific tennis player, to be one of the teachers. He became much in demand. In the summer, we sponsored tennis and hockey camps. Members of the original Boston Lobsters of World Team Tennis were among the draw in 1973 and 1974. They held open practices with their coach, the famous Romanian player Ion Tiriac. On occasion, as a favor, they would do a demo match; a few times, Ion and one of his players would play a short set with my friends and me. At the hockey camp, we had Phil Esposito and Ken Hodge. The Bruins stars, though, did present a problem – they couldn't resist straying over to the tennis camp to court the female Lobsters.

Although we were drawing more than a thousand clients a week to the club, our expenses outpaced our revenues. We simply couldn't compete with the subsidized state hockey rink down the road. I met with a vice president of Middlesex Bank, which held the mortgage on the sports complex. I told him that unless we could renegotiate the terms of the loan, we probably would have to discontinue operations and liquidate our assets. I explained that we needed an immediate decision because it was already June, when we ordinarily would be taking deposits for the fall season. Unless we were sure we'd be staying in business, we could not in good faith accept those payments. The banker agreed to a deal that would keep our interest payments the same, but lower our principal payments for five years. He said he would confirm the arrangement in writing, but gave us his word that it would go through. Based on that assurance, we began taking deposits for fall.

 A few months later, though, the vice president dropped a bombshell on us. He said that his board refused to renegotiate the terms of the mortgage. Flabbergasted, I said, "You gave us your word!" He offered no apologies.

Under the circumstances, we felt we had no choice but to shut down. Our biggest concern was that our members would be able to secure good court times elsewhere for the fall and winter indoor tennis seasons. We turned down an offer for our membership list from one club because it wasn't willing to provide that assurance.

Thanks to the good relations Genevieve had established with another nearby club, it agreed to accept our members and provide them prime-time slots. Even though the club didn't pay us for our list, we accepted the offer, and we refunded deposits to those members who didn't want to make the move.

Meanwhile, we were left with a fully outfitted sports club on our hands. We sold off all the equipment that could be moved: the hockey dasher boards (high-quality glass ones) to a rink in Canada, the compressors for the ice to a local buyer, and the artificial tennis turf to a club in Boston. The building was worth more than the outstanding mortgage, but we decided against putting it on the market. That would have meant continuing to do business with the bank that had betrayed us. Secured by the land and the buildings, the mortgage was non-recourse, allowing us simply to walk away from the property. With head held high, I went to the bank vice president and dropped the keys on his desk. The bank accepted the title, and it made money on the property. But I have no regrets. Life is too short to waste time with people who lack principles.

RADIN, too, ran into business difficulties because we couldn't continue to match the charges of two competitors that weren't unionized. Our warehouse workers and drivers were members of the Teamsters. Under the terms of their contract, they earned four times that of nonunion workers. Making matters worse, all our warehouse employees were classified in the same high-wage category as the over-the-road truck drivers. I tried to persuade the head of the union chapter in Boston to organize the workers at our competitors or else grant us wage concessions. Without a level playing field, I said, we would be forced out of business. The union was somewhat sympathetic, but wouldn't compromise. Over the next several months, then, we wound down RADIN's operations and helped our customers transition elsewhere. We did get a good price on our architectural gem, selling the building to a wire-coating company best known for its lobster traps.

All of this occurred in the late '70s and coincided with our repurchase of Shawmut, which we had sold to the Duplan Corporation a decade before. Fortuitously, since all the operations came under the umbrella of R.H. Wyner Associates Inc., we could offset the losses we had incurred from our forays into the furniture and sports businesses against the profits we eventually made after buying Shawmut back. Ultimately, we returned to a variation of the old name, calling the company Shawmut Corporation.

ANTHONY, AGAIN

I can't close out this chapter without returning to Mr. Pier 4. While Athanas and I never clashed in court, we did in his restaurant. About a year after we moved RADIN to Sudbury, a Shawmut customer from out of town asked me to take him to lunch at Pier 4. I tried to persuade him to go to another restaurant, but he was insistent. I crossed my fingers that we wouldn't run into Athanas.

We got off to an auspicious start, seated at a corner table. But after starting in on my bouillabaisse, I suddenly found blood gushing from my mouth. A piece of glass had wound up in the fish stew and cut my gums. Seeing my distress, a waitress came to my rescue. I told her not to make a fuss. Next thing I knew, though, I heard someone screaming at me. It was Athanas. He accused me of deliberately planting the glass and demanded that I leave the restaurant. I calmly ignored him, and the staff eventually brought me something else to eat. At least my guest found the incident amusing. I had already told him why I had wanted to dine someplace else.

Athanas would eventually get his comeuppance. He had an opportunity to make $80 million on Fan Pier through a hotel deal, but it unraveled in a series of messy lawsuits. Athanas would have been bankrupt had his political friends not bailed him out by building the federal courthouse there.

Today, the property is estimated to be worth well over $1 billion. To think, I once could have had it for a mere $1.5 million.

PART V: ON THE SEA

- **Captains Courageous:** It all started with a yellow canoe

- **A boat of our own:** Exploring the coast aboard Seabiscuit

- **Adventures in the Caribbean:** The more remote the better

- **Blasting through the waves:** In search of a better boat

CAPTAINS COURAGEOUS

Braving fumes, fog and a dog – while recharging our marriage

Sailing has given me countless hours of bliss, punctuated by hair-raising scrapes.

BOATING HAS BEEN A part of my life for almost as long as I can remember. It has provided me countless hours of idyllic bliss, punctuated by a few hair-raising scrapes that tested my nautical nerve and skill. It brought me closer to my father and to my sons and grandchildren. It nearly grounded my marriage before it got off to its start, but ultimately helped make it more seaworthy than ever. It introduced me to a prime minister and a senator – and exposed both my strengths and my weaknesses.

I received my first lessons in sailing from my father, but my formal education began when I was 12. I'd take the streetcar downtown (just a nickel for students under age 16) and stroll over to the Charles River Esplanade, where the Community Boating program was just getting underway. I believe the dues were just $1 a month. I first had to learn how to rig the sails and then how to trim them depending on the direction of the wind. After many apprentice sails with more experienced young sailors, I finally passed the test to sail solo up and down the Charles River Basin. The skyline looked very different than it does today. There were no skyscrapers in Back Bay; the old John Hancock building didn't go up until the late '40s.

It would make a better story if I could regale you with tales of how I romanced Genevieve while taking her sailing on the Charles, but it was just as well that we had kept our dating to dry land. I realized that on our honeymoon in Bermuda, when we chartered a boat to go fishing. The minute Genevieve stepped on the boat, she got seasick. I looked at her with some sympathy as she lay on the bunk below deck, but

I must admit that my appetite got the better of my chivalry. Though it was only 8 in the morning, I was already hungry. I asked my new bride if I could eat her lunch, seeing how her stomach was upset and she probably wouldn't have an appetite. Luckily for me, Genevieve didn't toss me overboard. As to the fishing, we had a pretty good haul. I particularly remember the moray eel, a long, skinny, feisty fish with razor-sharp teeth. It put up quite a fight before the crew managed to pitch it back into the water.

THE YELLOW CANOE

That honeymoon sail was to be our last for many years to come. I decided not to push it because I was concerned Genevieve would again become seasick. Then one day in 1966 she surprised me by purchasing a boat through the WGBH auction. I learned about it when I came home from work and the kids greeted me with a news bulletin: "Mommy bought a yellow canoe on Channel 2."

As Genevieve tells the story, I reacted by slamming the door and giving everyone the cold shoulder. That's probably true. Not that she could have known, but I had been intending to talk with her about research I had been doing into buying a small sailboat. Genevieve had unwittingly preempted any discussion. I was angry at myself for not bringing up the matter sooner, and even more so for crushing my family's enthusiasm.

It was a fine canoe, made by the famous Old Town Canoe Company. After I calmed down, with Genevieve's approval, we purchased a kit from the company to convert the vessel into a sailing canoe. I then gave Genevieve sailing lessons, and she was a quick learner. All was going well until I persuaded her to cast aside her qualms and take the canoe for her first solo sail. We were on Cape Cod in Phinney's Harbor by Mashpee Village in Bourne, where our family used to summer.

As Genevieve headed closer toward other boats, I yelled, "Look out! Look out! She doesn't know how to sail!" I was worried that she might make an unconventional move that would confuse other sailors. I hadn't bothered to consider how the warning might sound to Genevieve. She immediately lost all confidence and nearly capsized the boat in her haste to change course. It tipped, taking on water. But Genevieve was in wading depth, not far from the shore. There was no real problem, only a loss of face – more mine than Gen's.

GEN'S BRILLIANT IDEA

So once again, we went years without much sailing until, as before, Genevieve brought boats back into our lives. It happened at Marriage Encounter. As we bared and shared our souls, Genevieve said it bothered her that she was forced to share my limited free time with my golfing friends. "Why don't we find something we can do together, like sailing?" she asked. I was doubtful. "But you get seasick," I replied. Genevieve persisted, so we agreed to give it another try.

The America's Cup race was coming up in Newport, Rhode Island, and Genevieve suggested that we charter a sailboat to watch. My son Daniel and I picked up the boat in Bristol, Rhode Island, and set off for Newport to meet up with the rest of the family. Since we were sailing at night, we had to work together to identify distant buoys from their distinctive blinking lights. When we got closer to them, we could verify our sightings and plot our progress on our charts. This was long before the advent of GPS, which makes it easy to figure out where you are. Thanks to a steady wind, we didn't need the engine. The only sounds were the whoosh of the boat lazily cutting through the water and the slap, slap, slap of small waves rippling against the hull. After setting our heading for a buoy, we'd sit back and identify the constellations. With neither city lights nor clouds to obscure the sky, we enjoyed a rare view of the Milky Way. For three hours, we were in our own world.

Chartering the boat turned out to be a new challenge for me. Not only were my sailing skills a bit rusty, but I was taking on a strange boat that, at 36 feet, was 8 feet longer than anything I had sailed before. With the entire family aboard, we motored out of the harbor. Away from the congestion, I raised the sails. As they filled with the wind, the boat began to heel. That was perfectly normal, but Genevieve got nervous. "Straighten this boat up," she ordered. I tried to explain that the boat was designed to sail while tipped, but to no avail. "Straighten this boat up or take me in," she barked. In frustration, I said, "Genevieve, if you think I am doing this deliberately, why don't you take the helm?" Well, that was the cure. As soon as she took control of the boat, she felt at ease. The seasickness vanished. Genevieve proved to be a natural at the helm. In fact, over time, I came to feel more comfortable with her in control and me at the navigation station below.

But Genevieve's fear of sailing never totally disappeared – at least at the start of the season. Every year, as we would bed down on that first night on our mooring at the New Bedford Yacht Club in Padanaram Harbor, Genevieve would say, "I forgot that I'm scared to death of boats." And I'd reply, "Relax, we don't have to go anywhere for days." Inevitably, though, the next morning Genevieve would be over her jitters, and we'd set out to sea.

Taking the wheel was Genevieve's cure for seasickness.

LOST IN A FOG

That first charter expedition wasn't only memorable because of Genevieve's sailing epiphany. Several days later, our sons and I sailed out of Newport one misty afternoon for Block Island, Rhode Island. Suddenly, the fog thickened. When we reached the mouth of the harbor, we couldn't make out the town. It was too risky to turn back because we couldn't blindly navigate such a busy harbor. To find our way, we had to rely on a small portable radio direction-finder that came with the boat. We could get our bearings by tuning to designated frequencies of radio navigation beacons marked on our chart. By rotating the antenna until the signal was loudest, we could note the direction of the beacon. The idea was that by repeating this process with two or three beacons, we could fix our location by triangulation (seeing where the directional lines crossed on the chart). But before we could capture the second signal, the direction-finder was rendered useless when its antenna broke off.

At that point, we decided it would be too tricky to find our way to our original destination, Old Harbor, a small port on the near side of Block Island. Just beaching the boat wasn't an option. Unlike the smaller sailboats with rounded bottoms and retractable centerboards to which I had been accustomed, this one had a keel. We headed for the larger port on Great Salt Pond on the far side of the island.

While we couldn't see above, we could, in effect, peer below by using a depth finder. By comparing soundings to the depth charts, we followed a contour that took us around to the back side of the island. As I recall, I stationed one of the boys on the bow to keep an ear out for other boats. I had another blowing a foghorn on a regular basis. I had the third son keep his eyes peeled for a break in the fog that would reveal the island. I kept us under sail, rather than use the engine, so that we might eventually hear the waves lapping against the shore. That welcome sound came after two tense hours. Just then, several boats emerged from the fog, heading straight toward us. At the last minute, they veered away.

Later, we learned that they had targeted us because our foghorn sounded exactly like that of the Coast Guard station at the entrance to the harbor. What a disappointment we must have been for those other fogbound sailors!

After that close call, our luck ran out when the boat got stuck on a shoal near the shore. Just as we were starting to work our way free, a power boat materialized out of the mist. Aboard were a father and several teenage sons. We didn't know it at the time, but they were members of the famed DuPont family, which for generations had owned an estate on the island. To us, they seemed like a bunch of ordinary guys. Several climbed out and helped push us off. They then guided us into the harbor, which turned out to be very close by. We then heard the foghorn that matched ours. Before us, almost completed enshrouded in mist, was the Coast Guard station.

TROUBLE IN THE KEYS

The first sign of trouble was when I fell on my face as I stepped onto the sailboat.

We had leased the boat for a week's trip along the southern tip of Florida, our first charter since the Newport trip. Accompanying us were the Greenfields, Genevieve's sister Harriet and her husband,

Michael. The boat was tied up at the Florida Keys home of its owner, an Eastern Airlines pilot, whom we had found through a charter boat agent. This was long before charter companies were common.

As I was climbing aboard, Michael distracted me with a question about pillows attached to the boat. I was not only baffled by his question, but had trouble seeing what he was talking about because I was still adjusting to my first pair of bifocals. Between my fall and Michael's maritime faux pas (those "pillows" are called fenders), the owner took us for a couple of landlubbers. He pulled me aside to make sure I had some idea of how to handle a boat.

The second sign of trouble was a few days later, when I noticed that the starting motor made a grinding noise each time I switched on the engine. But since everything else seemed to be in working order and the sound was only momentary, I didn't give it much thought.

So off we went, with me at the helm and the others having a grand time chatting away. Navigating the Intracoastal Waterway was fairly boring. The scenery was monotonous, and much of the time I had to use the motor because many stretches of the channel were too narrow for sailing. No challenge there.

We headed south along the inland side of the Keys, stopping overnight in Islamorada, where we picked up provisions at a grocery store. The following day, we continued south. While everyone else relaxed and chatted, enjoying the beautiful weather, I continued steering at the helm. After four hours, as I had planned (though no one seemed interested in hearing my plans), I turned the boat to pass under a tall bridge that linked two of the keys and then headed back north.

When it came time to tie up for the night, I pulled into the harbor on the ocean side of Islamorada. "Where are we going to find a store here?" my companions asked. To which I answered, "Why don't we go to the same store we went to last night?" It took a while before it dawned on them that we had looped back to Islamorada. They had been so caught up in their socializing that they had been oblivious to where we had been going.

On our final night, we pulled into a fancy development known as Ocean Reef on the northern part of Key Largo. We anchored in what we thought was a sheltered area, just offshore. By then, the engine noise had me so worried that I called the boat owner and left him a message telling him where we planned to eat that night. We then set off in a dinghy for the restaurant, where the owner eventually found us. He told us that he had just motored out to the boat and looked it over. He brusquely dismissed my concerns about the engine and admonished me for leaving the boat's lights on. He said he had shut them off. I told him I had left them on so that we could find the boat in the dark.

As it turned out, the dark would be the least of our concerns. Thanks to a sudden storm, we wandered for what seemed like hours in the rain-drenched dinghy before we found the sailboat. It would have been much easier had the owner not turned off that mooring light. At one point, Harriet expressed alarm that we'd be stuck out in the middle of the harbor overnight, unable to find the boat or our way back to the dock. I didn't take offense. She hadn't had much experience at sea, so I could only imagine how scared she must have felt.

Once we did get back aboard the sailboat, Harriet announced that she and Michael had just remembered that he had to conduct surgery the next afternoon. I shuttled them ashore in the dinghy early in the morning so they could catch a cab to the airport. After that miserable night on the dinghy, I could understand why the Greenfields decided to cut short their trip. But they did have the courage to sail with us again, becoming regular guests over the years to come.

Meanwhile, we were due to return the boat the next day, but despite the owner's assurances, the engine refused to start. Though we could still rely on the sails, the motor would have provided greater control over the boat. The last leg of the trip, all while under sail, proved uneventful – until we were just within sight of our destination. One obstacle stood in our way: a closed drawbridge. After blowing the boat's whistle three times – the standard signal for alerting the attendant to raise the bridge – I raced forward to the bow so that I'd be ready to drop anchor for an emergency stop. The wind was directly behind us, and we had no room to maneuver.

At last, we heard the bell rings that signaled that the attendant was lowering the road barriers. Just then, a guy dashed across the bridge, clutching a squirming dog. Before he made it to the other side, the dog jumped out of his arms to the deck of the bridge. "Get off the bridge," I yelled at him as he chased the dog. "We're about to collide!" At the last second, he scooped up the pooch and rushed off. Miraculously, seconds before our mast would have been crushed, the decks parted.

A BOAT OF OUR OWN

Not even hurricanes keep us from our home away from home

"Seabiscuit," Norman Fortier, photographer.
Courtesy of the New Bedford Whaling Museum.

For our maiden voyage, we sailed Seabiscuit up from Florida. It was not a breeze.

IN 1982, GENEVIEVE, THE sailor-come-lately, surprised me by announcing that we really ought to buy our own boat. "Really?" I said. "What's the point of owning a boat? Every time we charter a boat, it seems like the owner is a New York Stock Exchange member – or an Eastern Airlines pilot – who has to slave away to get it ready for us."

But with Genevieve's encouragement, we fulfilled my lifetime dream and purchased a 54-foot Hunter cutter rig sailboat from Havencraft, Hunter's dealer in Sudbury. A cutter rig is similar to a sloop, but its single mast is set farther back, allowing for a larger forward deck and a larger jib sail. Since the boat had been used as a demo for two years, we arranged for the dealer to have it refurbished at the factory, in Alachua, Florida. When it was ready, we flew down to sail it back to Massachusetts from the nearby port in Cocoa Beach. We did the trip in weeklong stages, leaving the boat at marinas so we could fly home for a couple of weeks at our day jobs. On some stretches of sailing, our sons or friends accompanied us.

The boat could sleep eight, but Genevieve and I could handle it ourselves. By this time, she was firmly ensconced at the helm. She had proven herself in the heaviest of weather. In fact, I preferred to navigate and leave the helm to her.

We called the boat Wahoo, after a type of fish. After that maiden voyage, we learned that Wahoo was also a brand of boat, so we decided to change the name. Genevieve suggested Seabiscuit, which I thought odd. Why name a boat after a racehorse? But Seabiscuit is actually another name for the nearly indigestible crackers that once were the staple of sailors' diets. The father of the famed racehorse was Hard Tack, yet another name for the sea crackers.

During the first leg of the trip, a horrendous storm struck after we tied up at a Florida port. We considered leaving the boat because the wind and waves were so strong that we feared the docks to which we were tied would be swept away. I stayed up the entire night, helping others rein in their boats. By the next morning, the weather had calmed enough for us to continue our journey. At our next port, Daytona Beach, I struggled mightily with the anchor, having to lower and raise it several times before it caught on the bottom. That was before we bought a power winch. Then, when we went ashore, I suddenly felt dizzy. Someone called 911, and I was rushed to a hospital.

When I told the doctor about how I had spent the past few days, he said, "Look, I could keep you here for a couple of days to make sure you haven't had a heart attack." But he said that he saw no evidence that I had had one, and that he wasn't surprised I felt faint after what I'd been through. "It's your choice," the doctor concluded. "If you decide to go on with your trip, I won't try to stop you." And so we sailed on. Fortunately, the dizziness did not return.

'ALL HANDS ON DECK!'

Our son George joined us for the stretch into St. Augustine. There wasn't a spot for us in a marina, so we anchored offshore not far from several other boats. I put two anchors out, one on the bow and one on the stern, because the current was swift and would turn with the tide in the middle of the night. I got up at 5:30 a.m., as usual the first riser. Rather than wake up the others, I decided to get us underway on my own. After hauling up the 45-pound bow anchor, but before I could pull up the stern anchor, the strong current twisted the direction of the boat. I couldn't put the engine into gear for fear the stern anchor line would foul the propeller. At the mercy of the current, we were heading straight for another boat.

I yelled to its crew: "All hands on deck! We're about to hit you!" A very startled guy and two girls, all stark naked, rushed topside. Somehow, they managed to push our boat away. I was now free to raise the stern anchor and get underway. Meanwhile, George and Genevieve slept right through the show.

The next several hundred miles were uneventful (and G-rated). As we headed into Charleston, it was just Genevieve and me. I radioed ahead to the dockmaster, requesting that he stand by to help me come alongside and tie up. I explained that I was still getting used to the boat. I told him it was on its first voyage, and I was concerned about damaging it. When we arrived, no one was there. Pulling alongside the dock, we heard a painful scraping sound. A nail protruding from the rub rail that was attached to the dock inflicted the first scratch on our pristine boat. The blemish remained as an unpleasant reminder until the topsides were refinished after Hurricane Bob years later.

For much of the journey, we took the Intracoastal Waterway. We mainly used the engine because there wasn't enough room to tack back and forth. Whenever we came to a drawbridge, we had to sound our horn to notify the operator. Usually, we'd have to wait for two or three boats to line up before the bridge would be opened. If you're nervous that a drawbridge will open as you drive over it, imagine being below in a boat when a drawbridge suddenly begins to close. That's what happened at one bridge on our trip.

We were second in a line of three boats, whose crews we had gotten to know from sharing the same slow trek north. After passing under, I was alarmed to see the bridge closing just as the last boat came through. Like a biting pair of teeth, the sides of the bridge crunched into the boat's mast about 30 feet up. The boat's owner and I yelled and blew our air horns to get the bridge operator's attention, but he appeared to be more interested in chatting with a girlfriend. When he finally saw what was happening, he put the bridge mechanism in reverse. By then, though, the sails and rigging had become so entangled with the roadway that as the bridge halves opened they lifted the boat 20 feet out of the water. Gravity prevailed, slamming the boat back down. Miraculously, it remained afloat. Those onboard were shaken up, but otherwise unhurt. The Coast Guard towed it 30 miles to a repair yard. The bridge operator was fired, and the boat owner had to wait two months before he could resume his trip. There's a postscript to the story: Several years later, I ran into the unlucky skipper at a Harvard Business School reunion. It turns out we had been classmates.

When we pulled into Norfolk, home of the huge naval base, we had completed three legs of our trip. We left the boat and flew home. At the rate we were going, it would take several more legs to get to Massachusetts. I decided to do the final trip in one sprint, shortening the route by traveling offshore. At Friday night services at Temple Israel following our return home, I asked around for a volunteer to join the crew. A former temple president, Gerry Holtz, signed on. I also enlisted the top mechanic at Shawmut, Joe Cabral. A Cape Verdean and former merchant marine, Joe softened his tough exterior with a gentle manner.

BUFFETED BY A BEHEMOTH

Back in Norfolk, it was pitch-dark by the time we were ready to shove off. I hadn't sailed the boat in the middle of the night before, so I was a little apprehensive. Just minutes out of port, we were jolted by five piercing blows of a ship's horn – the signal for imminent danger. I looked up and saw silhouetted against the sky the dark shape of an enormous supertanker bearing down on us. There was no way that this behemoth could possibly stop, so it was up to us to scramble out of the way. But I didn't know which way to turn because I couldn't tell exactly where the tanker was headed. For a few nerve-wracking moments, I thought we might have to brace for a collision. I frantically tried to establish bridge-to-bridge contact, but didn't get through until the tanker passed by with just 50 feet to spare. In the dark, it appeared to loom over us like a mountain.

Now I was really gun-shy as we pulled into the offshore sea lane. Marked by ocean buoys spaced many miles apart, it's like an aquatic highway. Spotting a boat 10 miles away, I'd become very cautious until I knew its exact course. I'd get on the radio and announce, "This is sailing vessel Wahoo, near offshore buoy [so and so], looking north and seeing you. Do you see me, Cap?" And the captain would respond, "I see you." Then he would add something like, "I'll pass you two whistles," which means on my starboard side. Thus assured, I'd calm down.

It's particularly tricky encountering barges at night or in the fog. They are being either pulled or pushed by tugs. Sometimes a single tug is pushing or pulling more than one barge. The number and positions of navigation lights tell the story. If you misread those lights, you risk plowing into a cable connecting a tug and a barge. The tug, being less maneuverable, cannot alter course for you. Tugs are an exception to the rule that a boat under power must give way to one under sail.

Sailing day and night, we took 2½ days to reach port in New Bedford. In keeping with the tenor of the trip, we picked up our yacht-club mooring in the midst of a storm.

COMMANDING A CONVOY

Our adventures with Seabiscuit had only just begun with its maiden voyage. We got ourselves into some dicey situations both on our own and with other boats. As new members of the New Bedford Yacht Club, we joined its annual Down Maine cruise. We looked forward to a packed itinerary, exploring the many inlets north of Portland. After we arrived in Falmouth Foreside, Maine, our first destination, a heavy fog set in. Playing it safe, the cruise commodore called off an excursion the next morning to Christmas Cove. To keep up with the rest of the schedule, we would have to skip that port when we went out the following day. Our sons were with us, and I'd been looking forward to showing them the cove. I had never visited it before, either, but was enticed by photographs in guidebooks.

Since Seabiscuit had radar – rare on a sailboat in those days – I announced that we would make the trip and guide all those who wished to follow. Three boats joined us. We notified the captains when our radar showed that they had passed particular buoys, and we told them which ways to turn. Visibility was under 30 feet. Had we had GPS – still unavailable for ordinary citizens – we would have known exactly where we were. Without it, we had to rely on dead reckoning and our knowledge of the waters to determine which radar blips represented tiny rocky islands and outcroppings. A mile offshore, we broke out of the fog and basked under sunny skies. Maine fog typically just hugs the shore.

We loved Maine so much that for several years, Southwest Harbor was a second home for Seabiscuit. We'd leave the boat there in the summer and fly up from Boston for short vacations.

Sometimes, I'd go up with Joe Cabral, the Shawmut mechanic I mentioned earlier. Joe enjoyed the trips, and I enjoyed his company. I also felt more secure, because between the two of us, we could fix just about anything that might go wrong – and on our first voyages each spring, things often would go wrong.

For a number of winters, I stored Seabiscuit at Shawmut on a stand in a corner of the warehouse, where we installed a special overhead door that was high and wide enough for it to pass through. After hours, Joe and I would upgrade and renovate the boat's mechanics and electronics. I also knew that I could rely on Joe's physical prowess. He had a reputation as someone who could take care of himself. I heard one tale – a tall one perhaps – about how in a bar brawl he had picked one guy up by the ankles and knocked another 10 down. He might have been fearsome, but not to me; we were great friends.

Aboard Seabiscuit with our first grandchild, Samuel Wyner, George's son.

Genevieve's sister Harriet Greenfield frequently joined us, along with her husband, Michael.

BAFFLING BUOYS

One evening, our son James, Joe and I set out from Southwest Harbor to Matinicus, a remote island famed for its birds. As we sailed out of the harbor we encountered heavy fog, which shrouded a rocky route that is tough to navigate even under the best of circumstances. We had to rely on the buoys that marked the narrow channel. But when we came up to what I thought would be buoy No. 2, where we were to make a turn, it was marked No. 4. I made a wide sweep around, but couldn't find No. 2. As we searched, the seas became heavier and heavier.

I decided our safest option was to head for a harbor with distinct night markings to guide us in. It was late when we set on the new course, for Camden, Maine, and James went down to sleep. I, too, was exhausted, but couldn't leave the helm. Joe was plenty strong, but he wasn't tall. To man the wheel in rough weather, with the wind and waves coming right on the beam, you need long legs that you can plant far apart for stability. Otherwise, you might lose your grip – or worse – as the waves rock the boat from side to side. After a few more hours of the pounding, I had had all I could take. I spotted a shore light signaling in three-flash bursts. Based on dead reckoning, and the chart, I concluded this was the entrance to North Haven Harbor. If I was wrong, we might have found ourselves on the rocks. But, as we headed in, an unoccupied mooring emerged from the mist. We hooked it and hit the sack. The next morning, we saw that we were at the North Haven Yacht Club. Fortunately, the mooring had been designated for guests. Otherwise, we might have been rudely, if rightfully, awakened in the middle of the night had the assigned boat owner returned.

We did eventually make it to Matinicus. Later I learned why we had gotten lost. In a rare move, the Coast Guard had changed the numbering system for the buoys. The No. 2 buoy had become No. 4. I had been going by the old numbers – if only I had obtained the updates for my chart.

My son George and his wife, Barbara, on a foggy morning off the Maine coast.

TURNING LOBSTER RED

One summer we moored Seabiscuit in Stonington Harbor on Deer Island, Maine. Often, we'd sail from there to a series of mostly uninhabited islands, along a passageway designated on the charts as Merchant Row. We'd drop anchor for the night just offshore one of them, Green Island. The only drawback was an alarm clock in the form of a lobsterman who at 5:30 a.m. would rush by at full speed on his way to lay his traps every time we anchored there. We'd be left rocking in his wake. The proper etiquette is to slow down, but I guess he figured we were just tourists who didn't merit common courtesy. Inwardly, I developed a strong dislike for the inconsiderate man.

On one particularly humbling excursion to Merchant Row, we were accompanied by our son George and his wife, Barbara, a native of Maine. As I once again dropped anchor at my favorite spot, Barbara expressed concern that the water appeared too shallow. I assured her that I had always anchored there and that we'd be fine. We took our dinghy to the shore and explored the little uninhabited island. When we returned, the tide had gone out, and our boat – all 54 feet of it – was lying on its side, its 6-foot keel appearing like a tongue sticking out at me. The low tide exposed the fact that we had anchored over a rock. I was embarrassed – not just because I hadn't heeded my daughter-in-law's warning, but because of how incompetent I thought we must have looked to other boaters. I started cleaning the hull, hoping that it would look like I had deliberately upended the boat.

While I was out there scrubbing away, along came my nemesis, the lobsterman. He was motoring home after a day with his traps. And, of course, he was going at full speed. But this time that was a good thing: The waves kicked up in his wake lifted Seabiscuit right off the rock. In the future, I always took his early morning wake as a friendly reminder not to be overconfident.

Speaking of pride, we used to play bridge occasionally with a South Brookline couple. They would regale us with their nautical accomplishments, making us feel like amateurs by comparison. One day we were tied up on a mooring in Vineyard Haven Harbor when we saw them sail by. They waved to us, a bit haughtily I thought. We then watched as the wife tried to use a boat hook to grab the pennant of a vacant mooring nearby. Trouble was they were sailing so fast that the hook slipped out of her hands and was left dangling from the mooring. They could have easily swung by to pick it up, but presumably that would have been too humiliating. Instead, they sailed right out of the harbor, leaving their boat hook behind. That got me thinking about the price of hubris.

CRASH LANDING

While the consequences of missing a mooring are generally no more serious than mussed-up pride, they proved nearly calamitous once when we were sailing into Woods Hole on a trip with my brother-in-law Michael Greenfield. Just as we were entering the harbor, the engine quit. I spotted an empty mooring at the edge of the crowded mooring field. I told Michael that he should be ready to drop anchor in case we missed the mooring. I didn't relish the prospect of trying to maneuver without power among all of those boats. In all the excitement, Michael must have frozen. We missed the mooring, and he didn't drop anchor.

The only way I could avoid a crash was to sail straight through the harbor and run up on a sandbar, which I had spotted on the charts. As I did so, I saw people on shore waving frantically to warn me that I was heading aground. When we hit the sandbar, I dropped the anchor and the sail. Some people stormed out in their dinghies to berate me about my lack of seamanship. I must admit I felt some satisfaction when I saw their attitudes abruptly change after I explained the circumstances. Fortunately, Seabiscuit survived the abrupt landing unscathed. After repairing the engine, we floated away on the high tide.

We had our share of scares on the high seas as well. One was so serious that we put in a call to the Coast Guard. Along with friends Malcolm Gordon and his wife, Nan Miller, we were sailing from Southwest Harbor to Roque Island, Maine. That's up near Campobello Island, where FDR had his summer retreat. At mid-day, when we were well out to sea and the four of us were in the cockpit, acrid smoke started to billow out from below. I suspected that the problem was in the forward cabin, but its hatch could not be opened from the deck. As Malcolm tried to raise the Coast Guard, I took a deep breath and rushed below deck – past the cabins, the galley and the dining area – to the source of the smoke. Since it had to be watertight, the hatch was secured with four turnbuckles, each of which required a half-dozen twists to open. The smoke was so heavy that I could only make a few turns before having to rush the 35 feet back to the cockpit to gulp down fresh air. I must have made the round trip eight times before I was able to open the hatch. The source of the smoke was a saltwater pump I had installed to wash down the foredeck, which our dog Buttons had turned into his private head. The pump switch must have corroded, causing a short circuit that had turned the device on. But because the water valve was shut, it couldn't pump anything. The wiring got so hot that the insulation burned up. It glowed bright orange. Fortunately, nothing flammable was nearby. I switched off the electricity on the circuit to the pump, and the emergency was over.

Meanwhile, Malcolm had reached the Coast Guard – the Canadian Coast Guard in Nova Scotia. The hilly terrain on the Maine coast blocked our signal from reaching US authorities. It's a good thing we no longer needed help; the Canadian base was 75 miles away. Despite the ruined pump, the boat was good to go, and we completed our trip as planned.

Hurricane Bob swept Seabiscuit ashore in 1991.

BATTERED BY BOB

The worst punishment Seabiscuit ever endured was during Hurricane Bob in August 1991. The fast-moving storm blasted our home base in South Dartmouth with 100 mile-per-hour gusts. The wind and the 25-foot sea surge swept some 75 boats onto a bridge that spanned the inner section of Padanaram Harbor.

The day before, I had prepared Seabiscuit for the storm by lengthening and doubling the lines on our mooring to allow plenty of play so the boat could ride out the expected surge and turbulent waters. While Seabiscuit survived the surge, it was sideswiped by at least one wayward vessel that had broken loose from its own mooring. Then, as the winds reversed after the center of the storm passed through, the boat finally wore out its lines and was blown ashore.

Our insurance company had planned to lift Seabiscuit and several other boats with a heavy-duty copter brought up from Louisiana. I figured out a way to use the halyard winch to force the boat onto its side so that it could be floated out at high tide. Normally, the winch is used to raise and lower the sail. It controls a line (the halyard) that runs up through a pulley at the top of the mast and down to the top of the sail. For our makeshift rescue, we rerouted the halyard, disconnecting it from the sail and attaching it instead to a heavy anchor set way out from the beam of the boat. By tightening the halyard, we tugged the mast down and tipped the boat on its side. That freed the keel, which had been stuck in the sand. When the tide came in, I had Seabiscuit towed for $100 into deep water. As soon as we released the line from the anchor in the deeper water, the weight of the keel immediately righted the boat.

You might think the insurer would have been grateful that we had saved the cost of a $20,000 helicopter rental. Not a chance. The company proved obstinate when I tried to recoup the cost of repairs, arguing that it should only have to cover the cost of refinishing the side of the boat that had been scraped when it washed ashore. I protested that if just the damaged side was refinished, it would not match the other side, which had weathered the elements for nine years. "If we did both sides, you'd practically have a brand new boat," the agent told me. I responded, "OK, then, just make sure the refinishing job matches the look of the other side." In the end, the company relented and paid to refinish everything.

In the wake of another hurricane, when the boat had been safely secured in Boston, we set out for Padanaram after the weather had calmed down. Everything was fine until we exited the Cape Cod Canal. All of a sudden we were socked with steady 40-knot winds. That might not have been hurricane force, but when you're in a sailboat, it's really rough. Making matters worse, the driving rain was piercing us like needles. Barely in control of the boat, we pulled into Red Brook Harbor near Bourne. Boats were zigging

MR. FOGHORN

I know I have a reputation for being a high-tech guy, but one of my funniest sea stories involves relying on a very low-tech instrument: my voice.

We were traveling from Martha's Vineyard to Nantucket with Genevieve's sister, Harriet, and her husband, Michael Greenfield. When the fog rolled in, I discovered that my foghorn wasn't working. We spotted a large merchant ship looming in the murky distance.

"Don't worry," I assured everyone. "I can do a foghorn."

Cupping my hands together, I boomed, "A-hooooga."

Amazingly enough, the ship answered my call, but with the mechanical version.

and zagging on their moorings as we went by. We found an opening on a dock, where I threw a line to a fellow boatsman who had come out on the deck after spotting our predicament. He managed to fasten it down, but then it broke loose from Seabiscuit. That was my fault: I hadn't made sure the line was fastened on our end. It wasn't a big deal, because the strong winds were buffeting us toward the dock. Still, after we got ashore, my Good Samaritan delivered the final blow of the day: a long lecture about irresponsible seamanship. Never throw a line that has not been properly fastened, he admonished me. He was right. Even in extreme conditions, it's unwise to skimp on safety.

My father with Buttons on Seabiscuit.

Yet another "shiver me timbers" but fascinating experience came in the form of a whale that was as long as our boat. We were on our way to a landfall at Portland, Maine, and had just passed the tip of Cape Cod. The whale popped up about 10 feet away alongside us – so close that we could hear its heavy breathing. We imagined the worst – that it would dive and then burst up right under our hull. But we were lucky. Apparently, the whale was just looking for company. After about a half hour swimming to our side, it decided it had given us enough excitement for one day and went on its way.

TOASTING TEDDY

Before we bought our home in Martha's Vineyard, finding a place to moor our boat there was a bit like hunting for a parking space in downtown Boston. At Vineyard Haven, only two moorings in the inner harbor could accommodate the length of our boat. One belonged to Senator Edward Kennedy and the other to the man he had vanquished in the 1962 primary, Edward McCormack. Since neither of them had a home on the Vineyard, their moorings were frequently available. One afternoon, we were sitting on deck at McCormack's mooring when Kennedy and his new wife, Vicki, pulled in. Our boats were within 15 or 20 feet of each other – close enough for us to chat. We told them it was our anniversary, and Kennedy said it was theirs, too. It might have been their three-month or first-year, I don't recall for sure. I do remember, though, that their deck was abloom with flowers. We talked for a few minutes more, and they went down below. We didn't see them on deck again all weekend.

Another Vineyard encounter began on a less friendly note – and does not stand as one of my finest hours. Shortly before Genevieve and I expected to arrive at the island, I called the harbormaster to reserve a mooring. I was looking forward to tying the boat up and bunking down. I had had a difficult week at work, and sailing from Padanaram had been a tough slog through heavy seas. When I pulled up to the mooring, I found another boat already there.

Tired and irritated, I shouted to the other skipper, "You're on my mooring!"

"Well, I just wanted to tie on until the bridge opens in half an hour, so I can go into the lagoon," the fellow responded apologetically.

"Well, we reserved it, and we need it now," I snapped back.

Then he asked a question that totally disarmed me: "Say, aren't you my temple president?" (At the time, I was president of Temple Israel in Boston.) It was as if I had been slapped by a wave. Chagrined, I abruptly switched from being confrontational to conciliatory. I apologized for my gruffness and suggested that he tie up to our boat while he waited – something I ordinarily would have done had I not been feeling so tired and cranky in the first place.

There was no lasting damage to my relationship with my congregant, but the exchange left me troubled. I should never have let my foul mood get in the way of courtesy. Because I thought this man was a stranger, I allowed myself to lash out at him. I had been raised to conduct myself in a manner that was considerate, respectful, and beyond reproach regardless of whom I was with or who was watching. Ever since that incident, whenever I found myself about to unload on someone, I recalled those words: "Aren't you my temple president?"

Similarly, whenever I faced an ethical quandary about some business practice, I thought of the question my father would always ask: "Would you do it in Macy's window at the corner of Broadway and 34th Street?" In other words, even if an action were perfectly legal, how would it look to other people?

My mother drilled home a similar policy when it came to my wardrobe. I can still hear her scolding me: "You can't wear that underwear! What if you're in an accident and the doctors and nurses see that it's torn?"

Genevieve chats with her brother-in-law Michael Greenfield, as I take a well-deserved rest in our dinghy on Martha's Vineyard.

SAILING OFF INTO THE SUNSET

Looking back over nine decades of life, I'd say that some of the most relaxing times I spent were with Genevieve on Seabiscuit. Often, we'd escape on our own for a two- or three-day trip. Even in the early days, we worked up the courage to head out into the open seas. At first, Genevieve would wonder if we were lost when she swept the horizons and saw no other vessels. But she soon overcame those fears, just as she had her seasickness.

Besides, I was always updating the boat with the latest gear. I was among the first to install radar on a small boat. I also had one of the earliest semi-electronic chart plotters. It was hooked into a radio direction finder, which picked up signals from lighthouses. Each would emit a signature code. With two or more sources, I could figure out our location.

Long before renewable energy was the rage, we were recharging our batteries with photovoltaic cells and later windchargers (nautical windmills). We used our engines as little as possible, priding ourselves on getting by some seasons on just one tank – 100 gallons – of diesel.

There's nothing like the peace of hearing just the flapping of the sails and the lapping of the waves. Even in rough waters, our 54-foot boat stayed relatively steady as it bridged the waves.

I miss those summer weekends when we'd take Seabiscuit out to, say, the Elizabeth Islands. The chain stretched southwest from Woods Hole to Buzzards Bay. We'd anchor overnight in a secluded spot, perhaps Quicks Hole or Tarpaulin Cove.

And then we'd let the waves gently rock us to sleep.

THE LONG GOODBYE

This is how I nearly talked a buyer out of purchasing Seabiscuit.

We had been living at Rowes Wharf for a couple of years when Genevieve and I decided that we were no longer using the boat enough to justify keeping it.

I obtained permission to dock it right in front of the Rowes Wharf harborside restaurant, with a "For Sale" sign prominently displayed. A young German fellow approached me, saying he'd always wanted a boat like mine. My asking price was $129,000, very low for a boat of that size, and the buyer agreed to it immediately.

As we were sitting on the boat working out the details, he told me that he had never sailed before. I was aghast.

"I can't sell you a great big 54-foot boat like this when you've never sailed even a little dinghy," I told him.

"What do you mean you can't sell it? I'm giving you your asking price," he responded.

"It would just be unconscionable," I said. "You have no idea what you're getting yourself into."

He told me that he had grown up in Hamburg, surrounded by boats, but only now could afford one. Buying one was his dream. Realizing how dejected he was, I agreed to a deal: I'd find a mooring nearby, and he would keep the boat there and only sail it with me until I felt he knew what he was doing. For me, it was the ideal outcome: I still had Seabiscuit to sail, but without having to worry about maintenance.

That arrangement went on for a year or so, after which I lost track of the fellow. Then, a couple of years later, my secretary at Shawmut received a worried call from a woman in New Bedford who used to mend the canvas for Seabiscuit. She said she had spotted Seabiscuit in Fall River and was shocked by its condition. Finding it hard to believe that I would allow the boat to fall into such disrepair, she was concerned that I was sick.

And that was the last I heard of Seabiscuit.

ADVENTURES IN THE CARIBBEAN

*In which I learn lessons about diplomacy from
family, friends and a prime minister*

On one of our charters in the Caribbean, Genevieve practically had to fight to take the wheel.

I LOVED TO BE the host of our expeditions, but I learned that being a good one sometimes meant setting aside my best-laid plans. I first realized this after chartering a boat in St. Thomas in the Virgin Islands for a vacation with Genevieve's sister Harriet and her husband, Michael Greenfield. We crewed the boat ourselves. I thought it would be fun to sail over to St. Croix, a five-hour trip across open water.

As we were leaving the harbor, Harriet came up from below and demanded to be put ashore. "I'm not going," she said. "You can't do this to me." She wasn't comfortable about being out of sight of land, even for less than half a day. The rest of us had talked about the trip ahead of time, but she hadn't been part of the conversation. We hadn't intentionally excluded her, but we had made the mistake of assuming that she would be as delighted with the plans as we were.

I had spent a long time working out our itinerary, but Harriet's objections made me realize that I had lost sight of what was most important: people getting together to have a good time. At first, we tried persuading her to change her mind, but I didn't push it. Looking back, I'm glad we hadn't subjected her to what could have been a 10-hour round trip of misery. I can only imagine how terrified she might have felt miles from shore with no land in sight and no escape.

The experience also made me sensitive to something else: With just the four of us, two couples who were quite close, Harriet felt she could speak her mind. But in larger groups, people who are in the minority might be too intimidated to speak up or might feel as if they are being spoilsports. And then, completely unwittingly, we would turn what they expected to be an exciting adventure into a nightmare.

Genevieve's childhood friend Rose-joan Barron joins me at the wheel on a boat we chartered in the British Virgin Islands.

MAYBE I'M TOO NICE

Trying to be a good host (and husband) can be perilous to your health and sanity, I discovered on several Caribbean voyages.

In 1981, we cruised around the British Virgin Islands with Rose-joan Barron and her husband, Mort. Rose-joan and Genevieve have been friends since childhood. This was their first sailing trip together, and it got off to an inauspicious start. After picking up the charter, we sailed into Charlotte Amalie, where I stayed on board while the others ventured into town to explore and shop. I couldn't find a mooring, so I dropped anchor near a dock where the Cunard Countess cruise ship was tied up. Suddenly, smoke started to pour out of it, fireboats converged on the scene, and I was ordered to move my boat. I told them I wasn't sure I could pull up the anchor by myself since I didn't have a winch. A heavy wind was straining the anchor line, making it extremely difficult to haul up the anchor unless I was directly over it. I needed to be in two places at once: at the helm, nudging the boat forward to slacken the line, and at the bow pulling up the anchor. I felt helpless as fire captains yelled at me, water gushed from fire hoses and passengers scrambled ashore.

Fortunately, the fire was contained, and no one was hurt. But the commotion delayed my picking up Genevieve and the Barrons. Unaware of what had happened, they berated me for leaving them stranded. Some days you can't win.

Mort, though, redeemed himself later on that trip. We were anchored off of Norman Island, and I was taking a swim. As I was about to climb aboard, Genevieve leaned over to help me and her hat fell into the water. It was a broad-brimmed Tilley, lined with foam so that it could float – and float it did, swept along by a fast current. Genevieve told me to go after it. When I told her I didn't think I could beat the current, she upped the ante. She said she had tucked a $100 bill in the hat. That was enough to persuade me. By the time I caught up with the hat, I wasn't sure I could battle the current to get back to the boat. Mort happened to be in the dinghy, and though nautically challenged, he managed to get the engine going and come to my rescue. Afterward, I looked inside the hat. There was no $100 bill. Genevieve just didn't want to lose her favorite hat, but she was embarrassed that her ruse had put me in peril.

Finding a slice of paradise at Foxy's, a well-known, but remote, beach bar on Jost Van Dyke in the British Virgin Islands.

BRUSH WITH A WAR ZONE

Whenever we sailed, we preferred to avoid the crowds. We weren't interested in spending our time in port shopping and dining. We were happy to find someone in a little shack in a remote cove willing to spear us a lobster and cook it on a griddle. When GPS made it easy for inexperienced sailors to charter boats, we sailed to even more remote locations. There, we were less likely to run into sailors who didn't know the rules of the sea or how to read a chart.

That's what drew us to St. Vincent and the Grenadines, a chain of more than 30 islands, mostly volcanic in origin. In all, their land area is equivalent to twice the size of Washington, D.C., with the island of St. Vincent being by far the largest. The chain is part of the Windward Islands; St. Lucia is to the northeast, Grenada to the southwest and Barbados to the east. It's always the unexpected that makes trips memorable. Two adventures in the Grenadines come to mind.

A week before we were going to head down to the islands, I got a call from our partners for the vacation, the Greenfields. "I had a premonition," Michael said, "and I'm not going." In disbelief, I asked, "A premonition? What are you talking about?" Michael explained that he just had this terrible feeling about going on the trip. He was apologetic but firm.

With a boat chartered, we couldn't cancel the trip. We called Genevieve's other sister, Marjorie, to ask if she and her husband, Walter Levitan, wanted to go. A really sweet guy, Walter was a retired jeweler who, as I mentioned in an earlier chapter, was such a great tennis player that we hired him to teach at Sudbury Skating and Tennis. The Levitans enthusiastically agreed to go, but I wanted to make sure they knew what they were in for. I asked if they had ever sailed before. They said they had sailed to Nantucket on a 48-footer owned by mutual friends Harvey and Dotty White. Knowing that Harvey's boat was about the same size as the one we had chartered, I felt confident that the Levitans would be up for the trip.

We left St. Vincent on what should have been a two-hour sail to Bequia. The first thing that unnerved me was seeing Walter bait a small freshwater fishing rod with plastic worms. "Walter," I said, "you're not going to catch anything with that rod or with those plastic worms out here."

The second thing was Walter asking as we left the harbor why the ocean looked so funny, with all those waves. The seas were running as high as 3 to 4 feet. I told Walter that was normal. He said that on their Nantucket trip, the water had been flat calm – so calm that they had never hoisted the sails and had relied entirely on the engine. I began to have doubts that this cruise would be an enjoyable experience for our less than experienced crew.

About 15 minutes out to sea, I spotted a small squall in the distance and decided to reduce sail before it reached us. We would need to take in the roller reefing Genoa jib. I asked Walter to help with one of the winches. The operation required coordinated maneuvers. Walter was to hold the end of the line attached to the jib sail. Using a winch, he had to let out the line at the same rate at which I was winching in the jib's roller reefing line. Surprised by a sudden gust of wind, Walter let go of his line and it flew off the winch. The sail flogged out of control, and the line Walter had just freed struck him in the head. He decided it best to go below.

His departure left me to struggle on my own with the snapping sheet and the jib's menacing metal tip, which could have knocked me out or worse. Fortunately, with Genevieve at the helm, I didn't have to worry about controlling the boat. Luckily, Walter, the boat and I were spared any serious damage. Walter didn't leave the cabin for the rest of the day. But the incident confirmed my suspicion that I had overrated his skill level, so I revamped our plans for the trip.

We dropped anchor that night in Saline Bay in Mayreau. It can be a precarious spot because of twin hills to the north. They can turn the valley between them into a wind tunnel depending on the direction of the gusts. As a precaution, I put down two anchors in a V formation to keep us from dragging in the middle of the night. Another boat had been similarly anchored a good distance away. Then a third boat dropped anchor right behind my stern. In very windy conditions, I like to let out more anchor line. That way the anchor eventually grabs the bottom at a low angle, which makes it more secure. But with this newcomer anchored so close behind me, I didn't have that option. As a result, the anchors dragged along the bottom as the wind picked up overnight. Our lines became entangled with those of the neighboring boats.

After an uneasy night, with all of us taking turns keeping watch, we awoke to discover that tangled lines were the least of our problems. While we were bobbing in the waters off Mayreau, we heard over the radio that a revolt had broken out on nearby Union Island. Soon, a single-engine plane buzzed us, flying below the height of our masts. Had I brought my guests to paradise only to be strafed? In the end, the plane pulled away, apparently satisfied that we posed no threat. Maybe there had been something after all to Michael's premonition.

On another trip, we met the pilot and several members of the short-lived revolution. Making the introductions was the soon-to-be prime minister of St. Vincent, a good friend about whom I'll say more later. By then peace had been restored on Union Island.

HOW MANY DOCTORS DOES IT TAKE TO STEER A BOAT?

To my regret, I was persuaded to violate my small-group rule when my old friend Malcolm Gordon, a geriatric psychiatrist, told me that he and his medical colleagues had chartered a large sailboat out of Grenada. Besides Gordon and his wife, there would be a couple who were both psychiatrists and a psychiatrist whose wife was a surgeon. Malcolm said they would love to have Genevieve and I join them. I tried to put Malcolm off, explaining my reservations about sailing with big groups. "Come on," he said, "you'll help us make decisions; you'll be the navigator." I finally relented.

After we had been out to sea for a couple of hours, I asked the psychiatrist who had been hogging the helm to give Genevieve a turn at the wheel. "No," he said. Stunned, I replied, "What do you mean, no?" He told me that if he let go of the wheel, he'd throw up. Unless he piloted, he insisted, he'd get seasick.

"We're going to be out for 10 days, and we're in heavy seas," I responded. "It's just not going to be satisfactory for you to be the only one at the helm." At last, he stepped aside for Genevieve. But just a few minutes later, his face turned ashen and he was at the rail, heaving. That ended the argument. He had the helm all 10 days. Fortunately, Genevieve's many trips before had inoculated her against seasickness.

FIRE BELOW!

You never know for sure whether a boat is shipshape until you take it out to sea. When you charter a boat, you put up a damage deposit of $1,000 or more. As a result, people sometimes are reluctant to report problems for fear of being blamed and charged for the repair. If the charter company fails to inspect the boat, the next customer may inherit problems that could have been easily fixed in port.

For one trip out of St. Vincent, we had chartered a boat from Caribbean Sailing Yachts. When we were 35 miles out, just about the limit of our contact range with the company, the boat's engine started up on its own. It was as if a ghost had turned the switch. After a bit of effort, I managed to shut it off – only for it to start up again a few minutes later.

When I radioed the company about the problem, the employee on duty immediately blamed me. He asked me questions such as whether we were running the refrigerator at the same time as the engine (no). I began to get impatient. This guy was wasting time talking about blame while his company's boat – not to mention those of us aboard – might be in danger.

I diagnosed the problem to be a starter motor with a mind of its own, probably because of a corroded control switch. After the main motor kicks in, the starter is supposed to shut off. Since it didn't, it got hotter and hotter.

While I was still on the radio with the guy from the company, the starter erupted into flames. I told him that we had no choice but to douse the engine with buckets of saltwater. "Don't you dare do that," he yelled, fearing that the salt would permanently damage the motor. But we had no choice, unless we wanted to abandon ship and let it go up in smoke.

Ever since Malcolm Gordon told me that a hacksaw was a sailor's best friend, I had kept one in my utility bag. This was the first time I needed it. Sure enough, it saved the day. I shut down the starter motor by sawing through the heavy wires connecting to its power source. We then set sail for the nearest place where a mechanic could fly in and fix the engine. I was correct in my diagnosis; I got no more lectures from the charter company.

As scary as the story sounds, our lives were never in any danger. We could have always escaped in a dinghy. In the Grenadines you're never far from an island, and the natives are invariably welcoming.

Such was the case with another charter mishap in the Grenadines. Once again, we had rented from Caribbean Sailing Yachts. As was typical for the area, the seas were heavy and the winds fairly strong. Suddenly, I heard the sound of fluttering and noticed the boat straighten up from its normal heeling position under sail. I looked up and saw the mainsail come apart in strips at its seams. After years of baking in the sun, all the stitching let loose at once. That left us with only a headsail. The engine was of no use for the time being because I had been sailing so fast that water had been siphoned into the exhaust pipe, flooding the cylinders (a design flaw of the CSY 43 that we had chartered). It's very hard to maintain a course with just a headsail and no sail at the stern of the boat to balance the force of the wind. Capsizing wasn't a worry, though. The heavy keel would ensure that the boat always righted itself. But I had to fight that keel to steer. I radioed the charter company, which directed me to Princess Beach in Bequia, about 5 miles away, for repairs.

A couple of hours later we dropped anchor off the beach. Shortly thereafter, a young native man motored out to us in a dinghy and gathered the remnants of the sail. He said he would be back in the morning with the sail resewn. He proved true to his word.

That was not the last we were to see of that young sailmaker. The following year I was having a sail repaired at The Sail Loft in Martha's Vineyard. Working there as an apprentice was that lad from Bequia. We had a surprising and friendly reunion.

MY PAL, THE PRIME MINISTER

We made the trip from St. Vincent to Bequia many times, becoming regulars at the Frangipani, a restaurant and small hotel named for the fragrant flowering tree that is native to the area. The owner was a Canadian, Pat Mitchell, who was married to a prominent locally born politician, James "Son" Mitchell. A towering 6-foot-4, Mitchell was a member of the cabinet in St. Vincent when we met him. Born in 1930 and educated as an agronomist, Son came from a boat-building family. His father had disappeared in the Bermuda Triangle in 1938, adding to the mystery surrounding that region. Despite his political stature, Son would occasionally tend the bar at the Frangipani, and we became fast friends. He was intrigued by my thoughts on Town Meeting, how I viewed it as democracy in its purest form. And he talked of his own political dreams and ideals.

On one trip, we were anchored in a remote part of the Grenadines, off World's End Reef. Anchored nearby was the Mitchells' sailboat. The couple invited us onboard, and Son told me about his disappointment with the current St. Vincent government and his hope to provide a bigger say for the poorer residents of the county's outlying islands and others whose voices were ignored.

Sometime later, when I was back at my Shawmut office, I got a phone call. "Guess who this is," the caller said. I immediately recognized Son's voice. He told me that he had just been elected prime minister of St. Vincent, by a landslide no less. The inauguration was in two weeks. It was to be a big to-do, with a representative of the queen attending. "Would you like to join us?" he asked. As I said to Genevieve, "Who else would invite us to an inauguration?"

When we flew down, the last leg of our trip was in a tiny plane owned by Liat, the Caribbean airline; veteran passengers joked that the name stood for Luggage In Another Town because of the island-hopping airline's reputation for losing baggage. Although his inauguration was the next day, Son personally greeted us at the airport. That night we attended a lavish dinner hosted by the ambassador from Taiwan. On the menu were dishes made from fresh produce that the Taiwanese had taught the locals to grow. There were six couples in all, including the Mitchells and the St. Vincent minister of agriculture and his wife.

At the inauguration, we sat in the box with Son's family. All the officials wore white wigs at the hour-long affair. Afterward, the new prime minister invited us aboard a British naval frigate for a ceremonial cruise to his home village in Bequia. The whole island, it seemed, turned out to welcome him. Here we were, this couple from Brookline, with a front-row seat to the start of one of the longest prime ministerial reigns in Caribbean history.

Getting saddle sore in Canouan, part of St. Vincent and the Grenadines.

245

INTERNATIONAL INTRIGUE

After returning to the States, I followed up on an idea I had had at the inaugural banquet. I saw how St. Vincent came to revere the Taiwanese just for spending a little time and money to help with agriculture. I thought that since Israel was always looking for new friends, St. Vincent would offer a great opportunity. I called a cousin by marriage, Harold Katz, who was a lawyer with close ties to Israeli officials.

Soon after, an Israeli diplomat in New York contacted me to arrange a meeting with Son. I made the necessary introductions, and the diplomat flew down to St. Vincent. That led to the Israelis inviting St. Vincent's agricultural minister for a three-month visit. The next time Genevieve and I were in St. Vincent, the minister picked us up and took us all around the island, regaling us with stories about his trip to Israel. The Israel-Grenadines connection remains to this day. Just recently Israel announced it would be donating 15,000 banana plantlets to St. Vincent, part of a years-long agricultural project between the two nations.

Harold Katz himself has an interesting history. In the mid-1980s, Jonathan Pollard used Katz's office to make copies of secret documents for the Israelis. Harold has claimed that he knew nothing of Pollard's actions. He has since moved to Israel with his wife, my cousin Mimi, apparently for good. One story has it that Katz is concerned that he could face legal trouble back in the States. Another has it that the Israelis don't want him to return for fear of what he might end up saying. Meanwhile, Pollard was imprisoned for spying until being freed on parole in 2015.

Getting back to Son, we saw him again in 1986 when we were on a cruise to see Halley's Comet and he came aboard the ship to visit us. This was about three years after the United States had driven the communists out of Grenada, an island chain just south of St. Vincent and the Grenadines. Son told us that at his suggestion he had taken part in the invading armada so that it would not appear as simply a U.S. operation. He was aboard a small vessel from St. Vincent's token navy.

While under communist rule, Grenada generally barred Americans. I had heard that you could motor over to one of its northernmost islands, Petite Martinique, from St Vincent's Petit St. Vincent island. That was an opportunity I couldn't pass up. Petite Martinique had one large town, which was indistinguishable from those in St. Vincent, except for the many communist slogans plastered on the walls. While we were there, we ran into Son, who was visiting an aunt, I believe. This was before he became prime minister.

I nearly lost my childhood friend Malcolm Gordon when we got separated exploring a remote part of the British Virgin Islands.

WHERE'S MALCOLM?

My sailing companion Malcolm Gordon and I were always trying to outdo each other as we cast about for new places to explore. In the early '90s we found one – and for a time, I feared I would never see Malcolm again.

The spot was Anegada, 15 square miles of coral and limestone in the British Virgin Islands. The island is 70 miles northeast of St. Thomas. Its treacherous waters, filled with hidden reefs, have claimed 500 boats over the past three centuries. Until sailboats were equipped with GPS, the territory's government would only allow experienced sailors in the area. We got permission on the strength of our many years sailing in the Caribbean and the fact that Genevieve and I owned a large sailboat.

We made our first trip to Anegada in a boat that we chartered with Malcolm and his wife, Nan. As we approached, we encountered a long reef, beyond which we could see a large bay and a harbor. It was around noon, about time for lunch. With the sun directly overhead, its light penetrated the clear waters without any reflection, and we could easily distinguish between sand and coral. At another time of day, it would have been too dangerous to navigate among the reefs. As Malcolm called out directions from the bow, we weaved our way to the idyllic bay. No other boats were in sight. The only people around were a few natives on the shore.

While our wives made lunch, Malcolm and I took off in a dinghy to snorkel the reefs. We had to take turns, because we didn't want to drop anchor and risk damaging the coral. While I was out snorkeling, Malcolm suddenly took off in the dinghy. I was wearing a little vest that gave me some buoyancy, but bobbing in the water soon became uncomfortable, especially as my imagination began to race with fears about what might have happened to Malcolm. Five or 10 minutes later, he returned. He explained that as he was trying to shut off the engine, it wobbled and seemed on the verge of falling off the boat. "I didn't dare do anything but hold it until I could fasten it down," he said. We realized how foolhardy we had been; if we had both gone under, our wives would have been stranded.

A FORTUITOUS DIP

Our last trip to Anegada – and our final Caribbean adventure – was just over a decade ago. You could say we ended that chapter of our lives with a splash. Genevieve at the time was recovering from an operation. Dressed for dinner ashore, she stepped off the boat to board a dinghy. Somehow, though, she missed her footing and fell into the water.

Genevieve refused to allow an impromptu swim to interfere with our dinner plans, but we did break our "no tourist shopping" tradition. Still in her wet clothes, Genevieve bought an outfit at an apparel shop, and we continued to our dinner. On reflection, perhaps I should question if that spill really was an accident.

BLASTING THROUGH THE WAVES

How being a first adopter can be a real pain in the neck

Onyx – our Picnic Boat made by Hinckley Yachts – turned heads but left me with a very sore neck.

IN 1998, WE ABRUPTLY shifted from the age of sail to the jet age.

By then we had bought a house on the Vineyard and were taking out Seabiscuit less and less often. Toward the end, I was just sailing on my own several times in the summer; we were no longer up for those multi-day excursions. It no longer seemed worth the time we spent in spring readying the boat for launch and in fall securing it for winter. But Genevieve and I still had some spring left in our sea legs.

Hinckley Yachts, which had been building boats in Southwest Harbor, Maine, since the 1920s, had just introduced a line of jet-propelled vessels, called Picnic Boats. Jet boats suck water into a pump and then expel it through high-velocity nozzles. With its relatively flat bottom and lack of propellers, the Picnic Boat can operate in water as shallow as a few inches. I thought it would be perfect for exploring the craggy coast of New England and its many islands.

Besides, it was the latest thing in power boats – and I can't resist that. When we were vacationing in Palm Beach, Florida, I heard that Bob Hinckley, grandson of the company founder, was in town demonstrating the boat. I called him up and arranged for a test cruise.

Genevieve took the wheel, with Bob at her side, in the cockpit's plush swivel chairs. I sat back in the open stern. Anxious to see how the boat would perform, I urged Genevieve to take it out into the ocean. From my cozy perch, I pointed to the three-foot waves and yelled over the roar of the engine, "Faster,

faster!" As the boat plowed through the waves, I just felt an exhilarating flutter. They looked back at me in amazement. It was only later – after we owned our own Picnic Boat – that I came to realize what a jolting experience it could be at the helm.

When we had owned Seabiscuit, we would go out even in the rough waters that followed a storm. Such was the case once in Nantucket, where we had been staying with other boating friends. When it came time to leave, our friends opted to fly out and leave their motorboats behind. We weren't daunted by the four- to five-foot waves. At 54-feet long, Seabiscuit could bridge the tops of waves, rather than bounce up and down between them. The weight of the sails further smoothed out the ride. Had we owned the Picnic Boat then, we probably would have taken a flight, too.

About two years after we purchased the boat, which we named Onyx, I realized it wasn't for me. This happened while I was traveling alone from the Vineyard to Boston. All was fine until I exited the Cape Cod Canal and hit small, foot-high waves in the bay straight on. Traveling at 25 knots, I felt battered all the way to Boston as I flew off the top of each wave and slammed down in the trough before the next one. Afterward, my neck was so sore that I had to wear a Thomas collar for a week.

Something else made me a bit uncomfortable with the Hinckley boat. It wasn't that it was glitzy. It wasn't – just the opposite, actually. But its hefty price tag was widely known. We'd often be greeted with admiring glances and thumbs-up. I wondered if this had more to do with the apparent size of our nautical investment than with the quality of our seamanship. Remember, since childhood, it's been drummed into me not to show off wealth.

When we sold the boat, we made a profit. Hinckley couldn't keep up with the demand for his brand, so it was a seller's market. Two Hinckley salesmen with two potential customers bid up the price for Onyx. As far as I was concerned, someone else could enjoy the prestige – and the pounding.

Bluewater – our Glacier Bay catamaran – performed beautifully, but left passengers feeling topsy-turvy.

THE SCARY CATAMARAN

I made sure our next boat wouldn't rattle our bones. I settled on a 28-foot Glacier Bay catamaran, which our grandson Samuel named Bluewater. Its twin hulls sliced through the waves rather than bouncing off them. While the boat performed beautifully in heavy seas, many passengers found the ride disconcerting. When making a sharp turn, a catamaran feels like it's going to tip over. That's not the case with a single-hull boat, which leans into turns much as a bicycle does. The catamaran cannot lean. And when waves approach the side or the beam, the catamaran is more prone than other vessels to cause sea-sickness. It tips side-to-side, unlike a single-hull boat, which floats more gently up and down.

So many guest passengers reported feeling uncomfortable that I sold the catamaran after two or three years. I replaced it with a classic 15-foot catboat, which we named Katama Kitten, anticipating that in the future only experienced sailors would want to join me. But my favorite sailing companion, Genevieve, found it increasingly difficult to board as she developed issues with her mobility.

Sailing Katama Kitten, a 16-foot classic catboat.

AMPHIBIAN ADVENTURES

The last boat we purchased came with wheels. We called it Sealegs, which was also the brand name. We weren't worried about our boat being confused with others; as usual, we were among the first adopters. I first saw Sealegs at a winter boat show held at the convention center not far from Rowes Wharf. I visited the show mainly in hopes of seeing old friends from our boat-building days. Sealegs was displayed in a small booth tucked away in a corner. After looking it over, I told the exhibitor that now I regretted going to the show. I hadn't intended to buy a boat, but this one was perfect for Genevieve. By this time, she was finding it hard even to climb on and off boats at the dock. Sealegs would allow us to continue boating together.

Our loaner Sealegs in the July 4, 2010, Edgartown parade.

The 24-foot-long vehicle has a rigid bottom, inflated sides and three big, retractable wheels. It can travel up to 6 m.p.h. on land and up to 40 m.p.h. on water. A New Zealand company had initially built it for the military market. I bought one of the first civilian models.

In keeping with Wyner tradition, I immediately made note of possible improvements. For example, because it tended to bog down in beach sand, I suggested making the vessel all-wheel drive. After struggling with turns on narrow town roads when I drove it with our entire family in the Edgartown July 4th parade, I recommended power steering. The company incorporated those changes and several more I proposed in its new boats. I didn't receive a word of thanks. I only succeeded in cutting by a third the value of my now inferior boat on the used market. The manufacturer rejected my request to swap it at cost for a new one. Our boat was still practically brand new, with only a few hours of actual use. I was very disappointed. I had naively thought I'd be afforded the same customer-comes-first courtesy that I had provided at the Chestnut Hill Boat Company.

We keep Sealegs in our driveway, with its wheels raised so that the vessel itself is on the ground. We can adjust its height to accommodate boarding by passengers who aren't as agile as they once were. Passengers sit on the inflated edge and move their legs inside. Then we straighten the boat, lower the wheels, and we're off.

PART VI: PASTIMES

- **'CQ, CQ, this is W1PST':** Tuning in the world via ham radio

- **Paging Dr. Doolittle:** Playing Cupid for a sheepdog

- **Car talk:** From a cranky Rolls-Royce to the car of tomorrow

- **Confessions of an early adopter:** Getting the latest gizmos

'CQ, CQ, THIS IS W1PST'

In which I make a honeymoon splash, chat with a king and help defend Brookline

IN 1911, JUST 14 years after Guglielmo Marconi patented his first radio – my father was tapping out Morse code on his homemade set using a spark gap and a coil wrapped around a Quaker Oats box. That was a year before Congress took its first step to regulate amateur radio and nine years before KDKA in Pittsburgh went on the air as the first commercial radio station. In his teens, Dad was among the first and youngest American ham operators to qualify for a license. He assigned himself the call letters 1FF; prefixes had yet to be standardized. Whether it was an earthquake halfway around the world or a prizefight in New York, his neighbors looked to him for the latest word.

Now let's flash ahead to the late 1930s to the attic of a house on Dean Road in Brookline. By then, radio was big business, not just a bunch of amateurs tapping keys. Sets were in everybody's home, but mainly for listening, not broadcasting. Families spent evenings listening to shows like *Amos 'n' Andy* and *Burns and Allen;* swing bands led by Tommy Dorsey and Benny Goodman; or classical music courtesy of the NBC Symphony Orchestra. But I was as interested in what was inside the sets as what came out of them.

I got to know the owner of the local shop where my father took his radios for repair. If he couldn't salvage a set, he'd give it to me to scavenge. I would de-solder the components and sort them into cigar boxes I got from another shop owner I had befriended. I must have accumulated more than 100 boxes of parts. Mostly I built radios from scratch, sometimes fashioning chassis from aluminum sheets and punching holes in them for tube sockets. I bought some of my equipment at the original Radio Shack store, which was located on the site of what is now Government Center. I copied circuit designs out of the thick annual book published by the American Radio League, to which I belonged. Early on, my father would help me out, but this was one area where I soon surpassed him.

At first, I just built receivers, but in my last few years at Roxbury Latin I was taken under the wing of another radio enthusiast. Henry Cross was a year ahead of me. As neither of us played team sports, we'd sometimes find ourselves assigned to an activity like chopping wood behind the school. Henry would set down his axe and pick up a stick to scratch drawings of radio circuits in the dirt. That's how I learned radio theory, one of the requirements for passing the license test. I also had to know basic radio law and, most challenging for me, Morse code. The test required an ability to send and receive at least 13 words a minute. I mastered transmission, but had great difficulty with transcribing. Somehow, I mastered Morse just well enough to pass the test; afterward, I rarely used it. To the ham world, I became known as W1PST, the license the FCC assigned to me. The "W" signifies a U.S. amateur class, and the "1" that I'm broadcasting from a New England state.

TALKING TO TOMORROW

For security reasons, the government banned amateur radio during the war, so it wasn't until after 1945 that I became seriously involved in the hobby. Even with the first radio I built, which was just 50 watts, I could broadcast a signal that could reach around the world. Shortwave signals bounce back and forth between the earth's surface and the ionosphere. Think of the transmission as being like a stone skipping across the surface of a lake – except that the cosmos, not skill, dictates distance. When sunspot activity is high, the ionosphere is especially reflective of radio waves sent at ham frequencies. One of my first contacts was with a ham in Australia. I still remember the thrill when he said, "Jerry, it's tomorrow afternoon over here."

The postwar period was a boon time for ham operators, as the market was flooded with Army surplus equipment. My dad and I bought a BC-610 transmitter, which had been used by the Army Signal Corps, and we built a tower next to the garage. It was 15 feet higher than our three-story house and topped with a rotary antenna. My parents were supportive and the neighbors tolerant, considering that my transmissions occasionally came through on their TVs.

I also had a portable ham radio in my car. When I was driving Uncle Murray and several of his colleagues from New York to the factory, they asked me to demonstrate it. I picked up the mike and called out "CQ, CQ, this is W1PST." A ham operator who identified himself as CM9AA responded from Havana. He turned out to be an American named Phil Richards. We got to talking, and when I told him I'd be visiting the island around Christmas, he said he'd meet my boat. That was the start of the adventure-filled friendship I described in an earlier chapter.

'TURN OFF THAT NOISE'

While the car radio brought me together with Phil, it nearly doomed my relationship with Genevieve. When we were out on a date and I turned it on, she stopped me cold. "Why don't you turn off that noise?" she said.

But eventually Genevieve came to appreciate that the radio produced more than just static – and even passed the test for her own license (KN2OQK, with "2" for the area that included her home state of New York). I'm lucky she was such a good sport, because I took my hobby with me when I traveled. I liked to look up operators I had met on the airwaves. Before our honeymoon in Bermuda, an operator there told me the editor of *CQ*, the ham radio magazine, would be on the island at the same time as our trip. We got together, and the editor would occasionally stop by to visit afterward. One morning, I happened to be away when he knocked on the door. Thinking it was me, Genevieve, still in her nightgown, answered – both were a bit taken aback. That fall we honeymooners – W1PST and KN2OQK – were featured in *CQ* magazine with a picture of us coming out of the water in our scuba gear.

We were also featured in *The Boston Herald*, when Genevieve put both her professional PR and newfound ham knowledge to work. As Rudolph Elie reported in his "Roving Eye" column on November 29, 1955, she marched into the newspaper office to publicize an eight-day marathon in which "27 of Boston's leading amateurs" – myself included – sought to contact as many of our counterparts in Rome as possible. (The marathon had been organized by my father's friend Mark Bortman, who the following year would be named chairman of the People-to-People Civic Committee to promote international understanding by President Eisenhower).

Elie was intrigued that Genevieve herself had become a ham. Women in those days didn't have first names, at least so far as newspapers were concerned:

> Mrs. Justin Wyner, an attractive girl with a mass of dark hair and an animated way of talking … has hurled herself into her husband's hobby with enthusiasm – and no little forbearance as well. 'When we moved into our home,' she said with a laugh, 'we had the radio but no furniture.'

Genevieve went on to describe how she was just learning Morse code so that she could become a full-fledged ham. She reported having had made one radio contact, with someone in Cambridge. "I got stage fright, I guess," she told Elie. "I didn't know what to talk about." (See the Appendix for a copy of the article.)

I enlist George's help with my ham radio station.

HEAVEN HELPS ME

When we rented our first house, we took along the tower from Dean Road. But as soon as we owned our own property, the house on Marthas Lane, I went all out. With the help of a minister – who felt the higher he got, the closer he'd be to God – I poured a concrete foundation and assembled a triangular tower 85 feet tall, topped by a rotating 30-foot-wide boom antenna. To power the antenna, I bought an Army surplus prop pitch motor originally from a B-29 bomber.

We used a homemade crane to raise each piece of the framing, placing a pulley atop a jib pole that we tied to the tower. I was not comfortable with heights, so I left the aerial work to the minister. At one point, he dropped a wrench and, without thinking, asked me to bring it up. Realizing it would be churlish of me to ask him to retrieve it himself, I overcame my fears and made the climb up the tower. But I did have this vision of myself 80 feet in the air clinging to the rings, frozen in terror, waiting for the Fire Department to come to my rescue as if I were some scared kitty.

Today, when you can email or Skype just about any place in the world, it might seem quaint the way ham operators used to compete over the number of countries from which they'd received written confirmations of contacts, known as QSL cards. I would read ham radio magazines and bulletins to keep abreast of the latest equipment, projected broadcast conditions and lists of temporary stations operating in remote parts of the globe. I'd stay up half the night to talk to someone halfway around the world. Besides the sunspots, the time of day affected transmissions. To contact Southeast Asia, my best chance might be at 4:30 a.m.

Ham operators mail QSL cards to confirm radio contact. This is the one I used when I was living with my parents on Dean Road in Brookline.

LAYING CLAIM TO AN ISLAND

Many of us became hooked on what is known as "chasing DX," that is, contacting stations in countries where there were only a handful of hams. Colonies, such as the possessions of the British Empire, counted as separate countries.

After accumulating QSL cards from contacts in 270 countries, I set my sights on being the first ham operator to broadcast from Navassa Island, an uninhabited speck of land claimed by both the United States and Haiti. It counted as a separate country, with its own assigned call letters. If I were to broadcast from the island, thousands of hams would contact me to chalk up a new country credit. I enlisted the aid of a lawyer who had once worked with the FCC. I had met him when friends and I made an aborted bid to launch a television station in Lowell. He found out that no one had ever sought a ham license for Navassa and helped me obtain one. Thus, I became the proud owner of KC4AA.

The next obstacle was physical. The island was surrounded by deep water lapping against steep cliffs. The only access was a ladder that had been set into a 100-foot precipice to reach an old lighthouse. I learned that the groundswell at that time of year was very large. You might start your climb from the base of the ladder only to find water surging over your head when you were 50 feet up. I delayed making my trip until the end of the high groundswell season to avoid being stranded on the island. In the meantime, three chicken farmers from North Carolina had applied for a license after hearing about mine. Now that I had blazed the paperwork trail, they quickly got one. Being young and adventurous, they set up the first transmitter on Navassa. After that, I lost interest.

A MONARCH AT THE MIKE

It's surprising to learn of some of the people who were hams. Generally, people used just first names, but the call letters of famous people would leak out. I once spoke to Barry Goldwater, when he was still senator from Arizona. I also chatted with a king of Greece; he sent me a very nice QSL card.

One of my early contacts turned out to be a prominent Cuban diplomat in the pre-Castro era. Before my parents traveled to Cuba in the late '40s, I appealed to ham operators there for one who would let my parents speak to me from his or her home. Such requests were common in those days, when long-distance phone calls were expensive. I heard back from a man named Antonio. When my parents arrived in Havana, they discovered that Antonio was a distinguished elderly man who lived in a lovely house in one of Havana's finest neighborhoods. He graciously let them radio me back home. After their trip, my astonished mother said to me, "How could you call that man by his first name?" That man was Antonio Sánchez de Bustamante y Sirven, a lawyer whose resumé included serving as a professor, senator and judge of the Permanent Court of International Justice at the Hague.

Most of the time, the ham conversations were brief and about innocuous subjects like equipment and signal strength. Since we generally steered clear of politics, I could talk with people behind the Iron Curtain even during the height of the Cold War. But one operator whom I had regularly chatted with in a communist country made the mistake of saying "Jerry, things are changing around here for me. All the letters I receive now come to me opened, some even without envelopes." That was the last I heard from him.

CIVIL DEFENDER

Historically, ham radio operators have played a pivotal role in keeping communications open during disasters, natural or otherwise. I organized about 10 ham operators to create a communications division for Brookline Civil Defense. Remember, this was decades before everyone had their own cell phone. Outside of the police and fire departments, we were the only people with mobile two-way radios. We held weekly drills around town and mapped radio dead zones. We also helped out during major events like parades. I arranged for us to have an office in the building that had once served as the town's incinerator.

It was just up the street from our house on Marthas Lane. We got a license from the FCC, W1VBC; set up a radio; and built a tower. It has been years since Brookline Civil Defense depended on ham operators, but the tower still stands.

When you read the stories of pioneers in television, computers and the Internet, it's amazing how many of them were once ham radio operators. They spent their childhoods cooped up in attics, basements and garages stripping down old radios and TVs to build something better. They pushed the envelope on technologies not yet available to the general public – just as their children and grandchildren are doing today, only they're rewriting code rather than rewiring radios.

Ham radio isn't dead, though. Some of my old friends are still active operators. As it happened, a fellow resident of NewBridge is one of the radio hams who was part of that Brookline Civil Defense group: Dave Goldman, W1YSW.

PAGING DR. DOOLITTLE

I play Cupid for a sheepdog, mop up a Newfoundland and try to desegregate ducks

OF THE MANY CHARACTERS I've come across, some of the oddest, most endearing and most down-right troublesome padded into my life on four legs or a pair of webbed feet.

When I was about 10 and living on Clark Road in Brookline, we had a little fox terrier. Jack was loyal to a fault. Wherever we went, Jack followed. When my mother would take Betty and me sailing during our summer vacations in Buzzards Bay, Jack was not keen about being left behind on the beach. To our amazement, he swam – or should I say, dog-paddled – out to us. We had no choice but to scoop him out of the water and take him with us. Don't believe me? I have a movie to prove it.

But while Jack was very trusting, he was no pushover. One of our neighbors on Clark Road, a 12-year-old boy named Dick Smith, liked to toss pebbles from his window at Jack. He meant no harm; he thought it was a safe way of playing with our dog. Unfortunately for Dick, Jack could carry a grudge. One day when Dick was outside, Jack bit him. Now while Jack might have claimed he was provoked, he came very close to being evicted from the neighborhood. There was a lot of discussion between my parents and Dick's. Ultimately, Jack got a reprieve. As for Dick, there was no lasting harm. Indeed, he went on to make it big in business (CEO of the Neiman Marcus Group, among other achievements); as adults, our paths would often cross in Boston's philanthropic world. But Dick never did let me forget the day Jack nipped him.

CANINE IN THE CAB

After Genevieve and I married, we got an Old English Sheepdog puppy. Wendy was the gentlest dog you could ever imagine. My mother, who was fussy about most things, loved to take the dog with her when she went shopping. When our sons went to school, Wendy would follow them to the MBTA bus stop. When they hopped aboard, Wendy climbed on, too. On several occasions, Wendy stayed on the bus after the kids were dropped off at school. She rode until the end of the line, where the driver left her at a shopping center. We would then get a call from some storekeeper, who found our name and phone number on Wendy's collar, asking how we could possibly let our dog end up there. Genevieve, who was home with the baby, would respond, "I cannot come and get her. Please put her in a taxi and send her home."

One time, Genevieve's mother had just driven up from New Rochelle when she saw a taxi pull up to our house. In the back seat was Wendy, sitting straight up, her head as high as if she were a human. The cabbie then stepped out, opened the door, and Wendy jumped out. Needless to say, I was a bit peeved with the MBTA. I wrote the director a letter saying the bus driver should never have allowed the dog to come aboard. I said you wouldn't let anyone else on without paying a fare. I never did hear back from the T.

Since Wendy was a thoroughbred, we decided to find her a mate. We paid a breeder a stud fee and left Wendy with her for what we hoped would be a few amorous days. When we returned, she said nothing had happened and suggested that we take her dog home with us on the theory that Wendy would be more receptive on her own turf.

Our veterinarian prescribed a tranquilizer to help Wendy conceive. When Genevieve picked it up at the drugstore, the pharmacist gave her the fisheye since it was in her name. On it, the vet had written: Take two before mating.

I played Cupid so Wendy could have puppies.

It was summer, about 88 degrees, and we set aside the garage, which was next to our cellar, for the tryst. Wendy was in heat, and her scent drew dogs from all over the neighborhood. Howling with lust, they peered through the ground-level cellar windows into the garage. Meanwhile, I was inside trying to rev up the romance. It was extremely hot in the garage as I tried to keep this 60-pound dog in position for her suitor to make his move. But Wendy kept collapsing in a heap, so I draped her over a big bale of peat moss and brought her mate over to mount her. I steadied Wendy by holding her head. Instead of satisfying the vicarious desires of all those dogs outside, the lackadaisical suitor looked up at me and licked my face. It was very embarrassing – if one can be embarrassed in front of the canine world. I finally had to help him navigate the penetration. I couldn't believe it – it was like being in a nightmare, especially with all the other dogs howling to get in.

Later, after returning the male dog, I heard from his owner. "What did you do to him?" she asked. "All he does is sit in the corner and whimper." Whatever I did, it worked. Wendy gave birth to six pups. At first, I would stay up all night with the brood, because I was worried that Wendy would roll over and accidentally smother one of them. Sheepdog pups were selling for $500 each, and in those days $500 was a lot of money. I became so worried that in the middle of the night I called the vet for advice. He was not pleased to hear from me.

The pups, by the way, almost became famous. They were so cute that, at Genevieve's instigation, Captain Kangaroo invited them on his show. But on the eve of their appearance, they came down with dysentery; perhaps it was puppy stage fright. Eventually, they all recovered, and we sold them to people eager to own such mild-mannered pets. For a sheepdog, Wendy lived to a ripe old age, dying at 14 of a heart attack.

GUSHING WITH AFFECTION

After losing Wendy, we went to a dog show to find another pet. We decided not to get another sheepdog because there couldn't possibly another dog like Wendy. We were taken with Newfoundlands. They were big dogs, nearly twice the size of Wendy. After we brought one home, we discovered they have one drawback, one we might have learned about sooner had we asked why every Newfoundland breeder had a plaid handkerchief in his back pocket. We now know there are two kinds of dogs: wet-mouthed and dry-mouthed. Newfoundlands fall into the first category.

As it happened, I was town moderator when we owned the Newfoundland, whom we named Heidi. During the weeks before Town Meeting, the police were supposed to deliver town-related mail to me every day. I later learned that this was not one of the more popular assignments. The police would draw straws, with the officer who drew the shortest getting to play my postman. It wasn't that the police were afraid of Heidi. If anything, she was too friendly. The 180-pound dog would greet the officers by putting her paws on their shoulders and showering them with saliva as she shook her head in excitement. After delivering the mail, the poor officer had to go home and change.

Newfoundlands are also known as lifesaver dogs. If you take them on a swimming trip, they have to be restrained. Otherwise, they'll rush into the water, wrap their forepaws around you and try to take you back ashore as they vigorously paddle with their hind legs. While they may have thought their actions noble, they were in fact quite painful. Heidi could really rake your back with her hind-leg paws.

A gentle giant at 180 pounds, Heidi romped around the neighborhood in those days before leash laws. After she became afflicted by a hip problem, we had to make the heartbreaking decision to find her a new home. Her breeder helped us locate Newfoundland owners who welcomed Heidi, even with her hip problems, to their farm in Montana.

COP'S WORST FRIEND

Our next dog, a Scotch terrier we named Buttons, also had her run-ins with the police. One day an officer who was delivering the town mail thought that turning on the siren might amuse Buttons. It didn't. The siren drove her crazy. Afterward, she would chase police cars (and only police cars) and try to bite their tires. Even if Buttons were with us in the car, she seemed to have a sixth sense about the presence of a police cruiser. She would start barking incessantly and jumping up and down. I would look in the rearview mirror, and sure enough there would be a police car. It didn't matter whether the siren was on;

Buttons could even detect unmarked cars if the driver was in uniform. The local beat police officer tried to make amends with Buttons by driving her around in his car. It didn't work. As soon as she got out of the car, she growled and tried to bite the tires as the officer drove away.

Buttons doesn't cry fowl when Barnacles gets first dibs.

It wasn't just the police who gave Buttons fits. About the time we got her, our son James was in second grade and had hatched a few baby chicks as part of a school project. We ended up with a pet chicken, Barnacles, roaming the backyard. Sometimes when we set food out for Buttons, Barnacles would gobble it up first. The dog was so hungry that she would lick the food off of the chicken's beak. James took Barnacles to summer camp, where both apparently thrived. Later that summer, we asked a neighbor's son to watch over Barnacles when we went on vacation. We left her in our fenced-in backyard with feed and a little shelter. When we returned, there was no Barnacles, just feathers and chicken pieces scattered in the backyard. The young caretaker claimed not to know what had happened, but we suspect that he took his big dog with him into our backyard and couldn't control his pet.

I suppose I could sympathize with James's affection for the chicken. I had had my own feathered friends as a boy. Dad raised chickens on farmland next to our Stoughton factory. I got to know them on my frequent visits and gave them names. The trouble was that my father grew the chickens not only for their eggs, but for their meat. My mother made sure Dad never told me that the chicken we were eating for dinner had grown up on our farm.

PECKING ORDER

Speaking of fowl, the first pets that Genevieve and I had were ducks. Early in our marriage, when Genevieve was pregnant with George, we vacationed in Nova Scotia. We stayed at a little inn where we would feed a brace of ducks that would drop by in the evenings. I thought a duck would make a nice present for Gen. It turned out, though, that you couldn't buy just one duckling; you had to buy six. In the past, people would buy a single duckling for Easter and then let it die. The law was in place to ensure that duck buyers were serious about the commitment they were making.

I bought the required half dozen and brought them home. In no time, they bonded with Wendy. Everyplace Wendy went (this was pre-MBTA bus days), the ducks would follow and snuggle up to her. She didn't mind. And the ducks provided us with a garden service of sorts: weeding and feeding. They didn't eat the grass, only the broad-leafed weeds. But we had to be careful, because once they finished with the weeds, they started in on the flowers, including those of our neighbors. But that wasn't the worst of our problems. Over time, three of the ducks died, leaving one female and two males. Both the males had designs on the female. That would have been OK had they been living in a pond, but on land all the mounting left the female very sore. Thinking I could solve the problem, I got a bucket of water and put one of the males in with the female. The third duck got so excited that he too jumped in, nearly smothering the poor female.

I next tried to find another female. A fellow who lived near our factory trapped a mallard for me to bring home. Little did I know there was a pecking order among ducks. The original three ducks wanted nothing to do with the newcomer, despite her efforts to befriend them by following them around the backyard. In a futile effort to promote avian integration, I set up two pens, with a male and a female in each. That worked out fine – I suppose it was a case of love the one you're with – but when I put all the ducks back together again, the mallard was relegated to walking five paces behind the others.

I did try to make the ducks pay their keep. When the females laid eggs, they would reject the ones they didn't think would hatch. I thought the mothers were being too picky, so I gave the eggs more time by keeping them warm on our furnace. I accumulated a big collection of eggs – all of them, unfortunately, became hardboiled. No, we never chanced eating them.

Frustrated with the ducks, I tried setting them free at nearby ponds. But they kept coming back. I finally took them to live with a farmer in Easton. He swore that as soon as I left, they started marching back toward Boston.

Our latest four-legged companions: Barnaby and Boots.

CAR TALK

From a cranky Rolls to a smelly Volvo to the car of the future

IF MY LIFE WERE a filing cabinet, one of its quirkiest files would contain stories of the cars we've owned.

Now, while our current car is the all-electric Tesla – about the most advanced vehicle now on the market – our most memorable car was 30 years old when we bought it.

And one that looked much like it was driven by James Bond's nemesis Auric Goldfinger and his henchman Oddjob. While Genevieve and I may not have tangled with the celluloid spy set, we, too, had many adventures in our yellow Rolls-Royce.

Our Rolls story began one Saturday afternoon when we thought it would be fun to attend a car auction at the Larz Anderson Museum in Brookline. We hadn't intended to buy anything, but that changed when we discovered we could afford an antique Rolls.

We paid $3,500 for a 1938 Barker model, named for the coach maker that constructed the body. As it happened, 1938 was the Barker model's last year. With its roomy back seat and an interior trimmed with burl wood, our Rolls had some of the trappings of a limo. Fortunately, it did not have a divider between the driver and passengers – that would have been too glitzy for our taste.

We didn't buy the Rolls for attending fancy balls and dinners. We needed a second car for Genevieve to run errands and shuttle the kids around town. Its most distinguished passenger was our sheepdog, Wendy, who from a distance could have been mistaken for some dowager.

But still, we did worry a bit that the Rolls would be seen as a radical departure from our family tradition of not flaunting personal wealth. We bought Chevrolets and Buicks, not Cadillacs and Lincolns. At work, my father didn't want his car to stand out from those of his employees. Drawing attention to his status, he feared, would make him appear less approachable. My concerns about the Rolls turned out to be groundless. Rather than being turned off, the Shawmut workers seemed to get a kick from the novelty of the car.

Our classic Rolls graces Marthas Lane. That's me at the wheel with Genevieve.

CRANK CASE

Wherever the Rolls went, it drew a crowd. And on occasion, the audience enjoyed a bonus show, courtesy of a flaw in the engine. Normally when we turned the key, a small gear in a starter motor would engage with a giant gear, and the engine would roar to life. This giant gear, the flywheel, had some 100 teeth. At some point over the previous three decades, one of the teeth had gotten knocked off. If the small gear happened to engage the wheel just at the spot where that tooth should have been, the car wouldn't start.

We never knew when the gap would be a problem because there was no predicting its location when the big wheel stopped spinning the last time the engine was shut off. Think of it as our own Wheel of Fortune – or misfortune. In the case of the latter, Genevieve – invariably alone at a shopping center – would have to step out of the car to fix it. As an admiring crowd gathered to watch, she would open one side of the bonnet (the hinged panels that enclosed the engine), remove the hand crank tucked inside, bend down at the front of the car, fit in the crank handle and turn the main gear so that one of its remaining teeth would properly engage. It looked like a throwback to the days when drivers rotated a crank to start their Model Ts. We could have fixed the problem permanently, but that would have required disassembling the entire engine at a sum too princely for us frugal Yankees.

Another challenge of owning a 30-year-old Rolls was getting it repaired. I once took it into a Rolls dealer to fix a dent. The quote was for more than a thousand dollars because the body was made of aluminum. When I suggested using a little body putty and paint, I was pretty much shown the door. I had my local auto body shop fix it my way. I'm no purist.

When the distributor contacts needed to be replaced, I had to call Rolls-Royce in England. They told me that the car came with replacements, stored inside the directional signal lever. It sounded too simple, but I unscrewed the knob on the end and there were the parts. By the way, at the time our Rolls was built, American cars didn't come with directional signals; people just stuck their arms out the window before making a turn. When you flicked the Rolls signal, a little pennant popped out on the side of the car that corresponded to the direction of the turn.

Our Rolls had perhaps its finest and least finest hours on a trip we took to visit George at Camp Kirkland on the Cape. On the way down, it was like we were in a one-car motorcade. People cheered us all along the route. Their feet planted on the seats, Daniel and James stood up through the sunroof. They waved back at the crowd as if they were astronauts on parade.

The return trip was a different story. We broke down in the middle of the road. Instead of cheers, we drew sneers. Never mind that we were in a Rolls; we were holding up traffic. After a seemingly endless wait, a truck driver stopped and tied our car to his rear bumper. For 30 nerve-wracking miles, we were pulled along without any idea of what was ahead of us. Only at the last minute did we know when to turn the wheel or slam on the brakes. Somehow, we and the car arrived in one piece at a garage in Brockton.

After owning the car for about three years, we sold it – by accident. All that we had planned to sell was the yellow canoe that Genevieve had bought at the Channel 2 auction. A buyer came around who happened to be a distant cousin. After he agreed to take the canoe, I mischievously said, "Hey, we have a car that matches it." To our surprise – and the horror of the rest of the family – he offered to buy the Rolls. We sold it for what we had originally paid plus the money we had sunk into it. Genevieve worried that anything yellow that we owned would end up sold that day. Several years later, I tried to buy the car back for $6,000; the cousin wanted $20,000.

HEY, MOM, LOOK WHAT I FOUND!

The first car we bought after getting married was a purple station wagon. When it was shiny and new, it looked smart. After a few years exposed to the elements, it appeared so garish that we had it repainted. But what made it memorable wasn't the vehicle itself, but what happened inside of it.

To begin at the beginning, we should go back to when I became engaged to Genevieve. Considering that I was descended from a jeweler, I couldn't get her just any engagement ring. So, I went to the fellow who had supplied my grandfather with diamonds. After he let me take home six unmounted stones to examine for flaws, I chose a two-carat diamond. Now flash forward to early in our marriage when Genevieve looked at her hand and noticed the ring was gone. She had no idea where or when it had slipped off. After searching everywhere we could think of, I filed an insurance claim, and we received a check.

Some years later, as we were driving to the dealership to trade the station wagon in for a new car, we had to make a brief stop. Daniel, then 3 months old, was with us. We noticed that he was clenching something. Worried that he would swallow it, we opened his hand and discovered the diamond ring. Evidently, his tiny fingers had extracted it from the tiny crevice between the seat back and the seat. To think, had it not been for Daniel's last-minute discovery, we would have unwittingly given away a diamond.

I dutifully reimbursed the insurance company, explaining how we had found the ring. The company wrote back, expressing its gratitude, surprise and admiration. It seemed the insurer had never encountered such honest customers. The following year, the company rewarded us – by refusing to renew our policy. I guess we were viewed as too much of a risk because we hadn't looked hard enough for the ring in the first place.

THE ODIFEROUS VOLVO

It had been my habit to buy a new car every couple of years from Simonds Chevrolet in Stoughton. In 1968, I decided to move up to a Volvo. It was my first big purchase. The car had front-wheel drive, which was great in snow, and it had a reputation for safety and reliability. In the case of our car at least, it also came with a peculiar odor. But the only one who really noticed it was Daniel. Whenever he rode in the car for more than a short drive, he'd become nauseated. That was neither good for Daniel nor the upholstery.

I had the Volvo dealer check out the car and was told nothing was wrong with it. But Daniel's problem continued. The simple solution would have been to sell the car, but I couldn't see unloading a potentially harmful vehicle on an unsuspecting buyer. The only safe buyer would be Volvo itself. Having gotten nowhere with the Volvo dealer, I had my attorney write the company. We demanded that our car be replaced. Ultimately, Volvo agreed.

When the dealer asked what color car I wanted, I said anything but the one we had. I was worried that Daniel would associate the color with the nausea. You may recall that when I was sick as a child, I voraciously read Western-themed pulp magazines. Afterward, I would turn green at the sight of them. Anyway, despite my expressed wishes, the dealer gave us a car of the same color. Fortunately, Daniel had not been similarly traumatized. He did just fine with the new car.

And, as it turned out, we were lucky that the old one had made him sick. Shortly before we took delivery of the replacement Volvo, I asked the Stoughton Chevy dealer to check out the original car. He opened the hood while the engine was running and spotted gas spurting from a hose clamp near the fuel pump. What Daniel smelled was evaporating fumes. The dealer said he was surprised the car hadn't exploded. We all gave thanks to Daniel's super-sensitive nose.

THE FAUX CADILLAC

In 1981, Cadillac announced its answer to fuel-efficient luxury compacts: the Cimarron. My father, then in his mid-80s, and I were intent on being among the first to own the car. Big mistake. Our first-adapter instincts bought us a pair of lemons. The car, which was in fact a dressed-up Chevy Cavalier, came equipped with all the latest features, but was shoddily assembled.

After three years of taking the cars in and out of the shop, we sold them. Writing in *Time* magazine, auto critic Dan Neil said of the Cimarron: "The horror. The horror. Everything that was wrong, venal, lazy and mendacious about GM in the 1980s was crystallized in this flagrant insult to the good name and fine customers of Cadillac." The model didn't make it through the decade.

A JEEP WITH A MIND OF ITS OWN

And finally, there's the car that tied up traffic in all of Edgartown.

Genevieve had spotted a black Jeep Grand Wagoneer carrying a wedding party. With the bride in her gown and everyone else in formal attire, the car itself struck her as elegant, too. We bought one as Genevieve's car. Roomy and fun to drive, the Wagoneer had one serious flaw: It would inexplicitly stall out. This would even happen on the highway. Amazingly, when the Jeep stalled, we were always able to maneuver it safely out of traffic. After a short wait, we could restart the car as if nothing had happened.

But the Wagoneer was an accident waiting to happen. It was also a potential embarrassment, which brings me to the time it stalled in the one open lane on North Water Street in Edgartown. For that day, we were probably the least popular people on Martha's Vineyard. No drivers could move until our temperamental car decided to behave itself and let us start it.

As with the Volvo, the dealer's mechanics couldn't figure out the problem. They brought in a representative from the regional office. He couldn't find the problem either. In the end – to Genevieve's regret – we traded the Jeep in.

In its place, we bought a Lincoln SUV, the model that preceded the Navigator, from Steve Owen at Owen Motors in Dedham. It could seat seven people. Not that many years later, as the car was being serviced at the dealership, Steve approached us in the waiting room and asked, with tongue in cheek, "How can you be driving such an old car? Just leave it here and drive away in this new Mercury Mariner." We were taken back by his sales pitch since the thought of buying a new car hadn't even entered our mind. But Steve made the idea sound so simple and reasonable. When Genevieve expressed concern that the car would be too small to take the seven of us on our annual trip to Danbury for Thanksgiving, he said he would loan us a Navigator for the holiday (a promise that he kept for as long as we bought cars from him). We drove away in the Mariner that day and never looked back.

Whenever we take in a car to be serviced at Owen Motors, we joke that Steve will give us another offer we can't refuse. And one time he did, leading me to buy a Mercury Milan. I'd still be driving it now had not the Tesla come along.

Plugging in my first Tesla S model for a trip to the Vineyard.

ELECTRIFIED BY TESLA

I was introduced to the sleek all-electric car in 2012 when the family gathered at our Rowes Wharf condo for the Chanukah menorah lighting ceremony. My son Daniel handed me a key fob and said, "Dad, I want you to try out my new Tesla Model S." As I tooled around the waterfront, I was amazed. I had never driven anything like it. Like my dad before me, I was reluctant to buy a car my employees would resent, but I decided that the Tesla was so different that they would forgive me the indulgence.

Teslas were so popular that the manufacturer had a six-month waiting list for delivery. People were selling their reservations for earlier delivery dates on Internet auction sites for as much as $15,000. A Tesla representative told me I was eligible for a special three-month delivery window because, thanks to Daniel, we were already a "Tesla family." I put down a deposit, but after a few days I couldn't stand the anticipation. I called back the representative and asked whether I could get the car sooner if there were a cancellation. I explained that I was 87 and wanted to relish every day, but I was so looking forward to my Tesla that I found myself trying to rush the next three months. As it happened, he called back with good news: A New York customer had backed out and that car would be ready in a couple of weeks. But when I heard the car was red, I nearly backed out. You already know how my family feels about anything flashy. The red, though, turned out to be more of a maroon, which put both Genevieve and me at ease. We took delivery on the last business day of 2012 of car number 805 of the Signature series – placing it among the limited edition first 1,000 cars of the S model.

I would still have it today, but when Tesla came out with an all-wheel drive car in 2015, I traded for it. It is one of my best cutting-edge tools. The car is so computerized that the company can automatically download upgrades overnight. Thanks to one of them, the car now can literally drive itself.

Genevieve stands by our electric Smart car at the entrance to Rowes Wharf.

We became a two-electric-car couple in 2015, when we were preparing to move from Rowes Wharf to NewBridge. I wanted to find a small vehicle that Genevieve could drive around the Dedham campus. I first looked at enclosed golf carts and was surprised by how pricey they were. Then a friend recommended Smart cars, pint-size vehicles offered by the same company that makes Mercedes-Benz. Inside, it was roomier than a golf cart, not to mention more comfortable. And, with rebates, it was in the same price range.

Now the Smart car is our main vehicle on the Vineyard, a breeze to drive on the narrow roads and to park in tight spaces between the omnipresent SUVs. The only challenge was getting the car from Dedham to our Vineyard home. It has a stated range of 60 miles before requiring a recharge. I found that by driving at 50 mph, which reduced wind resistance, I could get 76 miles on a single charge. I drove to the Vineyard by making a pitstop at Shawmut in West Bridgewater for recharging. I just had to get used to all the other drivers passing me, but had the satisfaction of knowing that when it came to being green – both in terms of dollars and the environment – I was leader of the pack.

CONFESSIONS OF AN EARLY ADOPTER

From a hair-raising helmet to a high-tech drone

JUST OVER TWO DECADES before I made my entrance, the Wright brothers flew into history from the sand dunes of Kitty Hawk. In 1925, the year of my birth, commercial radio was in its infancy; television was still in the laboratory; and the word "computer" referred to people who counted, not to a device that can direct a spacecraft to within a few thousand miles of Pluto.

In August 2015, when I turned 90, my family gave me a Phantom Three Professional drone, which weighs 3 pounds and snaps photos and takes videos four times sharper than the image on a high-definition television.

Several months before, I had traded in my all-electric Tesla – number 805 of the original limited edition of 1,000 – for a new four-wheel drive model that literally sticks to the road, even on the snowiest of days, and gets us comfortably from Boston to the Vineyard on less than half of a single charge. It pretty much drives itself for miles at a time on the open road.

When the Apple watch debuted, I snapped one up. I stood in subfreezing temperatures for an hour to be among the first to get a new version of the iPhone.

Yes, I'm addicted to getting the very latest in technical advances in any field in which I am involved. Some people call them gadgets, but basically, I only acquire the latest developments in items that I use on a regular basis or that fill a previously unmet need.

I built my own radio receivers in the 1930s and my own ham radio transmitters in the late '40s, including one for my car. I talked on my own AT&T mobile car phone in the '50s; watered our lawn with one of the first in-ground home-sprinkler systems in the '60s; recorded television shows on the early Sony Betamax in the '70s; installed one of the first compact radar systems for sailboats on Seabiscuit in the '80s; put the early Palm Pilot through its paces in the '90s; and then, moving into the Apple family in the 2000s, acquired and continue to acquire the latest of their iMacs, iPads and iPhones.

PULSAR PIONEER

Back in 1972, Genevieve bought me the world's first digital watch, a Pulsar. Knowing my appreciation for technological advances, she immediately ordered one for my birthday after reading an article about the watch. The same day she gave it to me, the Pulsar was reviewed on *The Today Show* – we were indeed ahead of our time. A few days later, when I was checking the watch's illuminated red digits in a movie theater, I was startled to see that seemingly dozens of people had turned away from the screen to crowd around me and my Pulsar.

Some years later, after digital watches had become more common, I was intrigued by a new model from Citizen Watch Company that was advertised for sailboat racing. Looking forward to buying one for the competitions sponsored by the New Bedford Yacht Club, I was disappointed to see it labeled "water resistant" and not "waterproof." I feared the watch wouldn't stand up to stormy weather. I called the manufacturer's North American vice president and asked when Citizen would release a waterproof model. After assuring me that eventually, of course, one would be available, the executive said, "Mr. Wyner, if you keep worrying about the next generation, you'll die before you ever buy another watch." I've taken his message to heart ever since.

Others may wait until a product has been proven and refined. I like to do the test-driving myself. I don't bother myself with all the reviewers on the Internet who show off how smart they are by nitpicking about all that's wrong with a pioneering piece of technology.

A FAMILY TRADITION

Being an early adopter is in my genes. My father, as I describe elsewhere, was an early ham radio operator. He kept up with the latest technology related to our work at Shawmut, as did I. My son James, since taking the reins, has not only installed every worthwhile improvement in the industry, but has also directed the company in continually refining our processes and machinery. That has kept Shawmut at the forefront of technology and quality in its field.

In my earliest days at Shawmut, I watched in amazement as my father and his mechanical team would break in the most advanced knitting machine on the market, immediately modifying cams and correcting other design weaknesses. As a result, many manufacturers went to great lengths to debut their latest equipment with Shawmut to get our feedback.

Dad also was among the first in town to buy a television. On the links, he swung the latest golf clubs, and he hooked trout with the latest rods.

COSTLY LESSONS

We've had our fair share of duds. And sometimes my enthusiasm for improving the latest development can come back to bite me. As I wrote in an earlier chapter, we purchased the very first of a New Zealand amphibious boat called Sealegs. I suggested to the manufacturer relatively inexpensive modifications that would make a big difference in performance. The company almost immediately adopted my ideas in a later model, reducing the resale value of my version by a third.

Actually, it only grew fuzz.

In 1936, the Crosley Corporation touted a device, the Xervac, that purported to reverse balding by using suction to spur hair growth. My dad, who began balding as a young man, bought this helmet-encased vacuum pump. My mother became very alarmed when she saw me testing it. She thought it would pull all my hair out.

I did lose my hair, but not until decades later. As to my father, he actually grew some fuzz – but not any real hair – experimenting with the contraption. In short order, the helmet was relegated to the attic.

That's where I found it after his death. I tried it out again, with no discernible results. I hope that Mom wasn't too upset if at the time she had happened to glance down at me.

PART VII: MR. FIX-IT

- **Troublemaker:** Perils of communal politics

- **Diagnosing a hospital:** Money woes at Beth Israel

- **In the thick of the fight:** Jewish Community Council

- **My friend the Rebbe:** Charmed into doing good

- **The sand traps of Belmont:** Settling turf wars

- **Securing a home for Hillel:** Students left in a lurch

- **Eternal affairs:** Tending to Jewish cemeteries

- **A feather in my cap:** United Fund

- **A Gene McCarthy Republican:** My national crusade

TROUBLEMAKER

Caught in the web of communal politics

IN THE INTRODUCTION TO this book, I told the anecdote about spotting a fire in Dedham while I was on my way to work. What made it stick in my mind was that a crowd had pulled over to watch the flames engulf an old factory building, but nobody had bothered to call the fire department. I did.

So many of us go about our daily lives taking our community for granted. It's easy to assume that if there's a problem – that is, one that does not directly affect you – someone else will take care of it.

I'm the opposite. If I see a problem, I feel compelled to fix it. As I've described, I was raised in a family where community service was as much a part of life as going to school or work. It was that way for my grandfather more than a century ago in South Africa – the letter from his fellow citizens of Malmesbury bemoaning his departure for America attests to that.

When it comes to the communal world, while some people flee from struggling organizations, I seem to be drawn to them. Like an auto mechanic, I pull up their hoods and tinker with their engines. My personal life has often led to my involvement with community groups as well, particularly through our home on Martha's Vineyard and our condo on Rowes Wharf.

But I've learned that sometimes groups would prefer that I just leave my tools at home and my thoughts to myself. Thus, the lengthy list on my resumé is misleading. Among them are organizations to which I've devoted decades, but there are many as well for which my service could be measured in days if not hours. Still, those experiences are worth recounting here, if only as lessons in the foibles of human behavior.

SUFFOCATED BY HOT AIR

My shortest committee stint occurred in 1965, when I was among corporate leaders invited by Vice President Hubert H. Humphrey to a brainstorming session in Washington about helping minority businesses. After listening to one platitude-laden speech after another, I stood up and said that we had not all come to Washington to be preached to, but rather to discuss and vote on specific steps that could and should be implemented. Some people applauded my remarks and came up to me afterward to thank me for saying what they were thinking. But nothing was accomplished at the meeting. I resolved not to attend such conferences again.

I was similarly frustrated about five years later when I attended meetings of Action for Boston Community Development as a representative of the Jewish Community Council (now the Jewish Community Relations Council). We met at the Parker House, up the street from the Old City Hall. In that bastion of Yankee-dom, the subject of conversation was mostly Roxbury and Mattapan – an area that had in the postwar period gone from being heavily Jewish to predominantly black. But in an economic sense, the ABCD members (all of whom but me were African-American) had as much in common with the residents of that inner-city community as I did. Well wired into Boston's political establishment, they were fairly clueless about what was happening on the street. Much to their chagrin, a contingent of young protesters would regularly show up at the meetings to upbraid the leaders for being out of touch. While most of the ABCD members were gritting their teeth and glancing at their watches, I would ask the protesters to identify problems that needed to be addressed. Ironically, they came to look to me, the only white guy in the room, for moral support. It was kind of embarrassing. "He is the only one here who understands us," one of them said, pointing to me.

BATTLING FOR DIVESTMENT

For the professional staffs of educational, religious and other nonprofits, the lay leadership is often viewed as a necessary inconvenience. Some would rather have us write a $2,000 check than offer our two cents. I'll tell you some longer war stories in other chapters, but here are some examples of the skirmishes I waged.

Today, especially among Jews, divestment has become a dirty word because of movements to sell stock of companies linked to Israel or its businesses on the West Bank. In my day, the principal targets included Big Tobacco and companies that did business with South Africa, where blacks faced apartheid until 1994.

When I became a member of the board of managers of Combined Jewish Philanthropies in 1964, I proposed selling all the tobacco stocks in our portfolio. I said it was simply wrong to be profiting from smoking, echoing my father's argument when as president of Beth Israel he banned cigarette sales at the hospital gift shop. He pointed out that it was hypocritical for the hospital to make money from a product that was responsible for the cancer cases its doctors were treating. By the mid-1960s, the link between tobacco and cancer had been proven beyond doubt. I recall that as a young boy, though, tobacco's dangers were little known. Baseball players, for example, would endorse a cigarette brand, claiming it helped them perform better on the field.

My boyhood neighbor Dick Smith and others on the CJP board countered that we had no right to make moral judgments about the companies in which we invested; our job, they said, was to maximize our gains so long as what we bought was legal. But while never explicitly stating it was doing so on principle, the board did dispose of the tobacco stocks over the course of the following year. Sometimes things have a way of working themselves out quietly. Had there been a showdown over the issue, egos might have trumped reason.

As a trustee for Roxbury Latin School in the late 1980s, I advocated combating South African apartheid by selling the stock of any companies that failed to adopt the Sullivan Principles. Drawn up by Reverend Leon Sullivan a decade before when he was on the board of General Motors, the principles spelled out corporate conduct that promoted social, economic and political equality. The school's headmaster happened to be a minister, too, but he appeared reluctant to make a show of his clerical collar. In this case, he gave less weight to ethical values than to the financial considerations raised by board leaders. In private, some other trustees would tell me, "That's wonderful you're saying that, but I don't dare say that on the board." Besides making the moral case, I argued that divestment made financial sense, because the growing anti-apartheid movement was bound to sway other investors to pull out of uncooperative companies, ultimately driving down their stock prices. I also urged the headmaster to be emboldened by his esteemed colleagues at Harvard who were out marching against apartheid. After some hesitation, he changed his position, and we sold the stock.

MY HEBREW COLLEGE EDUCATION

On occasion, I've ruffled feathers by being viewed as too diligent about my board duties. After joining the trustees at Hebrew College in 1967, I was appointed chair of the adult education committee. Before I had even attended a meeting or talked with anyone about the curriculum, the college issued a brochure of the fall offerings with my name on it. I told college officials that while I didn't have an opinion one way or the other about what the brochure contained, I was very uncomfortable about anything going out with my name on it that I hadn't read.

To broaden enrollment, the college offered an informational session previewing the courses at five satellite sites in the suburbs. I decided to check some of them out. At a Lexington temple, the only people who showed up were the congregation's president and me. At another site, I found just a handful of prospective students. When the board next met, the president of the college announced that the satellite program had been a big success. He reported 50 people were at one site he had visited and 100 at another. To help us understand why there appeared to be such a disparity in attendance between the places he had visited and those I had, I suggested we have people fill out a sign-up sheet telling us about themselves and why they came. We would then have a better idea of which programs would generate sufficient income to cover their costs. The president, who had suggested the satellite courses in the first place, rejected my idea. Perhaps he feared negative feedback or, as a cynic might suggest, being found out if he tried to inflate attendance figures in the future.

It wasn't long before I was moved off the adult education committee.

Several decades later, Hebrew College's trustees were to find out the pitfalls of placing too much trust in a president. It was in the 1990s, when the visionary David Gordis came up with grand plans for building a new campus in Newton Centre. While David was bursting with great ideas, he needed someone to say, "We can't do all of them. Pick two." But the trustees were so enamored by their charismatic and brilliant president that they failed to do their homework. They didn't ask him tough but vital questions about finances and enrollment projections. The campus became a success in terms of participation, but it was so costly to operate that the college couldn't afford to keep up payments on the bonds that paid for it. David wasn't around by the time the college nearly drowned in red ink. The turmoil cost the American Jewish Historical Society – and me – dearly; more on that in a later chapter.

What happened at Hebrew College is a cautionary tale both for lay leaders and for the professionals who ostensibly serve them. When Temple Israel was shrinking the size of its board a dozen years or so ago, I cautioned Rabbi Ronne Friedman about the danger of being surrounded by a clique that worshipped the ground he walked on. He was a wonderful visionary, but he needed a strong board to provide a reality check. Otherwise, he could be blinded by his own brilliance and have no one to blame but himself. I can't claim any credit, but the board in recent years has proven to be very able, thoughtful and transparent in its actions.

ROCKING A BIGGER BOAT

I took my proclivity for getting on the nerves of educational leaders to a new level in 1987, when I was named to the board of governors of Hebrew Union College (HUC). The Reform seminary has campuses in Cincinnati, Jerusalem, Los Angeles and New York. Though I was honored to be considered for the board of such a prestigious institution, I asked the member of the nominating committee who had approached me how much I would be expected to contribute each year. It's a question I always ask before I join a board. That way I won't find myself saddled with obligations I cannot comfortably meet. We agreed on a figure, and it turned out to be a good thing that I had raised the issue. I was astounded to see the other governors nonchalantly write out six- or seven-figure checks when the president made an impromptu request for donations. It was almost as if they were trying to outdo each other in their displays of generosity.

At my first meeting, the president announced that the college was embarking on a $40 million capital campaign. I told him that in my experience, organizations don't set a target without first conducting a feasibility study. The president retorted that he knew what was needed, and it wasn't a feasibility study. He wanted my vote, not my thoughts. To my amazement, he raised much of the money in short order, all by himself. He knew from the outset which donors to tap. While he didn't officially appoint the board, he used his influence to line up members whose pockets were as deep as their loyalty to the institution. I had to admire the president's shrewdness, and I found much to admire about HUC. But the deeper I delved into its operations, the more I doubted its priorities.

The board rotated its meetings among the college's four campuses, which gave me an opportunity to meet with professors and other staff members at all of them. Particularly disturbing was that at the same time it was conducting drives for new buildings, HUC would plead poverty when faculty asked for raises in line with what their peers earned elsewhere. It became clear to me that the other board members had no conception of what was happening in the classrooms.

About a year after I joined the board, I further endeared myself to my fellow governors by torpedoing a vote to condemn Rabbi Alexander Schindler, the president of what is now the Union of Reform Judaism. Rabbi Schindler had criticized Yitzhak Rabin, then Israel's defense minister, after he was alleged to have ordered soldiers to "break the bones" of Palestinians who incited riots during the intifada of the late 1980s. Concerned about blowback at the Jerusalem campus, the governors wanted to distance Hebrew Union from Rabbi Schindler's comments because he served as an ex-officio member of the board. I objected to the resolution on grounds that the rabbi wasn't at the meeting to defend himself. Furthermore, I said that I did not disagree with his comments and was certain that other members of the board, whether they would be willing to voice it or not, felt the same way. I offered an amendment to the motion that effectively reversed its intent. I proposed that the board resolve to take no action or offer any comment on Rabbi Schindler's stance.

The board wasn't used to such public displays of disharmony. Typically, the president would make a motion, and the board, after brief discussion, would approve it. After I proposed my amendment – which directly challenged the views of the president – one aghast member rose and said, "This is terrible. We can't have these kinds of disagreements. We've never had them before." He suggested that the author of the resolution condemning Schindler step outside with me so that we might reconcile our competing motions. In response, I said, "I didn't fly all the way to California to have us never vote on anything. There is clearly a difference of opinion – there is no in-between. We should have a full and frank discussion, and then members should each vote their convictions." In the end, the original resolution was withdrawn because I wouldn't back down over my amendment.

Afterward, several board members told me they were glad I had spoken up. Among them was the rabbi of Temple Emanu-El in Manhattan, one of the nation's most prestigious synagogues. I asked them why they hadn't spoken up. I don't recall their responses, but I came away disappointed at how timid our supposed leaders were. It was a rerun of my experience at Roxbury Latin when I pushed to sell tobacco stocks. By the way, Rabin later denied making the "bones" statement; he went on to make his reputation as a peacemaker, for which he was rewarded with an assassin's bullet.

A few months after the HUC board contretemps I attended a lecture by Rabbi Schindler. He spotted me and stepped down from the podium to thank me for defending his reputation in his absence.

DIAGNOSING A HOSPITAL

Like the elevators we endowed, we experience Beth Israel's ups and downs

My grandmother Gussie breaking ground in 1931 for a building at Beth Israel's new site in Longwood.

WEARING WHITE GLOVES, a calf-length dress and a fashionable cloth hat, my grandmother prepares to drive a shovel into the lawn outside of Beth Israel Hospital.

The year is 1931, and the event is the groundbreaking for a power plant funded through the sale of life memberships to Beth Israel – a fund-raising technique Gussie Wyner originated and managed both for the hospital and for Hadassah.

Behind her stands Joseph Rudnick, chairman of the men's committee of the hospital. That a man is in the background is fitting. For it was women who had given birth to Beth Israel two decades before.

In September 1913, under the headline "Boston Will Have A Jewish Hospital," *The Jewish Advocate* reported: "After much debate in private, Jewish women have put themselves at the head of a movement to create a hospital in which the Jewish sick shall receive proper care, kindness and sympathy." The article listed the eight people at the organizing meeting. Among the names is "Mr. George Wyner," but that must have been a typo; all the others are listed by their husbands' names, but preceded by "Mrs."

At the time, the Jewish community was divided over establishing its own hospital. The impetus was the massive influx of immigrants, many of whom spoke only Yiddish and kept kosher. Furthermore, Boston hospitals resisted giving admitting privileges to Jewish doctors. However, few prominent Jewish men actively supported the hospital; most of them feared it would lead to further discrimination against both Jewish patients and Jewish doctors at existing hospitals.

GUSSIE'S LEGENDARY GUSTO

Gussie helped turn the tide of public opinion. Her role was noted by Judge Jennie Loitman Barron at the memorial service Beth Israel held for my grandmother in 1949. Judge Barron, speaking then as honorary president of the Beth Israel Women's Auxiliary, recalled how as a young woman she was encouraged by Gussie to promote the hospital.

In the Wyner family tradition, Gussie had seen a problem in the Jewish community's lack of access to medical care and had set about solving it. She was 43 at the time, and the hospital would be part of her life until her death 36 years later. Through her, it became part of the lives of my grandfather and father and me, too.

As I wrote earlier, it was the hospital that propelled my father out of real estate and into the textile business. Rudolph had originally planned to develop the mansion property that instead became the first home of Beth Israel in 1916. The hospital moved to its current Longwood location in 1928. A decade later, *The Boston Globe* touted the hospital as "one of the most remarkable health, educational, and charitable institutions in Boston." The article singled out the role of the Women's Auxiliary, for which Gussie served as treasurer from its inception in 1926 until her death in 1949.

"Mrs. George Wyner" appears in scores of newspaper stories about hospital fund-raisers. I wonder how many hundreds of cups of tea she drank in pursuit of contributions and how many celebrities she courted at public galas. At a 1938 luncheon at the Statler Hotel celebrating the auxiliary's annual fund drive, my grandmother sat at the head table with Massachusetts Governor Charles Hurley and Boston Mayor Maurice Tobin.

While the women did much of the spadework, the men held the prestigious titles. Beginning in 1918, George served on various incarnations of the executive board. When he stepped down as a member of the board of trustees, Gussie took his place. She held that position at the time of her death in 1949.

Several weeks after she died, 3,300 auxiliary members filled the floor and part of the first balcony of the old Boston Garden for the annual "victory luncheon" celebrating fund drives. After the invocation, "the record crowd stood in tribute to the memory of Mrs. George 'Gussie' Wyner, founder of the life membership fund," the *Globe* reported. Among those paying tribute was the luncheon's guest star, Milton Berle, then the reigning king of TV comedy.

PUTTING BETH ISRAEL ON THE MAP

My father was named to succeed his mother as a Beth Israel trustee. Israel Friedlander, then the institution's president, "pointed out how pleased the hospital trustees were that Rudolph consented to continue the noble tradition of the Wyner family," the *Advocate* wrote.

Rudolph also continued the noble tradition of finding and fixing problems. While Beth Israel had been widely lauded for opening its wards to rich and poor alike of all religions, the hospital had yet to establish the national reputation it now has for medical excellence.

Dr. Charles Wilinsky had been general director of Beth Israel since it had moved to its Longwood quarters in 1928. Often, the forceful leadership traits necessary to get an organization on its feet can inhibit its ability to mature. My father was skilled at removing egos from the equation. That trait – plus the fact that he wasn't a doctor himself – helped him forge strong bonds with the medical community. During his tenure as hospital president, from 1959 through 1961, Beth Israel discontinued its part-time affiliations with both Tufts and Harvard medical schools. Instead, it became a full-time Harvard teaching hospital.

As president of Beth Israel Hospital, my father in 1960 unveils a portrait of Dr. Felix Fleischner, who retired after serving as the hospital's radiologist-in-chief since 1945.

My father, being such a dedicated Harvard man, had been the driving force behind that transition. While it was in the works, he would tell me about negotiating with the dean of the medical school over such details as making sure that the hospital's various department chiefs were appointed Harvard professors. Genevieve tells an anecdote that captures his deep loyalty to his alma mater: After our son George received acceptance letters from Harvard, Yale, Princeton and Dartmouth, he asked my father's advice about which one to attend. My father answered, "What is the question? It is Harvard, of course."

Under his leadership, the hospital also launched a $7.5 million campaign ($61 million in today's dollars) to modernize and expand its campus. But when it comes to money, what I remember best is how Dad deliberately cost the hospital revenue. He ordered the hospital gift shop to stop selling cigarettes. When trustees argued that the decision would mean $25,000 a year in lost income, he said, "I don't care. We can't sell cancer and then say we're going to cure it." You may recall from an earlier chapter that I took up my father's anti-tobacco crusade.

CHANGING OF THE GUARD

Worried that my generation wasn't getting involved with the hospital, my father asked me to help organize the Young Executives Group as he would later do on behalf of CJP. Cliff Helman – whose father, Si, also was a hospital trustee – and I recruited others, including Zayre executives Stanley and Sumner Feldberg and Richard Smith, my childhood next-door neighbor. For many, it was their introduction to the Jewish institutional world.

Later, my leadership roles with Beth Israel and Temple Israel, along with my father's, converged when the hospital sought to increase returns on its endowment. We wanted to tap into Dick Smith's financial acumen by recruiting him for the hospital's board of managers. The son of a Midwestern drive-in theater owner, Dick had expanded his family's holdings into retail stores, bowling alleys and the General Cinema movie chain.

At the time the hospital approached him, Dick was already advising Temple Israel and CJP. When Dick said he was stretched too thin, my father came up with a solution: the Beth Israel, CJP and Temple Israel boards of managers would hold their meetings together as a new entity known as the Combined Board of Managers. That way leading investment gurus could volunteer for multiple boards at once. and our combined resources enabled us to hire financial consultants who would have been too expensive for our individual organizations. Although identically invested and managed, the funds were technically separate.

Thanks to Dick and later Seth Klarman and other money gurus, the portfolios produced fantastic returns. We became the envy of other Jewish organizations, some of which joined in. Eventually, the different groups found a way to merge the separate funds into the Jewish Community Endowment Pool.

DISSECTING THE BOOKS

In 1966, I was named to the Beth Israel board of trustees. Appointed to the finance committee, I arrived just as the hospital was grappling with an unanticipated operating deficit of $1 million, which today would be equal to more than $7.7 million. At my first meeting, the committee discussed how to reduce expenses, but appeared to have no interest in how the hospital had dug its financial hole in the first place. Not being one to hold my tongue – even though I was new to the committee – I argued that unless we pinpointed where the budget was going awry, we'd face greater shortfalls in the future.

Committee members agreed to engage Ernst & Ernst to analyze our expenses – though they weren't happy with the accounting firm's estimated fee of $25,000. They were even less happy when halfway through the study, Ernst & Ernst announced that the assignment was taking much longer than it had anticipated and projected that our tab would be $75,000. "Look what you've gotten us into," the other committee members said to me.

I was beginning to sour on the firm, too. If Ernst & Ernst couldn't predict expenses in its own realm of accounting, how astute could it be in evaluating ours? I managed to negotiate the fee down to $35,000. It was worth it. The company showed us where the money was leaking and helped us right our financial boat. But by then, I think, I had worn out my welcome on that committee.

Genevieve and I at a function benefiting Beth Israel Hospital.

A FITTING HONOR FOR GUSSIE

Over the years, my family has made numerous donations to Beth Israel. For example, we gave money for the maternity wing in honor of Gussie, who was, after all, one of the true mothers of the hospital itself. Later, we gave up the naming rights for the wing so the hospital could sell them to someone else. Another time we donated money for a registration desk, though I have no idea where it is or whether it's still there.

We really weren't looking for credit anyway, although my father did take delight in endowing elevators. He would joke that people in elevators had nothing else to do but read the nameplates. The trouble is, the plaques in the elevators seem to disappear over time. That was the case with the one my father endowed in the name of my mother (and later was renamed for them both). Now the hospital has so many buildings with so many elevators that Genevieve and I have lost track of the one that we endowed.

BARNEY IN OUR BED

One day in November 1990, Genevieve and I got a call from Barney Frank.

"Guess where I am," the congressman said. "I'm recovering at the Beth Israel in a bed that says it was donated by you and Genevieve."

We laughed and wished him a speedy recovery from what turned out to be a mild heart attack. We had known Barney, but weren't close friends, so the call came as a nice surprise.

A few weeks later, we heard from a friend that Barney gave a talk at the old Stoughton JCC about his experiences in politics and the reaction to his coming out as gay three years before. He also spoke about his heart attack, telling the crowd that he recovered in Jerry and Genevieve Wyner's bed. Afterward, people mischievously linked his coming out with his staying in our bed.

Barney and I had a good laugh about that several years ago when we chatted after he gave a talk at the Martha's Vineyard Hebrew Center.

IN THE THICK OF THE FIGHT

In which I try to save a neighborhood, stand up
to the JDL and do battle with CJP

IT WAS THE HIGHLIGHT of my tenure with the Jewish Community Council: I censored the speech of a Soviet refusenik.

The occasion was the 1972 Israeli Independence Day rally in downtown Boston. The day before, the refusenik had been involved in a brawl while touring the old Jewish neighborhoods along Blue Hill Avenue. I'll get into the details later, but I start out with the speech episode because it represents the convergence of the three struggles that dominated the agenda while I was at the JCC: the flight and plight of Jews in urban Boston; the movement to free Soviet Jewry; and the campaign to take Israel advocacy beyond the Jewish community. The JCC is now known as JCRC, the Jewish Community Relations Council.

Robert E. Segal, who had been executive director of the JCC since its founding in 1944, persuaded me to join the organization's administrative committee in 1967; I went on to serve as its president from 1971 to 1973. Bob graduated from college the year I was born. After a successful career in journalism, he switched to Jewish communal work in the 1940s, alarmed by the rise of Nazi sympathizers in Cincinnati (both a Jewish and German stronghold). When he took up his post in Boston, Bob contended with the likes of Father Leonard Feeney, who ranted against Jews in sermons delivered on the Boston Common. Intense and feisty, Bob ran the JCC with an iron hand. We got along because he saw me as an ideological soulmate. He also knew he could count on me to do more than just attend meetings.

'HELP ME, MISTER'

At one time, as many as 100,000 Jews lived in the Roxbury-Mattapan-Dorchester area of Boston stretching along Blue Hill Avenue. By the time I arrived at the JCC, the number was fewer than half that. Many, like my relatives, had moved to the suburbs as they became more prosperous. But in the mid-'60s, real estate agents, capitalizing on fears of crime, set about scaring the remaining white residents into selling their homes. It was called blockbusting. They would go up and down streets, urging homeowners to sell now before it was too late. They targeted Jews, believing they would be more willing to sell to blacks. The other dominant group in the neighborhood, Irish Catholics, were less likely to pull up stakes because of their ties to their parishes. Synagogues could pick up and move; Catholic churches couldn't – at least not without Archdiocese approval.

Accelerating the exodus was a reverse form of redlining. Pressured by the city over discriminatory mortgage practices, some 20 area banks formed the Boston Banks Urban Renewal Group to funnel federally guaranteed loans to blacks. However, BBURG, as it was known, only made the money available for homes within a circumscribed area that just happened to encompass much of what had been Jewish Boston. With little or no financial vetting, just about anyone could get a mortgage. Agents were practically taking vagrants off the street, provided they were black, and setting them up with homes. They would move in, fall behind in their payments and ultimate abandon their property. The real estate agents got their commissions. The banks got their fees. If homeowners defaulted, it was Washington's problem. Vandals and thieves stripped empty houses of fixtures. In the end, the neighborhood was like a war zone, with roving gangs preying on the vulnerable.

I recall visiting Woodrow Avenue, just off of Blue Hill Avenue, where four synagogues were then clustered. Even into the early '70s, these shuls would be packed on the High Holidays as their now-suburban congregants would make a pilgrimage back to the city. As the neighborhood changed and became polarized, the JCC had to hire security guards to protect worshippers. Checking out the arrangements, I visited one of the synagogues on Yom Kippur. It was standing-room only, but the rabbi noticed me in the back. "I see the president of the Jewish Community Council is here," he told the congregation. "I want to ask him to come up and speak to us." I gave an impromptu speech from the bimah about how the Jewish community still cared about the old neighborhood. As I was leaving, one of the few congregants who still lived in the area approached me. "Help me, Mister," he said. "I can't get out of the community." Over the next couple of weeks, I tried to find him a new home. But before I succeeded, I learned that he had been mugged walking to synagogue; shortly later, he died.

I was determined not to let a similar fate befall an elderly woman who called me for help. She lived in senior housing near the old Mishkan Tefila synagogue on Blue Hill Avenue; the temple had relocated to Newton in the 1950s. Her daughter used to visit her regularly. After one visit, the daughter discovered all four wheels missing from her car – one that her husband had just bought. That was the final straw. He would not let her make the trip again.

I appealed to Combined Jewish Philanthropies for help in moving her and other seniors. I argued that they were pretty much prisoners in their own homes and that it was up to us in the Jewish community to help them. To get me off its back, CJP responded in classic bureaucratic fashion: It formed a study committee. While I was appointed to it, I soon realized that the deck was stacked against me. The members were almost entirely federation professionals or their allies. We must have met 15 to 20 times. I couldn't get them to budge. Their attitude was that demographics would make the problem go away on its own. I countered that just because many of these people were in their 80s didn't mean they would die in the next couple of years.

Later, as president of the Hebrew Free Loan Society, I announced that I would use its funds to move the elderly woman. That really angered the CJP people, not that they had any power over the loan society. They contended that if I helped this woman, CJP would be pressured to bail out everyone else. In other words, I'd be shaming them into acting. Eventually, I found an apartment for her through Roger Stern, who owned many senior units in Brookline. The woman had enough money to pay her rent and living expenses. I believe she was the last Jew (and white person) to move out of her Roxbury building – one that once had been totally Jewish.

STUDENT SHOWDOWN

But my efforts amounted to just a few drops in the bucket. No one brought that home to me better than a group of students who protested at the General Assembly of the Council of Jewish Federations and Welfare Funds when it held its annual meeting in Boston. The year was 1969, when student activism – spurred on by the civil rights movement and opposition to the Vietnam War – was at its peak. Busloads of students descended on Boston to demand that the Jewish establishment wake up from its slumber. They lambasted leaders for a lackluster response to the ordeal of Jews in urban America and in the Soviet Union; for failing to support religious education; and for ignoring the voices of younger Jews like themselves.

Assembly organizers feared the students would shut down the event. Because I had served as president of Harvard Hillel and the Hillel Council of Metropolitan Boston, I was asked at the last minute to negotiate with the students. "You know these students better than any of us; see what you can do," said Judge Matthew Brown, who was chairman of the conference host committee and later CJP president. I spoke to the students outside the hotel where the assembly was meeting. We reached an accord that gave the students an opportunity to present their demands to a council panel and for one of them to address the assembly as a whole. I agreed to their request that as representative of the JCC, I would accompany one of their leaders on a tour of the Roxbury-Dorchester-Mattapan area so they could show me the places where problems were the worst.

A few days later, as I drove with the student leader through the decaying neighborhoods, I told him about the JCC's efforts on behalf of the remaining Jews. I don't think I succeeded in making much of an impression. He responded by cautioning me to remember the story of the last leader of the dwindling Jewish community in the Warsaw Ghetto. When he finally learned the truth about where the Nazis were sending his constituents, he hanged himself.

There wasn't much that I could say in response to that, but I did continue to keep the lines open between Jewish leaders and the students. Representing the JCC and to a limited extent CJP, I visited area campuses. At Brandeis, I met with an umbrella group known as the Concerned Jewish Students of Greater Boston. We talked for almost the entire night. Through such meetings, I came to appreciate that much of the students' criticism of Jewish leaders was right on target. Over time, the atmosphere became more trusting and less confrontational. CJP agreed to help fund some of the umbrella group's programs and its excellent annual handbook, *Jewish Boston*. Concerned Jewish Students became a JCC member organization, nominated students to sit on CJP committees and represented the Boston area's 20,000 Jewish college students on the Metropolitan Hillel Council.

I really had no idea how much the students valued my role until Bob Gordon, then leader of Concerned Jewish Students, presented me with the first copy off the presses of the 1970 edition of *Jewish Boston*. Above the table of contents was my picture and a dedication to me. I was touched, almost to the point of tears. I have received honors for service to other organizations, but this acknowledgement, so unexpected, stood apart. It showed how the simple act of listening could make a big impression. Genevieve, in her work overseeing human relations at Shawmut, would repeatedly use a phrase for this: "responding with empathy."

ELMA AND ME

As a goodwill gesture, CJP purchased the building complex that had housed Mishkan Tefila for $1.1 million and gave it to the black community for use as an arts and cultural complex. The JCC helped arrange the deal, and then we found ourselves caught in the middle when the good deed nearly blew up in our face.

Elma Lewis, a long-time arts educator and community powerhouse, accepted the gift, but after moving in blasted her benefactors. Miss Lewis was telling people all over town that the Jewish community should be ashamed because the buildings were in horrible condition. Although I had not personally been involved in the transaction, I went to see her as a representative of the JCC. She lit into me. "The roof is going to cost $500,000," she said. "The Jewish community gave me this thing, and they're getting all this good credit." On the outside, the building seemed in pretty good shape. But after she showed me the peeling paint and dripping ceilings, I told her that I would do my best to help her out. In the end, we left on good terms.

I again found myself cast in the role of peacemaker when I was asked to mediate a dispute between two black gangs. Even after the neighborhood had become predominantly black, CJP continue to sponsor a teen drop-in center on Blue Hill Avenue. It had become a refuge for a group of black kids who wanted an escape from neighborhood thugs. I was called in when workers at the center learned that these kids were about to get into a big fight with a street gang. The teens at the drop-in center accused the gang of getting their girlfriends hooked on drugs. Meeting with the teens, I was struck by their bleak lives. Many had no homes and were living in cellars. Some were runaways. They could hardly speak intelligible English, at least to my suburban ears. We managed to persuade them to avoid a confrontation with the gang, and the center focused on helping to straighten out the lives of the girls.

ACID ATTACK

In the late 1960s, blockbusting continued its inexorable spread south along Blue Hill Avenue into Mattapan. Many of the Jewish residents had only moved there within the last decade or so. Their single-family homes, a major step up from the triple-deckers they had left behind in Roxbury, would not have looked out of place in Brookline and Newton. Among the residents was a 28-year-old rabbi, Gerald B. Zelermyer, of Temple Beth Hillel. One day in June 1969, two black youths rang his Mattapan door. When he answered, they handed him a note and tossed acid in his face. Filled with expletives, the note began "dearest rabbi" and then ordered him out of town. Initially, he tried to keep the attack out of the news for fear of further stoking neighborhood tensions. But the editor of *The Jewish Advocate* got wind of it and persuaded Zelermyer to go public.

The news galvanized the JCC. Along with local rabbis, we urged the police to step up their presence in the area. Bob Segal called on residents to report any incidents to the JCC. By fall, the situation became even more toxic when the New York-based Jewish Defense League announced that it was setting up a branch in Boston to patrol the streets in the Blue Hill Avenue area. Boston's Jewish establishment, including the JCC, denounced the JDL as vigilantes who would only incite further violence.

At the same time, then-mayor Kevin White announced that the police would beef up surveillance. White insisted, though, that racism wasn't to blame for increased crime. "Victims of these assaults are both black and white," he told the *Globe*, "easy prey for young thugs of both races." Even Bob tried to play down race. "We reject, and we are confident that practically the entire Jewish community rejects, the false thesis that the issue before us is unique, that it is isolated anti-Semitism in Dorchester and Mattapan," he told the *Globe*, adding that people of every religion and race are victimized by crime in cities across American.

Still, in that same November issue, the *Globe* reported that 2,000 Jews had left Mattapan over the previous year.

'ARE WE NOT ALL GUILTY?'

Among the last holdouts was Rabbi Samuel Korff, leader of the Orthodox Congregation Kehillath Jacob on Fessenden Street in Mattapan. Rabbi Korff was administrator for the Rabbinical Court, where he made national headlines shaming a Jewish slumlord. But that didn't indemnify him from the turmoil in his own backyard. At the end of a service in March 1973, the rabbi was approached by a 79-year-old congregant, Charles Shumrack. "I hope the synagogue will be kept open," said the retired fruit dealer, who worshipped daily at the shul. The rabbi, according to a report in the *Globe*, assured Shumrack that it would "as long as you're alive and come to the synagogue." That night, Shumrack was found dead in his apartment, his home ransacked and rent stolen.

In his eulogy, Rabbi Korff said historians studying Mattapan would one day ask "how it was possible for a Jewish community of 40,000 souls to be emptied in the course of two years and how so much crime was concentrated in the short space of 40 blocks." He noted that it took Roxbury 20 years to become *Judenrein*, Dorchester 14 years and Mattapan only two years. The rabbi blamed the Jewish leadership both for its failure to anticipate the crisis and for its inadequate response. "Are we not all guilty of this crime?" he asked.

Not long after, Rabbi Korff moved his synagogue to Newton. He left behind a beautiful home in what had once been a middle-class community on the edge of Mattapan. He couldn't find a buyer who would come close to his asking price, the home's value had fallen so far so quickly. As the house sat unoccupied, vandals stole rugs, furniture, radiators, appliances and then the windows, toilets and even the boiler. Since the rabbi didn't have the money, the JCC spent $10,000 to board up the place to keep it from becoming a public spectacle. Imagine the headlines about a drug den that had been the house of a rabbi who had fled to the suburbs.

BRAWL ON BLUE HILL AVENUE

The plight of the inner-city Jews became intertwined with another major issue confronting the JCC, that of the Jews trying to flee the Soviet Union.

In May 1972, Soviet refusenik Boris Kochubievsky was among the star attractions at the annual Israeli Independence Day parade and rally downtown. The day before the big event, the Jewish Survival League, a JDL-like organization whose members dressed up in military-style uniforms, gave Kochubievsky a tour of the old Jewish neighborhoods of Boston. They stopped at what was once a popular venue for bar mitzvah celebrations that had since become a mosque for black Muslims. The refusenik stepped out of his car and started taking pictures just as a service was letting out. The congregants told him to stop taking pictures. But he didn't understand English and kept snapping away. He ended up on the ground being punched and kicked. Members of the Survival League came to his rescue, but not before a brawl had broken out.

That evening, Kochubievsky recounted the incident at an appearance at Temple Beth El in Newton. He said the persecution he had experienced in Roxbury was far worse than anything that had happened to him in the Soviet Union. He called Boston a terrible place for Jews and vowed to tell that to the crowd at the parade. Stephen Morse, the attorney for the JCC, had been keeping tabs on Kochubievsky's visit and tipped me off, as president, to the refusenik's plans for his speech. The Jewish militants saw this as a publicity coup; I saw it as a nightmare for the movement to free Soviet Jewry, not to mention a major distraction from the parade.

Since we were paying the fee for Kochubievsky's translator at the rally, I had no compunctions about directing him to take liberties with the refusenik's remarks. I told the translator, "Whatever he says in Russian, you tell the crowd he says, 'I've never been so well-treated in my life. I feel so fortunate to be here in America.'" And that's what happened.

I went to bed that night feeling pretty good about my last-minute maneuvering, only to be awakened at 2 a.m. by an angry MIT professor. The caller was a Russian immigrant and a member of the Jewish Survival League. When I asked him what business he had disturbing me in the middle of the night, he said, "You're the president of the JCC; I can call you any time I want to." His chutzpah reminded me of the lawyer who berated the general at the Pentagon for not paying my father's wartime contracts. I didn't let the outraged professor get to me. Mustering as much patience as I could, I explained that had we not intervened, the refusenik would have ruined what was supposed to have been a joyous event.

HEAD-TO-HEAD WITH KAHANE

I became involved in the Soviet Jewry movement early on at the JCC. At the urging of Rabbi Albert Axelrad, the young firebrand who headed the Brandeis Hillel chapter, I attended a meeting of the Student Struggle for Soviet Jewry on campus. Surrounded by big posters of the Star of David superimposed on the hammer and sickle, I spoke with the students long into the night. I came away impressed by their fervor, but concerned that their enthusiasm might get out of hand.

The Jewish establishment had thus far steered clear of what it viewed as a group of hotheaded students. I argued that instead of allowing the issue of Soviet Jewry to divide the Jewish community, we at the JCC should embrace it. I appointed Rabbi Samuel S. Kenner to chair our Soviet Jewry committee.

When it was announced that the Bolshoi Ballet would be performing in Boston, we learned that the Jewish Defense League planned to interrupt its performance at the Metropolitan Center (now the Wang Theater) with stink bombs. Rabbi Meir Kahane, the group's fiery national leader, was expected to attend. Through my grapevine, I discovered that Kahane was also to be at an event at the house of the father of

Alan Solomont (who become a major force in the Democratic Party). I met with Kahane in the kitchen of the Brookline home. I told him that the JCC would be picketing outside the Met. I said our message would be: By all means go inside and enjoy this beautiful ballet, but just remember that there are people in the Soviet Union who can't worship as they please, let alone move to a country where they can. Kahane said, "If we see the leadership of the community like you out on the picket line, we'll follow you; otherwise, we'll do what we want."

I had never been on a picket line in my life, but if joining one was the only way I could contain the JDL, I decided that I must. So, I stood out there along with other leaders, Jews and non-Jews, including Father Robert Drinan, the Roman Catholic priest and U.S. congressman. Kahane was true to his word: The JDL members who showed up peacefully joined our picket line.

Many of us also stood outside the Museum of Fine Arts, distributing leaflets and other protest materials, when it hosted an art exhibition from the Soviet Union. The head of the MFA was so impressed by our demonstration that he came out to thank us for being informative without being disruptive. He also asked for a couple of Save the Soviet Jewry T-shirts for his grandchildren.

Only on one occasion did I feel uneasy at a protest. That was when I was part of a Boston delegation participating in a march on the Soviet embassy in Washington. Although I was walking shoulder-to-shoulder with prominent leaders, my hair stood on end when I saw riot police marshaled at every side street. Other police came right up to us to snap our pictures. All we were doing was holding lighted candles.

POWER STRUGGLES

While I was able to work out an accord with Meir Kahane and the JDL, I often found myself at odds with the professional leadership of the Jewish community in those days. That friction has vanished in recent years under Barry Shrage's leadership of CJP. As I've mentioned in this chapter and elsewhere, hundreds of hours of my life have been wasted in CJP study committee meetings where the outcome was predetermined.

I saw no point in serving on a committee just to gab and listen to platitudes. I served on the American Jewish Committee's local board from 1960 to 1965. Besides chairing its annual dinner in 1962, I never felt I really accomplished anything at the AJC, I'm disappointed to say.

In contrast, thanks to my close relationship with Bob Segal, I was able to put my problem-solving skills to work at the JCC. When I became president in 1971, I was saddled with the delicate task of arranging Bob's departure as director. I liked him very much, but his autocratic ways had alienated CJP leadership and members of the JCC board. Besides, by then he had run the council for a third of his 66 years. I was able to negotiate a good retirement package for him. Herman Brown, who had directed the New York chapter of the American Jewish Congress, was selected from among a number of candidates by a search committee that I led.

While Bob was abrasive and assertive, Herman was affable and accommodating. Between me and Ben Rosenberg, the paid professional leader of CJP at the time, Herman was caught in a bind. A typical instance was when Ben told Herman that the JCC should take a public stance on some issue – now long forgotten – and Herman answered, "My president will want to present it to the council members for a vote." Ben essentially responded: "Lay people are to be manipulated and used to raise money. They don't make policy. We make policy. You forget what they say." I told Herman: "If we are a Jewish Community Council, then we have to represent the community."

I was a different sort of JCC president. Up until then, the lay leaders had indeed done the bidding of the professional staff. I did an unexpected end run. Herman told me that as soon as I was gone, he expected to be fired for following my directions. He was right, but he did make his mark.

WINNING FRIENDS FOR ISRAEL

Prior to becoming president of the JCC, I chaired the Greater Boston chapter of the American Israel Public Affairs Committee. This was long before American Jews had become polarized over Israel, with AIPAC on the right and groups like J Street on the left. AIPAC had grown out of the American Zionist Committee for Public Affairs, which was founded by Canadian native Isaiah (Si) Kenen, a legendary lobbyist for the Zionist movement and then Israel. Si and I developed a good friendship. Under his leadership, AIPAC gained a reputation with members of Congress as the go-to place for information about the Middle East and its publication *The Near East Report* was regarded as reliable and nonpartisan.

At the time I joined AIPAC in the 1960s, Israel's survival was by no means assured. We forget that during the Six-Day War, and, more so, the 1973 Yom Kippur War, Israel depended on its American lifeline.

During the Six-Day War, in June 1967, I got a call from Kenen at the national AIPAC headquarters to round up statements of support from Protestant ministers. I asked my rabbi, Roland Gittelsohn, whom I should contact. Roland said, "Here, call these three guys I marched with in Selma." That would have been during the civil rights protests. I called all three; not one would give me a statement.

I then realized we had a major public relations problem. We had to find a way to get Christian clergy on our side. As a result, the JCC started organizing goodwill trips to Israel. It was Herman who organized the first mission with ministers. Over the decades since, the trips have continued to win sympathy for Israel.

MY FRIEND THE REBBE

How I become front man for a Hasidic heath care charity

AFTER MY MOTHER'S DEATH in 1965, I committed to myself to recite the Kaddish daily, both morning and evening. Since our reform synagogue, Temple Israel, did not have daily minyans, I rotated among minyans at Kehillath Israel, Ohabei Shalom, and Temple Emeth, all in Brookline. One morning at Kehillath Israel I saw an old family friend, George Michaelson, who was saying Kaddish daily for his late wife. George asked if I had ever attended services at the Bostoner Rebbe's. "Who is the Bostoner Rebbe?" I asked. At his suggestion, I attended the Rebbe's Shabbos services the following night at Bais Pinchas in Brookline.

Just before the service, George introduced me to a distinguished-looking man with a long beard and an outfit right out of eighteenth-century Poland. He was Grand Rabbi Levi Yitzchak Horowitz, the 44-year-old second Bostoner Rebbe. His father, Grand Rabbi Pinchos Duvid Horowitz, had been the first. A native of Jerusalem, the elder Rebbe arrived in Boston in 1915. He took the name of his new hometown, as was the custom in Europe. Despite his august title and lineage, the current Rebbe immediately disarmed me with his easy smile and twinkling eyes. When we shook hands, it was the start of a friendship that would endure until his death in 2009.

The following Sunday, I got a call from the Rebbe. Saying he was sorry that we hadn't had a chance to talk much on Friday night, he invited Genevieve and me over to his house to have coffee and dessert with him and the Rebbetzin. When we arrived, Genevieve put out her hand to shake his, but he declined. Realizing that she must have broken Orthodox protocol, she apologized. The Rebbe responded, "No, I'm sorry." That was the way he was, ever gracious. He was not one who would call a Reform Jew a goy. Indeed, Jews of all stripes have been captured by his charisma, and some so inspired by his ways and wisdom to become more religious themselves.

However, our first chat had much more to do with the personal than the spiritual. We talked about our children, family histories and the community. I'm not sure if it was on that occasion or a later one that the Rebbe told me that as a child his goal had been to play for the Red Sox.

The president of the Rebbe's shul was a cofounder of Building 19, Harry Andler. One day Andler came out to Shawmut to buy our fabric seconds and remainders. He and my father dickered over the price until they were $2,500 apart. At that point, Andler said, "Why don't we settle it this way? Your son, Jerry, has become friendly with the Bostoner Rebbe. The $2,500 will make him and his wife, Genevieve, founders." My father said sure, and informed Genevieve and me of our new status. The title didn't really mean anything, beyond being a fund-raising gimmick. Still, we did go to a few more services. But in the end, we decided we didn't like praying separately; women sat hidden behind a mechitzah.

No one could say no to Grand Rabbi Levi Yitzchak Horowitz.

'YOU'LL RUIN THE DINNER'

But the Rebbe didn't forget me. He invited me over to discuss ROFEH International, the charity he had established to provide referrals and support services for hospital patients and their families. The name is Hebrew for "doctor," and the acronym stands for Reaching Out for Emergency Health. ROFEH raises much of its money through annual dinners, many of which honor doctors. That year's honoree was the chief of surgery at Beth Israel Hospital, Dr. William Silen. Knowing that I was a trustee of the BI, the Rebbe asked if I would chair the dinner and introduce the honoree. "Sure," I said, "but I've heard your dinners go on forever, with speaker after speaker. My father always told me that if you make sure a dinner wraps up before 9, everyone will go home happy, no matter what happens at it."

The Rebbe was taken aback. "You'll ruin the dinner," he said, worried that speakers would be offended at being rushed. I said, "Well, I assure you I'll be polite, but we'll have to control the number of people who speak, or many people will be so bored that they won't return the next year." He finally agreed to let me do it my way, but said he was sure he would get in trouble. The Rebbe had nothing to fear. He received so many compliments about the dinner that he asked me to host it the following year. And so began a hosting gig that lasted more than 15 years. In later years, when we would have two honorees, one medical and the other nonmedical, I co-hosted with Dr. Sumner Slavin of Beth Israel. He saw to the doctors, and I, to the other honorees.

Many of the honorees were surgeons who came from old Yankee families and had been pulled into the Rebbe's circle after he asked them to consult on a medical issue. It was impossible to say no to him. At least one doctor had flown to Europe to perform operations at his request. The Rebbe didn't ask them to work for free; rather, he was like a medical matchmaker, finding just the right specialist for a patient's illness. In many cases, the doctors' only contact with the Rebbe would be by phone. Before the awards dinners, I would arrange for the honorees to get to know the Rebbe and Rebbetzin in person. I also participated in the preliminary discussions to select honorees and other dinner speakers.

I streamlined the night's schedule by having routine business, such as recognizing the person who had donated the flowers, conducted while people were eating. Between the first and second course, we would introduce the nonmedical honoree, and before dessert, the medical honoree. After dinner, it would be the Rebbe's turn to speak. Many people attended just to hear him. He would talk movingly not just of ROFEH's work, but also of the importance of Jewish continuity and of a community he had founded in the Har Nof neighborhood of Jerusalem.

Except for the Rebbe, I held all the speakers to time limits. I had a reputation for being strict from being town moderator. I even made Alan Dershowitz toe the line when he was asked to be a guest speaker. I startled his secretary when I said her loquacious boss would have just 10 minutes to speak.

"Ten minutes?" she said.

"He can't say what he wants to say in 10 minutes?" I responded.

"Oh, of course, he can say it – he's a skilled courtroom attorney. But people will expect him to speak longer."

So, I said he could have 12 minutes.

MAKING EVERY DOLLAR COUNT

As it still is today, the benefit dinner was held at the Park Plaza Hotel in Boston. The event would draw 400 people, but most of the $250,000 it raised would come from the accompanying ad book. A number of wealthy Canadian families would purchase space in the book, for example, even if they didn't plan to attend. Unlike many other charities, ROFEH doesn't pick its honorees with an eye on the number of affluent guests they will attract. Just the opposite, in some cases. When doctors were honored, members of their staff would be welcomed as guests. Such was the case, too, for many distinguished Hasidic rabbis and scholars, who stood out in their traditional black broad-brimmed hats and garb. On some occasions, perhaps a fifth of the attendees had obtained complimentary tickets. Beyond that, the Rebbe wanted to keep the ticket prices low to make the dinner affordable to as many of his followers as possible. I persuaded him to raise the ticket price to $125, which still was only a fraction of the cost of many other fund-raising dinners in town.

ROFEH did an amazing amount with the few hundred thousand dollars raised from the dinners. It arranged for its clients to be treated by the best specialists in town. The patients covered their own medical costs, but volunteers would meet the families at the airport, find them places to stay and send them kosher food. Non-Jews, including, on occasion, Israeli Arabs, have been among the beneficiaries. Initially, the Rebbe turned his attic and the top floor of the synagogue into guest rooms. Eventually, ROFEH amassed enough money to buy an apartment house on Beacon Street near the synagogue. It was mainly to house families whose loved ones were being treated for cancer; sometimes their stays would last weeks, if not months. My son Daniel was among the donors; having had lymphoma treatment in Seattle, he could identify with the out-of-towners.

My relationship with the Rebbe didn't just revolve around the ROFEH dinners. He would often call me to see how my family was doing, even when he was in Israel for the High Holidays. When my father died in 1984, the Rebbe paid a shiva call and invited me to say Kaddish at his shul. I said I would come, but not for the morning service, for which I would be expected to put on tefillin. I explained that I felt inspired to put on tefillin on occasion, but was uncomfortable feeling compelled to do so. "If anyone tells you to put on tefillin, I'll ask him to leave," the Rebbe promised. I never did put his word to the test.

THE SAND TRAPS OF BELMONT

*In which I bring order to the tennis courts, spar
over shorts and perfect fast golf*

AFTER A GROUP OF my parents' Jewish friends purchased the Belmont Country Club, they found in the men's lockers old papers laying out club policy. Among the rules listed: Guests of the Hebrew persuasion are not welcome.

That was in 1944, when America was at war with the Nazis, a regime systematically massacring millions of Jews. Yet, at home, restricted clubs and hotels were commonplace. If Jews wanted to join a country club, they had little choice but to form their own.

My family didn't join Belmont until the following year. My mother thought it would be unseemly to establish a Jewish country club during wartime.

The founders of the club had their own qualms. They feared that Jewish charities would suffer if members cut back on donations to pay dues for the luxury club. So, the founders instituted a rule that members must, at a minimum, match their dues with a donation to the federation (now Combined Jewish Philanthropies). That rule applied to all members, including the sole Gentile, Charlie Pappas, the only holdover from the club's earlier days.

Over the decades, as the dues rose, the mandatory contribution was capped at $2,500. And, as more non-Jews joined, the club decided to allow donations to charities other than CJP. But the question of which charities qualified opened a new can of worms. At the urging of younger members, the club in the end decided to make the charitable donations optional.

MEMBERSHIP HAS ITS PRIVILEGES

In my single days, Belmont was the center of both my sports and social lives. On Saturdays at Belmont, I'd golf during the day and dance at night, most often with a girl from a Belmont member's family whom I'd just asked out there that afternoon. It was an informal atmosphere. Most of us had known each other since childhood, perhaps from Temple Israel or the Charlotte Orlov School of Dance. Some of our families went back generations together, first in Boston, later in Brookline and Newton. Although the Jewish leaders of Boston's business, legal and medical worlds were members, people didn't put on airs. They were brought up with the same philosophy as I was – to avoid flaunting your wealth or status. There were not a lot of people with big egos looking for recognition.

David Bernstein, the head of American Biltrite – which, like Shawmut, was based in Stoughton – headed the Greens Committee. The joke was that if a ball of his ever landed in a trap, he had the trap removed. But when it came to the important things, such as supporting the community, his family would quietly shore up one charity after another.

With few decent restaurants in the Boston area beyond Locke-Ober, the country club was our dining destination of choice. The maître d' was a little bald-headed fellow who was always bowing and scraping. The room could accommodate 250. It was packed on Thursday nights, when families had to fend for themselves because it was the traditional day off for maids. Otherwise, most people I knew rarely ate out, except for the occasional dinner party at the home of friends or relatives.

TENNIS TSAR

I took Genevieve out to dinner and dancing at Belmont when we were dating. She was one of the few girls from a nonmember family whom I ever brought to the club. After we got married, we took out our own family membership. Thanks in part to her urging, Belmont got serious about tennis. When Genevieve saw the condition of the clay courts, she was appalled. Pointing out that she came from a true tennis-playing family, she said their club, Fenway Golf Club, would never tolerate the courts deteriorating as ours had. I complained to David Bernstein. His response: "You are now chairman of the tennis committee. You fix it."

Built on what was once a swamp, the courts had suffered from years of neglect. Few members even cared about tennis, much less played it; they were all golfers. To me, the courts presented an irresistible challenge. Spending little money, but a lot of time, I restored them to pristine condition. From there, so it appeared, we would need to rent a heavy roller, like those used for paving roads, to pound down the clay. After scouring tennis court suppliers, I found a less expensive but just as effective alternative: a small vibrating power roller that the board agreed to purchase.

As head of the tennis committee, I decided that we should establish a dress code in keeping with other respected tennis clubs of the day. Dismayed at seeing people on the courts in their bathing suits, I insisted that everyone wear tennis whites. The blowback was immediate. The club president wrote me a letter saying that I couldn't tell members, especially the senior ones (I was deemed a junior member until I turned 34), what to wear. I used my own money to buy sets of tennis whites in different sizes for men and women. I had my friend Stanley Snider, who was then in the lumber business, build a little tennis house for people to change in. I declared that from now on everyone had to come with whites or change into one of ours. Game, set, match.

Genevieve holds a trophy she won at a Belmont tennis tournament.

We hired a locally prominent tennis pro named Arnie Brown, who put us on the tennis map. Our timing couldn't have been better, as this was just when America was swept by tennis fever. Genevieve's practice on the Belmont courts helped her keep the game that she had when she was young. Over the years, she would become a leading player on the town tennis team in Brookline.

BENDING THE RULES

While I was a stickler about dress on the tennis courts, I was a bit of a wardrobe rebel when it came to the links. Playing golf in Bermuda on a family trip, I took a liking to the British custom of wearing Bermuda shorts and long socks. Even the police wore them. At fancy dinner parties, men would come dressed in a modified tuxedo that included Bermuda shorts and long stockings. On that trip, I bought a Bermuda shorts golf outfit. When I wore it for the first time on the Belmont course, I was sent back to the locker room. I couldn't persuade club officials that what was formal enough for the British should be acceptable to Belmont. It wasn't until a decade later, well into the '60s, that the club allowed shorts.

My father was also a bit of a rebel on the Belmont links. He and his friends – Charlie White and Mark Bortman, among others – would regularly play very early on weekend mornings. All of them had cardiac troubles, so they took along a flask of whiskey. It was for medicinal reasons, of course. By the time they finished up, they were all feeling pretty good, especially Charlie and Mark. I guess their medicine didn't come with instructions.

While my father's gang perfected medicinal golf, they also set an early standard for ready – or fast – golf. Typically, a foursome is the max for a game so that one group doesn't tie up the links. Dad's group of five played so fast that no one questioned them. Besides, they were usually first on the links.

As junior members, my friends and I had to tee off before 9 a.m. There were 20 of us, who would split up into foursomes every Saturday and Sunday morning. I always played with my closest friend at the time, Paul Lubell, but we varied the others in our foursome. When we all turned 34, and were thus eligible to play later as senior members, I was the only one who chose not to sleep late; I wanted to have more time later to spend with my family. Since those in my father's group were all early risers, I joined them.

As our ranks thinned over the years, it got down to my father; his friend Al Franks, a clothing retailer turned entrepreneur; and me – and the pace of play increased dramatically. We'd tee off at 7 a.m. and finish before 9. We made it a goal to be at the 10th hole by 8 a.m., because that's when the club would let people start on the back nine. We didn't rush our shots, we anticipated them. We'd always have the right club ready for the next hole. And as we approached a hole, we let players putt out, rather than waste time by taking turns after each shot. We also didn't get hung up as to who was entitled to shoot first for each round. You'd be amazed at how much time we saved with these little changes. Interestingly, "ready golf" as it has aptly been named, became a sport for many, including the first President Bush.

The only problem was that on occasion one of us got out ahead of the others and was in the path of the ball. Once, Al knocked out one of my father's teeth. Another time, my Dad stroked a ball that smacked Al in the rear; for the next week, it pained him to sit down. I guess we were lucky that no one got killed.

Since we were so quick, the caddies loved us. Years later, I happened to be touring a fancy new course on Martha's Vineyard called The Vineyard Golf Club. When I introduced myself to its developer, Owen Larkin, he said, "Wyner? Would you be part of that father-and-son group at Belmont that we all fought to caddy for? You played so fast we would be back in time to get a second loop." So our reputation was still alive!

A CLUBHOUSE DIVIDED

In recent years, the leadership of Belmont has shifted from hands-on businessmen to lawyers and financiers, and I think the club has suffered for it. The new power structure lacks the experience of the old in managing people and staying on top of day-to-day details. As a result, standards have slipped, both in services and maintenance.

By 2010, the club was faced with a decision about whether to renovate or rebuild its clubhouse. As often happens when people rise to leadership positions, they assume that they know what's best for the general membership. They become tight-lipped, taking the attitude that the members would only become confused by the nuances of the decision-making process. That's a good formula for making bad choices, as Belmont has painfully learned.

Club leaders appeared to exaggerate the problems with the existing facility to bolster the case for replacing it. While the cost of renovation was pegged at $7 million, they said it would be more like $9 million. And at that price, they argued, the club would be better off spending $12 million for a new building and then not have to worry for years about capital expenditures.

By the following year, the price tag for a new building had soared to $18 million. Before anyone had a chance to protest, work had started on demolishing the old clubhouse. The new building wound up costing $28 million. Debt service alone nearly swallowed all the annual dues income.

If I had been younger I might have run for president, because the club became splintered with recriminations over how it got itself into this $28 million mess. Fortunately, my son James, who had recently joined so that we could play together, served as the voice of reason. He pointed out that the club's biggest problem wasn't the size of the bond for the building, but rather the size of the membership. Thanks to steady hikes, the club had outpriced itself. Many people had left, and few were taking their place. James said that if the club attracted 100 new members, it would be back at the level of a decade before and able to spread costs over a larger base. He persuaded the club to offer new memberships at a reduced price, with the goal of eventually lowering everyone's payments.

A little over a year later, the club appeared to be back on a solid footing. James, who was not interested in holding any office, has since gradually stepped out of the picture. Not many people even remember the role he played in fixing the problem. Like me, he's more interested in solutions than in fanfare.

Teeing off in 2018: my 73rd opening day at Belmont.

WHAT WOULD HILLEL SAY?

Rallying support for an orphaned campus group

CONSIDERING THE TENS OF thousands of dollars that Combined Jewish Philanthropies invests annually in area universities these days, it's hard to believe that in the not-too-distant past the federation balked at bailing out campus Hillel chapters.

Hillel had not yet established a chapter at Tufts when I was a student there. I became involved with the organization in the 1960s through the usual route: I was drafted onto the board by my father. Our family had been involved with the Harvard chapter since the early 1950s.

It was at Hillel that my sister, Elizabeth (Betty), then an undergraduate at Radcliffe, was introduced to her future husband, Melvin Mark, by the chapter's director, Rabbi Maurice Zigmund. And when they were married in the garden of our family home, it was Rabbi Zigmund who conducted the ceremony. I got to know the rabbi even better during our summer vacations on Martha's Vineyard, where he served the Hebrew Center on a part-time basis.

So, when I became president of the Harvard chapter in 1966, I was no stranger to the institution or its staff. That was a time of transition at the popular conservative minyan, and I was drawn to the challenge.

BUILDING ON A DREAM

The first big change came with the retirement of Rabbi Zigmund after two decades at the helm of Harvard Hillel. He was succeeded by Rabbi Ben Zion Gold. Since arriving at the chapter as associate director in 1958, Rabbi Gold had dreamed of moving its quarters closer to the center of campus. He thought Hillel could play a larger role on campus that way. In addition, Hillel was bursting at the seams where it was. As a temporary solution, it moved from 5 Bryant Street to 1 Bryant in 1969.

Much to his credit, the rabbi came up with a plan to swap Hillel's Bryant Street property for two small buildings Harvard owned on Prescott Street. Although Gold hadn't known it at the time, one of those Prescott buildings held a significant place in Harvard's Jewish history. Before it was turned into offices, the building in the 1920s had been home to a kosher restaurant and to residences for Jewish students.

As a show of support for the Prescott Street proposal, my father, Genevieve and I pledged to the building fund that we would endow a biblical garden there in memory of my mother, who had died in 1965. But that never came to be. While the Prescott Street plans were still in the design stage, Rabbi Gold and my designated successor as Hillel president, Henry Morgenthau III (a television producer and son of FDR's treasury secretary), turned to a more practical swap with Harvard. The new site, at 74 Mount

Auburn Street, had been home to the former Iroquois Club, which had catered to undergraduate elites. The building required costly renovations, but Robert Riesman, who succeeded Morgenthau, footed much of the bill. Riesman and his parents were longtime friends of our family. I was pleased to see Bob honored when 74 Mount Auburn Street became the Riesman Center for Harvard Hillel in 1979.

AN ORPHANED ORGANIZATION

As I wrote earlier, my tenure at Hillel was marked by transition. It was moves on the national, not local, scene that would prove most vexing.

B'nai B'rith, which had been supporting Hillel chapters nationwide since the 1920s, decided in the late '60s that the student organization was no longer a priority. That left local Hillel chapters, including those at Harvard, Boston University, Tufts, Northeastern and Brandeis, in the lurch.

I assumed that Boston's Jewish leaders would consider the Hillels to be important not just to the students, but to the community at large. After all, the organization nurtured the next generation of Jews. To my surprise, when I approached Combined Jewish Philanthropies to replace the support we had been receiving from B'nai B'rith, federation leaders were less than sympathetic. They argued that since most of the estimated 25,000 Jewish college students in the area weren't local, Boston's community had no obligation to support them. In response, I pointed out that many of our children attend college out of state. Wouldn't we want local federations to support the Hillel chapters at their schools?

At that time, CJP was more territorial and less open-minded than it is today. Lacking the commitment to community building that it would later embrace, the federation resorted to its old trick for making unpleasant things go away: It formed a special committee. I served on it, along with academic representatives of area university faculties. At meeting after meeting, committee members expressed support for CJP funding. But somehow that message didn't resonate with the CJP representative who served as notetaker on the committee. She appeared to tailor her summaries to suit the blinkered views of the CJP leadership.

Leonard Kaplan, my father and I consulted with national Hillel leaders and with members of the more vocal local chapters, such as those at Harvard and Boston University. Working with CJP, we came up with a solution that would secure funding for area Hillels and provide the federation what it needed for its comfort: a sense of ownership. As a result, in 1971, CJP dramatically boosted its support in return for oversight of a newly formed Hillel Council of Metropolitan Boston, which in turn dispersed funds to the campuses. When I completed my term as president of Harvard Hillel, Leonard Kaplan asked me to succeed him as president of the metropolitan council. I accepted, eager to take on the challenge of keeping Hillel afloat in one of the nation's biggest college towns.

The success of the plan was cemented when the Hillel council agreed to CJP's recommendation to hire Rabbi Richard Israel as its full-time executive director. The rabbi, who had been Hillel director at Yale, brought a wide-ranging background, an inquisitive mind and a strong sense of social activism to the job. In 1974, he traveled to the Soviet Union to help set up a network for refuseniks. A beekeeper and marathon runner, he also found time to write several books, including *The Kosher Pig and Other Curiosities of Modern Jewish Life.*

MARCHING ON HARVARD

On September 16, 1979, my son George was among several hundred students marching through the streets of Harvard University. They weren't carrying protest signs, but rather Torah scrolls.

Their destination was 74 Mount Auburn Street, the new home of Harvard Hillel that, as I recounted earlier, Rabbi Ben Zion Gold had been seeking for decades. Speaking at the dedication ceremony, Harvard College dean Henry Rosovsky noted that Jews made up a quarter of the student body.

By then, Hillel was drawing as many as 400 people to Shabbat services and an astonishing 3,000 to its High Holiday services. To accommodate the crowds, the chapter used Harvard's Memorial Church and occasionally other area churches. I recall attending several of them with George.

In 1994, Hillel moved to its current home, Rosovsky Hall, designed for the chapter by Moshe Safdie. The internationally famed architect would later design the Newton campus of Hebrew College, where – as I describe in another chapter – I had a pocketbook-draining experience with him when I relocated the archives of the Jewish Historical Society.

I'm pleased to say that yet a fourth generation of Wyners has become involved with Hillel as our grandchildren attend college. Most recently, George's son, Samuel, while enrolled in an architecture program at the University of Miami, traveled to Israel through a Hillel Birthright trip.

ETERNAL AFFAIRS

Tending to the wishes of the living and the dead

IN AMERICAN HISTORY, BOSTON Mayor John Francis "Honey Fitz" Fitzgerald is best known as the maternal grandfather of President John Fitzgerald Kennedy.

In Wyner family lore, he holds a less celebrated position.

In the early 1900s, my grandfather George Wyner and other leaders of Congregation Adath Jeshurun approached Mayor Fitzgerald for a permit to open a cemetery in West Roxbury.

"It's going to cost you sheenies $10,000," the mayor is said to have told them.

Whether that's true or not, I can't say. Fitzgerald was also known as a champion of immigrants and to have wooed Jews with election circulars in Yiddish. But my dad often repeated the anecdote as the younger Kennedys climbed to political prominence.

After buying the property and paying the $10,000 (or whatever combination of fees and bribes were required), the machers of Adath Jeshurun faced another big decision: Who was going to buy the first cemetery lot? Perhaps they feared the Grim Reaper was watching.

But not my grandfather. He purchased the first site and defied superstition by avoiding occupancy for nearly 40 years, outliving most of the other founding machers.

Meanwhile, minding the cemetery became another Wyner family tradition. My father would join the cemetery board and, of course, bring me on, too. I've been its treasurer since 1964.

In the 1960s, our biggest concern was that the cemetery endowment would be raided to repair the synagogue. By then, most of the members of Adath Jeshurun – like those of other Roxbury-Mattapan synagogues – had switched to suburban temples.

Among my fellow committee members were lawyers Ben Trustman and Leonard Kaplan. They arranged to have the cemetery established as a separate entity, assuring its upkeep. But other synagogue boards were not as foresighted. When the Vilna Shul's original congregation dissolved in the mid-'60s, the money set aside for the perpetual care of its cemetery disappeared. According to one account, the last man out the door sent the money to yeshivas in Israel.

Just looking at the state of the various Jewish cemeteries clustered around Adath Jeshurun, I could see that something had to be done to protect the graves of Boston's first large wave of Jews. I recall one summer day visiting my family's plot with Genevieve when we spotted an older fellow tending to the cemetery next door. The following year, he was gone, and that neighboring graveyard overgrown.

I urged the leadership of Combined Jewish Philanthropies to address the cemetery problem while there was still an opportunity to do so. CJP then set about tracking down leaders of declining or closed synagogues. They were persuaded to designate CJP the default final trustee of their perpetual care funds in cases where no one else held the responsibility. In 1984, the federation spun off the Jewish Cemetery Association of Massachusetts. JCA started out managing 17 cemeteries; now, it cares for 115.

FAITH VS. FAMILY

My cemetery concerns didn't end with upkeep. As more Jews began to marry outside the religion, including our own sons, I began to think about where their families would find final resting places.

Since Adath Jeshurun was an Orthodox cemetery, only Jews could be buried there. I asked the wisest religious authority I knew, the Bostoner Rebbe, whether we could change the rules. He said that to do so would be unfair to the people already buried there and would upset the Orthodox community. In effect, the cemetery had an eternal contract with its inhabitants. They went to their graves expecting to be exclusively among their Jewish brethren.

But the Rebbe, as he inevitably did, had a solution: If we could acquire adjacent land, we would not be bound by the existing "contract." There, we could provide lots for families that included non-Jews. We would, however, have to install a visual boundary, such as a walkway, to distinguish between the cemeteries.

As it happened, because the cemetery had already been near capacity, we had been looking to acquire any available adjacent land. We had purchased a somewhat dilapidated house next door on Baker Street, tore it down and obtained approval from Boston's Zoning Board of Appeals to use the property for gravesites – which were snapped up in no time. There was still room to expand, though. Marshall Dana, a good friend, was at the time the only other active trustee of Adath Jeshurun's cemetery. Like mine, his grandfather had been a founder of the synagogue; and like me, he wanted to be able to accommodate non-Jewish relatives at the cemetery.

When the house next to the one we had razed went on the market, we purchased it and sought approval to tear it down to make way for more gravesites. This time, though, the city turned us down in the face of stiff neighborhood opposition. The organizer was a young Irish immigrant, Conal Crowley.

Marshall came up with a plan. He discovered that over the years Conal had quietly purchased four houses on the street adjacent to the cemetery. All in poor condition, he had painstakingly restored them. He installed his family in the first one, which was next to the house we had just bought, and rented out the others. Marshall suggested that we appeal to Conal's business instincts. We offered him an attractive price on our house if he would be willing to sell us the rear halves of all the properties and rally the neighbors behind our renewed attempt to win zoning approval.

Conal liked the idea, but wasn't sure he could swing the purchase. After we offered even better terms and favorable financing, he agreed. (Like my father, Conal went by the adage "Never pass up a chance to buy a neighbor's land; you may never have the opportunity again.") We then resubmitted our application to the city.

While Conal had had his own agenda for originally objecting to the cemetery expansion, we knew that we could allay the concerns of the other neighbors. It wasn't a matter of anti-Semitism, but rather understandable fears that the cemetery extension would only increase the problem of teens partying among the gravesites, which at night were unsupervised.

After Conal laid the groundwork, I spoke about our plans before a neighborhood meeting that drew 100 people. "When our families established the cemetery many years ago, they never expected that our people would one day be marrying your people," I told the crowd. "We just want to make sure that we can have them buried here together when their time comes, but we can't do so without having this extra land."

Conal then got up and endorsed our revised plan. He pointed out that it would save a house from being razed and that he would assume the responsibility, with our authorization, to contact the police if he spotted rowdy teens. His kitchen looked right over the cemetery.

To my surprise and delight, many of the people whom I had met at the local meeting showed up at City Hall to support our renewed request to the Zoning Board of Appeals. One after another, they spoke at the microphone; not one expressed opposition. At their urging, their local state representative appeared on our behalf. Afterward, everyone came up, all smiles, to congratulate us.

TRADITIONS, NEW AND OLD

Originally, I had expected that I and other members of our family, when our time arrived, would be buried together at Adath Jeshurun's cemetery. Genevieve, though, made a persuasive case for making Temple Israel's cemetery in Wakefield our final home. We had both been presidents of the temple – as I'll discuss in a later chapter – and had educated our children there. And, at the Wakefield cemetery, we'll be joining my mother's parents, sisters and brothers.

But even so, I expect to continue, for so long as I am able, the Wyner-Dana partnership in the care and maintenance of Adath Jeshurun Cemetery. Marshall's son, Myer, shares my enthusiasm. We are furthering the work started by our families more than a century ago.

A FEATHER IN MY CAP

How I put my mind and body to work for the United Fund

YOU WON'T FIND IT on my resumé, but my career as a civic volunteer began when I was in fourth grade.

My mother was a captain for the predecessor of the United Fund. Each year, the captains were given cards with the names of their neighbors who had donated before. I helped out by taking the pre-filled cards around to the neighbors and asking them to donate again. I would also distribute blank cards to anyone else in the house who might want to contribute. The charity would present a red feather to anyone who gave money. Few people made big donations, but I noticed that sometimes at the grand old homes on Fisher Hill, the maids would give me four dollars while their employers would offer half as much.

Years later, I recounted that experience to the president of United Way as evidence for why the organization had to do a better job of publicizing all that it does. That way its volunteers wouldn't be treated as just another person going door-to-door with a pushke (that's a tin can for accepting alms, for those who don't know their Yiddish).

I dress up as a Puritan on Red Feather Day – all in a good cause.

When I was editor of the Tufts college paper and learned about the United Way Fund drive, I agreed to head it up. On Red Feather Day, the opening of the campaign, I dressed up as a Puritan, complete with stockings, cape, black wig and buckled hat (which I still have). Several community newspapers printed pictures of me soliciting donations in my colonial get-up.

I left the Puritan hat at home when Genevieve became a United Fund captain and assigned me to make the rounds with the cards. At the end of the year, the volunteers assembled to critique the campaign. I noted that we were missing a lot of possible contributors and suggested improvements for the following year. As a reward for opening my mouth, I was asked to chair the Brookline chapter's fund drive for the next year, 1960. When I accepted the job, I had no idea what I had gotten myself into – a recurring theme in my life.

According to our books, we were supposed to have more than 1,000 volunteers, but in fact the real number was far smaller. Many people had left messages with the United Fund offering to make donations, but no one had followed up. I discovered that numerous donation cards had gone missing, taken by so-called volunteers to Florida, where they had gone for the winter.

The collection system was such a mess that I persuaded my father to allow me to take a four-month leave from my job at Shawmut to straighten things out. Otherwise, I was worried I would be the first campaign chairman to bring in only a fraction of the annual goal.

In some cases, I would personally visit a home and come back with a $1,000 check. That only fueled my obsession with the thought that there were many other people out there willing to give, if only someone would ask. In the end, we exceeded the goal, raising as I recall $85,000, a very large sum in those days.

I WAS A GENE
MCCARTHY REPUBLICAN

When it comes to party politics, I upset the punch bowl

A button from my short-lived campaign for Gene McCarthy in 1968.

OK, I'll officially come out of the closet: I'm a liberal.

For many years, I played down my leftist leanings so that my conservative friends would take me seriously.

I served on Brookline's Republican Town Committee from 1964 to 1998, hoping to help the party shed itself of lingering associations with Barry Goldwater's extreme right-wing presidential bid. Just as they are today, the Massachusetts Republicans during those years were less conservative than the national party, and the state's Republican governors tended to be moderate, if not liberal. They provided a much-needed check on the state Legislature, which took many a crooked turn under decades of Democratic domination.

But, still, I got into hot water with some of my fellow committee members in 1968. I was a strong opponent of the Vietnam War, which put me at odds with Richard Nixon, who was coasting toward the GOP presidential nomination. The one Republican who might have stopped him, Nelson Rockefeller, was still smarting from the pounding he had taken from Goldwater in 1964.

I was persuaded to support Eugene McCarthy by my friend Arnold Hiatt, who was active in Democratic politics and would later become president of Stride Rite shoes. My dad suggested that a write-in campaign for McCarthy among Republicans might just persuade Rockefeller to run. Brookline School Committee chair Viola Pinanski, who had attended every national GOP convention since 1952, agreed to hop aboard the write-in campaign. Over a couple of months in early spring, we took out ads in major national papers, urging Republicans to write in McCarthy if Rockefeller didn't enter the race.

As I recall, we were astounded to find that a full-page ad in *The New York Times* would cost $35,000. My father-in-law, Max, placed it for us through his ad agency, Weiss and Geller. Fortunately, the ad included – at Max's suggestion – a coupon seeking contributions. Our message resonated with so many people that donations paid for the next ad. We continued to include coupons, enabling us to buy ads up until the Massachusetts primary on April 30.

Around noon on the day of the vote, Rockefeller announced that he had changed his mind and would run. Home-state favorite Governor John Volpe, the only Republican listed on the state's GOP ballot, received 29,663 votes, but lost to Rockefeller's 30,903 write-in votes. Nixon came in third with 26,021 write-in votes. McCarthy still wound up with 9,501 GOP write-in votes. Imagine if Rockefeller had stayed out of the race. McCarthy, the liberal Democrat, might have made Massachusetts history by winning its Republican primary.

I continued to support McCarthy until after the Democratic Convention, when I switched to Hubert Humphrey. Meanwhile, I had to fend off efforts to toss me (albeit gently) from the Republican Committee. I justified my write-in campaign for McCarthy as still being part of the Republican primary. I ended up staying on the committee long enough to be sent to the GOP state convention in 1998.

I'm still a registered Republican, though I rarely vote that way.

PART VIII: BROOKLINE CITIZEN

- **My first campaign:** Learning from the Old Guard

- **Friendly fire:** Running against a friend for moderator

- **Jerry's Rules of Order:** Putting democracy into action

- **Battles of Brookline:** Matters weighty and wacky

MY FIRST CAMPAIGN

How ringing 500 doorbells changed my life for decades

WHO KNOWS? IF I hadn't gone to post-confirmation class at Temple Israel, I might not have entered politics.

The teacher was a wonderful man named Reuben Lurie, who packed into one lifetime enough accomplishments for five. He served as a Superior Court judge, commissioner of correction and head of the state parole board. For more than half a century, he played a leading role in raising the level of public discourse as a leader of the Ford Hall Forum, which hosts free lectures and debates.

As it happened, Lurie first broke into the headlines around the time he was teaching my class. He exposed several Boston politicians for filling campaign coffers by extorting public employees. But for me, what comes to mind is not a hard-charging lawyer, but an engaging man with a warm, smiling face.

A dozen of us attended that Sunday morning class at Temple Israel. We sat around a table, just as we would at a college seminar. We talked mostly about current events and public service, much as the temple's rabbi, Joshua Liebman, did in his sermons. Lurie didn't dominate the discussion, but rather prodded us to speak our minds. He appeared genuinely interested in what this bunch of 15-year-olds had to say. Without being preachy, he impressed upon us the preciousness and fragility of democracy. By his actions, he reinforced the lessons I had learned at home about integrity and the importance of giving back to the community.

My parents knew and respected Lurie. I'm not sure how close they were, but he made me feel as if he had a special connection with me. That link would figure nearly a decade later into my decision to run for Town Meeting. At that time, he was a selectman in Brookline. I cannot recall exactly how he was involved in launching my political career. He may have suggested to my parents that I run, or perhaps my father had urged me to seek out Lurie for campaign advice. Whatever the case, the judge was delighted that I was thinking of running and was very encouraging. He has always represented to me the ideal of a public servant.

RINGING 500 DOORBELLS

My political career didn't exactly get off to a roaring start. I was a year out of Harvard Business School and just starting to get my feet on the ground at Shawmut. I was living with my parents at their home on Dean Road. The residents of my precinct were predominantly old-line Yankees, along with town workers who, though small in number, could decide a close vote.

In those days, you had to ring at least 500 doorbells to get elected to Town Meeting. Despite wearing out my index finger and considerable shoe leather, I went down to defeat in my first two tries, in 1949 and 1950.

Each precinct sent 15 representatives to Town Meeting, elected to staggered three-year terms with five seats contested each year. Well, they weren't exactly contested; the incumbents usually won.

A former classmate of mine from the Rivers School, Bill Tyler, was trying to break into Town Meeting at the same time I was. After our second defeat, his father, Roger, a veteran Town Meeting member, told us not to be discouraged. He clued us in to the fact that two representatives would likely step down in the middle of their terms. When vacancies occur between elections, the precinct's remaining Town Meeting members caucus to fill the positions.

Lo and behold, Bill and I were chosen. I suppose it was because we had both proven our interest with our previous campaigns. Had our precinct been as contentious as some of the others, we probably would not have had it so easy. We did, however, have to face the voters in the next election.

I took nothing for granted, reintroducing myself throughout the precinct. When people answered the door, they nearly all welcomed me. I would say who I was and hand them a campaign pamphlet. I wasn't running on any particular issue, just that I wanted to be of service. I don't recall feeling shy or intimidated, but I was aware that in most cases I was much younger than the people whose support I sought.

Besides the gracious brick colonials owned mostly by the Yankees, I visited the triple-deckers off Eliot Street that housed, in many cases, town employees and their families. There I didn't go door-to-door, but instead sought out influential employees at the recommendation of politically savvy friends. I particularly remember seeing a Mr. O'Reilly. When he answered his door, I asked him for his support, and he responded in a heavy brogue: "You're the only one who has come here to ask for a vote. You'll get the votes of all nine of my family." He invited me into his home and introduced me around.

The next day was the election. I got to the polls before they opened, determined to be the first one to vote. But as I was standing there, I heard someone behind me mutter, "For 40 years I've been the first to vote, and now I'm not." I turned around, and there was Mr. O'Reilly.

I was the second person to vote in the precinct that day.

During the last year of my three-year term, Genevieve and I as newlyweds were temporarily living in Hyde Park. I realized I was bending the rules, but felt justified doing so since we intended to move back to Brookline just as soon as we found a house.

We were settled on Marthas Lane in South Brookline when I ran for re-election in 1956. Although we were now living in a different precinct, I could still campaign on my Town Meeting experience. The precinct was less of a closed club than my previous one. I made important political connections with activists who attended Temple Emeth in South Brookline, where being Jewish was an asset. I rang a lot of doorbells; mailed out a card introducing myself; and won without any major difficulties.

THEY ACTUALLY TOOK ME SERIOUSLY

In addition to Town Meeting, Roger Tyler was a member of the board of the Brookline Taxpayers Association. At his recommendation, Bill and I were invited to join the board as well. In those days, the association was held in high esteem for being unbiased and doing its homework. It was not a knee-jerk anti-government group like the Tea Party types of today. It served as a watchdog for waste, but was not obsessed with cutting taxes.

Through the association, I learned how government really worked in Brookline. I was assigned to keep tabs on Parks and Recreation. I tried to make every commission meeting, so I could understand the issues and watch how the department's budget evolved from start to finish. As with Town Meeting, I didn't come in with an agenda. I was more concerned with efficiency than policy. Was the parks superintendent exaggerating the workload to pad his payroll with friends? Could programs be scheduled to make better use of time and equipment? For first-hand knowledge, I often went out into the field.

As they assembled their budget proposal, commission members would ask me how I thought the Taxpayers Association would react. At first, I was surprised that they would care what some young whippersnapper had to say. But they took me – or at least my group – seriously. As a result, the association had a surprising amount of influence over Park and Rec's policies and budget.

BIG BEN

A dominant figure in Town Meeting during my early years was Ben Trustman, a Harvard Law graduate who was just a few years younger than my father. Trustman was a senior partner at Nutter McClennen & Fish. In later years, Trustman became a philanthropist, benefiting the arts, medicine and education. His wide-ranging resumé included serving as president of Hebrew Teachers College and Combined Jewish Philanthropies – as well as being a founding director of World Jai Alai.

Just as Temple Israel always seemed to find the right rabbi to suit its changing needs, Brookline was blessed with moderators suited to their times. Trustman brought order to what for many had seemed a chaotic Town Meeting process. An expert on municipal minutiae, he co-wrote the defining book *Town Meeting Time: A Handbook of Parliamentary Law* (you can still find later editions on Amazon).

Though relatively short in height, Trustman was a commanding, even intimidating, presence. He had definite opinions about what should come before Town Meeting, and saw his role as moderator as largely supporting the administration. That wasn't necessarily a bad thing: Much more than in later years, the selectmen back then were among the most accomplished residents in town. They viewed themselves as trustees of a very special place and worked hard to preserve it as it was. But while I don't doubt that Trustman believed he was serving the best interests of Brookline, catering to the establishment did amount to cronyism. While he would let the selectmen chairman ramble on for 30 minutes, he would cut off people who weren't among the insiders. As a result, the conservative viewpoint received much more airtime in Town Meeting than the liberal.

Trustman made little effort to get to know a broad cross-section of the town. Not only did his reserved personality make him appear unapproachable, he made himself literally inaccessible during the three weeks before Town Meeting. It was then that he always seemed to be away on vacation.

Except for giving town officials and some longtime Town Meeting members seemingly limitless floor time, Trustman ran a tight ship. He prided himself on keeping Town Meetings to as few nights as possible, even if that meant debating into the wee hours of the morning. Many members had jobs to get to the next morning, so they couldn't stay for the votes. As the minutes ticked into the night, Town Meeting would become less and less representative.

THE POWER OF PERSUASION

Personally, I got along well with Trustman. I was a known quantity, thanks to his friendship with my family and service with my father and later with me on various Jewish community boards.

As moderator, Trustman had the authority to appoint the 30 members of the town's budget and finance committee, the Advisory Committee. In 1961, he named me to that powerful board. As the elected year-round stewards of the town, the selectmen were better known, but the Advisory Committee had greater clout when it came to influencing Town Meeting on matters of both money and policy.

At the time I joined the committee, it was chaired by a man with a sharply different leadership style than that of Trustman. Charles Hubbard III taught me how to run a meeting without dictating its actions. His example served me well when I became chairman in 1966.

Traditionally, the committee had waited until budget season to sit in on the meetings of the various town departments. Hubbard accepted my suggestion that we take the same approach as the Taxpayers Association and assign committee members to monitor department meetings year-round. By being in on the process from the start, we would be seen less as adversaries and more as a resource. We would compare notes at the Advisory Committee meetings, assembling a picture of the town's overall budget needs. I was assigned to my old stomping grounds, Parks and Recreation, so I picked up from where I had left off as a representative of the Taxpayers Association.

By working closely with the individual town departments, Advisory Committee members could help shape their budgets. It was a bit of a balancing act: The natural temptation would be to identify with our assigned departments, but we had to keep in mind the town's overall finances. Still, the process seemed to work — too well in the eyes of some. Observing how closely the final town budget followed our recommendations, a local newspaper editorial fulminated about the excessive power of the committee. I called the editor and said, "What power? We're advisory. The only power we have is the power of persuasion. If people listen to us more than anybody else, you ought to worry about the other people."

When I became Town Meeting moderator, I made sure the Advisory Committee maintained its vigilance through my power to make appointments. I made it clear to prospective members that if they missed more than three meetings in a year, I would deem that the equivalent of their having submitted their resignation. The only acceptable excuse would be a temporarily disabling illness or another unpredictable event. Typically, the committee met monthly, but before Town Meeting it might convene several times a week to hear from department heads and article proponents. The run-up to the annual Town Meeting in spring coincided with tax season. As a result, many accountants – whose skills would have been particularly valuable – weren't able to serve on the advisory committee.

CASUALTY OF WAR

As I said, Trustman was the right moderator for his time, but that time ran out in the late 1960s. That was when the baby boom generation began to come of age, teeming with anti-establishment furor.

In retrospect, Trustman should have bowed out one term earlier than he did. Had he done so, he would have left office with accolades rather than acrimony. The town's liberals became a bloc too powerful to ignore as North Brookline increasingly became home to young professionals, many connected with the area's universities.

At his last Town Meeting as moderator, a large contingent pushed for a resolution calling on the president to withdraw the troops from Vietnam. Trustman ruled the proposal as being out of order, saying the matter was beyond the town's authority. Alan Sidd, then head of the Democratic Town Committee, stood up and challenged the moderator. Trustman, departing from his normally austere manner, shot back: "I can yell louder than you." He then requested and accepted a motion to adjourn. After an abrupt voice vote, he declared the meeting to be adjourned. Before anyone could react, he marched out. Sidd was left standing there, his clenched fist raised, along with those of many other irate representatives.

But the bullets flying halfway around the world would continue to ricochet in Brookline. And I stepped right into the middle of the fray.

FRIENDLY FIRE

In which I vie with a close colleague in a close race for moderator

THE STYMIED VIETNAM WAR resolution became an issue in the 1970 election for town moderator. I entered the race not because of my opposition to the war, but because of the way Ben Trustman had shut down the discussion. I argued that Brookline had taken a stand on the Boston Tea Party two centuries before, so why shouldn't it vote on Vietnam? I campaigned on the platform that I would guarantee true democracy in Town Meeting, where people would really debate, not just make speeches at each other. I vowed that meetings would end at a reasonable time and be spread out over consecutive weeks, rather than jammed together over several nights.

I had established credibility with voters some years earlier by founding the Town Meeting Members Association, which instructed new representatives on such procedural matters as how to draw up an article, make an amendment and secure time to address the assembly. When I was moderator, I turned those lessons into a handbook.

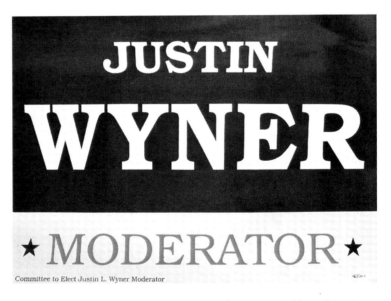

I first ran in 1970, vowing to bring true democracy to Town Meeting.

KEEPING MY OPPONENT'S SECRET

My election opponent happened to be a good friend of mine, Dan Rollins, who trumpeted his long experience as town counsel. Indeed, I owe much of what I know about municipal law to Dan and the selectmen's longtime executive secretary, Arthur O'Shea. Along with the assistant executive secretary,

Dick Leary, we would pull all-nighters crafting a report that detailed the sometimes clashing recommendations of the selectmen and the Advisory Committee on each Town Meeting article. That report had to be printed in time to be distributed to each Town Meeting member before the sessions began.

Because of my close ties with Dan, I found myself called upon to do something unusual for an election candidate. Shortly before we were to appear at a voters' forum, I received a call from Dan's wife, Selma, with whom I had served on the Advisory Committee. She told me that Dan had just had a mild heart attack and would be hospitalized for an undetermined period. He would have to miss at least one forum and possibly more, but still intended to stay in the campaign. Concerned that her husband's election chances would be jeopardized if word got out about his illness, she asked me to help keep the news under wraps. "Sure, Selma," I said. We concocted some excuse for his absence from several events, and his health never became an issue.

I had two people running my campaign, coming from very different segments of the community. The official manager was Anne Gowing, an old-guard resident who cherished Brookline's character and government. While many of her peers shied away from politics, she felt strongly enough to rally behind candidates sympathetic to her cause. The other was Joanne Blumsack, a member of PAX, a liberal social action group, and a savvy campaigner. One of the first things Joanne said to me was that I had to do streetcar stops. I told her that wasn't my style. I felt uncomfortable foisting myself on people who had no way to avoid me. But Joanne insisted that the commuters would welcome me. Waiting for the trolley, they're a captive audience with nothing else to do (this was decades before iPhones). So, I got up early in the morning and made my way up and down the Beacon Street stops, over and over saying, "Hi, my name is Justin Wyner. I'm running for moderator. I hope you'll consider voting for me." Not one person refused to shake hands with me. Everybody smiled, and some people talked about the issues. I did this for many days, shaking hands with many hundreds of people. I enjoyed it.

'HERE COMES JUSTIN WYNER'

To solicit votes from municipal employees, I visited their homes in the town's public housing complexes. A couple of town workers who were enthusiastic supporters of my candidacy accompanied me through the warren of apartments, one going ahead to knock on doors. Everyone who answered knew him. "Here comes Justin Wyner," he would say. "He's running for moderator." I think I ended up with just about everyone's vote.

Touring the public housing taught me a lesson in how building design affects people's behavior. While demographically all the complexes were similar, they differed in character. I noticed that the garden-style, four-unit buildings were quiet and graffiti-free. Not so in the 150-unit high-rise, where anonymity allowed vandalism to flourish.

Even with the public workforce behind me, it appeared on election night that I had fallen short. The first count showed that I had lost by 42 votes out of 10,000 cast. I called Dan to congratulate him. Then, an hour later, election officials announced they had made a mistake. The 42 votes had been posted to the wrong column. It was I who had narrowly won. I think if I hadn't charmed Dan with my initial call of congratulations, he might have asked for a recount.

JERRY'S RULES OF ORDER

Bringing my own brand of democracy to Brookline

WHEN I TOOK OFFICE as moderator, the Vietnam resolution, as expected, was at the top of the agenda. I laid down ground rules, giving each side the opportunity to speak for a total of 30 minutes. Each speaker would have three minutes. I urged everyone to stick to the resolution itself and be sensitive to the fact that there were people in the room who had family fighting in the war, perhaps even children who had been killed or were missing.

"We really don't want this to be all about whether what they did was wasted," I said. After that, I called for a roll-call vote. The tally was 110 for, 54 against and 3 voting present. Brookline's call for withdrawing American troops from Vietnam was now on the record. It wasn't until three years later, in March 1973, that the last military unit left the still embattled region.

POWER TO THE PEOPLE

I have no shortage of opinions on any number of topics, many of them deeply held. But when I chaired an organization, be it the Rowes Wharf condo association, the Temple Israel board or Brookline Town Meeting, I believed it was my duty to put my own agenda aside and concentrate on helping every member become fully informed and involved. By staying above the fray, I found I could be a more effective leader.

Sumner Kaplan, the late judge, state representative and Brookline selectman, once told me that if I was placed in a position of power, I should use it. His tenure as a selectman reflected the pitfalls of that approach. Often in the minority on a given issue, he would make fiery speeches on behalf of progressive causes. But when he assumed the chairman's seat, bully pulpit tactics backfired. If a chairman appears too partisan, opponents question whether they can get a fair hearing and would-be supporters wonder if they're being steamrolled.

By contrast, Ben Trustman wielded the power of town moderator in more subtle ways. Instead of trumpeting his views, he would choreograph the debate to give those on the side with which he sympathized more opportunities to speak, at the most opportune times. He was so adroit at it that no one could ever call him out for playing favorites.

Calling Town Meeting to order early in my career as moderator.

I didn't come to Town Meeting with a personal agenda. Sure, I had my opinions. But rather than getting my way, I found it much more satisfying to help the town find its own way. If Town Meeting is run properly – and from my experiences in Sudbury and on the Vineyard, it often is not – this governing body comes closest in America to representing the true wishes of the citizens. Yes, some members might vote out of self-interest, but as a whole I believe they look out for what's best not just for their street or precinct, but for the entire community. I have presided over meetings where I thought I knew what the outcome should be, but after hearing all the points of view aired was quite comfortable when the decision went another way.

I'm a fix-it man, as I've shown in other aspects of my life. At the factory I would tinker with machines to make them more productive and foolproof; I looked for ways to do the same for the mechanisms of town government.

The factory-town comparison can only go so far. People aren't machines. They don't always behave logically; they're prone to letting feelings blind them to facts. I found that one of my best tools was my ear. I publicized that every Monday night I'd be home by the phone. Anyone could call me then about town business. I would stay up half the night, if necessary, talking to residents. I did this in part for selfish reasons; it could save me a lot of aggravation down the line. I learned about problems before they had time to blow up into full-scale furors. From a practical standpoint, the policy also worked to confine most moderator-related calls to one evening a week, albeit a long one.

MY NETWORK OF EARS

I wanted to know everything that was going on in town that potentially could become an issue. If I heard someone was upset about something, I would give him or her a call. Perhaps there had been a misunderstanding. Once something goes public and people stake out their positions, it's hard for them to backtrack even when presented with the facts.

By putting my feelers out, I also hoped to avoid surprises. I recall one evening when Town Meeting spent more than two hours debating some zoning matter. Just as we were about to vote, a woman far in the back stood up. When she pointed out how the proposal would affect her property, she surfaced a larger issue that hadn't occurred to any of us. We adjourned and went through the entire debate again the following night. We probably would have avoided that extra night's debate had I known of her issue in advance.

People would call me for help in drawing up an article or an amendment. Regardless of whether I agreed with them or not, I'd outline how to write the motion in a way that wouldn't be ruled out of order on some technicality. If it was something that I felt was beyond the bounds of Town Meeting, I would explain why. And I made a point of assuring people on all sides of an issue that I would keep our conversations confidential. By earning the people's trust, I became a more effective leader.

If you're consistent in what you do, then you won't find yourself challenged by too many wise guys. I promised to provide equal time for all points of view. During my first year, some skeptics kept stopwatches on me, but I had my own stopwatch, too. I wasn't a nitpicker. If someone asked to make one last point when his or her time was up, I would allow it. But when people abused that privilege, I'd take them aside and say, "I have not wanted to embarrass you, but next time I'll give you a 30-second warning and if you run through that, I'll cut you off, even in mid-sentence." People would complain to me, "How could you give that bunch of pinkos as much time as you give the selectmen?" But in the long run, I think people felt the system worked.

ENOUGH WITH THE SPEECHES

As I emphasized to Town Meeting before the Vietnam vote, I wanted to make sure that people addressed each other's arguments. If members habitually stuck to prepared statements, I would use my prerogative not to recognize them. In the past during fractious meetings, a contingent would step outside when the opposition took the floor. When I took over, I wouldn't allow people to speak if they hadn't been present through the entire discussion – even if they had signed up ahead of time. "This is a debate, and not a series of speeches," I would tell them. "How can you respond intelligently when you didn't actually hear what somebody said?" And to make sure they couldn't use calls of nature as an excuse for missing an argument, I had the proceedings wired to a speaker placed in a small bathroom directly below the stage. Anyone who went to that bathroom would be counted as present and allowed to continue to participate in the debate on the current article before us.

The moderator had a lot of leeway in Brookline. Town Meeting procedure was guided by tradition, not Robert's Rules of Order. I made some very controversial rulings, but suffered comparatively little fallout because I took great care to explain the reasoning behind my decisions. Once, after I had made a ruling, the auditorium echoed with loud groans. I asked for a show of hands about whether people wanted me to reconsider. Seeing the vast majority of arms shoot up, I reversed myself – even though as moderator, as I explained to the meeting, I was under no obligation to do so. Unless I was upholding a point of law, I felt I had no right to thwart the will of Town Meeting.

On other occasions, though, I stepped in when I felt a potential resolution was well intended but misguided. During the 1973 Yom Kippur War, for example, some people thought that because I had backed Town Meeting's right to vote on the Vietnam War, I would be similarly inclined to allow debate on a resolution supporting Israel. I told supporters of the motion that while I personally was pro-Israel, I didn't believe it was appropriate for Town Meeting to take a stand about another nation. I also pointed out that the vote could backfire even if it were to pass. Say, for example, the vote was 65-35. That sizable opposition could be misconstrued as being anti-Israel when many dissenters may have felt as I did that such matters shouldn't go before Town Meeting. In the end, the proponents decided not to pursue the resolution, and I escaped the onus of ruling it out of order.

NO DILLY-DALLYING

On one point I was a real stickler: starting on time. Previously, if Town Meeting was scheduled to begin at 7, it usually wouldn't get underway until 7:30 or 7:45. People would come on time, but chat outside. I decided that the entire building counted as Town Meeting, including the steps outside. We would count everyone in and around the auditorium, and I would start the meeting once we arrived at the magic number for a quorum. After a couple of sessions where 50 or so people wandered in late and missed key votes, the tardiness problem was resolved.

I also kept the meetings moving swiftly by applying common sense to counting votes. If a measure required approval by a two-thirds majority, I would first ask those opposed to stand. If only a modest number stood, I would count them out loud. I would then ask those in favor to stand and would count out loud until it was clear that the necessary threshold was reached. Bearing in mind the town clerk's latest count of those present, I could make a reasonable estimate of the tally. I'd announce, say, "180 for, 20 against," and bang the gavel. "Motion passed." I earned a reputation for my quick count. If the vote appeared at all close, I would declare, "The chair is in doubt," and request a count by tellers whom I had appointed at the beginning of the meeting. I always wanted people to feel comfortable with the process.

No matter how much I tried to be fair, I had my share of critics. Passions ran high at Town Meeting, and a few members did take their anger out on me. People have asked me how I put up with the nasty insults. The answer is that I remembered back to my childhood when my mother told me not to give other kids the satisfaction of knowing when their taunts stung. Genevieve would put it another way: Obsessing about my critics allowed them to live in my head rent-free.

So, whenever a Town Meeting member spoke rudely to me, I made sure to respond as respectfully as I could. I found that courtesy could be mightier than the club.

THE BATTLES OF BROOKLINE

Matters weighty and wacky put the character of the town to the test

WHILE COMPARED WITH THE rest of the nation Brookline was fairly united in its opposition to the Vietnam War, the town was still roiled by battles closer to home. Debates over rent control, condo conversions and rezoning dominated my first tenure as moderator. At stake was the very character of Brookline. Would rising housing costs drive out the middle class and seniors on fixed incomes? Would high-rise apartment buildings overshadow leafy neighborhoods? Would retail development in Coolidge Corner turn it into a mini-downtown Boston?

The various controversies surfaced social and political divisions in the town. Rent control pitted the left against the right. The old-line Yankees in such areas as the affluent Middlesex Road neighborhood feared a power grab by left-leaning North Brookline. Empty nesters resented footing the bill for costly school projects. Landlords felt singled out to bear the burden of keeping the town affordable.

The answers weren't easy, and the trade-offs were many. After rent control was imposed in the early 1970s, landlords increasingly converted apartments into condos. That led to a series of measures to curb tenant evictions. Meanwhile, efforts to keep Brookline affordable and suburban had repercussions elsewhere. Higher property values and increased commercialization would have expanded the town's tax base and perhaps taken the steam out of anti-tax groups. Several times over the decade they waged successful referendum fights to reverse Town Meeting decisions for school construction.

The archives of *The Boston Globe* from that period contain dozens of articles about heated Town Meeting deliberations, taxpayer revolts and prolonged court battles. But among the only times my name appeared in the *Globe* was in December 1977, when I asked Town Meeting members if coffee and doughnuts should be sold at future sessions. In response to overwhelming support, I offered to buy the first time around. "Let's see: that's about 50 cents for each of 252 town meeting members," wrote reporter Robert B. Kenney. "Say, don't you think the selectmen could help out? Maybe an appropriation? After all, town moderator is an unpaid post."

The lack of publicity suited me just fine. As I said before, I saw my role as making sure Town Meeting members were well informed and had equal access to the floor. I was the stage manager, not the puppet master.

SHAPING THE TOWN'S FUTURE

Perhaps the most important issue, at least from the standpoint of long-lasting impact, that Town Meeting considered while I was moderator was zoning. OK, I can see readers' eyes glazing over. But think about it: Brookline today might look like a very different place had it not been for the rules we passed four decades ago. Imagine Beacon Street lined with 17-story buildings or the town's many small residential buildings, two-family houses and stately Victorians replaced with drab, utilitarian shops and apartment houses.

In January 1974, Town Meeting passed a series of articles that amounted to a major "downzoning" of Brookline. They were aimed at curbing high-density building. This was not something I took lightly, because it meant reducing the potential value of some property without the owners having the legal recourse available in non-rezoning issues. For example, where once a 17-story building could be built, now only one half that size or smaller would be permissible. For nine months, a special commission met with neighborhood groups to present details of the zoning changes. I asked for visual presentations to be as clear and precise as possible. I made sure to speak with everybody who raised concerns and to provide them a chance to address Town Meeting. Just before Town Meeting convened, I took the unusual step of sitting down with the Planning Board. I suggested ways to modify its presentation, such as by using transparent overlays with their maps to highlight each zoning change. I wanted to make sure that even the least technical-minded Town Meeting members could see what was at stake.

Over four sessions in January 1974, Town Meeting considered a 142-page warrant, containing more than 100 zoning changes. In the end, nearly four fifths of the changes were approved.

THE TROUBLE WITH GARY

With more than 250 members, Town Meeting inevitably had its quirky characters – few more so than Gary Kayakachoian. In the 1970s, Gary moved from covering Brookline politics for *The Boston Globe* to participating in them. A man of boundless energy and passionate convictions, Gary never left any doubt where he stood. Restraint was not among his strengths. Nor was the sense of knowing when to quit a fight.

Gary served as the mascot for the anti-tax forces around town and was a driving force behind the referendums that quashed school construction plans. Particularly nasty was the 1975 battle over building the Lincoln School. Two teachers – a mother and her daughter – posted signs around town urging approval of the school. Gary followed them around. He'd wait until the teachers were out of sight and then tear down the posters. Eventually, the pair caught on and confronted him. Gary claimed that the mother rebuked him as a "god-damn dirty Jew." He said he answered, "I'm not a Jew; I'm an Armenian." To which, he said, the mother responded: "That's even worse."

Gary was so infuriated that he asked the School Committee to have the mother and daughter fired for being prejudiced. Rebuffed, he approached me about his intention to propose that Town Meeting oust the daughter, who was a representative. Although I explained that a question of residency was the only grounds for challenging Town Meeting membership, he refused to back down. I told him: "When you get up, I'm going to ask you if you're rising for the point about which you and I have spoken. If you say yes, I'm going to have you seated. I'm not going to let you say one word about her. And if you won't sit down, it is within my authority to have you carried out by two Brookline policemen."

True to his word, Kayakachoian did attempt to move for the woman's ejection. But I ruled him out of order before he had a chance to say her name. That still wasn't the end of it. Kayakachoian hired a lawyer and filed suit, demanding that I call a Special Town Meeting to hear him out.

The suit was still pending when I stepped down as moderator in 1982. But I left on a high note, with several hundred people turning out to honor me at an event held at the Greek Orthodox center. It was organized by Ann Jackson, one of my biggest supporters (and the principal of my sons' JCC preschool). I was presented with the gavel that had been wielded by moderators in Brookline for 75 years. On it was inscribed: "Presented to the town of Brookline by the Brookline Post No. 11 American Legion, March 17, 1931."

It was a good thing I held on to the gavel. Another of Gary's passions – saluting the flag – would trigger a chain of events leading to my return as moderator.

THE PLEDGE OF DIVISION

My successor was Carl Sapers, a longtime friend and colleague in town government. As moderator, I had appointed him chair of the Advisory Committee, and he had done an excellent job. Although reelected twice as moderator, Carl had a rockier time in the job than I did.

A notable example was the infamous row over the Pledge of Allegiance. When I was moderator, we had a tradition of opening Town Meeting by singing the national anthem. In 1983, after terrorists blew up a Marine barracks in Beirut, a Town Meeting member asked Carl if he would open with the pledge. After floating the idea among the members for a couple of weeks, he sent out a letter saying that feelings on the matter ran so deep that reciting the pledge would be too divisive. Carl was all too right about the divisive part.

At the next Town Meeting, several members defied Carl. As they stood to recite the pledge, some others jeered. Proponents called the pledge an affirmation of patriotism; opponents called it tantamount to a loyalty oath. I privately suggested to Carl a way to defuse the controversy: Ask Town Meeting to decide between reciting the pledge and singing "The Star-Spangled Banner." That would avoid a strict up-or-down vote on the pledge – and head off a controversy likely to draw unwelcome attention to the town. Carl had no interest in following my suggestion.

Sadly, the dispute put Brookline in the national spotlight, with the nuances of the debate lost in the shadows. It dragged on for the remainder of Carl's term. At the start of every Town Meeting, Gary and other self-proclaimed patriots would taunt the moderator by waving U.S. flags.

In 1991, a group of conservatives in town approached me about challenging Carl in the next moderator's race. "He's just arrogant and arbitrary," they said. "We're fighting with each other, while before you had us all working together." I balked at first. I said if I entered the race as the conservatives' candidate, I would lose my reputation for independence. They suggested I call PAX, the liberal group in town. PAX members, too, urged me to run. We then had a kitchen cabinet meeting with representatives of the left and the right. People who hadn't talked to each other for years gathered in the same room to strategize on my behalf. Among them was Gary. "What are you doing here?" I asked him. "You're still suing me." He dropped the suit.

I visited with Carl before I entered the race. I told him about the people pushing me to run. "I'm the one who got you elected, but they seem to think it's time for a change," I said to him. But Carl wasn't deterred. On Election Day, I ran into him at the polls at Runkle School. I said we might as well stand next to each other as we greeted the voters. "You know, Jerry," he told me, "I'm spending my son's inheritance for this thing."

I beat him 2-1, but our friendship survived.

One of my first orders of business after taking office was resolving the pledge dispute. I suggested a compromise. Just before the official start of Town Meeting, I would stand and lead the pledge for whomever wanted to participate. The cable TV camera would be focused just on me, so no member would feel stigmatized for joining or not joining in. Then we would open the meeting as usual by singing "The Star-Spangled Banner." After an hour's discussion, the plan passed by a 105-85 vote, putting to rest the decade-long dispute.

ONE LAST JOB

Town Meeting started in Brookline decades before there was a United States or a U.S. Congress (and no, I wasn't a member then). Thus a few archaic articles remain on its agenda. We would begin the annual session by routinely approving an article stating "that the number of Measurers of Wood and Bark be two." During the colonial era, the measurers of wood and bark marked trees owned by the crown. The first time I stepped down as moderator, I asked the selectmen if I could be appointed to one of those now ceremonial posts. Thus, under Town of Brookline on my resumé you will find: "Measurer, Wood and Bark, 1983-1985."

PART IX: SWEPT UP IN HISTORY

- **Keeping history alive:** How I was drafted into the AJHS

- **Wandering Jews:** Finding a new home

- **The biggest show of my life:** Taking history on the road

KEEPING HISTORY ALIVE

How failing to say no changed the past quarter-century of my life

IT WAS THE ULTIMATE fix-up job.

It has occupied much of the past quarter century of my life, provided me with some of my most rewarding and most frustrating experiences, introduced me to the rarefied world of the super-rich and super-diplomats and cost me more hours and dollars than I'd care to count.

It all started because I couldn't bring myself to say no to Bernie Wax. Bernie was the longtime executive director of the American Jewish Historical Society, a lovable fellow if not the most meticulous administrator. For years I had been able to plead other obligations when turning down his invitation that I join the AJHS board of trustees. But by late 1987, I had run out of excuses. Besides, I thought, it might be fun. There didn't appear to be much heavy lifting, and I could enjoy the perk of their library on the Brandeis campus.

My father had been a member of the society, but for him it involved little more than paying dues and receiving its quarterly publication. With so much of our own family history bound up with that of the Jewish community, we were naturally interested in the subject. But aside from establishing a book fund in my parents' name for Harvard's Judaica Collection, most of our philanthropic efforts and time had been devoted to health, social service and religious causes.

A day or so after I said yes to Bernie I received an anxious call from Phil David Fine, a feisty lawyer who was then AJHS president. "Thank God, you're there," Phil said. "I'm putting you on the administrative committee. I hate to tell you, but there's a meeting this afternoon." It was at the office of accountant Sherman Starr, who was the society's treasurer. Among others present was attorney David Pokross. I had known both men through my work with the Jewish community.

As we settled down to business, they told me that the society was in a financial bind. They were thinking of borrowing from restricted endowment funds for operating expenses. Hearing that, alarm bells sounded in my mind. I had always been told that touching any kind of endowment was a no-no. Dipping into endowments reduces an institution's future income stream – and it can become habit-forming. I was particularly uncomfortable with tapping a restricted endowment, which would have had contractual limitations on the use of income and/or principal. But here I was a newcomer, and these two men were not only prominent leaders of Boston's Jewish community, but also highly esteemed in their respective professions. "I don't want to tell you what to do," I said, trying to keep my tone as casual and non-confrontational as possible. "I respect you fellows. You've all had successful careers. Let's pretend I never came. You should do what you think is appropriate."

Before I could put on my jacket, they said, "Come on back. We'll forget about that." And the conversation turned to other matters. Perhaps, they, too, had been uneasy about the endowment option. If anything, my response might have served as the final shove that forced the society to recognize that it could no longer dodge its financial difficulties with accounting maneuvers.

PASSING THE HAT

That moment of recognition came at the next meeting of the trustees, the first one that I attended as a member of the board. It was held in 1992 in Washington, D.C., to coincide with a ceremony marking the AJHS's centenary and honoring the authors of a five-volume history of Jews in America that the society had commissioned. The mood at the board meeting itself was far from celebratory, though. Sherman startled the members by saying that the society didn't have the cash on hand to meet payroll. He suggested passing the hat, asking each trustee to donate what he or she could. An uproar ensued. The society had never been this desperate before. During a recess, David took me aside. "Everybody's very upset," he said. "Since you're new to the board and have no connection to the past here, we'd like you to chair a blue-ribbon committee to fix things."

David, wittingly or unwittingly, knew just which of my buttons to push. I couldn't turn him down. Here was a chance to right a ship. I approached the challenge in much the same way as I had when I took the reins of Vanta 40 years before. I studied the society from top to bottom, looking for ways to do things more efficiently, raise more money and better fulfill the mission.

I began a daily routine that would last for the next decade. Before starting my day at Shawmut, I'd spend an hour or two at the AJHS offices at Brandeis. That added quite a few miles to my commute; Waltham was in the opposite direction from West Bridgewater, where Shawmut had relocated in 1984.

The first thing I discovered was that things were worse than I had thought. The accounts were being kept by Stanley Remsberg, a wonderful fellow who became a good friend. But his education – a doctorate in American history – had not equipped him with the knowledge to draw up a balance sheet. He never could give me a straight answer when I asked how much we had and how much we owed. I tried to ease him back into historical work while bringing in a person to straighten out the books. Gradually, the true financial picture became apparent. For some time, the society had been spending more money than it was bringing in. Stanley's solution was to put off bills, leaving some unpaid for as long as two years. We needed $250,000 to erase our debts and start over with a policy of spending no more than we received.

I broke the grim news at a gathering of trustees in the spacious Prudential Center apartment of Bill Ginsburg and his wife, Ray. Sherman was asked about launching an emergency fund drive, but said that was not possible. Instead, he suggested selling the society's most valuable asset, seven colonial-era portraits of the Franks-Levy family. They were reputed to be the oldest suite of family portraits of American colonials – Jewish or non-Jewish – still in their original frames. Although the portraits were rarely displayed, they were the society's trademark possession. In response to that suggestion, Ken Malamed, a trustee from California, put Sherman on the spot: "Either you raise the money or give up the responsibility for being treasurer."

Ken then proposed that 10 people in the room each pledge $25,000, payable over the next five years. Ten of us, including Bill, Ken, David, Sheldon Cohen (a former U.S. commissioner of internal revenue) and I, signed pledges. So that we could clear the books immediately, I suggested that we borrow the full amount. On the strength of the pledges, I obtained a loan from First National Bank, where Shawmut did much of its business. After paying off the debts, I announced that we would never again spend money that we didn't have. We would budget with actual, not fantasy, figures.

(In 2006, the society did sell the paintings. But the decision was not made out of financial desperation, but rather out of recognition that the few times they were displayed did not justify the high expense of storage and maintenance. The Walton family of the Walmart chain bought them for $3 million for its Crystal Bridges Museum of American Art in Bentonville, Arkansas, where Jews and non-Jews alike can appreciate the collection's significance in U.S. history. As a condition of the sale, the museum agreed that the paintings would always be on display and featured prominently.)

THE WAYWARD LIBRARIAN

Besides heading up the emergency blue-ribbon panel, I chaired the library and archives committee. That gave me another window into the society's laid-back operations. When our librarian asked me to approve his shopping list of books, I said I wanted to put it before the entire committee. He was taken aback. In his many years there, he and the previous chairman had always made those decisions themselves. More likely, I suspect, he made the decisions and the chairman rubber-stamped them.

Left pretty much unsupervised, the librarian, an Orthodox Jew, had purchased the books that interested him, regardless of their relevance to American Jewish history. His ambition was to collect every book published in Hebrew in the United States. When he began this enterprise in the 1970s, the society already owned almost every Hebrew book printed in colonial and early national America. Continuing the project must have seemed logical. But with the invention of the photocopier, dozens of small presses started cranking out facsimile editions of obscure eastern European rabbinic commentaries. Nearly our entire annual $15,000 book budget was going for reprints – a huge waste of money and precious shelf space for a library of American Jewish history. Over the years, the librarian had accumulated 5,000 volumes of these reprints, mostly purchased from Brooklyn publishing houses. They filled most of our bookshelves. We were so squeezed for space that historic records had to be stuffed into air conditioning ducts or trucked away for remote storage. We tried to sell the reprints, but there were no buyers. I even offered them as a gift to my good friend the Bostoner Rebbe. "What would I do with them?" he asked me, expressing incredulity at the librarian's acquisitions and pointing to several shelves of similar books in his own library.

Our librarian was very displeased with the turn of events. Just as I was about to arrange friendly terms for his departure, he developed pancreatic cancer and quickly succumbed. He left behind a wife and many young children. We had a pension plan in place to take care of them, but members of the librarian's Orthodox community persuaded us to supplement it because of the size of the family. This we did for many years – one more financial burden on the society, but the humane thing to do.

GORBACHEV TELLS HOW HE LET OUR PEOPLE GO

I don't want to leave you with the impression that my experience with the AJHS has been one long headache. On the contrary, I was buoyed by the friendship and partnership I forged with Michael Feldberg, as well as by the dedication and friendship of my fellow board members, including David Pokross, Ron Curhan, Arthur Obermayer, Alan Edelstein, Sheldon Cohen, Ken Bialkin, Sid Lapidus and Dan Kaplan. Over the years, Genevieve and I have become close to them and many of their spouses. Indeed, Dan Kaplan and his wife, Renee, are now two of our closest friends.

Thanks to Dan, I've had a front-row seat to history. Take, for example, the behind-the-scenes story of the massive Jewish exodus from the Soviet Union that started in the 1980s after Mikhail Gorbachev assumed power. I believe it was told in public for the first time two decades later at two AJHS programs that Dan conceived and planned while he was president. The first, a dinner honoring George Shultz, secretary of state under President Ronald Reagan, and the second, featuring both Shultz and the former Soviet leader. The tale begins in, of all places, Iceland, as Shultz told us at the dinner in his honor.

The fall 1986 Reykjavík summit was initially considered a failure, but has been subsequently credited for laying the groundwork for breakthrough nuclear arms treaties between the Soviet Union and the United States. Less known is how it put human rights high on the agenda of the two superpowers.

Shultz said that public posturing had stymied negotiations. Protests in the United States on behalf of Soviet Jews had put Gorbachev in a position where he feared his people would see him as caving under American pressure.

Reagan, who had famously called the Soviet Union the "Evil Empire," managed to defrost relations with Gorbachev during a stroll between negotiating sessions. As Shultz told us, Reagan said, "Mr. General Secretary, let me ask you a question: If we were invaded by enemy aliens from outer space, would you come to our rescue?" Somewhat astonished, Gorbachev responded yes. To which, Reagan said, "And the United States would do the same for the Soviet Union." In this manner, Reagan shifted the focus from diverging interests to common interests. The two men grew so comfortable with each other that by the end of the walk they were on a first-name basis.

Following up on that conversation, Shultz said he approached Gorbachev about the Soviet Jews. He told the Soviet leader that Reagan recognized that the controversy had become a public problem for him. "I promise you," Shultz said he told Gorbachev, "that if you decide to allow the Jews to leave, the president of the United States will offer no comment whatsoever about it – that it will be your decision, as it should be."

Shultz said that as a test of America's good faith, the Soviets could start by removing barriers to the emigration of another oppressed group, Seventh-day Adventists. Gorbachev agreed. And after seeing that Reagan had not seized on the opportunity to gloat, he opened the gates for the Jews.

At the AJHS event several years later where he joined Shultz, Gorbachev expanded on why he let the Jews go. He said something like this: "I decided that if we wanted to become the kind of a country that I think we should be, how could I be telling any of our citizens that they don't have the freedom to move?"

THE POWER OF A HUG

Impressed by my efforts to restore the society to good health, fellow trustees began floating my name for the presidency in 1993. I wasn't looking to become president. Still, thanks to my experience on the blue-ribbon and the library committees, I probably knew more than anyone else about the inner workings of the organization. However, my emergence on the scene had upset the expectations of a veteran trustee. As treasurer, Sherman Starr thought he was in line for the presidency. I had heard from someone else that Sherman and his wife, Jill, had been spreading word about town that I was trying to shove him aside and that I lacked qualifications for the job. I told my source that I didn't want Sherman to know that I was aware of what he and his wife were up to. Making an issue out of it would have only led to a public spat, which would do neither us nor the society any good.

When I next saw the Starrs at a trustees' meeting, I went out of my way to give Jill a big hug and Sherman a warm handshake. I must have surprised them, as that seemed to put an end to their behind-the-scenes criticism. Concerned about any lingering bitterness, I met with Sherman to explain the situation as I saw it. I told him that the current president, Ronald C. Curhan, had encouraged my efforts to revamp the society's operations and that as I was in effect running the place, many of the trustees felt I should succeed him. Sherman said he felt he had earned the presidency because of all the years he had put in. I said it was no honor to be president, just a lot of work. I made it clear that I would take the job, but I would hate for the society to lose him. He backed off on the presidency and remained active with the organization, but our relationship was never as close as it once had been.

A PERFECT PARTNER

What could have been a source of friction but turned out to be very much the opposite was my relationship with Michael Feldberg. Michael was named executive director of the society shortly before I took office as president. He came with good credentials as a historian and author, but little experience as an administrator.

Now I tend to be a micromanager. If I see that something's not getting done, I jump in to do it. But it was the executive director's job to oversee the day-to-day operations of the society. So, I helped Michael set priorities. He was a very willing learner, and our working relationship soon developed into a personal one as well. To this day, he is one of my closest friends.

I started Michael with a Franklin Planner, then the time-management system of choice among businesspeople. My son James had just successfully introduced it to Shawmut's top management. He had learned about it when he worked for the consulting firm McKinsey & Co. After the Franklin Planner was incorporated into Palm Pilots, I purchased the handheld devices for Michael and me. Later, I donated money to the society so that Michael could take an intensive course in nonprofit management at Harvard Business School. Under the program's rules, the nonprofit's president was required to enroll, too, so Michael and I studied together for a week at my alma mater on the Charles.

We came up with ways to make the society more valuable to scholars and useful to the public at large. Self-assured, Michael didn't feel threatened by my suggestions. When it came to executing our ideas, he was superb. Thanks to his academic background, he had far more credibility with scholars than I did. Michael spoke their language. Among his accomplishments was shepherding through our project to create and publish the mammoth two-volume encyclopedia *Jewish Women in America*. Its more than 800 biographies formed the core of the encyclopedia now posted on the website of the Jewish Women's Archive.

Michael and I also revamped the society's fund-raising strategy. Impressed by the phenomenal success of the Amherst-based Yiddish Book Center, we consulted with founder Aaron Lansky and then brought him onto our board. Lansky was a master at direct-mail campaigns. Defying the conventional wisdom that a fund-raising letter should be concise, he would write three or four pages. He realized that he would get nowhere by making abstract appeals to save Yiddish literature. Instead, he told stories that grabbed the reader's attention. For example, he sent out an alert that the last surviving Yiddish linotype machine, which had been accumulating dust in the New York basement of the *Daily Forward*, was about to be junked, but could be preserved if he raised $50,000. Lansky played both on donors' guilt and on their desire to feel that could make a tangible difference. His strategy was similar to that of Save the Children, with its magazine ads featuring a starving waif and the line, "You can help this child or you can turn the page."

Our most successful appeal was for a portrait of Rachel Levy, whose son Uriah P. Levy was the first Jewish commodore in the U.S. Navy. An ardent admirer of Jefferson, the commodore purchased the former president's beloved home Monticello in the 1830s and spent three decades and a small fortune to restore it. His widowed mother made it her home, and she was buried there. When we learned that the Levy portrait was going to be sold in Europe, we sent out a letter saying we needed $45,000 to purchase the painting and keep it here. We wound up with $180,000 in donations.

Besides being able to tell a good story, we had to target the right people. We traded our donor lists with those of other Jewish organizations through a list broker, who cross-referenced the names to weed out duplications. We coded our return envelopes so we could determine which donor list they came from. Typically, if you get a 1.5 percent return on a mailing you break even. We had the greatest success – 8.5 percent – with a list for the preservation fund of the Eldridge Street Synagogue in New York City. I later learned that my father's parents, George and Gussie Wyner, were married there.

By experimenting with various styles of fund-raising letters and testing out different lists, we eventually accumulated 9,000 donors who were regularly giving a total of $125,000 a year ($250,000 in today's dollars).

A MYSTERY IN THE BODLEIAN

Helping our British counterparts celebrate their 100th anniversary, we turned up what appeared to be a centuries-old case of theft.

In 1993, the AJHS sponsored a trip in honor of the centennial of the Jewish Historical Society of Great Britain. Among the highlights was a lecture in London's underground war rooms by historian and Churchill biographer Martin Gilbert.

Later, we went to Oxford, where at Michael Feldberg's request the university's Bodleian Libraries pulled out their oldest Hebrew-language books. After about 20 of us assembled at a table drinking Cokes, a staff member rolled in a batch of books packed into a shopping cart, just like the kind you'd find in a grocery store. As we were eating, he started handing them out. Noticing that these books dated back to the Middle Ages, we quickly pulled our cola off the table.

As one of our group, Justin Oppenheim, looked through the books, he opened a front cover and spotted his surname. He was astonished to find that some of the books had come from the library of a famous twelfth-century ancestor of his, a rabbi who had lived in a Germanic state at the time of the Crusades. We were too polite to express our suspicions that the Oxford libraries must have received the books thanks to returning Crusaders, who were notorious for plundering the Jews of Europe.

MENDING FENCES

Besides straightening out our internal operations, we had a number of fences to mend. To strengthen ties with Jewish history scholars, we resurrected the society's academic council. Jonathan Sarna would become chair, a position that would give him a seat on the board of trustees. Prodded by the historians, we put the society's publication back on a quarterly schedule – a process that took some time, as we had fallen two years behind. We enlarged the role of our academic council members by inviting them to give talks during our quarterly trustee meetings.

To further bolster our scholarly bona fides, we invited outside experts to assess our collection and programs. They included Charles Berlin, bibliographer in Judaica at the Harvard College Library; Malcolm Freiberg of the Massachusetts Historical Society; Michael Grunberger, Judaica librarian at the Library of Congress; Abe Peck, assistant director of the American Jewish Archives; and Joan Rosenbaum, director of the Jewish Museum of New York.

We established liaisons with local Jewish historical and genealogical societies, which had felt neglected by the AJHS. At that time, there were about 115 of them – almost all spawned by the society in its early days. We also expanded the concept of holding our meetings in various cities across the country to raise our profile and dispel the growing impression that we were dominated by a Northeast clique.

We went international as well, sponsoring trips for members to Czechoslovakia, Morocco and England, for example. In an accompanying story, you can read how one of our members discovered books at Oxford that had been looted from his ancestors.

Meanwhile, we turned our attention to our immediate neighbor, Brandeis. Except for Jonathan Sarna's students combing our archives, we barely existed so far as the university was concerned. We weren't listed in campus brochures. We weren't a stop on campus tours.

And, as we were to learn to our surprise, we very much weren't part of the university's plans for the future.

WANDERING JEWS

In which I discover who my friends are and tie the knot with the Yankees

"JEWISH HISTORY SOCIETY TO Build at Brandeis," read the headline of a February 23, 1964, story in the *Boston Globe*.

The story went on to say that the American Jewish Historical Society, then based in rented quarters in New York, would build a headquarters housing a library, archives, study facilities and administrative offices on the Waltham campus.

"Decision to relocate was by unanimous vote of the society's executive council," the article stated.

If it had only been that simple. The real story behind the society's move from New York is a chapter in itself in American Jewish history – a tumultuous one with repercussions I would contend with three decades later. So before I go on with my story, I'll take you on a detour back in time.

THE BATTLE OVER BOSTON

In the early 1960s, the AJHS was running out of room in its New York offices when it received a timely bequest from a former president. Boston lawyer Lee Max Friedman left the society $1.6 million, with the hope that a portion of the money would go toward a new building. Dr. Abraham Sachar, an AJHS trustee and the founding president of Brandeis, invited the society to build on a prime hilltop spot on his campus. Less than two decades old, Brandeis was already gaining a national reputation as a home for Jewish studies. The trustees polled the society's membership – which was disproportionately New Yorkers – about making the move. As you might imagine, New Yorkers weren't thrilled with the idea of the society relocating to Boston. Tempers ran so high, I'm told, that a scuffle erupted as opponents tried to grab the ballots as they were being counted. Although the poll backed the Brandeis site, a dissident group rebelled and challenged the trustees' authority. There also was a court fight. In part to appease opponents, the society purchased the land from Brandeis and the building, designed by noted architect Max Abramowitz, faced away from the university, symbolizing the society's autonomy. The building opened in 1968, fronting onto a nondescript service road at the edge of the campus.

Three decades later, in the mid-'90s, I sought to rectify that ill-conceived compromise. I had an architect draw up a rendition of the building reorienting it to face the campus with a glass-enclosed museum. The renovation plan also called for increased storage space so that we could house the university's archives as well as our own.

I showed my plan to Sachar, who had been friends with my father and who, even in his 90s, was still a force to be reckoned with. He expressed enthusiasm, even after I told him that I estimated the cost at $3 million. "That's nothing, Jerry," he told me. "You and I will go across the country once, and we'll get that money." But he said we should do one thing first: Ask Dr. Samuel Thier, who was then Brandeis president, to proclaim the AJHS archives a precious resource on campus. Sachar also said I should assure Thier that we would not solicit people who had not already fulfilled their pledges to Brandeis itself.

Clutching the architect's drawings, Michael Feldberg and I arrived at Thier's office for an appointment. He invited in Dr. Jehuda Reinharz, then provost but soon to be president. I presumed that Thier invited Jehuda because he was also a scholar in modern Jewish history. I quickly learned that he was not an ally. After I made my pitch, Jehuda scoffed, "Precious resource? That's the worst archive I've ever seen." (To give Jehuda his due, the archive had not always been as organized as it should have been.)

In retrospect, it was obvious that the pair had heard about the society's past financial woes and had been counting the days until we were forced to close. The two Brandeis administrators might have already been making plans for the building and the collections, too. It probably came as a shock to them when I showed that we were alive and kicking. But although we weren't asking the university to contribute a cent, I couldn't even persuade the pair to get out of their chairs and examine the architectural plans I had spread out on a table. Their concluding remark was, "Why should I help you if I don't own you?"

We left the office stunned. Despite Jehuda's disparaging remarks, I knew from the committee of visiting scholars we had recruited that we had a worthy collection. I had just invested five years working to fortify the society's stability. I had counted on Brandeis being our partner as we spread our wings. But the administration left little doubt that what it valued was our building, not us. I realized we'd have to find a new home. But my next move was to shoot myself in the foot.

In the chapter on Town Meeting, I stress the importance of keeping everyone informed. A simple heads-up phone call can avert weeks of damage control. I was so surprised by my meeting with the Brandeis brass that I failed to practice what I had been preaching by needlessly antagonizing one of the society's staunchest supporters, Jonathan Sarna. As I've said, Jonathan often sent his students digging into our archives. His idol was Jacob Radar Marcus, the Jewish history scholar and former AJHS president. Jonathan had every reason to expect to be kept in the loop about the society's future. But I was in scramble mode. I called Ruth Wisse, the eminent Harvard scholar, to sound her out about moving to her campus. We had a pleasant chat, but she was noncommittal. Afterward, she called Jonathan. And that's when he first learned that this organization in his backyard, one that he so valued, was planning to pack up and leave. Jonathan exploded. He marched into Michael's office and told him it was his responsibility to knock some sense into "your president, Justin Wyner."

Michael immediately called me, and I slapped my forehead over my foolishness. Just as with the kerfuffle over the AJHS presidency, I first wanted to defuse matters before they escalated into a public dispute. I instructed Michael not to tell Jonathan that I knew about his outburst. Over the following months, I made it a point to reach out to him more and more. Meanwhile, I used a back channel. Jonathan's mother, Helen, was working at the time as a librarian at the AJHS. I asked her to let her son know that I really didn't want to move from Brandeis, but given the attitude of the university administration, I didn't see a future there.

In the end, my misstep caused no permanent damage to our relationship. Jonathan continued to be a tremendous advocate and resource for the AJHS, graciously carving out time from his busy schedule to speak at our events.

The real drama was yet to come, with a new cast of characters.

NEW YORK CALLS

Given the society's history, it was ironic where our search for a new home would ultimately take us. I got a call from Bruce Slovin, then head of the YIVO Institute for Jewish Research. Bruce wanted us to join forces with his and similar organizations to establish his dream of a Center for Jewish History in New York. Slovin had previously approached my predecessor with the plan, but our circumstances had clearly changed.

I told Bruce I thought it was a terrific idea, but made it clear that at best the only money we could contribute toward a new building was whatever we got from selling our current one, and that even being able to do that was unlikely. Slovin said that YIVO and a third interested group, the Leo Baeck Institute, could raise the necessary money by selling their Manhattan buildings. But he said the project wouldn't make sense without the AJHS as a partner. We agreed that the AJHS would not be expected to contribute to the new headquarters. It was also stipulated that if in the future the joint operation liquidated its assets or benefited from refinancing, the contributing organizations would be fully reimbursed before any remaining funds were split equally among the partners. I won over the AJHS trustees – many of whom were from the Boston area – by modifying the plan to retain the New England records at our building on the Brandeis campus. We had already discovered that if we were to abandon the building, we'd take a bath. Under the deal that had brought the AJHS to Brandeis, the society had agreed that if it ever left, the university could buy the building for the original cost less 3 percent a year for the period we occupied it. After 30 years, then, we would have received next to nothing for a building that had just been appraised at $2.4 million.

With the AJHS board backing the partnership, I turned to helping Bruce with the fund-raising. I approached Joan Rosenbaum, director of the Jewish Museum in New York, about teaming up with us. At the time, the museum was displaying our prized portraits of the Franks-Levy family. Joan suggested that the new center could house the museum's broadcast archives. Further, I envisioned that any alliance with the museum would mean access to its wealthy donor base. Our discussions had gone so far that the museum's board chairman had accepted my invitation to join the AJHS board. But then it all fell apart.

While I was talking to Joan, Bruce was recruiting the Yeshiva University Museum. When Joan heard that the Yeshiva museum would be part of the center, she abruptly broke off our budding relationship. There's no love lost between those two museums, which view each other as competitors. The Jewish Museum garners its support from some of the city's oldest Jewish families. The Yeshiva museum is run by relative newcomers, the Orthodox Jews and their descendants who fled the pogroms and the Nazis.

Still, the Yeshiva museum was a strong addition, with its collection spanning centuries of Jewish history. And a donor provided $3 million toward its move. But Bruce had made the deal without consulting anyone. While a friendly, generous and caring fellow, he would continue to infuriate colleagues with surprise faits accompli.

WOWING THE RICH

I helped Bruce raise additional money by making trips to New York to show "wow" items from our collection to potential donors. Bruce found wealthy Jews to host cocktail parties in their posh Manhattan apartments. I had never realized just how fancy kosher hors d'oeuvres could be. The high point of the party came when I slipped on my cotton archivist gloves, opened my dispatch case and pulled out documents dating from 1580. They were trial records of the Spanish Inquisition in Mexico, which lasted until 1820. In many cases, the defendants were women. I would tell the crowd stories about the fate of the heretics, how those found guilty of secretly practicing Judaism might be burned alive at the stake, while those who had admitted to practicing their faith would be killed first and then burned. But what most impressed the guests was that we Jews had been part of the New World almost from the beginning. I would then take out the pièce de résistance, the only copy in her own hand of Emma Lazarus's ode to the Statue of Liberty, "The New Colossus," the society's single most precious holding.

From real estate sales and fund drives, we raised enough money to purchase a building off Fifth Avenue between West 16th and 17th streets from the American Federation for the Blind. We then renovated and expanded it at a cost of $40 million, $30 million of which we borrowed. We estimated that our shared operating costs would be $1 million a year, but they've ballooned since to $8 million (but that's another story for another book).

The reason I toss out all these figures is to underscore a missed opportunity. At one point, New York University expressed interest in taking over the center as part of a plan to expand Jewish studies. NYU would have retired the center's debt and paid its operating expenses. But negotiations bogged down largely due to objections raised by the Yeshiva University Museum. Things became really nasty. It struck me that the Eastern European Jews who didn't join the Irgun in Palestine came instead to New York to do battle.

By 2000, when the Center for Jewish History opened to the public, it housed a total of five institutions, the last being the American Sephardi Federation.

Back in New England, Brandeis argued that by moving the bulk of the archives to New York, the AJHS had triggered the terms of the original deal and was obligated to sell the building for a fraction of its value. By this time, Ken Bialkin had succeeded me as AJHS president. After some unpleasantness, the society negotiated a sale price of $400,000. Thoroughly renovated, the building now is the Mandel Center for Studies in Jewish Education.

Now we faced the question of where to house the society's New England archives. Area universities were only slightly interested in the archives, and in some cases, we would have had to pay them. Then, as if in answer to our prayers, David Gordis, president of Hebrew College, approached me at a meeting of the college board, of which I was a member. Excited about the campus he was then planning for Newton Centre, he said, "We'd love to have you here. You'd be an important addition. You don't have to put up anything."

As president of the college, David may have had a lot of influence, but he didn't have the final say. When Mickey Cail, the chairman of the board, heard about the money we had received from Brandeis, he demanded that we turn it over to Hebrew College. When I explained that the money was already committed to New York, he said, "That's your problem, not ours." If Hebrew College did not provide this new home, he argued, we would not have been able to move out and sell the building.

I went down to New York to see if we could get some of our money back. I said that Genevieve and I were willing to donate $200,000. George Blumenthal, a fellow AJHS trustee, offered $100,000. When I returned to Boston, I told Mickey that $300,000 was the best we could do. He still wanted the rest of the money. In the end, he agreed to my promise that if the New England branch of the historical society held a capital campaign in the future, Hebrew College would get 25 percent of the proceeds until we'd paid off the remaining $100,000.

A FINICKY ARCHITECT

I thought things were finally settled, but I hadn't reckoned on the expensive ego of a big-name architect.

Hebrew College had hired Moshe Safdie to design its new campus. Safdie wanted control over everything, even the furnishings of the rooms. He insisted that we purchase desks that conformed to his style and refinish our shelves to his specifications. He added to our cost by dictating the location of the desks. His plan may have been aesthetically pleasing, but it made wiring for computers much more expensive. In the end, Genevieve and I had to donate an additional $120,000 for the refit.

Sad to say, the story only gets worse. Hebrew College would turn out to be just a temporary home. David Gordis had overreached with the new campus. Mesmerized by his enthusiasm and visionary plans, his trustees had failed to do their due diligence. Within a few years after the campus had opened, it became increasingly clear that the college was in way over its head. I discovered this when David asked me to join the college's finance committee. As talk turned to probable default on its bonds and an uncertain future, I decided that I had better find a new home for the archives, and I resigned from the committee because I felt my responsibilities to the AJHS presented a conflict of interest.

I again made the rounds of local universities, contacting Wellesley, Tufts, Boston University and Northeastern, but a regional Jewish archive wasn't really a good fit for any of them. Then one day, after dropping Genevieve off at her hair salon, Vidal Sassoon, I took a walk down Newbury Street and noticed a sign for the New England Historic Genealogical Society. It was located in a tall, narrow building that was originally built for a bank. I thought perhaps the old-line Yankees would have room for us and our New England archives.

It turned out they did. Not only that, they recognized that our archives would complement theirs. Many of their members were researching Jewish ancestors in their tangled family trees. And so in 2010, Jewish Boston moved in with Brahmin Boston at – if history were a map – the intersection of Blue Hill Avenue and Newbury Street. In 2018, the archive was reconstituted there as the Wyner Family Jewish Heritage Center.

THE BIGGEST SHOW OF MY LIFE

Introducing a million people to American Jewish history

PRESERVING HISTORY IS A tough sell. I found it difficult to persuade people why we needed money for material that had already been processed and put away. It's not a flashy cause, like rescuing a precious work of art. I felt like I did when I was I was soliciting money for the upkeep of the Adath Jeshurun cemetery. Descendants of families who had not purchased perpetual care plans would say, "You're not going to let my grass go to seed in the middle of the cemetery, whether I pay you or not."

We needed a way to make our archives come alive. The 350th anniversary of the founding of the first permanent Jewish community in America provided just the opportunity.

BATTLING PREJUDICE AND PIRATES

First, a little history about those earliest American Jews. They landed in New Amsterdam (now New York) in 1654. They were refugees from Recife in present-day Brazil. When Jews first settled there in the late 1630s, it was a Dutch colony, recently conquered from the Portuguese. Jews could worship freely and even had a synagogue. In early 1653, the Portuguese, who had colonized much of the surrounding area, retook Recife and reinstituted the Inquisition. If the Jews wanted to continue practicing their religion, they faced the choice of exile or death.

The Jews of Recife chose exile. Over the remainder of 1653, they were allowed to emigrate, and several hundred did so. One group of 23 adults and children hired a captain to take them to Holland on his ship, the *Ste. Katrina*. As the most dramatic version of the story goes, somewhere in the Caribbean, pirates robbed the passengers of all their valuables. After a stop in Jamaica, the voyage was diverted to New Amsterdam.

The Jews were not welcomed by Peter Stuyvesant, who was the director-general of New Amsterdam. The captain asked Stuyvesant to force the Jews to pay him even though they had no funds. Writing to his bosses at the Dutch West India Company, Stuyvesant complained that if he allowed the Jews to stay, he'd soon have the Papists and Quakers at his dock. The company, some of whose investors were Dutch Jews, rebuffed Stuyvesant. Once allowed in, the Jews successfully campaigned to be treated like any other citizens. Enjoying the right to worship as they pleased, they accepted the obligation of paying taxes and insisted on being allowed to serve in the militia on the same basis as Christians.

Until then, every other city in the New World was populated by people who had sought religious freedom, but only for themselves. New Amsterdam became the first religiously pluralistic city. It remained so after the city was taken over by the British, who then applied pluralistic policies to their other holdings.

In effect, the Jewish settlement in New Amsterdam set the stage for true religious freedom in America. Those 23 Jews broke the gates wide open.

The From Haven to Home *exhibition at the federal courthouse in Boston's Seaport District in 2005.*

GOING IT ALONE

The AJHS had mounted celebrations for the 250th and 300th anniversaries of the arrival of the first Jews, but for the 350th it joined forces with other organizations for what was hailed as the largest exhibition ever about Jews in America. Called *From Haven to Home: 350 Years of Jewish Life in America,* it opened in September 2004 at the Library of Congress. Besides drawing on the extensive collections of the AJHS and the Library of Congress, the exhibition included resources from the National Archives and the American Jewish Archives.

When I approached David Solomon – Michael Feldberg's successor as AJHS executive director – about moving the Library of Congress show to New York and then Boston, he replied he could do better with just the society's resources (he did just that in New York; the results were underwhelming). By then I was no longer president of the society, so my clout was limited. "It's your thing; you do it," he told me.

I returned to Boston and considered my options. Quickly, I realized it was unrealistic to remount the original exhibition here. The precious manuscripts and other original material required a temperature-controlled environment that only a few institutions like the Museum of Fine Arts could provide. But the MFA wasn't interested. Besides, remounting the original exhibition presented enormous logistical, not to mention insurance, problems.

I found my answer in the catalog to the Library of Congress exhibition. Nearly 250 pages in length and the size of a cocktail table book, the catalog is filled with essays, paintings, posters and vintage photographs. Turning its pages is a virtual tour of American Jewish history. We could mount an exhibition using full-scale facsimiles from the catalog. As it happened, Michael Feldberg had helped assemble the Library of Congress exhibit and was now working with me at the AJHS New England branch. Michael obtained the necessary permissions for the facsimiles, culled the historical materials, wrote new descriptions and – in collaboration with Gill Fishman, a good friend and leading exhibition designer – created new display panels.

I wanted the exhibition to be located someplace where not just Jews, but everyone would see it. Michael contacted officials at the new federal courthouse, named for the late Congressman John Joseph Moakley, and arranged for us to use the atrium. It was a spectacular space, with its bank of multi-story windows overlooking the harbor in South Boston.

Gill, who had designed other exhibitions with Michael, estimated it would cost $400,000 to $500,000 to mount the show.

BUDDY, CAN YOU SPARE $10,000?

I had participated in capital drives for Temple Israel and Beth Israel, but never one for a single exhibition. I had never been comfortable soliciting money, in part for personal reasons. I was wary of putting Genevieve and myself in a position where we'd feel obligated to make comparable contributions if the donors later approached us for their causes. But I viewed this exhibition as being in a category of its own – a chance for Jews to show their fellow Americans that we've been in the New World from the start, that our story of immigration is in many ways very much like those of the Irish, the Latinos, the Germans, the Italians – you name the ethnic or religious group.

Armed with the Library of Congress catalog, I launched my one-man fund drive with a visit to the Combined Jewish Philanthropies building. Just before I went into the private office of Barry Shrage, the CJP president, I ran into my friend Arthur Segel, a real estate developer, Harvard Business School professor and philanthropist, who asked me what I was doing there. After hearing my plans – and without my asking him – Arthur offered $5,000 toward the project. I said I would take it on a conditional basis. Wary of getting sucked into another pit as I had at Hebrew College, I vowed not to start work until I had raised two-thirds of the projected cost.

After seeing the catalog and hearing about Segel's pledge, Barry offered $25,000 on behalf of CJP. The next day I had a meeting scheduled with Marshall Dana and his sons, Myer and Alan, regarding the retail property their company managed on behalf of the George Wyner family trust. The Danas asked me what I had been up to lately. I told them about the exhibition and, again without my having to ask, they offered $75,000.

Within the next few days, I received two $25,000 pledges, one from my good friends Herb and Joan Schilder and the other from my then golfing companion, Gale Raphael. I now had a total of $155,000. That plus the $75,000 Genevieve and I had planned to contribute brought us almost halfway to our goal. We might just pull this off, I thought. Over the next six months or so, I went down my list of Jewish philanthropists, usually meeting them at their offices to show off the catalog. It became easier and easier – the bandwagon effect. When people heard that so-and-so had pledged, they wanted to jump aboard, too. As an incentive, I said that those who donated by a certain time would be listed on the entrance panel to the exhibition. We put out a Boston version of the original Library of Congress catalog. It includes a list of donors – just about every big name in local Jewish philanthropy is on it.

THE MONEY MEN

While I remain a trustee of the national AJHS, I rarely get down to New York for its meetings. They are held now on a late weekday afternoon for the convenience of the many members who work on Wall Street or in other corporate positions. It's not worth it for me to make the long trip for a two-hour meeting.

When my friend Dan Kaplan came on the board in the mid-'90s, he gave me the courage to raise the issue of donations with fellow board members. He said that so long as we were consistent in what we asked, we could make donations a prerequisite for the honor of serving on the board. The new rule did not apply to existing members, though.

Over time, contributions from trustees have become the core funding source for the society. I'm not sure that that has been all to the good. Many of the trustees today serve out of philanthropic duty rather than any special interest in Jewish history. I would now feel a bit out of place on the board that I once headed. However, I continue to be inspired by Sid Lapidus. After Dan succeeded him as society president, Sid became the chairman of the board, a position that he has held ever since. Sid, whose personal Jewish history collection is world-renowned, truly grasps the value of the society's mission.

FROM DREAM TO REALITY

Meanwhile, Michael headed up a full-time team that spent 18 months preparing the exhibition boards. They trained 60 volunteer docents. In retrospect, I marvel, who would have thought we would have an exhibition worthy of docents?

We created 16 two-sided, 8-by-8-foot curved display panels. Mounting the photographs and the text turned up unexpected problems. The glue didn't always hold, air bubbles emerged, posters curled. I suggested laminating techniques we had mastered at Shawmut to solve some of the problems.

As donations rolled in, the costs escalated. For example, Facing History and Ourselves had enthusiastically offered to prepare a curriculum for public school children visiting the exhibition. But the Brookline-based organization expected to be reimbursed and presented us with a bill for some $20,000. Then there was the unplanned expense for a video. And not long before we opened, courthouse officials surprised us with an expensive request. We had to make the exhibition panels portable so that the space could be cleared within 15 minutes for special events. To do so, we designed and installed an apparatus with wheels for the exhibition platforms. We also inserted small doors atop the 8-foot wide panels so that security officers could peer through to check for hidden bombs.

When the exhibit opened in September 2005, we held a dinner at the courthouse that drew everyone we had hoped for. Sid Lapidus, the AJHS president at the time, was very supportive and addressed the gathering. Other speakers included Barry Shrage, Jonathan Sarna and me.

We hosted at least one noon lecture a week to coincide with the exhibition. Held in the jury room, the lecture almost always filled the 200 seats. Local Jewish groups organized related events. *From Haven to Home* became the focus of visits by thousands of schoolchildren who visited the courthouse as part of its justice program for urban children. Teachers used the Facing History curriculum to prepare the children ahead of time.

Besides school groups, more than 15,000 tourists and local residents viewed this collection of photographs, paintings and diagrams depicting how a handful of Jews grew into a community of more than six million. But what was particularly gratifying was seeing how people of all backgrounds identified with our own struggles and achievements. Michael told me of overhearing a Latina girl as she translated and explained the panels to her mother, likening their own story of immigration to that of the Jews.

TAKING THE SHOW ON THE ROAD

Sid Lapidus was struck by the possibilities of touring the show and offered encouragement on behalf of the AJHS. Having had a tour in mind from the beginning, I had recommended designing the panels so that all 16 could fit into a 54-foot trailer truck. Over the past decade, the exhibition has been viewed by more than a million people in Denver, Las Vegas, Boise, San Diego, Detroit and Manhattan.

The Vegas visit was in part thanks to Sheldon Adelson's sister, Gloria Rita Field. When she saw the courthouse show, she was so enthusiastic that she persuaded the casino mogul to contribute $85,000 toward the cost of bringing it to his adopted hometown (Sheldon grew up in Boston). After the opening party in Las Vegas, Sheldon and his wife, Miriam, spent more than two hours scrutinizing every panel in the exhibition. Gloria passed away shortly later. Had she survived, I have no doubt she would have succeeded in persuading her brother to underwrite the cost of sending *From Haven to Home* to city after city for many years to come.

When not on the road, the exhibition is stored at the University of Denver. There, different sets of panels are displayed on a rotating basis. Meanwhile, an online version of *From Haven to Home* can be found on the Library of Congress website. Thus, the Jewish journey continues into cyberspace.

PART X: RINGSIDE AT TEMPLE ISRAEL

- **The profound and the petty:** Up close with the rabbis

- **Big man on the bimah:** How a synagogue really runs

THE PROFOUND AND THE PETTY

In which I learn that rabbis are only human

MY MOTHER WASN'T THE boasting sort, but we can forgive her for noting in her wedding diary that "Rabbi Levi quite justly said we were the best couple he saw in the last twenty years."

Harry Levi had been the senior rabbi at Temple Israel in Boston for a dozen years when he married Sara Goldberg and Rudolph Wyner in December 1923. He was two years shy of 50 and revered as one of the leading rabbis in not just Boston, but the nation. With the advent the following year of radio broadcasts of his sermons, he endeared himself to Bostonians of all religious persuasions.

No wonder my mother wrote in her diary how pleased she was when he complimented the newlyweds for their "manner," adding that "he felt very optimistic for our future." There clearly was mutual affection. In later years, my parents would host Rabbi Levi at our home, often for a game of bridge.

Over the decades, my family has had ties with many area synagogues, from the Blue Hill Avenue shul, built on property purchased by my paternal grandfather, and the Crawford Street Synagogue, where my maternal grandfather was a founder, to the Martha's Vineyard Hebrew Center, the religious home away from home for Genevieve and me. Temple Israel, though, has been at the center of my religious life, from my childhood days fidgeting in its pews at its Commonwealth Avenue home to my service as a trustee and president of the current Longwood Avenue campus.

Both my mother and her mother were long-time members of the Temple Israel Sisterhood, which held lunches that at their peak drew 350 people. My father was a member of the Brotherhood and a temple trustee – and I would follow in his footsteps. When I was around 12, I remember attending father-son events sponsored by the Brotherhood, such as an evening of boxing matches held in the temple social hall. The dads, dressed in tuxedos, would cheer on the sweaty boxers as they traded blows in the ring. Hugely popular among our children was the annual movie at Chanukah. A Brotherhood member with a Hollywood connection would arrange a special screening of a Disney film before it hit the theaters.

When Rabbi Levi was in the pulpit, Shabbat services were held on Sunday mornings, as was the custom with the Reform movement then. He had a mellifluous, almost heavenly voice. I could imagine him conversing with the Almighty. He spoke with such passion and vividness that he could make even mundane topics come to life. One sermon has always stuck with me. It was about how easily we can fall prey to bad habits. A habit, he said, starts as a gossamer thread, then becomes stronger and stronger until it's a rope that you can never break. Those words would come back to haunt me in my struggles to quit smoking.

At that time, Temple Israel included little Hebrew in its services and didn't offer a bar mitzvah program. I studied for my bar mitzvah with a tutor, Mr. Lieberman, from Congregation Kehillath Israel in

Brookline, the Conservative shul where my mother's parents were members, and made my debut at the bimah there. Afterward, I continued studying Jewish history and traditions at Temple Israel. My confirmation class was the first taught by the renowned Rabbi Joshua Loth Liebman, who had succeeded Rabbi Levi in 1939.

Rabbi Liebman was a short man with a towering intellect. When he gave his sermons, he became so animated that he would stand on his tiptoes as he drove home a point. He moved Shabbat services to Friday night and regularly packed the house. The Boston newspapers ran accounts of his sermons and speeches, such as his address to the annual congregational dinner in March 1941 when he warned of the impending destruction of the European Jewish community:

> I am not at all convinced that Boston Jewry has been awakened to the new world which we, in Israel, face. We are an orphan people. Our older brothers and sisters in Europe have been broken and liquidated. … Are we Jews in this age going to allow a 4,000-year-old culture and religious vision to go down, to be smashed, because we awaken too late?

A talk Rabbi Liebman gave titled "The Road to Serenity" came to the attention of Richard L. Simon of Simon & Schuster. The publisher had him turn it into a book, *Peace of Mind*, which connects religion and psychiatry. My Uncle Eddie, who ran the Ritz-Carlton, made sure a suite at the hotel was always at the ready for the rabbi if he needed a writing hideaway. In October 1947, Rabbi Liebman's book hit the top of *The New York Times* best-seller list. It was still on the list at the time of his death two years later.

THE PERILS OF PRIDE

Temple Israel has always taken pride in its top-notch rabbis. They have been very different in personality and style, but each has been well-suited for the congregation of his era.

That's not to say that they were immune from controversy. As I entered the ranks of temple leadership, I came to see that rabbis can have their moments of both greatness and pettiness. Like anyone else, they can allow their egos to blind them to reason. And their patience can be worn thin by querulous board members, the conflicting demands of congregants and the fishbowl scrutiny of their every action.

I also observed how emotionally invested congregants can become in their clergy. No matter how learned and prestigious a rabbi may be, what often counts most with congregants is their own personal experience. In some cases, their only contact with the clergy may be at life-cycle events, times of joy, like a wedding, or of sadness, such as illness and death. The rabbi comforts family members when they are most vulnerable. It's not a question to them of whether there's a better rabbi. That rabbi is best because he or she is there for them. Based on these experiences, congregants develop tremendous loyalty for their rabbi.

Ego and emotion can be a volatile mix, one that can inflame minor disagreements and misunderstandings into major disputes. I found myself in the midst of the battlefield on more than one occasion during my nearly five decades in temple leadership.

I became a trustee of the temple in 1964, carrying on the family tradition as my father became less active in the temple's governance. Fifteen years later, I was surprised when my father told me that a number of people at the temple thought I should become the next president. The fellow who really wanted the job, Sumner Rodman, was a few years older than me and had served as vice president. But the nominating committee picked me after receiving many letters on my behalf. I finally felt as if I were my own person in the temple community, not simply my father's son – and this was 1979, when I was 54 years old.

FROM IWO JIMA TO LONGWOOD AVENUE

Now back to my tales of tumult. The first occurred during the tenure of Rabbi Roland B. Gittelsohn, who served as senior rabbi for nearly a quarter-century. The rabbi came to Temple Israel in 1953, already nationally known because of the stirring sermon he gave in the aftermath of the Battle of Iwo Jima.

Rabbi Gittelsohn was the first Jewish chaplain appointed by the Marine Corps. At age 35, he accompanied 70,000 American troops in their fierce five-week campaign to dislodge the Japanese from the heavily fortified Pacific island. Jews accounted for 1,500 of the Marines, but as chaplain the rabbi ministered to soldiers of all faiths.

After the battle, the division chaplain asked Rabbi Gittelsohn to deliver a sermon at a combined religious service dedicating the Marine cemetery on Iwo Jima. But anti-Semitism was still rife in that era, and other ministers objected to having a rabbi preach over the graves of Christians. Rabbi Gittelsohn presented his sermon at a Jewish ceremony attended by fewer than 100, but it was so eloquent that the words would be passed along to millions. It was publicized in *Time* magazine, entered into the Congressional Record and for many years broadcast annually on Memorial Day by national radio commentator Robert St. John. This is an excerpt:

> Here lie officers and men, Negroes and Whites, rich men and poor, together. Here are Protestants, Catholics, and Jews together. Here no man prefers another because of his faith or despises him because of his color. Here there are no quotas of how many from each group are admitted or allowed. Among these men there is no discrimination. No prejudices. No hatred. Theirs is the highest and purest democracy.

While in the Marines, the rabbi was known as "Red" Gittelsohn because of his hair. At the synagogue, some suggested the nickname also aptly captured his fiery sermons. While rabbis Levi and Liebman employed logic and passion to persuade from the pulpit, Rabbi Gittelsohn's sermons at times came off more like a scolding. He lashed out at those he viewed as standing in the way of social justice. He marched alongside black ministers from Boston for civil rights in Selma, Alabama. He railed against the Vietnam War before doing so became fashionable.

Rabbi Gittelsohn was not afraid to bite the hands that fed him, displaying particular contempt for unethical business owners. On Yom Kippur, he would admonish them to beg for God's forgiveness. His condemnations were so sweeping that on the way home from temple, as Genevieve extolled the beauty of the service, my father and I would pick apart the sermons.

But it was when the rabbi strayed from national politics into temple politics that he ignited a firestorm at the synagogue.

The prologue for this drama began peacefully enough in 1961, when the nominating committee for temple president held an open meeting for congregants to suggest candidates. My father was part of a group that favored Bob Levi, the son of Rabbi Levi. It wasn't nepotism; Bob had served on the temple board for years. Other congregants, however, wanted to elect Frank Cohen, also a suitable candidate. As my father told it, no one had really felt it necessary to fight over who would be temple president, a position that in other years had often been hard to fill. To keep matters harmonious, his group suggested that Frank serve first and then Bob. Everyone agreed, but no one thought it necessary to put anything in writing.

A POLARIZING LETTER

In 1964, when Frank's three-year term ended, my father and his group went before the new nominating committee again to put forth Bob, citing the informal agreement. This time the committee not only refused to endorse Bob, it wouldn't so much as consider his candidacy. The attitude seemed to be: Where do you get the nerve to tell us whom to pick?

Perhaps my father's group had been naïve to think the understanding from three years before would carry any weight, but the committee's belligerence only made matters worse. While the committee had its eyes on another candidate, Lloyd Tarlin, it could have headed off the controversy by at least agreeing to consider Bob. Summarily rebuffed by the committee, Bob's supporters decided they had no choice but to exercise their right under temple bylaws to nominate a candidate independently. Thus, the battle was engaged: Lloyd versus Bob.

To the astonishment of many, Rabbi Gittelsohn took the stance that the election was not so much about the temple presidency as it was about him. He sent a letter to congregants accusing Bob's supporters of conspiring to remove him as senior rabbi. Where he got that idea, I still don't know. But while some of us didn't appreciate the rabbi's broadsides against business leaders, we didn't have a hidden agenda. We simply felt that Bob deserved a turn as temple president, and we were disappointed that Rabbi Gittelsohn was casting the election as a referendum on himself.

The rabbi's letter succeeded in making the election much more heated than it would have been otherwise. Some 2,500 congregants showed up for the election. I served as floor manager for Bob. Frank, the outgoing president, allowed the meeting to get away from him. Lloyd's supporters spoke for 45 minutes, while we got a third of that time. By the time I complained, it was too late to make up the difference. Touted as the rabbi's protector, Lloyd won.

The election left bruised feelings – largely thanks to the rabbi's meddling. But in time, relationships healed. Indeed, my father and Rabbi Gittelsohn carried on a lengthy correspondence over the years about various issues, such as the growing schism between secular Jews and the ultra-Orthodox in Israel. After the rabbi retired, he and my father occasionally socialized. I interviewed Rabbi Gittelsohn for his oral history. We had a great time together. He and his second wife had us to dinner at their retirement home.

On the fiftieth anniversary of Iwo Jima, Rabbi Gittelsohn read portions of his eulogy at a ceremony in Washington, D.C. It would be his last major public appearance.

ANOTHER EMBATTLED RABBI

Whatever lessons Rabbi Gittelsohn letter had taught about the perils of clergy charging into lay affairs apparently were not passed on to his successor, Bernard Mehlman. And once again I got caught in the cross fire.

Rabbi Mehlman, then 41, came to Temple Israel in 1977 after making his mark in Washington, D.C., overseeing the rapid expansion of Temple Micha and promoting the efforts of an experimental interfaith, multiracial seminary. The rabbi's success at community building appealed to Temple Israel. Up until then, its clergy had presented services as if they were performances and the congregants an audience. Rabbi Gittelsohn was known to stop and glare at latecomers, occasionally lecturing them. To attract more families, the temple sought to make services more participatory and activities more inviting. Among his first acts, Rabbi Mehlman moved the main evening service to 5:45, early enough for young children to attend with their parents.

The rabbi told temple leaders that to be more effective, he needed to operate with a team. He won their approval to bring along his former intern, 30-year-old Rabbi Ronne Friedman. Initially, the pairing was a great success, but the mentor-protégé bond ultimately led to a rancorous congregational divide.

First, some background: Wind back the clock to 1939 and the end of Rabbi Levi's 28 years at the pulpit. In keeping with synagogue tradition, congregational leaders announced they would conduct a national search to replace him. They wanted a spiritual leader with a reputation worthy of a synagogue that was not only New England's largest Reform temple, but also one of the most prestigious in America.

Many congregants, though, were disappointed that the associate rabbi, Beryl D. Cohon, had not been promoted to the top job. He had been at the temple nearly a decade. In a congregation as large as that of Temple Israel, many members, especially relative newcomers, felt much closer to Rabbi Cohon than they had had to Rabbi Levi. It had been Rabbi Cohon who had officiated at their weddings, presided over their funerals, and provided solace during times of trouble. Dispirited about being passed over and placed under the authority of a rabbi nine years his junior, Rabbi Cohon marched into next-door Brookline and established Temple Sinai. About a third of Temple Israel's congregants followed him.

That schism led Temple Israel to establish a rule that assistant rabbis could serve no longer than three years, with a possible limited extension as associate rabbi. After that, they would have to find a post elsewhere. Thus, fledgling rabbis would know from the start that Temple Israel would offer a training ground, but no more.

Now let's return to the 1980s. Like Rabbi Cohon before him, Rabbi Friedman became a popular figure in the congregation. In recognition of his success in revamping the religious school, the temple extended his employment after five years by naming him to the new position of director of education. Subsequently, I was asked by temple leaders to sound him out before his contract next came up for renewal. Having served many years on the temple board and as its president from 1979 to 1982, I got to know both Bernard and Ronne well, which is why I feel comfortable referring to them on a first-name basis.

A DIVISIVE ULTIMATUM

"I would really like to stay, but you can't afford to have me anymore," Ronne said to me at the outset of our talks. With his decade-plus experience now, he was eligible to serve as senior rabbi at a large congregation. Under the guidelines of the Central Conference of American Rabbis, he could probably earn as much as $275,000 plus receive housing. He said to forgo such an opportunity "wouldn't be fair to my children." Noting that he expected that Bernard would be retiring within a few years, Ronne offered to continue at lower pay if the new contract named him as successor.

I explained that the congregation probably would not be willing to make an exception to its practice of conducting a national search. While I told Ronne that he might still be selected, there was no way to guarantee that. We talked about how he might find great success at another synagogue. I wished him well and we parted with a warm handshake.

Much to my surprise – as well, I think, to Ronne's – Bernard stepped in the next day and said that it was important to him that Ronne stay. He suggested a co-rabbinate. He went so far as to say that if Ronne went, he would leave, too.

That got a lot of prominent congregants who were close friends with Bernard very upset. It also angered Ronne's many admirers. But for many it wasn't a question of "do you love Rabbi Friedman?," but rather of preserving the principle of conducting a nationwide search. This was no mere formality. The search process also served as a vehicle for the temple to reassess its needs and priorities. Besides, to make Ronne heir apparent would only haunt him later, with detractors grumbling that a search might have turned up a better candidate.

As divisions became more bitter, Irving Rabb, Herman Snyder and I asked Bernard to help defuse the situation. He backed down from making threats about quitting, but still pushed for a contract that would make Ronne his successor. A majority of the board of trustees agreed, leaving it to the congregation to cast the final vote.

Dismayed by the discord, Ronne began expressing second thoughts about the contract. By nature, he sought to bridge divides, not create them. I had thought from our conversations that we had an agreement that he would tell the congregation that he loved the temple too much to allow such dissent to go any further and was withdrawing from consideration. But on the day of the vote, he met me near the temple entrance and said he felt it was too late for him to withdraw from the fray. He said he didn't want to let down his supporters after all the effort they had invested in him. The congregation made the decision for him; it voted against renewing his contract under the terms he'd specified.

Even though I had spoken out before the vote about the importance of a national search, my relationship with Ronne was such that we could have a friendly breakfast the next morning. I said, "Ronne, you're going to get out on your own, and you're going to be a top candidate here when the time comes." And indeed, that was how it turned out.

But meanwhile the congregation was in turmoil. With the rabbi embittered and the temple leadership polarized, a committee of 30, including Genevieve, was named to figure out how to restore unity. It took months before the members advanced from talking *at* one another to *with* one another. I believe

Genevieve was instrumental in cooling the tempers. As she did when she guided human resources at Shawmut, she deployed the underrated skill of listening. It's not just a matter of telling people, I hear you. Rather, it requires restating their concerns so they know they've been understood. As Genevieve was the one person all sides respected, she was proposed for temple president. The congregation agreed.

Bernard remained rabbi until 1999. By that time, Ronne had served five years as senior rabbi of Temple Beth Zion in Buffalo, where he was credited with spurring a resurgence in membership. Sure enough, he was one of our top candidates to succeed Bernard. As a member of the search committee, I checked out his references in Buffalo. Time and again, people told me about his inspiring sermons. That came as a surprise to me, as that was one area where he hadn't impressed me during his earlier service at Temple Israel. I realized something had happened to him in the years that he was gone.

Still, Ronne was no shoo-in for the job. When the search committee voted on its choice for rabbi, I was on holiday in the Galapagos. James Segal, who was then temple president, insisted that I join the meeting of the committee by ship-to-shore telephone. During the 45-minute discussion, I backed Ronne – so I played a role in both the rabbi's departure and his return.

I recall telling Ronne's parents when he left Temple Israel that this was the best thing that could happen for him – and when he came back, his mother told me, "You were right."

It wasn't just his sermons that impressed me, it was also the way he approached the congregation. "Jerry," he said to me on his return, "I want you to give me the names of everybody who is still angry about what happened and angry about my coming back. I want to personally reach out to each one of them." So, I gave him the names of half a dozen people, including Herman Snyder, an elderly past president. Shortly after that, Herman told me, "It is really amazing. Ronne actually came to see me, and I now feel entirely different about him, and quite comfortable."

BIG MAN ON THE BIMAH

Taking the heat, sharing the warmth as temple president

IN 1979, THE NOMINATING committee of Temple Israel was considering two candidates for congregation president. In the end, I was selected over Sumner Rodman, an extremely nice fellow who had recently been a vice president. I think they settled on me because, being younger, I represented a new generation of leadership.

It was a time of change for the congregation. We were becoming accustomed to the ways of our new senior rabbi, Bernard Mehlman, who arrived from Washington, D.C., with his assistant, Ronne Friedman. They came from a much smaller congregation, which fostered a more close-knit atmosphere than we had had at Temple Israel.

The ways of the new clergy sharply contrasted with those of our retiring rabbi, Roland Gittelsohn, as I touched on in the previous chapter. Both were social activists, but whereas Rabbi Gittelsohn stood out on the national stage, his successors encouraged congregants to engage in local protests and community service work. While that was just what we needed to appeal to an emerging generation of congregants, some of the older members were not comfortable with the rabbis' more aggressive "boots on the ground" approach.

I had served on the temple's board of trustees since 1964 and, in the eyes of many of the older board members, had shown myself able to relate to the broad spectrum of trustees and congregants.

That quality was especially needed at the time, as the congregation had been splintering into interest groups. The first group consisted of older members who had been brought up in a more traditional style of Reform Judaism than that practiced by Bernard. The second group, a younger generation, liked the rabbi's more participatory services, which incorporated more Hebrew and singing (changes that many older members found to be off-putting). A third faction had rallied around the cantor, a holdover from Rabbi Gittelsohn's era, in a clash developing between him and the new rabbi over the division of responsibilities.

When I took office, my priority was to change the perception among many congregants that the temple's leaders were just a remote bunch of old-timers. I made myself accessible and encouraged all congregants to feel they could play a role in temple governance.

I took a leaf from my experience as town moderator. I not only established telephone hours for people to call me, but also acquired office space at the temple. I announced I would be available there every Monday afternoon from 3 to 6 and even later if necessary. I invited congregants to stop by with or without an appointment.

I chose to sit on the bimah every Friday night for the entire service and, with the clergy's support, took over the responsibility for presenting the weekly rundown of temple events – a practice that has been continued by my successors. I made a point of welcoming congregants to chat with Genevieve and me at the Kiddush after the service.

To broaden leadership opportunities, I instituted a policy of having committees rotate their chair positions. Some veteran committee leaders had become a bit stuck in their ways. The rotation system allowed me to shake things up without making anyone feel as if he or she were being singled out.

With the clergy, I tried to create a climate of partnership. Rabbis are naturally protective of their pulpits, on guard against well-meaning but meddlesome boards. When I heard some of the clergy say they felt overwhelmed by the number of hospital visits to congregants, I offered to share in the responsibility. I was gratified to see how much the congregants appreciated the temple president stopping by.

The duty to visit the sick was among the flashpoints involving the cantor. He didn't see it as part of his responsibilities. Nor for that matter did he feel obligated to teach in the religious school. But he did find time to earn money on the side, singing at outside engagements. Bernard tried to rein the cantor in a bit, asking him to coordinate his music with the sermon topic of the evening. Having received complaints, particularly from Bernard, about the cantor's outside jobs, I felt I had to intervene. I said to him, "We're paying you a big sum, and you're our precious resource. People are attracted to our services because they want to hear you perform. With or without the additional compensation, you cannot perform at different venues all over town because that would diminish your special value to us, not to mention reduce the time you have for your duties here." Quietly and over time, the cantor agreed to pull back on his outside activities.

THE ONE WHO SAID NO

I told the rabbis that they should avoid situations where they would have to say no to a congregant. "Let me take the heat," I said. That way people who weren't happy would just wait out my term rather than clamor for a new rabbi. My intervention was particularly welcomed by the clergy when I enforced the temple's policy of only hosting funeral services for members and their families. The temple was such a desirable venue that were it not for our restrictions we would have turned into just another big funeral parlor.

Early on during my tenure, Judge Matthew Brown, who had served as president of Combined Jewish Philanthropies, asked if we could make an exception for Irving Saunders. The respected real estate mogul had left the congregation three years before his death. Matty said the family was willing to pay back dues if necessary. I said it wouldn't be fair to make an exception for families that could afford to post-date membership. Besides, I asked, what would we say to all the families whose requests for exceptions we had denied in the past? The matter was resolved when Bernard agreed to lead the service at a funeral home, thus acknowledging the Saunders family's long history with the temple. I told family members that we would have loved to have hosted the services, but we had to be consistent about our policy. Afterward, I was heartened to learn they rejoined the temple.

I always found that being even-handed in enforcing policies was the best way to avoid offending people. That's not to say I believe rules should be set in stone. New circumstances may call for new rules, but the rule makers must be deliberate and open about changes. Otherwise, they're asking for a heap of grief.

FRIDAY NIGHT SHOCK

After my term as president had ended, a situation arose that demonstrated the perils of surprising people with policy changes. On a Friday night long before gay marriage became legal, one of the rabbis astonished many congregants by inviting a pair of women to the bimah to receive a blessing because, he announced, they were to be wed in a religious ceremony conducted by our clergy the following week (though not at our temple). I think that the congregants were even more startled when after the blessing the women kissed each other on the lips.

I later told Bernard that I personally had no problem with gay marriage, but rather with his failing to consult with the board before taking what was considered at the time to be such a radical step. Had he prepared the congregation in advance for his change in thinking about same-sex marriage, that night's event would not have caused such a stir.

Interestingly, while the temple clergy were ready to embrace gay marriage, they were not yet ready to preside over an interfaith wedding. Some years before, Bernard had asked me, in my capacity as a justice of the peace, to officiate at the wedding of the cantor's sister to a non-Jew. The service was not held at the synagogue, but all the temple's rabbis attended.

Speaking of hot-button social issues, as president, I struck a blow for women's rights. It came as I was helping the temple install a computerized database by tapping into Shawmut's mainframe. I noticed that in the case of families, the temple's mailings were all addressed to the male head of household. To remedy that, I wrote a simple computer program that printed the label with the names of both the husband and the wife, rather than, say, Mr. and Mrs. Justin Wyner. I even went a step further, each month alternating which name came first. As you can see, I had come quite a way from the time when I quashed Genevieve's hopes for a newspaper job because I thought people would think I couldn't support the family on my own! Later, I led the change in the bylaws that gave both husband and wife a vote at congregational meetings.

As president, I also made a point of emphasizing the appearance and upkeep of the building. At the time, we were breaking in a new executive director. I told him whenever I spotted trash on the stairs or in the corridors, I picked it up. I said he should head off any need for that. I urged him to walk the halls with the janitor and then assign him the role of twice daily making the rounds of the building to take care of even the smallest details. I drilled home the point that first impressions shape how people perceive a synagogue. It might not be a matter of Talmudic law, but we don't want people surprised to find, as I knew had happened more than once, no toilet paper in the stalls.

DUES AND DON'TS

As operating expenses and salaries soared over the years, Temple Israel increased its dues. But it always made sure that ability to pay did not stand in the way of membership. Still, for reasons of pride and privacy, it could be difficult for someone who had suffered a sudden financial setback to ask for a discount. Traditionally, the congregant would only have to confide in the temple president, and just that one time. Each president would pass along to the next the names of those congregants – and there were relatively few – who had been granted relief.

I went to great lengths to make people feel comfortable as we discussed what they could afford. It didn't always work out, though. One man told me that he had the resources to pay the dues, but that he should be able to pay a lower amount because he just went to services during the High Holidays. "That's only worth $1,000 to me," he said. I explained to him that we were willing to be flexible about our fees, but only in cases where people lacked the wherewithal to pay the full amount. "It's one thing for you to tell us what you can afford," I added, "but quite another to say you will only pay what membership is worth to you."

In the years since I served as president, dues decisions have increasingly been left to the executive directors. I hadn't wanted to go that route. Just as with the rabbis, I wanted to minimize situations where the director would have to say no. Besides, I doubted he or she would have done so in the face of someone pleading financial hardship – it wouldn't have been worth the grief. And that has proven the case: Now, more than half the congregants pay reduced dues.

KEEPING THE RABBIS KOSHER

Speaking of money, when I first took office, I struck a sensitive nerve with our clergy when I raised questions about the Rabbis' Discretionary Fund. Congregants donated to it in recognition of special services performed by the clergy, such as presiding at weddings, bar and bat mitzvahs and particularly funerals. Under their contract, the rabbis couldn't accept this money directly to spend for themselves. Some years, more than $50,000 would flow into the fund, but nobody was keeping track of how it was flowing out.

Generally, the clergy used the money to cover the cost of out-of-town professional meetings or to help a worthy cause in a pinch. I pointed out that the synagogue could get into hot water if the money went to a cause that fell outside of its mission and skirted laws governing tax-deductible charities. In the end, I prevailed upon them to allow me, as the sole representative of the lay board, to review the expenditures on a confidential basis. On occasion, when I heard the staff say they couldn't afford some program or project, I would suggest that they tap the fund if I knew enough money was available. I tried to avoid appearing intrusive, and the clergy accepted my suggestions on occasions that really mattered to me.

Receiving money could be just as dicey as spending it. When a wealthy widow offered a substantial gift to create space for a new temple museum, she insisted on being named lifetime chair of the committee overseeing it and the right to designate its members. I persuaded the board to turn down the gift, because committee positions should not be for sale. The board agreed. But when no other donor came forth, I felt guilty. In the end, Genevieve and I contributed in her place. It was just another example of how good intentions often seem to lead us down unexpected – and sometimes expensive – paths. We weren't interested in having Wyner emblazoned on walls in prominent places. But after the museum finally opened, we felt good that our names were associated with a project that so many people seemed to enjoy.

* * *

Temple Israel continues to play an important role in the extended Wyner family. As it had with my sister and me, the synagogue educated our children in the traditions and beliefs of our people. Later, I felt privileged to serve as its president and help strengthen it. As I described in the previous chapter, I then watched with admiration as Genevieve took on the presidency in an even more contentious time. And more recently, Genevieve and I have had the pleasure of seeing members of our family's latest generation take their place at the bimah as we celebrated the bat mitzvah of our granddaughter Lam An and the bar mitzvah of our grandson Oliver.

A fourth-generation Wyner at Temple Israel bimah: Celebrating Lam An's bat mitzvah are (from left) parents Giang and James; cantor Roy Einhorn; Lam An; Rabbi Jeremy Morrison; uncles George and Daniel; and grandparents Genevieve and me.

PART XI: BODY AND SOUL

- **Healthy skepticism:** Mother knows best

- **Trying not to be morbid:** Lessons in life and death

- **One of the Chosen:** Taking pride rather than offense

- **The Holy Land:** Following in the family's footsteps

HEALTHY SKEPTICISM

When it comes to medicine, mother knows best

I WAS JUST 3 years old when my family was rocked by a death that never should have happened. My mother had delivered a healthy girl at St. Elizabeth's Hospital in Brighton – Beth Israel didn't have a maternity ward at the time – but within a couple of weeks the baby, named Marjory Kraus Wyner, was dead. Someone had administered the wrong medication. This was 1928, long before malpractice suits became routine. I don't know the details of how the error occurred. My only memory is of my mother crying – something I rarely saw.

After that experience, my mother became extremely vigilant about health matters. She no longer would take a doctor's word for granted. When I was in the hospital to have my tonsils and my appendix out, she stayed by my bedside. (I carried on that practice, sleeping in Genevieve's hospital room whenever she had to stay overnight.)

Mother didn't just keep an eye out for her immediate family. When her brother Harry started complaining of stomach pains, she felt his family didn't take him seriously enough. Ironically, his wife, Florence, was the daughter of Dr. Charles Wilinsky, who for many years was director of Beth Israel Hospital. My mother was right to be concerned. Uncle Harry died of intestinal cancer.

I've followed my mother's example of being proactive about medical care and of recognizing that doctors are human like the rest of us. When she had cancer, I read all I could about the disease and arranged to bring in an expert from New Orleans to provide a second opinion. I also did my own research when my sister had breast cancer, which she overcame, and pancreatic cancer, to which she succumbed.

I saw the fallibility of doctors when one diagnosed my father's chest pains as resulting from a heart attack and sent him to the hospital. Just as he was about to receive blood-thinner medication – the typical treatment for heart blockage – an intern took a close look at Dad's fingernails. The color and texture can reveal a lot about a person's health. After checking, the intern determined the problem was internal bleeding from ulcers. "If we'd given you those blood thinners," the intern said, "you'd be dead."

My father, by the way, hated it when doctors were condescending. When he was hospitalized at 87 and asking about his prognosis, a doctor said, "What do you want me to do Mr. Wyner, make you younger?" Dad shot back: "Younger I've been, doctor; make me older."

THE 25TH SPOT

When I became involved with the medical community through Beth Israel, the American Cancer Society and the Bostoner Rebbe's ROFEH International, I took full advantage of the connections I made.

363

Employees at Shawmut knew they could come to my father or me when they had medical problems, because we would find them the best specialists. Thanks to the second opinions we arranged, one man avoided massive brain surgery and another having his liver removed. Most important to me, though, is that medical networking helped save my son Daniel.

Daniel was just 34 when he was diagnosed in 1993 with a form of lymphoma, the disease that had killed my father about a decade before at the age of 89. My dad had a form of the disease that progressed rapidly. Sadly, he died just a few years before a chemotherapy treatment was developed that might have prolonged his life. Daniel had a form of lymphoma that moved much more slowly, but was much more difficult to treat. The survival rate was just 25 percent.

Keeping up the spirits of my granddaughter Madelyn while her father, Daniel, undergoes cancer treatment in Seattle.

After the diagnosis, Daniel did everything imaginable to take care of himself. He stuck to a special diet that included seaweed and other unusual foods, for example. But his condition continued to deteriorate. At the time, I was on the board of the American Cancer Society and was among the lay-people serving on its allocations committee. As I result, I became familiar with who was doing what in cancer research. I talked to specialists at different hospitals to obtain different schools of thought. But it was thanks to a communications mix-up that I found the doctor who would be instrumental in helping Daniel conquer the disease.

I asked Dr. David Rosenthal at Beth Israel, a hematologist/oncologist and future president of the American Cancer Society, about a particular doctor. Rosenthal misheard the name I gave him. "Oh, you mean Ron Levy," he told me. I responded no, but asked who he was. Rosenthal explained that Levy had previously worked in Boston, but had since opened a research lab at Stanford. "You should call him," Rosenthal said. "He's doing interesting stuff."

Levy was harnessing the body's own immune system to target cancer cells and obtaining promising results with lymphoma. I called the Stanford lab and spoke with a member of Levy's team. She told me that one opening happened to remain in a 25-subject study. Daniel flew out to Stanford and snagged that precious spot. His lymphoma was put into remission for two years.

While being treated at Stanford, Daniel developed a close relationship with Levy's top assistant, Dr. David Maloney. By the time the lymphoma had reemerged, Maloney had moved to the Fred Hutchinson Cancer Research Institute in Seattle. There, Daniel underwent one of the first bone-marrow transplants involving the patient's own marrow. It was removed from his body, purified and then reinjected. For three months, Daniel was kept in extreme isolation, both for his own protection and that of others. The treatment temporarily made him radioactive, and removing the marrow had left him without an immune system. We had to talk to him through a lead door. In keeping with his normal manner, Daniel was very stoic through it all. Rather than giving in to self-pity, he expressed his determination to become cancer-free.

Daniel, in recovery mode, with Lorna and their daughter, Madelyn.

Along with Daniel's wife, Lorna, and young daughter, Madelyn, Genevieve and I moved out to Seattle for the duration. We made the Marriott Residence Inn downtown our temporary home. When Daniel was released, it was the last night of Chanukah. We celebrated in our room at the hotel. The menorah, with its full complement of candles aflame, sat in front of a picture window. Suddenly, we heard a bang. The candles had overheated the inside layer of glass, cracking it into a perfect menorah pattern. When I told the manager I would pay for the damage, he refused to take any money. We thought of the stunning pattern of cracks as a sign that Daniel would enjoy a full recovery. Several years later, when I was having prostate cancer treatment in Seattle, we returned to the hotel. Daniel and I ran into the same manager. We again apologized about the window. He said, "I thought it was a tremendously symbolic thing, and I never fixed it."

A CHANCE DIAGNOSIS

It was only by chance that doctors discovered I had prostate cancer. In the winter of 1997-98, I learned through the cancer society that Dr. Paul Church was conducting a study at the Deaconess Hospital to see whether ultrasound could detect prostate cancer better than a digital rectal examination. Although

I knew of no one in my family who had had that form of cancer, I volunteered for the study. The doctor noticed a speck on the ultrasound that was not evident in the digital exam. He recommended a biopsy, but my urologist at Beth Israel Hospital, Dr. William DeWolf, dismissed the suggestion.

DeWolf had been regularly doing my prostate-specific antigen (PSA) test. The results had been holding steady at 1.6, well below 4, the top of the normal range. I took his advice to return in a year for another check. When I did, the score had risen slightly to 1.8 – still in the normal range – but DeWolf felt a slight lump. This time, he agreed that a biopsy would be wise. It turned out that I indeed had prostate cancer, but at a modest level. As you might expect, I then embarked on a crash course about the disease, reading every book and scientific study I could find on the subject. I talked to a wide array of specialists, who offered conflicting advice. At Dana-Farber, specialists suggested radiation therapy; a Beth Israel doctor recommended hormone treatment. Other options included cryogenics, freezing the tumor, and radical prostatectomy, removing the prostate gland altogether. I surprised the doctors with the depth of my knowledge and the scientific papers I cited. I suppose I'm not one who believes too much knowledge is a dangerous thing, but it can complicate decision-making.

Ultimately, like Daniel, I ended up in Seattle. Dr. John Blasko, a radiation oncologist, had spent 10 years perfecting a treatment that involved using thin needles to place radioactive seeds directly into the prostate gland in and around the tumor. The five-year survival rate for Blasko's technique was the same as that for a radical prostatectomy. His procedure offered a key benefit: overnight recovery. Rebounding from the traditional treatment, major surgery, took much longer and could be accompanied by permanent complications. Too good to be true? Well, in my case, it turned out to be not so simple. The reason had to do with a different part of my body: my chest.

SPAGHETTI SCARE

Even though Blasko's treatment was minimally invasive and could be performed on an outpatient basis, I would still have to be knocked out. So, I had to be screened by an anesthesiologist. He asked me if I suffered from acid reflux. At the time, I had been experiencing heartburn, which I attributed to my stressful schedule. I told him I had been taking Gelusil and other indigestion medications. He said he would insert a breathing tube through my mouth as a precaution in case I had an attack of reflux while I was under sedation. That would avoid the risk of my accidentally choking.

The anesthesiologist's question about acid reflux nagged at me. So, I asked my physician at the time whether he, too, believed I suffered from acid reflux. He told me that he thought I did. When I said that I still wanted to see a cardiologist to make sure the condition wasn't something more serious, he expressed indignation that I doubted his diagnosis. That didn't stop me from going to Beth Israel's head of cardiology, Dr. Julian Aroesty, whom I knew from my work on hospital committees.

I recounted to Aroesty a disturbing experience I had had just the week before after having a plate of spaghetti at a Newton restaurant. It was the middle of winter. When we stepped outside into the frigid air, I was overcome by horrendous heartburn. I spent 10 minutes sitting in the car drinking Gelusil before I felt well enough to drive. The cardiologist said that didn't sound to him like a simple case of heartburn. He suggested doing an angiogram to check the blood flow to my heart. It was a Friday, and he arranged the procedure for the following Monday morning. "There's a guy at the hospital who is the best in the world," he assured me.

Monday morning, I found myself dressed in a surgical gown and laid out on a gurney watching a television screen tuned to a probe of my arteries. I could have been sedated, but I wanted to be fully awake so I could watch the procedure and be involved in any decisions that might arise. The doctors injected me with a dye that they could follow as it circulated through my bloodstream. For a few minutes, the dye spread at the expected pace. But then it hit a roadblock in one of the arteries, with only a tiny amount seeping through. The medical team said that that blockage explained the agony I had felt in the restaurant parking lot. The frigid temperatures had shrunken the already narrowed blood vessel, completely blocking the flow. What I felt to be heartburn was in fact angina pain.

The doctors said they could place a stent in the vessel to keep it open. Despite the serious situation, I retained my sense of humor. I asked what brand of stent they planned to use. "Why do you care?" they responded. I explained, somewhat tongue-in-cheek, that my daughter-in-law was descended from the family that founded Johnson & Johnson, so I felt a sense of brand loyalty. They said that the J&J stent wasn't flexible enough for that area of the vessel. I wasn't in a position to argue. As I watched the screen, they installed the stent. That allowed the dye to flow freely, but soon it hit another blockage. I readily granted permission for the doctors to install another stent.

At the end, they said, "If you really want a J&J stent, we can put it between the other two to finish off the procedure." My feeble attempt at a joke got me three stents instead of two. The entire procedure took perhaps 45 minutes. I haven't had chest pains since. Nor have I gotten around to telling my daughter-in-law about how I did my part for J&J.

PROSTATE ROULETTE

Now to return to my prostate. After I had the stents installed, the doctors put me on blood-thinner medication to keep clots from forming before I healed from the procedure. When Blasko heard I was on the medication, he said he would have to postpone the operation. Without the benefit of today's electronic detectors, doctors then could only be sure they had seeded the entire prostate by pricking the adjacent bladder wall. Normally that results in very mild bleeding into the bladder that's easy to control. But it can be severe if the patient is on blood-thinners.

The problem with delaying surgery was that the radioactive seeds that would destroy the cancer cells had already been ordered. You can't just go on Amazon and have them delivered the next day. Nor can you just stash them in the freezer until they are needed. There was a narrow window of time between when the seeds arrived and when they would lose their radioactive potency. The seeds scheduled for my procedure had a half life of only 27 days. Blasko and my cardiologist worked out a compromise date for me to stop taking the blood thinners. Otherwise, the procedure would have been delayed by at least four months because the manufacturer of the seeds couldn't keep up with the increasing demand for them.

Normally, the prostate procedure is routine. You go under anesthesia at 10, and the work is done by noon. At 2 p.m., you can leave the hospital. The next morning you return for the doctor to make a quick check for complications and schedule a follow-up for a year later. As I said, that's what normally happens. My body, against our hopes, still retained residual amounts of the blood thinner medication. As a result, I experienced extensive bleeding in my bladder, producing a dozen clots that my body would somehow have to pass. Over 24 excruciating hours in the hospital, I was administered gallons of saline solution to promote urine flow through a catheter that felt as if it were the width of a garden hose. (It was probably more like a half-inch in diameter, but considering where the tube was inserted … well, you get the picture.)

But after it was all over, I didn't regret my decision to turn to Blasko. A heart specialist couldn't have been expected to know that his medication would conflict with a particular treatment for prostate cancer. I've always believed that the worst action is inaction. Some prostate specialists had recommended no treatment at all, prescribing instead "watchful waiting." For me, that would have been the ultimate agony.

By the way, Blasko's method has since become one of the main procedures of choice for prostate cancer, including at hospitals in Boston.

DOCTOR'S RX: SHUT UP

My mother's advice served me well when I suffered another form of cancer. She would say if you ever find that your voice is hoarse for a prolonged period, see a doctor. In 2012, I suddenly found it more and more difficult to speak. My doctor recommended that I see Dr. Harsha Gopal, who had been a leader in nose and throat care at Beth Israel for three decades. Much to my alarm, he matter-of-factly inserted a tube with a remote camera up my nose to peer down my throat. Over several visits to his Chestnut Hill office, I was forced to get used to these nasal invasions, but they were not pleasant. After his first look, Gopal said the culprit appeared to be a benign polyp on a vocal cord. He said he could remove it with a laser, but he advised holding off. It was possible that the polyp would go away on its own if I didn't speak for four or five weeks. So, I kept quiet for the prescribed period. I couldn't even whisper, which Gopal said would do more damage than speaking.

The timing was bad; a number of business matters demanded my vocal participation. Ever the researcher, I discovered iPad applications that would speak for me. With a tap, I could choose among several standard spiels I had typed in, such as one explaining why I couldn't speak. The funny thing was that people understood me better when I used the artificial female voice.

Unfortunately, the polyp failed to succumb to the silent treatment. Gopal told me he'd have to numb my throat and then zap it with a CO_2 laser. Despite his confidence, I felt uneasy and sought out a second opinion. After surveying all the throat specialists in Greater Boston, I found only one who had what I considered sufficient experience in my problem, Dr. Steven Zeitels at Mass General Hospital. My physician, Dr. Steven Flier, told me that as far as he knew, Zeitels devoted himself to research, making rare exceptions, say, for prominent singers.

THE MAN WHO SAVED MY VOICE

I figured I had run out of options. I'd go with Gopal. He had assured me it was a simple procedure, and he had been doing it for 30 years. On the Friday before my Wednesday date with the laser, someone told me about a TV news segment describing how a revolutionary procedure had restored the voice of the British singer Adele. She was going to perform at the Grammys that Sunday and credited a Boston doctor for her recovery. That doctor was Zeitels.

I quickly found out all I could about what made Zeitels special. Unlike Gopal and most laryngeal surgeons, Zeitels does not use a CO_2 laser. The downside of that instrument is that it emits a continuous beam that can be very powerful; turned up high, it can pierce a hole in a cement floor. Zeitels uses a potassium-titanyl-phosphate (KTP) laser. Its first advantage is that it automatically pulses, reducing the risk of "overcooking" the surgical site. After administering a pulse, Zeitels checks the results and then, if necessary, fires another one. Second, the laser emits a green beam that only affects the red cells – the ones likely to be diseased – and thus spares healthy tissue.

As I wasn't in the same class as his other patients, such as Cher and Steven Tyler, I figured I would need some pull just to get Zeitels's attention. I first tried to locate a golfing friend of mine, Arthur Goldstein, who was one of the most influential trustees of the Partners HealthCare System. Then serendipity struck again. Mervin Gray, a member of our Marriage Encounter Havurah, happened to call Genevieve to ask how I was doing. Mervin had noticed that my voice was hoarse when our group had last met. After she told him about my problem, Mervin said that Zeitels had successfully treated him for throat cancer five years before. When Genevieve told him how I was trying to find someone with enough clout to reach Zeitels, Mervin said. "What do you need pull for? I don't think you need any pull." Mervin volunteered to contact Zeitels for me, calling back shortly later to say I would be Zeitels's first appointment on Tuesday. It could have been sooner, but the doctor had that date with the Grammys.

Zeitels turned out to be anything but the stereotypical aloof, arrogant giant of medicine. Slightly balding with a mustache and a closely trimmed beard, he put on absolutely no airs. He was warm and humble. We hit it off immediately. Soon we were on a first-name basis.

After an examination, he told me that the polyp might very well be a malignant growth. He said that had I undergone the operation I had originally scheduled, the surgeon would likely have found the cancer and used the CO_2 laser to remove surrounding tissue as a precaution. That could have left me mute. Steven, as I called him now, said that with his laser he could zap the problem area with little risk to my voice.

A week later, I went under Steven's laser. An hour after the operation, I woke up from the anesthesia. My voice was back to normal, but I was cautioned to rest it for a while. At the follow-up appointment, he showed me a video of my procedure. It was like mud being hosed off a shiny car fender. The machine just went click, click, click – and the growth was gone.

Genevieve and I have since become good friends with Steven, cheering him on as he goes from success to success. He has teamed up with an MIT chemical engineer to create a polymer that could cure some children born mute and restore the voices of adults scarred by extreme use, tumors and botched operations. If the procedure passes scientific muster, it will provide flexibility to stiff and paralyzed vocal cords.

Julie Andrews, who had undergone numerous unsuccessful operations to restore her glorious voice before seeing Steven, is honorary chair of the board of directors of his Voice Health Institute. It has held benefits on both coasts, including one that Genevieve and I attended at Club Passim, where singer after singer recounted how the doctor had saved their careers. Google co-founder Larry Page, who has suffered repeated bouts of vocal-cord paralysis, has contributed more than $10 million to Steven's work.

If only the mechanics of health care funding could keep up with medical research. Just before my procedure, Steven told me, with some embarrassment, that we had a payment problem. The only insurance he accepted was Medicare, and he had just learned I was on Shawmut's Blue Cross plan. "What kind of guy at 87 doesn't have Medicare?" he asked me.

Steven said he stopped taking Blue Cross after saving a singer's "$75 million voice." "I only got $600 for the operation, and the fellow wouldn't even pay the copay," the surgeon told me. "I decided if I take Medicare, I'll be taking care of all the people who are needy."

With apologies, he said he would have to charge me his regular fee of $10,000. I was happy to pay, knowing full well that much of the money would be plowed back into his research. Steven is not living high off the hog; he works all the time.

Incidentally, when I turned 65, I did go on Medicare. But I dropped it after my doctor was reimbursed just $35 for a visit. I thought, what's this? I'm suddenly being charged as if I were a charity case? So, I switched to the company plan and work just enough hours to cover the premium.

One other takeaway from my experience with Steven Zeitels: Remember how intimidated I was about making an appointment with him? That experience helped me understand why I had to work so hard as town moderator to persuade residents that I was indeed approachable.

TRYING NOT TO BE MORBID

Lessons I've learned on how to live – and how to die

I HAVE ENJOYED THE good fortune to live beyond 90 with my faculties intact. The downside has been experiencing the loss of many relatives and friends. They approached death, as they lived their lives, each in their own way.

Cancer claimed many people on my mother's side of the family. I remember the day at Beth Israel when the biopsy results came in on a lump in my mother's breast. Dr. David Freiman, the head of the Department of Pathology, was a good friend of my parents. When he came out to tell my father that my mother had cancer, Dr. Freiman had tears in his eyes. Despite an operation, the cancer reappeared in her bones. Especially her last year, she suffered intensely. Still deeply private, she kept her condition secret to all but her immediate family – not even telling her siblings. She continued to attend family gatherings, concealing the excruciating pain she felt when moving about. Mother died the way she lived, her spirit strong to the end.

My sister, Elizabeth, twice overcame breast cancer. But in 2010, about a decade after the second bout, she was diagnosed with pancreatic cancer, which rarely lets its victims escape. Once diagnosed, she remained as active as possible. She didn't want to miss a day of living life. Over her last days, she invited all her relatives and close friends over to her house to say farewell. To ease their discomfort – which seemed to concern her more than her own – she talked about her philosophy of life. "This is it," Betty said. "I'm happy with what I've done, and I just wanted to say goodbye to everybody." And then she said goodbye to me.

I didn't say goodbye to my father. I remained by his side, but I felt that to say goodbye was to suggest I was giving up on him. I'm sure, though, he knew it was the end. He fell into unconsciousness, and I was out of the room when he died. My nephew David was with him.

My grandfather George died in the best possible way: as he was lacing up his shoes to go fishing. Although it was the middle of winter – the second day of 1943 – he had intended to make the long detour from his Ritz-Carlton apartment to his favorite spot at Long Pond in Plymouth before heading into work at his Tremont Street office. The Wyner family didn't shield children from death. Indeed, the night before my grandfather's funeral, his casket lay in the living room of our house on Dean Road (somewhat to my mother's chagrin). Heavy snow kept many people from visiting, except for the extended family. In keeping with Jewish tradition, a man called a shomer prayed over the casket until late into the night. Uncle Sol, the municipal judge, arranged for the town to plow out the area in front of the house for the funeral procession.

Death was treated differently in Genevieve's family. She recalled coming home one day to find her mother forlornly sitting on a soapbox, a simple ritual in keeping with Orthodox tradition. She asked her mother what was wrong. Finally, her mother told her that her own mother had died.

I'm now past the age my father was when he died. Sometimes when I wake up in the morning and feel a bad headache or new pain, I wonder if I should call a doctor. I realize, though, that you can't do that all the time. I just remind myself, "Hey, you're 92." On other days, I'll go down to the gym to work out, and people will say, "Oh boy, you're an example for me." But then I knew a woman at Rowes Wharf who at 101 still worked out regularly with a personal trainer in the gym. More than once she whispered conspiratorially to me: "Don't tell my son that I came down here without my cane!"

As you get older, you realize that every day is special. You can waste a few when you're younger. But at my age, you ask yourself each night: What did I do today?

I'm reminded of Jacob Rader Marcus, who was a predecessor of mine as president of the American Jewish Historical Society and a professor of American Jewish history at Hebrew Union College in Cincinnati (where he mentored Sarna). We became fast friends when at my first meeting of the college's board of governors he pulled me aside to ask about people he knew in Boston like Rabbi Bernard Mehlman. When I became AJHS president, he told me to feel free to call him for advice after he was done working for the day. He said that would be at 11:30 or 12. I assumed he meant noon, but it turned out he finished around midnight. Whenever I called, he'd say, "Let me get comfortable, and we'll talk." He kept me up late, but I learned a lot from him.

For some time, Jacob had been working on a three-volume history of American Jews. At 98, he told me that he worried whether he would live long enough to finish the final volume. So, I said to him, "My understanding is that if you have a holy purpose, the Lord will keep you going. Why don't you make it a 20-volume set? Then you'll live to the proverbial 120."

One day in 1995 he just fell asleep and died. He was 99.

ONE OF THE CHOSEN

In which I confront anti-Semitism – real and imagined

MY FATHER USED TO tell me the story of when he went fishing with his dad and caught a lesson about anti-Semitism.

They had hired two local boys, aged about 10 and 12, to row them around Long Pond in Plymouth. My father and grandfather asked the boys about their lives and their outlooks. They discovered that the youngsters knew little about the world outside their town. They couldn't even name the president of the United States. And when asked if they knew what a Jew was, they offered this definition: "a dirty old man with a beard." They had no idea that the people they were rowing around were Jewish.

My dad didn't think those boys were anti-Semitic, only ignorant. That was often my experience as well with people who made anti-Semitic comments. Once I talked with them, I realized that many of them had never met a Jew and were just repeating what they had heard growing up. I've also found that ignorance cuts both ways: Jews sometimes assume prejudice to exist where it doesn't at all.

I don't want in any way to minimize the damage inflicted by hatred. It was anti-Semitism that drove my grandparents out of Eastern Europe. I came of age during the Holocaust. As a Jewish leader, I witnessed the ugly demise of the Jewish community in Roxbury and Mattapan.

While I was growing up, some hotels still posted signs saying that Jews were not allowed. When we visited with my mother's parents vacationing in the White Mountains in the late '30s, I noticed a sign outside the Maplewood Hotel in Bethlehem, New Hampshire, that said: "No Hebrew Clientele." The small sign was posted in an almost casual fashion on the front lawn, much like those that say, "Keep Off the Grass." Perhaps such a sign suited a town named for the one where – according to Christian teachings – Jesus's family was told there was no room at the inn.

Genevieve recalls that when she traveled with her brother, a competitive tennis player, they would often encounter restricted hotels. Her mother's attitude was to stay anyway. "We'll tell them when we leave," she would say.

But looking back, I encountered relatively little anti-Semitism compared with my peers. While my family was prominent in the Jewish community, especially my grandmother with Hadassah and Beth Israel Hospital, we did not socialize exclusively with Jews. And within the Jewish community, my father served as sort of a bridge between Lithuanians (Litvaks) like us, who had settled mainly in Boston, and the German Jews, who had arrived earlier and were established in Cambridge. For example, two prominent members of Belmont Country Club who were of German-Jewish heritage – Frank Vorenberg, president of Gilchrist's, a venerable Boston department store, and Alan Steinert, regional distributor for RCA and Whirlpool – rarely spoke to anyone but my father.

ISN'T EVERYONE JEWISH?

Until I was 5 or 6, I thought we were like everyone else. I just assumed that everybody broke challah and said Kiddush on Friday nights. We did not identify it as being Jewish or not. When the McAuliffe brothers on Clark Road taunted each other by saying "dirty Jew," I didn't take it personally. I didn't even realize the phrase was anti-Semitic. I just thought it was something you called people when you were angry. I soon discovered that was not the case. Mad that my mother was making me do something I didn't want to do, I called her "a dirty Jew." She was shocked. When my father came home that night, she told him, "Justin has to start Sunday school right away."

Our Passover ritual was to attend the first-night seder at the house of my mother's parents. On the second night we were with my father's parents at Sunset Lodge, a retreat on Lake Massapoag in Sharon then owned by Louis and Mae Dubinsky. It was a huge affair, with as many as 400 people. I don't remember much about the seder itself, but I do recall wandering around the basement of the lodge and discovering a room filled with slot machines. They've been a mystery to me ever since.

I became aware of the Nazis through a trip to the dentist. It was in 1934, the year after Hitler took power. After the checkup, the dentist gave me a little toy automobile. It was an innocent enough gift, but when my mother turned it over, she saw it had been made in Germany. "We don't touch anything made in Germany, because they are mean to Jews," she declared, and tossed the toy in the trash.

At my elementary school, Runkle, Jews were in the minority, and they accounted for only a handful of students at Rivers, the private school I next attended. I don't recall being bullied because of my religion, but I did notice at Rivers that people looked at me as though I were somehow different. One of my few idols at Rivers was Melvin Gordon, who was about four years my senior. He played football at Rivers and later at Harvard. Melvin followed his father into the hosiery manufacturing business, but switched from socks to sweets when he got married. His wife, Ellen, comes from the family that owns Tootsie Roll. He shared the title of company CEO with his wife until his death in 2015.

At Roxbury Latin, the one possibly veiled reference to my religion was a quotation attributed to me in the yearbook, saying I could get you a blazer cheap. I had found a company at 600 Washington Street that was willing to sell us school blazers at a cut-rate price. My year's class was the only one that I know of that had its own blazers. Years later, I still cringe a bit when I read that line in the yearbook.

TESTING MY FAITH

I experienced anti-Semitism of both the unintentional and the intentional kind at Tufts. A guy in my dorm the first year loved to tell jokes. He could be very funny, but sometimes he would tell jokes about Jews. When friends told me they thought he was anti-Semitic, I defended him. He seemed too nice a guy for that. I knew he came from the Midwest and assumed he grew up without meeting any Jews. I took him aside and told him that I was Jewish and that his jokes about Jews made me uncomfortable. I never heard him tell a Jewish joke again.

My only consequential encounter with anti-Semitism at Tufts was with a professor of organic chemistry, Paul H. Doleman, who was also head of the chemistry department. Chemistry was my major, and organic was to be my specialty. I took one of his courses over the summer. Doleman scheduled finals for Yom Kippur. I told him I could not take the test that day because of the holiday. He said he gave makeup exams only if students were ill. Take the test with everyone else or score a zero, he told me.

I appealed to the college president, who instructed the professor to give me the makeup. It was a killer test, compared with the one my classmates were given. That put a big dent in my otherwise high marks. The following year Doleman again scheduled finals on a Jewish holiday, and he again gave me a killer test. Had it not been for my marks in those two classes, I would have graduated magna (high) or summa (highest) rather than cum laude (with honors).

Doleman, I later learned, also served on the nominating committee of the Longwood Cricket Club in Chestnut Hill. Until he stepped down, the club had had no Jewish members.

'THAT JEWISH FELLOW'

I didn't know many Jews at Tufts, but made it a point to change that after overhearing my name while standing in the line at the school cafeteria. A group of Jewish commuter students were talking about what they thought was an absence of Jews among campus leaders. I suddenly realized that they did not recognize me as being Jewish. To rectify that, I joined Avukah, a Zionist group that at the time was the only Jewish organization on campus. Hillel had yet to come along, and I wasn't interested in joining either of the two Jewish fraternities because I found the fraternity system as a whole too limiting.

After I entered the business world, I occasionally would hear anti-Semitic comments, but found I could silence them pretty quickly. During the Korean War, I took a trip to the Philadelphia Quartermaster Depot to bid on contracts to make long underwear that was crucial for winter combat. Many of my competitors were from Gentile-owned manufacturers, including P. H. Hanes, Jockey, Munsingwear and Standard Knitting Mills. After the bidding, they said, "Come on, Jerry, let's have lunch at the Union League Club." An elite club to this day, it didn't welcome Jews back in the '50s. But I wanted to be friendly, and so went along. As we were sitting around the table, some of the others began talking about an out-sider who had made a bid. They referred to him in what seemed like a derogatory way as "this Jewish fellow." I hesitated about reminding them that I was Jewish. If I did, I thought, they would probably say something like, "Well, you're different." At last, though, I did speak up. I said I had no problem with their talking about whether someone had appropriate business ethics or policies, but I did have a problem with their associating that with his religion. As I had expected, they quickly assured me that they didn't think of me in that way and that they each had many Jewish friends whom they admired.

Today, no one would dare refer to someone as "that black" or "that Jew" or even "that woman." Back then, I think many of those who used the word "Jew" did so with a mixture of prejudice and envy. It was shorthand for someone sharp in business. I suspect many of them had never really gotten to know anyone who was Jewish.

WYNER-STYLE KOSHER

At another luncheon, the fact that I was known to be Jewish had very different consequences. This one was held by Waltham's board of trade. I was invited after Vanta – the Shawmut subsidiary I ran early in my career – moved to Waltham from Newton. Lobster was on the menu. Following the Wyner family's expansive definition, shellfish is not exactly kosher, but not exactly *treif*, either. My father reasoned that the kosher restriction was no longer relevant because it stemmed from the pre-refrigeration era when spoilage was an ever-present danger and that, unlike pork, shellfish was not specifically forbidden in the Torah. Still, for such rationalizations, Genevieve would call us "Yankee Jews." But most non-Jews don't know that shellfish is treif to more observant Jews. Unfortunately for me, a rabbi was among my fellow diners at the Waltham luncheon. When he was asked if he wanted lobster, he declined. When the waiter got to me, I declined as well. I felt it would only confuse people if I tried to explain the intricacies of Reform Yankee Judaism.

Wyner-style kosher, though, can be very strict, as my father discovered to his embarrassment. Just after his discharge from the Navy, he met his dad at a lunch counter near the train station. When my father ordered a ham sandwich, my grandfather, without saying a word, stood up and walked out. My father didn't finish the sandwich; in fact, he never ate a ham sandwich again so far as I know. He recounted the story to me, and it had a profound effect. It drove home the importance of respecting our ancestors, who had been dishonored by being forced to eat pork.

There was only one time that I ate pork, and I felt that God would have approved. When I visited our factory in Puerto Rico during the 1950s, I would immerse myself in the culture. I believed that you could not understand a people without developing a taste for the food that they liked. I sampled all types of Puerto Rican cuisine, except for pork dishes.

One weekend, I was staying by myself at the Villa Parguera on the south side of the island. I ordered a dish that I had come to particularly like, *estofado de cabrito* (roast stuffed nanny goat). Surprised by my choice, a young native-born lawyer at another table told me how pleased he was that I had ordered local cuisine. We got to chatting, and I told him my story. A little later, he came over and said that his mother wanted to invite me to their home in the mountains so she could prepare a native meal.

When I arrived, she greeted me with great enthusiasm and told me she had been cooking all day for this unusual American her son had told her about. The dish turned out to be pork. Seeing the pride in her face, I felt that God would not want me to disappoint her by declining the meal. So, I ate with relish, including the second helping she offered, and made sure to leave nothing on my plate. What better way could there be to show my appreciation for her efforts to please a stranger? For the record, though, I did try my best not to enjoy the meal too much.

BREAKING INTO THE CLUB

To return to the subject of ignorance, it can be responsible for misperceptions about prejudice. My father thought that clubs took on an exclusive veneer not so much out of hatred or bigotry as to avoid disturbing anyone's comfort zone: They wanted to admit only people who were already part of the larger social circles of their members. In the case of hotels, he said, the owners might have barred Jews for the sake of snob appeal. Ironically, many people thought the Ritz, because of Uncle Eddie's rigorous reservation policy, didn't admit Jews.

My father's policy was never to assume anything about membership rules. He encouraged me to join the Harvard clubs in Boston and New York, which were viewed as Yankee bastions. Dad said that people saw names like Cabot and Lowell on the membership committees and figured that anyone with a name like Goldberg or Cohen didn't have a chance. In fact, my father had joined the Harvard Club back in 1915. He called a couple of people on the membership committee, told them he had just graduated and asked if they could become acquainted before he applied for admission. They responded immediately with an invitation to get together. Soon after that, he was in the club. He was followed by several other Jews, including his brother-in-law Sol Wyner and friend Ben Trustman.

Decades went by without any other Jews applying until I broke the phantom barrier. In 1948, after I had graduated from business school, my father suggested that I, too, should join the Boston club. He knew a top executive of First National Bank of Boston, John Toulmin, who was on the membership committee, and recommended calling him. This was an era when you could do such things without it being considered pushy. After a very cordial meeting with Toulmin, I was easily admitted. When a friend said to me, "How'd you get in there? They don't take Jews," I replied, echoing my father. "It's not that they don't take Jews. It's that the nominating committee people don't know any Jews."

It didn't take the Harvard Club long to realize that Jews offered a potentially large pool of recruits, and it appointed Trustman, by then a prominent attorney, to the nominating committee. Within a few years, the club not only had many Jewish members but had elected one of them president, Sidney Miller.

Decades later in the 1970s, when I was making almost weekly trips to New York to drum up laminating business for our factory and either staying in hotels or taking the train back the same day, my father urged me to join the New York Harvard Club and make it my base of operations. By then, we no longer had a New York office. As a graduate of the business school, I was eligible for membership, but the club had very few Jews (my uncle IA Wyner, among them) and was viewed as being very exclusive. I asked two acquaintances to sponsor me: Elliot Richardson, then a member of President Richard Nixon's Cabinet, whose wife, Anne, I knew from Town Meeting, and Ames Stevens, a textile firm owner with whom we did business. With their backing I got in, and the Harvard Club became my New York base. As there weren't cell phones in those days, I told colleagues that they could reach me by calling the club. Our competitors, most of whom were New York-based, didn't know what to make of a guy who didn't have a local office and lived out of the Harvard Club. When they lost business to me – an upstart from Boston – they assumed that I was paring prices to the bone. I told them that if I ever found out that I was quoting prices as low as theirs, I would be very disappointed. It was a matter of pride for us that we won our customers through prompt delivery and top quality.

Conducting a family seder in the '90s at our Impact 2000 house in Newton.

KADDISH AND KINDNESS

Besides closing doors – or seeming to close doors – being Jewish opens them as well. I discovered that during the 11-month mourning period when I would attend synagogue daily, morning and evening, to say Kaddish for each of my parents after they passed away. It was through my father that I had come to appreciate the meaning behind the ritual. I was commuting with him to work during the mourning period for his parents. On the way to work and again on the way home, we would stop at a shul. As our route took us through Roxbury and Mattapan, we would vary the program by visiting different synagogues. Since membership in the smaller places was inexpensive, we would often join, even if we knew we were unlikely to return. Already in the 1950s, it was clear that synagogues in that once thriving area were falling on hard times. On occasion, we would find there were not enough men to form a minyan. When we explained why we came, a regular would sometimes step outside on the street and call out in Yiddish: *"A Yid vil machen Kaddish"* (A Jew wants to make Kaddish). Often, men who had just left after the regular morning or evening service would return; it was considered a great mitzvah to make a minyan for a mourner.

My father in his later years: He cautioned me about the hazards of Kaddish.

After seeing me say Kaddish for the full 11 months after my mother died in 1965, my father told me not to do the same for him. "I want you to promise me that after 30 days, you'll break the chain," he said. "Otherwise, 10 months down the line, you'll be racing in a car to get to a morning or evening service to say Kaddish, so as not to break your perfect record, and accidentally kill someone. You can't put that on yourself."

As I traveled frequently on business, it was inevitable that I would be away at some point while saying Kaddish for my parents. I discovered that synagogues, even overseas, treat you much differently if you say you're in mourning. When I walked into the Great Synagogue in Amsterdam, I was initially brushed off as being yet another tourist. But when I said I wanted to say Kaddish, I was welcomed to the service they were holding in a small chapel. Afterward, I was given a tour of the sanctuary, during which the cantor went out of his way to sing to me from the bimah. I thought, wow, this really is something. But shortly after I returned home, the cantor wrote me. He wanted help finding a job in America.

While I was saying Kaddish for my mother, I had to visit Manchester, England, to see a business partner. I was concerned that I would miss the evening prayer because I had arrived at the airport at 6 p.m. I phoned the office of the local dayan (the Jewish equivalent of a bishop for the area) and explained my situation. I was told that I was too late for the service, but members of a study session that night would be happy to join me afterward in a brief evening service (Maariv) so that I could say Kaddish.

I should note that in Britain, most Jews are either Orthodox or Conservative. When I arrived at the synagogue, the people in the group asked about my shul back home. I decided it would be better to refer to my affiliation with Kehillath Israel, a Conservative congregation in Brookline, than to my main synagogue, Temple Israel in Boston, which is Reform. To my surprise, one of them said he had a daughter who lived in Coolidge Corner, and another had a distant relative who lived in the area. The Jewish world is full of connections.

They then asked me to lead the service. I was a bit nervous about that, but managed OK. Afterward, they offered to pick me up at my hotel in the morning so I could have a kosher breakfast. I politely declined. I later read in a Manchester Jewish paper that the local dayan had just made a controversial decision to ban a team from a Jewish soccer league because its members came from a Reform synagogue. Thinking back to the impromptu prayers I had led, I wondered how my fellow worshippers would have reacted had they known I was Reform.

ACCUSED OF A SHONDA

On a few isolated occasions in America, I felt uncomfortable while saying Kaddish in unfamiliar synagogues. Close to where I was staying in Miami was a storefront Lubavitch shul. For the morning services, I put on a yarmulke and tallit. A man next to me asked why I was not putting on tefillin, and he kept insisting that I put them on. He said it was a shonda – a shameful act – not to put on tefillin. I might as well take off my yarmulke and stamp on it, he said. I told him that what he was doing was worse: He was interfering with my prayer.

When we vacationed at Mashnee Village in Buzzards Bay, I would occasionally attend a small shul in Onset, where my father's family had summered when he was a boy. In the 1950s and 1960s, Rabbi Joseph B. Soloveitchik prayed at the shul during summer vacations. While Rabbi Soloveitchik is revered as a brilliant Talmudic scholar and as the founder of the Maimonides School in Brookline, I witnessed him at one of his less eminent moments. It was a Friday night in 1966 following my mother's death. For the Shabbat Kiddush, according to Jewish ritual, children are to partake in the wine. Apparently, that night, the children hadn't finished their glass. The rabbi considered that a great affront and vociferously expressed his outrage. That was the last time I attended services there. I continued paying my annual dues, until for the fourth year in a row, the synagogue misspelled my name. I decided that if the leaders really considered me to be part of their congregation, they should at least get my name right.

Even when I wasn't saying Kaddish, I enjoyed the international benefits of being Jewish. When a textiles expo was held in Düsseldorf in the late '60s, I felt conflicted about visiting Germany, as the Holocaust was still very much in the recent past. By the time Genevieve and I decided to attend, all the hotels were booked. The expo's travel department informed us that we could stay in a private home. That made me even more uncomfortable. I didn't want to spend the trip wondering if my hosts or their parents had been complicit in the annihilation of my fellow Jews. After some hesitation, I wrote the organizers about my concerns. Genevieve was startled by my frankness, but I wasn't the only one with such reservations. I heard back from a person who identified herself as head of a committee established to reach out to Jews. She said they would arrange for us to stay at a Jewish home for the aged, which was hosting other Jewish mill owners.

Our room was gorgeous – nothing like what you would expect in a nursing home. To my embarrassment, I discovered I was out of the local currency. When I asked the head of the home where I could change money, he insisted on advancing me some $1,000 in German marks. Even though he had never seen me before, he said, "Just send me a check when you get home." What a wonderful fraternity we Jews live among – that people have that kind of trust.

THE HOLY LAND

In the footsteps of Moses, Gussie and my favorite childhood author

ON OUR FIRST VISIT to Israel, we could see, but not visit, Old Jerusalem.

The year was 1966. Along with Norman and Eleanor Rabb, Genevieve and I led a tour sponsored by the Young Executives Group of Combined Jewish Philanthropies. From our balcony at the King David Hotel, we could gaze beyond a stretch of no-man's land at the Old City. But for the taxis and honking of horns, I could imagine that I was looking at a scene right out of the Bible.

It was almost more inspiring to me than when I returned to Israel after the Six-Day War – this unreachable Jerusalem that I could see from afar was so full of life. My family history was out there. My grandmother Gussie's father and grandfather were buried somewhere out there. My grandmother herself had worked for Hadassah projects when the land was still called Palestine.

Our guides took us up to the roof of a Catholic convent next to the border with East Jerusalem, then under Jordanian control. From our perch, we had a sweeping view of the ancient city. And a half dozen Arab soldiers had a close-up view of us. I was startled to see them lying prone on a building fewer than 15 feet away, pointing their rifles at us. On this peaceful day, it was a shocking reminder that we were in a nation that any day could be at war.

JOURNEY UNDER JERUSALEM

Returning to Israel after the Six-Day War to deliver a paper on laminating at the International Conference of Knitting Technologists, I fulfilled my lifelong dream of retracing Richard Halliburton's 1920s trek through Hezekiah's Tunnel, which I had read about as a boy.

The tunnel was believed to have been built in the eighth century BCE by the biblical King Hezekiah to provide the city access to water in case of a siege. Considered an engineering marvel, it meanders for 2,000 yards from Gihon Springs to the Pool of Siloam. Tunnelers worked from each end, meeting up almost precisely at the intended spot, guided by people on the surface listening to the sound of hammering.

When I wrote ahead to Israel's Department of Antiquities for permission to tour the tunnel, the officials essentially responded, "Be our guest." They told me that they had yet to explore many of the hundreds of tunnels that ran under the city. At that time, surprisingly, Hezekiah's wasn't high on their list. A guide who had previously helped my father put me in touch with an Arab antiquities dealer in the Old City. The dealer assigned an Arab boy to lead me through the tunnel. Accompanying us was Gerald Varley, an English colleague of mine from the knitting industry. The dealer gave me the impression that we would be among the first tourists to explore the biblical marvel since the Six-Day War.

GUSSIE'S LEGACY

In another chapter, I recount how my Aunt Frances and her daughter, Anne, helped Austrian journalist Otto Zausmer and his wife flee the Nazis for America. A dozen years later, as an editor for *The Boston Globe*, Otto reported from Israel on the "New England Village of Ben Shemen." Rising on a bluff overlooking the Mediterranean, the village was home to orphaned children. "[N]ot too long ago the cornerstone was laid on the highest point of the bluff for a George Wyner (Boston) community center, which will provide a playroom, reading room and many other facilities," Zausmer wrote.

Actually, the center was to be named not for George, but for Gussie, who had died a few years earlier. My father had donated the money at the urging of Mrs. J. A. Gordon, a Brookline woman who had spearheaded fund-raising for the village. Decades later, when we visited the village, we found the community hall, but it was Mrs. Gordon's name that appeared on the main entrance. On a side entrance, we found my grandmother's name.

I doubt Gussie would have made a fuss over where her name appeared. She was more concerned about the children. And, according to a May 14, 1949, *Globe* article, it was Mrs. Gordon's idea to build a children's village. "Hadassah women, by their fund-raising, were able to transport Jewish orphans from Europe to Israel, but due to the increasing influx of immigrants, many children had to live in tents," she told a regional conference. New England Hadassah chapters raised more than $100,000 for the village. "In the near future," the article reported, "the cornerstone will be laid for the first house in the name of Mrs. George (Gussie) Wyner, who was one of the first to subscribe to a unit." My grandmother had died just a month before the article appeared.

We started out at the Pool of Siloam on the south slope of the city. Wearing just a bathing suit, I waded through the pool to stairs that led to the tunnel. With only my guide's candle for illumination, we walked deeper and deeper into the tunnel. In several places, I had to duck to avoid hitting my head on the ceiling. I became accustomed to the cool water, which occasionally came within two feet of the ceiling. The walls were chiseled and regular in shape. The only sound was the rustle of the water as we passed through it. Looking back, I'm surprised I didn't feel claustrophobic, but I was probably too excited to be nervous.

When we reached the spring at the other end, we tromped up ancient, but still sturdy, stone stairs to the surface. Afterward, we returned to the store of the antiquities dealer and celebrated our trip. The jolly owner presented us with a gift of fresh green figs. Those figs gave me the worst diarrhea I've ever had. Halliburton hadn't warned me about the runs.

FLEECED WITH A SHEEPSKIN

On that trip, I had another adventure – this one above ground in Hebron. I went to an old Arab shuk, an open-air marketplace where all kinds of stuff were on sale. I had never been in such a hurly-burly atmosphere. An Arab kid caught my attention with an array of sheepskins laid out before him. I bought one for $10. I should have known something was amiss when afterward he went leaping through the shuk waving the money and shouting ecstatically. Back in my hotel room, the reason smacked me in the nose.

The sheepskin stank, and the odor was getting worse by the minute. As I learned later, that was because it hadn't been cured. An Arab doorman at the hotel suggested that I rub milk into the skin. I went out on the balcony, sheepskin in hand, and took his advice, but it didn't work. So, I wrapped it up and decided to worry about it when I returned home.

I gave the skin to Daniel as a gift. He seemed to treasure it, but Genevieve was revolted by the smell. I asked Sumner Milender, a longtime friend who owned a tanning business, if there was anything we could do about it. He said it was too late, but Daniel loved the sheepskin anyway and wanted to keep it. He has since told me that he lost track of it. For all we know, it could be tightly wrapped in plastic in some family box that we haven't opened in years.

IN THE FOOTSTEPS OF MOSES

When Israel and Egypt made peace in 1979, I said to Genevieve that we had better get over to Mount Sinai before it's returned to the Arabs. Along with about 10 others, we signed up for a guided tour. A van took us to a motel at the base of the mountain. It was right below Saint Catherine's Monastery, built in the sixth century at the spot where the Bible says Moses witnessed the Burning Bush. Visitors could visit the site, located in the monastery's garden. The monks there were under a vow of silence, which had its disadvantages. When I sat down, a monk approached me making all sorts of gestures. At last, a guide came to my assistance. I had violated a religious law by sitting with my legs crossed.

That night, we slept on cots all together in one large room. Just before we went to sleep, an Arab man came by hawking something. Our guide translated, asking if any of us wanted to book a camel for the climb. I said to Genevieve, "Why don't you get a camel?" She declined, saying that no one else had seemed to want one. So, I said, "I'll take a camel."

We were anxious to get to sleep because we were to get up at 4 a.m. to complete the climb in time to see the sun rise from the summit. Just as I fell asleep, the others jostled me awake. They said I was snoring and made me move my cot outside. It was under the stars and quite nice. I was embarrassed, though. No one had ever complained to me about snoring before; maybe I had been getting a cold.

Anyway, at 4 a.m., as scheduled, we all got up. I mounted the camel's saddle while the sleepy beast was still curled up close to the ground. In the near total darkness, I felt queasy being jostled about as my ride went through various gyrations to unfold its knees and stand. With a camel boy leading me, I rode while everyone else climbed up through the dark. After a while, I heard someone say, "I wish I had ordered a camel." It was Genevieve. I said to her, "You take the camel." And she said, "Really?" I assured her it was OK, so the boy had the camel lower itself for the exchange.

There were still hundreds and hundreds of steps to climb. Huffing and puffing, I reached the top. But when I looked around for Genevieve, neither she nor the camel was in sight. I didn't know what to do. The sunrise was beautiful, but all I could think about was Genevieve. Finally, I spotted a little speck way down below. As it came closer, I realized it was Genevieve. She was climbing all by herself.

She told me that about a quarter of the way up, the camel boy had announced that that was as far as he would go. After making Genevieve dismount, he just left her there – all alone in the dark. She crawled next to a rock until it became light and then walked up. Without a flashlight, she had been nearly frightened to death. But by the time she made it to the top, she wasn't angry, just relieved.

The top of Mount Sinai was a big anticlimax. There were three little unkempt chapels and a cave said to have been used by Moses. I can't say that I felt the presence of God. I had felt more in awe at the base of the mountain looking up – it was like the feeling I had had on my first trip to Jerusalem when I could look at the Old City, but not visit it.

GRAVE HUNTING

My ancestors on Gussie's side of the family first ventured to Palestine in the 1800s. Both her father and grandfather are buried in the Holy Land. We never found the grave of Gussie's grandfather, but we knew that her father, Rabbi Avraham Yitzhak Edelman, had been buried on the Mount of Olives in 1927.

After the '67 war, my father spent weeks looking for the grave. While today, you can find gravesites online, back then no central clearinghouse of records existed. They were kept by individual burial societies. Just as my father was about to give up, he was approached by an old bearded man whom he had questioned weeks before. "Mr. Wyner, I think I've found it," he said, showing a penciled-in ledger entry listing the location. That led them to the grave. But the cemetery had been pillaged by the Jordanians, who had used the headstones to build latrines and to pave paths. Fortunately, my great-grandfather's stone had yet to be so ignominiously recycled. My father and the guide found it in a pile with other stones. My father had it restored and rededicated.

Some years later, I visited the Mount of Olives to see the grave for myself. I had a map made by my father that specified that the stone was so many paces from a certain chapel in a certain cemetery. Despite carefully following the instructions, I couldn't find the grave. Not that I should have expected to. The open hillside was a sea of gravestones, all laid flat in the Sephardic tradition with just inches between them. I could make out the delineations that divided the sections belonging to the various burial societies, but I couldn't find the right chapel.

Visiting my great-grandfather's grave with my son Daniel and granddaughter Madelyn in 2004.

I spotted a young bearded man, dressed in a traditional black suit. Instead of trousers, he wore knickers. Those savvy in such things could have identified his yeshiva from the pattern on his socks. When I asked him for help, this fellow, who was dressed like an 18th-century Pole, pulled a walkie-talkie out of his pocket and started chattering away in Hebrew. He then took me to another cemetery. I noticed that to give them prominence, restored gravestones rested on one or more levels of chiseled limestone blocks. My great-grandfather's had been among the first to be restored. Sitting on only a single layer of blocks, it appeared nearly lost among surrounding stones that had been restored more recently and were elevated higher. My newfound yeshiva friend told me that for $100 he could rededicate our stone and make it higher than all the others. I told him it would be fine just to bring it to the same level as its neighbors.

On my most recent visit to the grave, in June 2004, I was accompanied by Genevieve and by our son Daniel and his wife, Lorna, and their daughter, Maddie. While we were there, we had the Arab caretaker clean the stone and reblacken the Hebrew inscription. But more important, Maddie had a chance to see the grave of her grandfather's great-grandfather.

APPENDIX

1. Letter of citizens of Malmesbury, South Africa, to George Wyner on his family's departure to America in June 1899:

2. Letter from my father to me on my 20th birthday:

August 6, 1945

Dear Jerry:

            In thinking of your twentieth birthday, I cannot
refrain from bringing to mind the past years of your childhood and boyhood. From the stormy night of your birth, when
the rain and lightning deluged and crashed about the hospital
on the hill, and your little mother went so bravely, and
hopefully into the unknown trial of her first motherhood, to
the day, when bedecked in cap and gown, you became a Bachelor of
Science, with all the privileges and immunities of that degree.

            Whatever the past, it is always gone without recall.
Being twenty or sixty, a man has within his grasp only the
present. But with his present he makes his future. With his
"today", he makes his "morrow". We hope that your future will
find you a happy, well integrated man,--happy in the true
intelligent sense,--a leader of men, calm, respected, leading a
life of achievement and contribution in your chosen field. We
hope that you may carry on to great achievement.

            You have an obligation to fulfill. Your past career
has shown that you have extraordinary natural gifts of mind and

NEW YORK SALES OFFICE
I. A. WYNER & CO., 1441 BROADWAY

SHAWMUT WOOLEN MILLS

MILLS AT STOUGHTON, MASSACHUSETTS

August 6, 1945

-2-

character. It is your duty to live so that you may make the most of them, it is your obligation to make the most of them. It is our prayer that you will be strong, that you will by strength of character solve any problems that come into your life, and leave to the puny and the weak the escape from life through fixation and rationalization.

In your twentieth year may you bring forth in great measure your inner strength, and cleave strongly to what God has given you, to the people that it was ordained that you should lead. May you by your strength give strength to us also, and to your young sister, so that she may follow you in a life of happiness and intelligence and accomplishment.

May the years unfold for you in blessed pattern, until with God's grace, you stand face to face with your own handsome boy on his twentieth birthday, and as you look into his clear eyes may yours be the great satisfaction that you have contributed to his life neither chaos nor confusion but self assurance, character, strength, and happiness. May you, as you stand on that day, and place your hands in blessing upon his head, know the true sense of the immortality which God gives to mortal men.

God Bless You.

Affectionately,

Daddy

RHW:L

3. My Uncle Edward Wyner's 1947 tongue-perhaps-in-cheek memo to Ritz employees on proper bar attire for clientele:

March 24, 1947

STREET BAR REGULATIONS

The employees of the Street Bar evidently have not been able to understand our request as to patronage. We will try it again and make the language as simple as possible.

1. AGE We do not want young folks to patronize the bar. Some of the young folks are over 21 but do not look it; that makes them still young folks and we cannot serve them. We cannot help it if the person is over 21, unfortunately he looks young and others will not know he is over 21, and other parents will not know he is over 21, and other patrons will not know he is over 21 and so they may complain to the licensing board that the Ritz serves young folks under 21 because the young man does not look over 21. So you know he is over 21 and the young man knows he is over 21, but all these other people do not know he is over 21 because he does not look over 21. We do not want to be criticised, so this poor young man cannot be served. Maybe he will never look over 21 and the poor man will go through life without ever getting a drink at the Ritz bar.

2. CLOTHES We do not want the young men even when they are obviously over 21 and eligible to be served because of their age, who are not properly dressed. Not properly dressed means the college boy uniform of odd coat and pants. Odd coat means a coat not part of a regular suit. It is sometimes called a sport jacket. It usually comes in bright patterns and is very appropriate dress for college wear; that is, on the college campus going back and forth from the classroom, in and around Harvard Square in the stores. It is not, however, the proper dress to patronize the Ritz bar. If you are still in doubt as to what a sport coat or odd coat is, the Manager's office will have several samples to show you and it may be that one will fit you and you can buy it so that you will always know what an odd coat and sport coat is. When I last looked in the Ritz bar I counted 22 of them and when I asked the waiter who had been there for many years how come they were there, he said there weren't any sport coats in the bar. This waiter has just been appointed vice-president of one of the largest clothing concerns in the country.

3. STAGS We do not want a lot of young men pulling up 8 or 10 chairs, or even 4 or 5 chairs, around a table unaccompanied by either their parents or lady friends. We do not want young men alone. A stag is a man who comes unaccompanied by members of the other sex. The reason we do not want them is that students should be in college studying for their examinations. We don't want to encourage their drinking. We do not want to make them welcome here to feel that we want their patronage, that we want their money, that we want them to spend their time here instead of in their rooms, studying. Through this policy we will win the respect and regard of their parents, their teachers and the college faculty and of all the nice people in the city. Perhaps you, too, have or will have a boy in college and you will be gratified to know that the proprietor of the local saloon has discouraged your son from drinking and has helped him to stay at home to study.

4. WHEN CAN COLLEGE BOYS BE SERVED College boys can be served whether they look young or not when they are with their parents or when there are older people in the same party. College boys can be served wearing odd coats when they are with their parents or there are older people in the party.

-2-

No amount of rules or regulations can be a substitute for common sense or good judgment. If you haven't got this you have no business being a waiter in the bar. You have no business being a waiter anywhere. Despite any rule or regulation there will come a time when it will be common sense to make an exception. I bring this out because one of the waiters recently said he was confused with the odd coat regulation because Mr. Thomas Yawkey, age 45, the gentleman who owns the Red Sox Baseball Club, made it a practice to come into the bar with a sport coat. The waiter said that Mr. Yawkey looked young and he was not sure whether or not he was a student. He said that after a consultation with other employees in the bar it was decided to serve Mr. Yawkey without asking him for his automobile license. I think that this discussion and the right conclusion is ample testimony that we have the basis of building up a fine crew in the bar who can logically think a problem out. It was not easy to decide whether or not Mr. Yawkey was a student because there are many veterans attending colleges whose ages are two or three years older than the normal college age, but I insist that if it was decided to serve Mr. Yawkey that that is proof enough that we are getting somewhere.

Actually there is nothing wrong with a sport coat, the Duke of Windsor wears them and many other men who are considered to be well dressed. I do not consider myself in this group. The reason we pick on the sport coat is because it is the common uniform of the college boy and in that way we can reduce the college boy patronage. When these college boys grow up to be the important men of the country this hotel will probably be a garage but they will nevertheless have more respect for it when they look back at our policy and no doubt, if they live in the vicinity, will store their car here as a token of their appreciation. Some of the waiters suggested that as long as there were empty tables why keep anybody out. My answer is that under the policy under which the bar has been operating there will be more and more empty tables and we will all be out. On the last evening I happened to look in at the bar, I noticed a group of half a dozen young men, all resplendent in their odd coats, walk out of the bar with drinks in their hands to the lounge where they hoped to greet some other members of the odd-coat fraternity. When I asked the waiter at the door how come he let them walk out, he said he did not see them. I then asked him how come he didn't see them if he was at the door. He said he was at the door but at that moment he was taking care of the dozen tables in the front half of the room. The only moral I can give you from this story is that it is difficult for a waiter to take care of a dozen tables and be working at the door at the same time. In this case, not only could the members of the odd-coat fraternity walk out with the six drinks, they could have walked out with 11 tables and the man at the door could have been serving his 12th table.

In addition to all this, there are the usual drunks, effeminate men, sometimes referred to as "fairies", whose patronage we do not solicit. There are ladies who have chosen the oldest profession in the world to make an easy living and there is the racketeer, the bootlegger, the cheap man about town, the person who just does not belong in a place where the goal is respectability, decency, pleasant surroundings, a clean wholesome atmosphere and a place where one can take a drink and retain his self respect.

4.   My commencement address at Roxbury Latin in 1985.

Justin L. Wyner's Commencement Address

I am deeply honored to have been selected as your commencement speaker.

Roxbury Latin has had a very significant influence on my life, both directly and through the influence of my father, who was in the Class of 1912. We were associated together in business for almost forty years, until his passing this last year. It was actually more a joyous friendship than a business relationship — and his feelings about the School and the disciplines it gave him were passed on to me, both while I was in attendance and during our later years together. It was thus very meaningful to me that the School ended up giving us our diplomas together in 1970, when it decided we had indeed proven ourselves worthy and eligible, having left the school early to enter college directly, and subsequently received bachelor degrees with honors.

And so I know that both you and your family must have a great sense of pride and satisfaction as you sit here today. You competed amongst many to be accepted at Roxbury Latin. You have now successfully completed one of the most thorough and difficult secondary school curricula and, as I understand it, you have all been accepted to enter a college or university.

All of you are very special people. Each of you has received a very special God-given gift of ability and, with the assistance of Roxbury Latin, an opportunity to develop it to its fullest. It is important both to you and all of us that you take full advantage of both.

The School has asked me, as a longtime graduate, to come back and share with you some of the supposed wisdom I have gained in the period between leaving Roxbury Latin and now — some thoughts that might help you make an even more meaningful start in the outside world.

I will try my best, but am somewhat chastened by an amusing story I fortuitously heard over this past week. A teacher asked a young boy to write about Socrates. The young man made it short — he wrote, "Socrates was a Greek Philosopher who shared his wisdom with others. They poisoned him."

Our local community, our country, and the world contain many capable people, but only too often they are too retiring, too lazy, or just too selfish to give of themselves and we end up with second or third rate leadership. The results can range from just plain mediocrity to the total loss of freedom and totalitarian rule.

We need good men like you. I believe your special gift of ability and of opportunity obligates you to share some of yourself with us all. You are our hope. If you are not willing to be the trustees of your school, church or synagogue, or local hospital, then who? If you are not willing to put your shoulders to the wheel for the United Fund or the American Cancer Society, then who? And if you are not willing to run for town meeting, alderman, or even senator, governor, or president, then how can you or any of us complain of the lack of qualified candidates?

I spent almost 30 years working in the Town Meeting in Brookline. I was chairman of the Finance Committee, and more recently, Moderator for 12 years. Town Meeting, if run correctly, can be the true grass roots democracy — but only if it becomes a process where people with different points of view come together, not only to speak their piece, but to listen and try to understand the concerns, needs, and feelings of others, and to try to reach a creative compromise.

I guess that experience has made me somewhat obsessed with the idea that we have a very precious and delicate asset in our democracy. I have to say to you that I have never felt I had the right to miss voting in an election, and I haven't missed voting in a single local, state, or national election in my life; but more important, I felt it was my duty to make a thorough study of each candidate and make a knowledgeable choice. If the candidates were mediocre, then it was even more important that I made that difficult choice and not abdicate the decision to a group of political cronies.

I believe that it is important to understand that our country basically operates within a two party system. The creation of a third party has, in some cases, even ended up as counterproductive. Many people in recent years have been so disgusted with the pettiness of party politics that they have disdained any party affiliation and registered as "independents." But the choice of candidates is really made within the party, and by the time we get around to voting, even in a primary, the candidates have been picked. If they are poor choices, we have only ourselves to blame.

Join a local Republican or Democratic city or town committee — involve yourselves in the process. When you have done your best to provide the best candidates on both sides, then you can be independent and vote for the best candidate, regardless of party.

You would be surprised how much influence a few hard working people can have. In 1968, when our country's continued participation in Viet Nam was an issue, I organized and was national chairman of the Republicans for Senator Eugene McCarthy for President. He was a popular anti-Viet Nam candidate running in the Democratic presidential primary. We wanted to convince New York Governor Nelson Rockefeller that he should offer himself as an alter-

The Headmaster, Justin Wyner, and Mrs. Wyner.

nate to Richard Nixon in the Republican primary. We succeeded. At 12 o'clock noon, half way through primary day in Massachusetts, Rockefeller finally agreed to come into the race. It was interesting that, if we added up the write-in votes for McCarthy and Rockefeller in the Massachusetts Republican primary, they exceeded the number of votes for Nixon. Would we have actually nominated a Democrat as the Republican candidate if Rockefeller had stayed out? Who knows! Anything can happen in Massachusetts. Needless to say, Rockefeller didn't win the national Republican nomination either, but we did have some effect and gave an additional air of legitimacy to the Viet Nam issue that had up to then been considered by many as the cause of hippies and malcontents.

You owe it to us all to keep yourselves well informed on every issue, and to work for change when it is for the cause in which you believe. Remember, I am not telling you what stand you should take on any issue (there are always at least two sides) — but only that you take the time to listen to all points of view and then, having formed your own decision, to use the process to influence our direction.

Anyone who has gone through this "Ancient Latin School" has to have developed a great appreciation for tradition; but just because we have done something for a long time, doesn't make it right — either then or now. It is only a few years since the civil rights march on Selma, Alabama. Imagine that in our country 20 years ago there were many places where blacks could not use the same toilets or sit down in a restaurant with whites. They had to see a movie from the balcony, and a public bus would not start up unless they were seated in the rear — and none of that changed until our country was 180 years old!

You have to concern yourselves with the hungry, the homeless, the helpless, the oppressed, and the environment, whether here or in Afghanistan, Ethiopia, or South Africa. You have to make up your mind and then influence our government's policies, whether here or in El Salvador or Nicaragua.

Every little bit can help. For the second year in a row, our little manufacturing plant will farm seven acres next to its factory and send the entire harvest each day to Boston's kitchens for the homeless — the Pine Street Inn, Rosie's Place, and St. Anthony's Shrine.

A number of years ago, I was driving down Route 1 in Dedham on my way to work, and I came upon a crowd of several hundred spectators in cars stopped to watch 50 foot flames leap out of the roof of a building set back a few hundred yards from the highway. As I looked on for a moment, I realized that there were no firemen fighting the fire. It seemed ridiculous to contemplate — but I thought maybe everyone thought someone else called the fire department. I went to a pay phone and called the Dedham Fire Department and, sure enough, they knew nothing about the fire. Fortunately, no one was hurt, but the building was gutted by the time the firemen arrived. Since then, I have never assumed anyone has done even the most obvious.

On the more tragic side, we can all recall reading about at least one instance where someone was crying for help, no one wanted to get involved, and he or she was unnecessarily lost. Stop and care, and you will never have that pang of regret and shame when you read in the morning paper about a tragedy that could have been avoided if only someone cared.

When I first started to earn my own living, my father told me that I should begin to respond to every request for charity, with a contribution, no matter how small. I followed his advice. It has always given me a very good feeling, and I recommend it to you. Of course, nowadays with computerized mailing lists, I have had to modify the policy because 80% of the appeals I receive through the mail are duplicates. Remember, even here at Roxbury Latin, your education was paid for, to the greatest extent, by those generous graduates, parents, and friends who came before you. When you can, try to pay it back so that it will be there for someone else.

I know from my own experience that you will soon discover that the knowledge, discipline, and training you received here will make even the most difficult of college level curricula seem very easy to handle in comparison. Roxbury Latin has taught us all self discipline and how to study. It is a unique gift from our School that will give you a freedom many of your new college classmates will not have — that extra time to make the most out of all that a college has to offer, not only in your courses of study, but in the way of extra curricular activities and participation in all phases of the campus community.

You are about to enter into some of the most exciting years of your life. I found them so — and if I had only appreciated what truly great years they really were, I would have stopped to savor them even more. But every new phase of your life will be exciting; when you start a career, when many of you start a family; and I understand, when you have grandchildren. As the popular song says, "The best of times is now." Take the time to enjoy it.

Just two final thoughts. None of us is perfect. We all make mistakes. We have to be accepting of both ourselves and others. One of the worst mistakes we ever made in our business was when we brought in someone who was extremely well qualified, but had such an inflated idea of his own reputation that he believed he could never make a mistake. Not only couldn't he learn from mistakes he would never acknowledge, so that he was doomed to repeat them, but the morale of everyone was destroyed because he had to shift the blame. No matter what his talents, he was useless to us.

Be accepting of yourself and of others. Have humility. Life is different from school. You don't have to know all the answers — and there are many correct answers to the problems of life. Humility and the ability to listen to others will bring you great success.

Lastly, your reputation and integrity are worth more than all your money in the bank. You can always start again to earn more money — but believe me, you can never start again to regain your integrity. Long after your records in Roxbury Latin are forgotten, every act of bad faith and broken promise will follow you. Too often people feel, "If it isn't in the contract, forget it," or "if my attorney can interpret things differently than I know it was to be, it is okay." Let your word be your bond — it will bring you great dividends.

So today you don't have to decide what you are going to do or be in life. You probably shouldn't try. But you can and should decide the kind of person you are going to be.

6

5. Boston Herald column about Genevieve Wyner's enthusiasm for ham radio:

THE ROVING EYE
By RUDOLPH ELIE

Radio Hams Busy Raising Rome This Week

A tall girl in a tweed coat and snow boots came marching in here the other day with what looked like a phone book under her arm and, evidently mistaking me for the city editor or someone, handed over a carbon copy of a news release.

"Boston's amateur radio operators or 'radio hams' as they are better known," it read, "are joining in the Hub City's Salute to Rome through a unique program of direct radio contacts with Italian 'hams.' In an eight-day marathon event to contact as many Roman stations as possible, 27 of Boston's leading amateurs are saluting Rome with voice and Morse code contacts across the Atlantic."

Novice License

"Are you one of the hams?" I inquired, before re-directing her to the city room.

"I got my novice license just two days before I was married in July," she said. "It's my husband who's the real ham. All I can do is get Cambridge or someplace nearby and I even get stage fright doing that."

So I forgot all about the city room and grabbed her myself. After all, how often do you run into people who get stage fright talking to Cambridge on the radio?

My visitor turned out to be Mrs. Justin Wyner, an attractive girl with a mass of dark hair and an animated way of talking who has hurled herself into her husband's hobby with enthusiasm— and no little forbearance as well. "When we moved into our house," she said with a laugh, "we had the radio but no furniture. We're just beginning to get that now."

They also had a 50-foot radio tower but it apparently isn't tall enough to suit Mr. Wyner, who is director of communications for the Brookline Civil Defense, for they are now looking for a house. "But it has to be on top of a hill," Mrs. Wyner explained, "a high one."

Rag Chewer

Even so the 50-foot tower is potent enough for Mr. Wyner to carry on conversations with hams all over the world. "He's had lots of conversations with people lasting an hour or more, so he's a member of the Rag Chewers," Mrs. Wyner explained. "Those are hams who have talked an hour or more." Her husband's call letters are W1PST, the W1 indicating New England, and he has a power of one kilowatt.

"Right now," she said, "I can only do five words a minute in the Morse code and you have to be able to do 13 before you can pass the test to make you a full fledged ham." But she made one contact in Cambridge (her home is in Hyde Park) and it scared her to death. "I got stage fright, I guess," she said, "but I'm getting over it now. I didn't know what to talk about."

The hams themselves, it appears, are at no loss for words, especially those in the advanced category of the Rag Chewers. "First they talk about reception," said Mrs. Wyner, "how they're coming in and all that. Then they talk about their equipment. They're always getting something new to add to the rigs, you know, there's never any end to that. They talk about their work and how they feel and, of course, about the weather. They talk about that all the time."

Mr. Wyner has made many contacts behind the Iron Curtain, with Yugoslavia and Russia and elsewhere. But they never talk politics. "If we ask a question along those lines they say the reception isn't coming in so good. But we get Moscow a lot and all they talk about is how wonderful everything is there nowadays."

Special Cards

The current concentration on contacting Rome by the local 27 hams, with participation also by the radio clubs of Harvard and MIT, is all part of the week-long activities of the promotion in goodwill, and special cards, called QSL cards, have been printed for the occasion. These cards, which confirm a radio contact by mail, seem to be highly coveted by hams everywhere, and the special QSL's have been signed by Mayor Hynes for forwarding to Roman hams contacted by the local ones.

Most of the conversations are carried on in English or in the Morse code, it appears, but I gathered during this week many of the local hams will have Italian speaking hams on hand to speak directly to the Roman hams. Whether a non-licensed person can speak over a ham's equipment I forgot to inquire, but there are many regulations in connection with amateur broadcasting, and one of them seems to be that Mrs. Wyner has to get her full license before next July. "Learning the code is an awful challenge," she said. "It's pretty hard to do."

But Mr. Wyner's long interest in hamming has proved a very satisfying thing, for during their honeymoon in Bermuda all the hams he had previously contacted there put on parties for the Wyners. "We had a wonderful time, but we've got radio friends all over the place."

Although she is valiantly learning the code, Mrs. Wyner doesn't know very much about the mysterious workings of a ham's radio rig. "I can't do anything with wire," she confessed, "and don't know anything about the equipment either. In fact, when my husband's equipment began to arc the other day I ran out of the house."

THE BOSTON HERALD
TUESDAY, NOVEMBER 29, 1955

6. The Jewish Advocate's editorial upon the death of my father, Rudolph Wyner, written by editor Bernard Hyatt:

THE JEWISH ADVOCATE, THURSDAY, MAY 31, 1984

Rudolph H. Wyner

Rudolph Wyner, Jewish community leader for long years and Boston textile mogul who died last week, was a man of many attainments. Learning and wit dwelled side by side in his personality, and style and substance were keynotes of his philanthropic and industrial contributions. His innovative flair and gentle determination found expression in the moulding of his own high character, in the response to the needs of the times of the several textile mills he headed, and in his guiding the Beth Israel Hospital, which he led as president in the early Sixties, from an institution of expanding service to one also of research as it became a Harvard affiliated teaching hospital.

The sound foundations of Boston's civic society as well as our Jewish community were built of the hard work and intelligent vision of such people as Rudolph Wyner. Their passing from the scene should remind us not only of their accomplishments but also of our responsibility to continue in the wise and generous courses they have charted. We are fortunate, too, that Mr. Wyner has left in his children and grandchildren heirs capable of such leadership.

7. My resume:

JUSTIN L. WYNER

Born: August 6, 1925
Married: Genevieve Gloria Geller, July 3, 1955

Education: Tufts College, BS in Chemistry, 1946; Harvard University, MBA, 1948

Sons and daughters-in-law: George and Barbara Wyner of Belmont; Daniel Wyner and Lorna Stokes of North Scituate, R.I.; James and Giang Wyner of Brookline

Grandchildren: Samuel, Hannah, Madelyn, Lam An and Oliver

Affiliations: Harvard Club, Belmont Country Club, Farm Neck Golf Club (Oak Bluffs), The Boathouse (Edgartown), The Colonial Society

Occupation: Chairman Emeritus of the Board of Shawmut Corporation, West Bridgewater, Mass.

National Activities

American Jewish Historical Society
President, 1993-1998
Trustee, Executive Committee, 1987-2016
Chairman, Boston Overseers, 2000 to date
Chairman, Library and Archives, 1988-1993
Chairman, Nominating Committee, 2003-2012

American-Israel Public Affairs Committee
Advisory Council, 1967-1971
Chairman, Greater Boston Section, 1967-1971

American Assoc. for Textile Technology
National Board of Governors, 1970-1973

National Knitted Outerwear Association
Chairman of Standards Committee, 1950-1968
Director/Honorary Life Director, 1950 to date

National Fabric Laminators Association
Founder and Director, 1960-1978

National Jewish Community Relations Advisory Committee, 1971-1973

Union of American Hebrew Congregations
Director, 1979-1982

Yoo-hoo Chocolate Beverage Corp.
Director, 1967-1977

Republicans for Eugene McCarthy for President, National chairman, 1968

Hebrew Union College
Member, Board of Governors, 1987-1992

Local Civic and Professional Activities

Town of Brookline
Moderator, 1991-1994; 1970-1982
Chairman Advisory Committee, 1966-1970
Town Meeting member, 1950-1982
Measurer, Wood and Bark, 1983-1985

Martha's Vineyard Hospital
Trustee, 1999-2002
Chairman, Governance Committee, 1999-2002

Residences at Rowes Wharf
Member, Board of Managers, 1999-2015
President, 2001-2015

Brookline Civil Defense
Director of Communications, 1948-1971

American Cancer Society
Board of Directors/Mass. Division, 1984-1997
Grant Allocations, 1990 to date

Brookline Community Council
Director, 1957-1961

Republican Party
Brookline Town Committee, 1964-1998
Delegate to Mass. Republican Convention, 1998

Action for Boston Community Development
Board of Directors, 1971-1972

Brookline Civic Association
Director, 1988-1991

Brookline Rotary Club
Man of the Year, 1982

Brookline Taxpayer's Association
Director, 1958-1961

Justice of the Peace to Solemnize Marriages

Brookline United Fund Campaign
Chairman, 1960

Beth Israel Hospital
Board of Overseers, 1997 to 2000
Trustee/Honorary Trustee, 1966-1997
Task Force on Gerontology, 1991-1992
Finance Committee, 1972-1980

Beth Israel Deaconess Medical Center
Board of Overseers, 1997 to date
Executive Committee, 1997

Katama Association, Edgartown
Executive Committee, 2005-2015
Chairman, Ponds and Harbors, 2005-2015

Governors Committee on Juvenile Justice
Member, 1991

United Way of Massachusetts Bay
Public Member of the Corporation, 1988-1993
Development Committee, 2004-2008

New Center for Arts and Culture
Advisory Committee, 2002-2009
Board of Overseers 2009-2010

New England Historic Genealogical Society
Councilor, 2014 to date

New England Knitted Outerwear Association
Director, 1949-1960

Roxbury Latin School
Trustee, 1985-1989
Headmaster's Council, 2014 to date

Wharf District Task Force
Board and Steering Committee, 2001-2010

Wharf District Council
President, 2010-2015

Boston Redevelopment Authority
Member, IAG Aquarium Garage Project, 2010

Local Jewish Organizations

Adath Jeshurun Cemetery Association, Inc.
Treasurer, 1964 to date

American Jewish Committee
Board, 1960-1965
Chairman of annual dinner, 1962

Combined Jewish Philanthropies
Trustee/Honorary Life Trustee, 1964-1999
Board of Managers, 1989-1999
Social Planning and Allocations, 1961-1964
Scholarship Committee, 1972-78
Lifetime of Leadership Award, 2014

**Jewish Community Relations Council
of Metropolitan Boston**
President, 1971-1973
Administrative Committee, 1967 to date

Hebrew College
Chairman, Cultural Affairs, 1977-1978
Trustee/Honorary Trustee, 1967-2012

Hebrew Free Loan Society of Boston
President, 1972-1988

Israel Bonds
Campaign Cabinet, 1992-1993

Hebrew SeniorLife
Board of Trustees, 2017 to date

Hillel
President, Council of Metro Boston, 1968-1971
President, Harvard Hillel, 1966-1968

**Jewish Community Relations Council
of Metropolitan Boston**
President, 1971-1973
Administrative Committee, 1967 to date

Martha's Vineyard Hebrew Center
Finance Committee, 2002-2005
Nominating Committee, 2009

New England Chassidic Center
Man of the Year, 1991
Chair, ROFEH Annual Dinners, 1986-2014

Temple Kehillath Israel
Trustee/Honorary Trustee, 1967- 2008

Temple Israel
President, 1979-1982
Trustee/Honorary, 1964 to date
Chairman, Board of Managers, 1983-1995
Chairman, MASCO Garage Committee, 1981-90